Mining Childhood

Massive headframes known as gallows frames marked the entrances to underground mines in Butte.

Mining Childhood

GROWING UP IN BUTTE, MONTANA, 1900–1960

Janet L. Finn

Montana Historical Society Press

Helena, Montana

Front cover photograph: A boy and the Neversweat Mine. Samuel Hamilton, photographer, from Harry C. Freeman, *A Brief History of Butte, Montana the World's Greatest Mining Camp: Including a Story of the Extraction and Treatment of Ores from Its Gigantic Copper Properties* (Chicago, 1900), 71

Cover and book design by Diane Gleba Hall
Typeset in Adobe Caslon and Bitstream Grotesque
Printed in the United States

Distributed by the Globe Pequot Press, 246 Goose Lane, Guilford, Connecticut 06437, (800) 243-0495

12 13 14 15 16 17 18   10 9 8 7 6 5 4 3 2 1
978-0-9801292-5-0

Humanities **MONTANA**

This project is funded in part by a grant from Humanities Montana, an affiliate of the National Endowment for the Humanities. The findings and conclusions in this publication are the views of the author and do not necessarily represent the views of Humanities Montana or the National Endowment for the Humanities.

Library of Congress Cataloging-in-Publication Data

Finn, Janet L., 1956—Mining childhood : growing up in Butte, Montana, 1900–1960 / Janet L. Finn.
p. cm.
Includes bibliographical references and index.
ISBN 978-0-9801292-5-0 (paper : alk. paper)
1. Children—Montana—Butte—History—20th century. 2. Children—Montana—Butte—Biography. 3. Butte (Mont.)—History—20th century. 4. Butte (Mont.)—Biography. 5. Working class—Montana—Butte—History—20th century. 6. Copper mines and mining—Social aspects—Montana—Butte—History—20th century. 7. Butte (Mont.)—Social conditions—20th century. 8. Butte (Mont.)—Social life and customs—20th century. I. Title.

HQ792.U5F54 2011
978.6'6803—dc23
2012003270

This project is funded in part by the Burke Family Foundation and by a grant from Humanities Montana, an affiliate of the National Endowment for the Humanities.

To the people of Butte, who have so generously shared their lives and stories to make this book possible

Contents

Acknowledgments   xi

INTRODUCTION The Meaning and Making of   1
Childhood in Butte, Montana

CHAPTER ONE Children of the Hill   15

CHAPTER TWO Mining Childhood   64

CHAPTER THREE Saving Children   111

CHAPTER FOUR Child's Play   135

CHAPTER FIVE School Days   178

CHAPTER SIX Learning to Labor   216

CHAPTER SEVEN Memories of a McQueen Childhood   249

CHAPTER EIGHT Childhood Matters   278

Notes   291

Bibliography   303

Photograph Credits   310

Index   311

Acknowledgments

IT TAKES a community to write a book about childhood. The idea for this book was sparked through conversations with Ellen Crain, director of the Butte-Silver Bow Public Archives (BSBPA). The generous, ongoing support of Ellen, administrative assistant Lee Whitney, photograph collection assistant Aubrey Kersting, and the BSBPA staff and volunteers made this project possible. Even in the midst of construction of their new state-of-the-art facility, they were willing to help me at every turn in tracking down documents, scanning images, suggesting possible source material, and providing ongoing insights, feedback, food, and drink during both the research and writing phases.

At the heart of this book are the personal recollections of childhood shared by so many longtime Butte residents. I am grateful to Kay Antonetti, Micah Downs, Helen Evankovich, Danette Harrington, Betty Henderson, Robert Hole, Tom Holter, Dolores Kangas, Tom King, John Mazzola, Linda Raiha, Kevin Shannon, Lucille Sheehan, John "Skeff" Sheehy, Steve Sherick, Bonnie Stefanic, Vadis Stratton, Shirley Trevena, Laurie Ugrin, and Gina Zanchi for sharing personal and family stories of growing up in Butte with me. I am also thankful to the many Butte residents whom I interviewed in researching my earlier book, *Tracing the Veins*. While their names are not used here, their insights were critical in shaping *Mining Childhood*.

The extensive collection of oral histories maintained by the BSBPA proved to be a treasure trove of data on childhood in Butte. Thanks to Mary Murphy and Ray Calkins for spearheading the oral history project over thirty years ago and to Jim Harrington for introducing generations of Butte young people to the power of oral history. Their many contributions to the BSBPA oral history collection were invaluable to this project. Likewise, John Astle's work in gathering one hundred years of human-interest stories from Butte provided a rich resource for uncovering special moments of children's lives.

I am indebted to Andrea McCormick for providing introductions and photographs and for her important work in publishing so many stories in the *Montana Standard* over the years that capture the vitality, diversity, and uniqueness of Butte's people young and old. Likewise, I am grateful to Nancy Gibson, Ann Ueland, and the wonderful staff at the Belmont Senior Center. They welcomed me to the center and introduced me to many Butte residents who regularly take part in the center's activities. Lunchtime conversations created great opportunities for learning more about childhood in Butte from the Depression Era to the post–World War II years.

It is a privilege to work with the staff of the Montana Historical Society in the publication of this book. The incisive and insightful feedback from Montana Historical Society Press editor Molly Holz and reviewers David Emmons and Mary Murphy has been crucial in the direction and development of *Mining Childhood*. Glenda Bradshaw's careful and artful eye for photos has brought the stories of Butte childhood to life in poignant and compelling ways. Graphic designer Diane Gleba Hall designed a book worthy of its subject, and assistant editor Christy Goll lent her considerable talents to making all the parts of production and publicity come together.

Support for this book came in many forms, and I am thankful to all those who made it possible. Humanities Montana provided funding for the publication of *Mining Childhood*. Ryan Tolleson-Knee, chair of the University of Montana School of Social Work, and David Forbes, dean of the College of Health and Biomedical Sciences at UM, supported my request for a reduced teaching load in spring 2009, which enabled me to make numerous trips to Butte. Students in my "History of Social Policy, Justice, and Change" course served as captive audiences for presentations based on the research for this book and helped identify themes and issues for further development. Conversations with colleagues Lynn Nybell, Jeff Shook, Kerrie Ghenie, and Jim Caringi were critical in developing the discussion in the "Saving Children" and "Childhood Matters" chapters. Elizabeth Urschel's review of an earlier draft provided rich food for thought at a critical juncture in the writing process. Carrie Johnson opened her Butte home to me for months on end. Finally, thanks to my husband, Dave Ames, for his support, humor, and insight and for sharing the joys and frustrations of writing with me.

The Meaning and Making of Childhood in Butte, Montana

SATURDAYS at the Montana Laundry—the pungent smells of industrial detergents, oil rags, bleach, dry-cleaning chemicals, and hot irons on asbestos padding fuse into a single aroma as familiar to me as my father's hand. Some days I play with the antique cash register or color in a corner of the room-sized safe. Other days I neatly stack dozens of crisp, white napkins, bundling them in plain brown paper and carefully tying them with string for a late-afternoon delivery to a Butte restaurant. And then there are the bar rags, which do not require such tender care in packaging but which always require personal delivery.

Anticipation battles with anxiety as we lock up the building and head for the laundry truck. I scramble to my perch on the engine cover, my back to the windshield, ready to hold on to the laundry cart so it doesn't get away from us on the corners as we make the deliveries. First stop, Charley Judd's New Deal Bar, located a mere block from the laundry. We pull into the alley and up to the back door. It is a good sign if I get to come in. Free Cokes, a Hershey bar, and a chance to spin myself dizzy on a black Naugahyde barstool. "Wait here, I'll just be a minute" is a sketchier proposition. Dad's sense of time isn't so good on Saturday afternoons. "Just a minute" could be an hour, and then I'll have to decide whether it is worth creeping in the back door and making my way among the regulars to find him. Moods could shift in "just a minute." Good stories could seldom be told in "just a minute." A lot of Cokes and Hershey bars could be consumed in "just a minute." Sometimes our first Saturday afternoon delivery is also our last.

I grew up in Butte, Montana, in the 1960s, when underground mining was giving way to open-pit mining, and dynamite blasts at

the Berkeley Pit punctuated the noon hour each day. My own childhood memories served as a starting point for thinking about *Mining Childhood*. In earlier writing, I have traced the connections of
copper, culture, and community from Butte to the Anaconda Company copper-mining town of Chuquicamata, Chile, and explored
the wealth of women's contributions to Butte's history.[1] While children played on the edges of those accounts, they were not center stage.
Children were occasionally seen and seldom heard. As I reflected on
my own childhood experiences, it struck me that a focus on childhood
is a missing piece of the Butte story. Over the past few years, I have
been involved in research on the ways in which the lives of children
and ideas about childhood are shaped by the historical, political, and
cultural contexts in which we live. The idea of *Mining Childhood* came
out of my own questions about growing up in Butte and my recent
studies of childhood.[2] How might an exploration of childhood in Butte
provide insights about the ways in which meanings of childhood and
experiences of children were shaped by mining life? In turn, how might
stories told from a child's-eye view provide new insights into Butte's
history? *Mining Childhood* seeks to answer these questions.

Butte's story has been told many times. It is by and large a mas-
culine story, marked by the grit and danger of hard-rock mining, the
power plays of Copper Kings, and the intrigues of organized labor.[3]
Women have often been cast in cameo roles as matrons of boardinghouses and madams of bordellos.[4] If the voices and views of women
have been muted in this history, the experiences of children and stories
of childhood have been largely silenced and erased. Little is known
about children's experiences of mining life; of the ways in which class
politics, labor strife, and gender and ethnic relations insinuated themselves in the everyday lives of children; or of the ways in which children
contributed to, critiqued, and perhaps changed their life circumstances.[5]
Mining Childhood reveals children as keen observers and active participants in community life. Their accounts of work, play, family, schooling,

ethnicity, and neighborhood life offer fresh perspectives on Butte.[6] They remind us that children are not sheltered from the "adult" world around them; they are shapers of that world. Accounts of childhood reveal that growing up is serious business. At the same time, they offer lessons in resilience, optimism, and possibility.

The smokestacks and headframes of Butte's copper mines fill the city's skyline in 1914, during an era when thousands of its men worked in tunnels and shafts beneath the city.

Mining Childhood explores the social history of childhood in Butte from 1900 to 1960 with particular attention to the lives of working-class children whose families were most directly affected by the ups and downs of copper mining. These years mark the rise and decline of Butte's fame as the "Richest Hill on Earth," when the veins of copper coursing deep beneath the city's surface created thousands of jobs for miners and untold wealth for the Anaconda Copper Mining Company (ACM). I explore experiences of children and ideas about childhood from Butte's turn-of-century industrialization through the Progressive Era, World War I and its aftermath, the Great Depression, World War II, and the gradual decline of the copper industry in the postwar years. Drawing from a broad range of archival materials and oral histories, I strive to bring the lives of Butte's younger residents to the fore and offer readers perspectives from the vantage point of children and childhood.

Research as Detective Story

It seemed to me that Butte might serve as an ideal microcosm for exploring questions of twentieth-century childhood. Butte provides a dynamic setting for examining how children fit into the seemingly adult world of labor, immigration, urbanization, and industrial capitalism that shaped the social, cultural, and economic contours of early-twentieth-century America. I was also curious about the ways in which powerful events, which form parts of larger, and often contested, community or national collective memories, are addressed in accounts of childhood. I wanted to explore children's perspectives on Butte in particular and

Life in a highly industrialized environment shaped Butte children, who lived daily immersed in the sights, sounds, and smells of mining and smelting.

aspects of twentieth-century social, political, and economic life in general that would otherwise remain invisible. I started asking questions. How did life in Butte shape childhood experience? How might an exploration into mining life over time inform our understanding of the ways in which twentieth-century ideas about childhood were created, communicated, and contested?

I began to approach the project as a detective might, seeking to uncover and dislodge hidden stories of childhood. I sought clues in the collections of the Butte-Silver Bow Public Archives (BSBPA), which include records of the Paul Clark Home, the Soroptimist Home for Children, early county poor fund reports, county health and welfare records, coroners' reports, and school, parish, and social organization records. Butte's numerous newspapers also provided ample material for probing questions of childhood. I was teased by hints of a story and frustrated by dead ends, missing puzzle pieces, and competing "truths." I pored over the extensive BSBPA oral history collection in search of stories of childhood. I traced connections among multiple accounts of growing up in Butte, identifying repeated stories, shared experiences, and common memories. I also extracted some unique gems—some were intimate, individual stories and others were part of larger stories, suggesting a near-mythic quality of a particular event or collective memory.

As I worked my way through the maze of materials, I found I had more questions than answers. For example, when and under what circumstances is one considered to be a child, and what privileges and protections does that status entail? How do adult notions of childhood relate to the realities of children's everyday lives? How do popular and professional accounts of children's education, health, welfare, recreation, and labor reveal insights into underlying ideas about children, their capacities, and their vulnerabilities? How does one's class positioning, citizenship, or ethnic and gender identity relate to one's experiences of childhood? Under what circumstances are young people's voices and views recognized? How were these questions addressed in early- to mid-twentieth-century Butte?

Over the course of the project, I reviewed the transcripts of dozens of existing oral histories. The oral histories capture the reminiscences of adults reflecting on their childhoods from the vantage point of senior years. Some of the oral histories were conducted in the late 1970s and early 1980s with older Butte residents who were born near the turn of the twentieth century and who grew up when Butte was a youthful and boisterous metropolis. Some, conducted in the mid-1980s, focused on middle-aged adults and those approaching retirement years who were trying to make sense of life in Butte with the absence of copper mining as a driving force. Some of the richest oral histories were those conducted by young people over the past fifteen years—high school and college history students—who took the opportunity to learn more about the lives of their grandparents and great-grandparents. It is here that the expertise of the interviewers truly shone through. Informed by their own youthful vantage points, the interviewers often got to the heart of matters, posing questions about childhood experiences that elicited candid and poignant responses from their elders.

In addition to these resources, I also drew from a series of interviews I conducted in the early and mid-1990s to learn more about gender, labor, and the rhythms of mining life in Butte as they were shaped by labor contracts, strikes, and layoffs. As longtime residents recounted stories of hard times during strikes in the 1950s and 1960s, their memories often shifted to their childhood experiences during the Great Depression or the 1934 or 1946 strikes, which left indelible impressions. In 2009 and 2010, I conducted another twenty interviews with Butte residents ranging in age from sixty to ninety-four. In these interviews, I probed specific memories of childhood and was rewarded with provocative insights into schooling and work, family and neighborhood, fun times and difficult times, sickness and health, celebrations and struggles, birth and death, and the tastes, smells, and sounds of life in the Mining City. It is from these many stories that *Mining Childhood* was crafted.

Oral histories provide evocative insights into the experiences and memories of childhood. On the one hand, oral history accounts speak from a "life in review" perspective. The layering, merging, and fission of memories create a complex individual and collective archeology of childhood. One's recollections of both painful and pleasing childhood moments are reimagined and recounted from an adult perspective. Children and adults alike are in a constant process of re-storying their lives through the recounting of memory and experience. Certainly, there is the ever-present possibility of a nostalgic gloss over memory and history when looking back to one's childhood from the perspective of a thirty-, sixty-, or ninety-year-old. That child's-eye view is reinvented in the present, shaped by knowledge of outcomes, and crafted in a differing historic moment where differing notions of childhood prevail. At the same time, those details of memory and history that are dearly held and deeply embedded contain their own truth to the individual historian. And those memories, taken collectively, provide key insights into the social worlds of children and the meanings of childhood.

Butte's rich archival and oral history materials offer fascinating and fragmented clues into childhood. They are ripe with intriguing hints about what children are and what adults think they ought to be. They offer insights into the everyday worlds and worldviews of children. And they are always, at best, partial, as is this project. Readers will bring their own views and experiences of childhood to bear, posing questions and pondering insights that go beyond the scope of this book. It is my hope that *Mining Childhood* provokes a sense of wonder and reminds readers of the possibilities that open when viewing the world from the perspective of a child.

Thinking about Childhood: A Theoretical Perspective

Mining Childhood is informed by the work of historians and social theorists who have shown that ideas about children and childhood are products of particular historical, political, and cultural contexts.[7] Rather than a universal, biologically driven stage of development, childhood can be better thought of as a socially constructed concept that is culturally and historically contingent and subject to change.[8] Childhood, according to Judith Sealander, is a system of adult understandings about the young, and children grow up constrained by those understandings.[9] Adults create public policies, institutions, and practices based on prevailing understandings of childhood that, in turn, profoundly shape the everyday lives of children. However, children are not simply passive recipients of social experience. They are actively engaged in shaping the world around them, including ideas about childhood.

The work of social historians of childhood has shown how the lives of children are shaped by the particular social, economic, and political conditions in which they live and how children make sense of and engage with the social world around them. As Elliott West demonstrates in his insightful history of western frontier childhood, children were shaping not only their own lives but also the process of settlement of the West. They relished independence and managed responsibilities. They contributed their labors, created their own entertainment, became intimately familiar with their environment, and influenced their parents' commitments to education and moral instruction.[10] Similarly, in their study of frontier children, Linda Peavy and Ursula Smith address the ways in which children gave meaning to the harsh conditions of daily life, participated in the family economy, and developed the practical knowledge and skills that fostered resilience.[11] Anna Davin, in her study of working-class childhood in London, argues that an understanding of childhood—in particular, its historical and social contexts—demands careful consideration of the role of the State in regulation of family life and control of children.[12] Elizabeth Faue and Lucy Taksa suggest that studies of children's experiences can inform understandings of labor history by illuminating the ways in which class identities are formed and ideas about one's relationship to labor are transmitted in families, neighborhoods, and communities.[13]

Children on the frontier, like these two little girls, contributed their labor, created their own entertainment, and influenced their parents' commitments to education and moral instruction.

These insights have informed my approach to *Mining Childhood*. In this project, I pay attention to the role of the State in shaping family life and children's experience. I look for ways in which children acquired knowledge of ethnic identity, class consciousness, and gender relations in their everyday experience. I consider how children were both constrained by prevailing notions of childhood and an active force in determining what it meant to be a child. The focus here is on children and youth from infancy through teen years. However, an understanding of childhood cannot be described or contained simply by parameters of age. Instead, stories of children and childhood reveal how very young children often take on adult responsibilities and how the boundaries between notions of child and adulthood can be very blurry.

Constructing Childhood: A Historical Perspective

Ideas that adults hold about children and childhood have shaped the way we behave toward young people, structure their everyday experiences, and create policies, institutions, and practices to care for and control them.[14] In mid-nineteenth-century America, views about children and youth were being shaped in the context of a rapidly changing world. Immigration, urbanization, and the rise of industrial capitalism created fundamental changes in the nation's urban centers. Millions of foreign workers and their families were immigrating to the United

States. Differences of nationality, ethnicity, and religion intersected with class- and gender-based differences, and children as well as adults were marked by those differences. Children of the emerging middle class were coming to be seen as precious "innocents" in need of guidance and protection. In contrast, children of the urban poor and working classes, often left to their own devices while their parents worked long hours, were more likely to be seen as potential sources of trouble and in need of discipline. They became the targets of intervention by a cadre of reformers known as "child savers" who operated with missionary zeal to contain, control, and convert these "little wanderers." At first, private charities took up the cause of child rescue, but the plight of children soon became a concern of the State as well.[15]

Some reformers called for separate institutions for needy and dependent children. A veritable building boom of children's asylums and orphanages took place across the country in the mid- to late nineteenth century.[16] Others expressed concern over the cost-effectiveness of asylums and feared that a "contagion effect" would result from the confinement of large numbers of lower-class children together in the same institution. They advocated for the placement of children in homelike settings where they could be inculcated with wholesome family values. Children's Aid Societies began the practice of removing children from poor, urban families along the eastern seaboard and placing them with rural farm families in the Midwest.[17]

By the late nineteenth century, reformers embraced a notion of childhood as a distinct life stage that demanded adult protection and intervention to ensure that every child had a supervised, appropriate, and "sheltered" childhood.[18] Turn-of-century reformers worked tirelessly to expand the reach of both voluntary organizations and the State into the lives of children and families, promoting professional approaches to children's health, discipline, development, schooling, labor, and play.[19] They saw children, especially the children of the poor and working classes, as susceptible to forming bad habits and at risk of influence by the dangers and temptations of the streets, and they organized to intervene.[20] Their efforts were emblematic of the Progressive Era, a period of activism and reform spanning the 1890s to the 1920s that emphasized the application of advancements in science, medicine, and technology to address social problems and promote human betterment.[21]

Reformers also sought to intervene in the lives of children who were abused, neglected, abandoned, or exploited. Until the 1870s, no legal standards existed for the protection of children. The first formal legal interventions on behalf of children came under actions of the New York Society for the Prevention of Cruelty to Animals in 1875, with the argument that children, like animals, are a form of property and that they share with animals a fundamental helplessness. In the wake of the initial cases, a nationwide movement was launched to create Societies for the Prevention of Cruelty to Children and Animals in every state.

Turn-of-century child advocates called for new approaches to troubled youth that recognized both their rights and their vulnerability.[22] In 1899 the first juvenile court was established in Chicago, launching a new wave of reform across the nation. A philosophy of *parens patriae* guided early development of the juvenile court, wherein the State was seen as having both a legal obligation and a right to protect children, stepping in to discipline and guide errant youth and accept responsibility for their welfare when their own parents failed to do so.[23] Reformers around the country identified, organized, and supervised play as a potential deterrent to youth crime and called for establishment of playgrounds and organized group activities to promote children's moral, physical, and social development that kept youngsters off the streets and thus off the path to delinquency.[24]

During this same time, other trends were shaping societal views of children. As labor unions gained in strength, child labor came to be a political issue not only for the safety and well-being of children but also because child labor could be used to hold down the wages of adults.[25] In 1902 social reformers Lillian Wald and Florence Kelly organized activists in the New York settlement house movement to advocate for changes in state law to protect children working in the street trades. From their efforts, a national child labor committee was formed, and state-by-state legislative efforts addressing child labor were undertaken.[26] Labor leader Mary Harris "Mother" Jones was an outspoken advocate against child labor. Well-known for her strident and charismatic organizing of coal miners and railroad workers, she also engaged in highly public campaigns to protect children working in the Pennsylvania textile mills. For example, in 1903 she organized a "children's army" of young mill workers and marched them from Philadelphia to President Theodore Roosevelt's Long Island summer home, making a grand public display of the crime of child labor.[27]

Hand in hand with laws to protect children from labor exploitation came efforts to promote free compulsory education. By 1910, 88 percent of American children ages ten through fourteen attended school for some part of the year.[28] Public schools not only provided children with basic academic skills but were also seen as important institutions for socializing children to a common "American" experience. Through their participation in schooling, children also experienced a growing significance of peer groups and age-graded social ties.[29]

Children and youth were becoming the subjects of professional study and public policy aimed at ensuring their health, education, and well-being. Psychologists were studying children's development and offering professional guidance to parents on children's psychological conditioning. In 1904 psychologist G. Stanley Hall announced the "discovery" of "adolescence," which he described as a unique stage of development characterized as a biologically driven time of "stress and storm" that left young people particularly vulnerable to trouble.[30] Adolescence became a popular topic for advice columnists and educational and mental health professionals seeking to keep older youth from turning to deviance and vice.

Policy makers and child advocates gathered in Washington, D.C., in 1909 to participate in the first White House Conference on Children, wherein the twentieth century was declared "the century of the child." Children's health, welfare, and education were key topics of public policy making.[31] The U.S. Children's Bureau was established in 1912, bringing a cadre of professional researchers and advocates together to focus specifically on issues of child well-being.

By the 1910s and 1920s, new forms of media were also shaping children's lives. First movies then radio provided public entertainment, and children were eager audiences. Historian Joseph Hawes argues that a new version of American childhood was emerging at that time, marked by a national youth culture and recognition of children and youth as consumers. The market in movies, toys, and games targeting children and youth was expanding. At the same time, child advocates worried about the influences of these new forms of entertainment on children. They redoubled efforts to study children's mental health and development and encouraged the expansion of organized activities, such as Boy and Girl Scouts, to structure children's after-school and summer time.[32]

The Depression years, marked by widespread poverty, took a tremendous toll on children.[33] Rates of child malnutrition rose, and hunger was an everyday reality. Hard times forced many children out of school. Children tried to make sense of the dramatic changes in their lives, such as being forced from their homes when their parents could no longer pay the mortgage or rent. For example, children at a Philadelphia nursery school invented an "eviction game" in which they would systematically pile their toys in one spot and then pick them up and move them to another. As they told their teacher, "We ain't got money for rent, so's we've moved into a new house. Then we got a constable [sheriff] on us, so we's moving again."[34]

New Deal public policies paid particular attention to the needs of children and youth. Over two million young people around the country took advantage of employment opportunities offered through the National Youth Administration. The Social Security Act, passed in 1935, provided federal funding for services for abused and neglected children, services for crippled children, and programs for maternal and child health.[35] The beginnings of economic recovery could be seen in a renewed attention to children as consumers by the late 1930s. In 1937 *Snow White and the Seven Dwarfs*, the first full-length animated feature film, was released, and the comic book, a new genre of entertainment targeting children and youth, was launched with the arrival of *Superman*.

The 1940s began with the White House Conference on Children and Youth in a Democracy. Fears regarding the growing radicalism of youth during the Great Depression and the international surge in fascism in the 1930s prompted policy makers and youth advocates to again examine youth-focused policies and institutions. With the United States' entry into World War II, however, adult preoccupations shifted, and children and youth were recognized as national assets and called upon to fulfill their patriotic duties. Young people were key players in war-bond stamp and scrap-metal drives around the country. With sixteen million Americans called to military service, war became a central part of children's everyday lives and consciousness.[36] Demands of wartime also prompted federal support for child care, given the numbers of women working in war-production industries. For a time, nursery schools, day care, and after-school programs enjoyed both funding and broad-based support.

The 1950s saw growing concern over the development and well-being of young children, and public funding for preschools and kindergarten followed. High school graduation rates continued to rise. Cold War politics and sentiments also stirred adult concerns about children and youth. Fears about young people's propensity for trouble led to renewed social science interest and public debate about juvenile delinquency. Fears about the lagging competitiveness of American children in comparison with their Soviet counterparts were stirred in professional debates and popular media, such as Rudolph Flesch's controversial 1955 book *Why Johnny Can't Read*.[37] While schoolchildren were captivated by *Sputnik*, the first satellite to orbit the earth in 1957, and knew the name of Laika, the first "space dog," policy makers fretted over their scholastic

Danette Harrington and her uncle Otto Stallman enjoy fresh snow in winter 1948.

aptitude. In 1958 the National Defense Education Act was passed with the goal of improving student performance in math, science, and foreign languages.[38]

Children's health became a centerpiece of public concern as the worst polio epidemic in American history swept the country in 1952, with fifty-eight thousand cases reported and more than twenty thousand people left with mild to debilitating paralysis.[39] In 1952 Jonas Salk developed the first polio vaccine, and by 1954 nearly two million American schoolchildren had participated as test subjects in field trials of the vaccination.[40] With the passage of the Polio Vaccine Assistance Act in 1955, large-scale vaccination programs were implemented around the country.

By 1960 the United States was poised for profound change as the first of the postwar "baby boom" generation reached their teen years. Young people gained unprecedented access to higher education and were quickly becoming a social and cultural force to be reckoned with. At the same time, policy makers were turning their attention to the widespread nature of poverty and inequality affecting America's children. Ideas about children and childhood were changing, sparking a sense of both loss and possibility.[41]

As this brief overview illustrates, concepts of childhood are dynamic. They shape and are shaped by public policies, social institutions, and the actions of young and old alike. Changing notions of childhood and child-related policies and practices did not come about without struggle and resistance. The story of childhood in Butte provides not only a unique view into the Mining City but also a window into the ways in which modern notions of childhood were constructed and contested and the ways in which children themselves played key roles in those negotiations.

Mining Childhood takes readers on a journey to diverse contexts and moments in time to tell the stories of early- to mid-twentieth-century childhood in Butte. Chapter 1, "Children of the Hill," provides a historic overview of Butte with particular attention to the place of children in the story. The chapter offers a child's-eye view of key events in Butte's history and considers how social, political, and economic forces shaping life in Butte left their marks on the bodies and psyches of children.

Chapter 2, "Mining Childhood," explores the myriad ways in which the power of mining insinuated itself into the everyday lives of children. Many Butte children grew up with a keen awareness of the labors and landscape of copper mining, which provided them with a unique local knowledge and shaped their understanding of family, community, work, danger, fairness, and the boundaries of belonging and difference. The chapter also speaks to the ways in which ethnic identity and the social space of neighborhoods shaped experiences and memories of childhood. It provides us with a child's-eye view of life in Butte.

Chapter 3, "Saving Children," examines the ways in which adult reformers sought to intervene in the lives of "other people's" children. The chapter explores the work of charities and State-based organizations involved in the care and control of Butte children and youth from the turn of the century to the 1950s. It highlights activities of the State Bureau of Child and Animal Protection, the Paul Clark Home, early youth court, the Junior Service League, and the Soroptimist Home for Children. These efforts reflect deep concern for children growing up around the dangers of urban life; they also reveal underlying assumptions about class and gender that shaped understandings of poor and working-class children's lives.

Chapters 4, 5, and 6 draw heavily on oral histories to capture childhood experiences of school, play, and work. Chapter 4, "Child's Play," enters into the worlds of children at play. It addresses the ways in which Butte youngsters played with and around the dangers of mining life and forged their identities in the process. Children of Butte have had a longstanding reputation of being hardy survivors, socialized from infancy to thrive on tough terrain. Themes of risk taking and resilience reverberate through their accounts. Children's stories reveal both tough and tender moments as they established their turf, protected siblings, built alliances, and negotiated power.

Chapter 5, "School Days," explores childhood accounts of schools and schooling. The stories speak to children's joys and miseries as students, their keen impressions of teachers and classmates, and the lessons they learned, which were not necessarily those being taught. This chapter also examines ways in which broader issues regarding education in the early- to mid-twentieth-century played out in Butte and considers the various ways that children acquired political education both inside and outside the classroom.

Chapter 6, "Learning to Labor," investigates the place of work in the lives of Butte children. Accounts of paid and unpaid labor have a central place in stories of childhood. This chapter considers the ways that Butte children learned to work, the necessity of their labor for their families and community, and the lessons in responsibility, economics, and justice learned along the way. Accounts of childhood entrepreneurship are also suggestive of a certain power and autonomy that children gained through their labors.

Chapter 7, "Memories of a McQueen Childhood," is based on the rich oral history of Steve Sherick, who grew up in McQueen in the 1930s and 1940s. Sherick's remarkable eye for detail and storytelling prowess bring Butte childhood in the post-Depression era vividly to life. He captures the sights, sounds, and smells of his tight-knit neighborhood. Sherick offers an evocative view of working-class culture, ethnic identity, and community ties and tensions. His story reveals ways in which children negotiated the everyday demands and opportunities of schooling, play, and work.

Chapter 8, "Childhood Matters," reflects on the lessons about children and childhood gleaned from Butte's history. This chapter addresses the ways in which the landscape of mining shaped the geography of childhood, the relationship of mining to both trauma and resilience in children's lives, and the capacities of children to give meaning to their experiences, understand and negotiate relations of power, and invent possibilities to not only survive but to thrive in this harsh terrain.

Mining Childhood attempts to put flesh and bones on the notion of "modern childhood" as it was experienced in Butte. As you the reader begin this journey, I invite you to look at Butte from the perspective of a seven-year-old circa 1925. John Sheehy was born in 1918 and grew up on the Butte Hill. In recording his memories of childhood, Sheehy wrote:

> It is the mornings I remember chiefly from the years of my boyhood in Butte, Montana. Especially the winter mornings—winter in the sense of lots of snow on the ground and temperatures around the zero mark. In my bed, piled with blankets, only my head sticking out, I reveled in the warmth and anticipated the chill which would greet my first steps out of bed. I used to dress quickly, long johns, which were already on since I slept in them; a shirt made by my mother, which she called a waist; then my knickers (all kids wore knickers then, which came as a set with a coat—I wore them until the seventh grade when I got my first "long pants"); then long black stockings; and finally high shoes with metal catches on their top halves for cross-lacing, or else high-button shoes, which required a buttonhook to fasten. A sweater, coat, and cap and I was ready to brace the elements.[42]

Readers, it is time to grab your coats, put on your hats, and brace the elements.

CHAPTER ONE

Children of the Hill

Situating Children in Butte's History

The Hill wasn't much to look at in the daytime, all red and yellow dirt that had been dug up and piled around. At night it was pretty. When it got dark The Hill was sprinkled all over with lights because the mines worked twenty-four hours a day and they kept the lights on in the mines yards and along the roads. Some goofy poet sent in a poem to the Standard *about The Hill at night and they printed it. I forget how it went except that it said the lights at night made Butte look like "all the stars in heaven fell on The Hill." That's too mushy, but there were a lot of lights.*

—Richard K. O'Malley, *Mile High, Mile Deep*

From Mining Camp to Metropolis

BUTTE, MONTANA, was once known as the "Richest Hill on Earth" thanks to the rich veins of copper that coursed deep beneath its surface. At the turn of the twentieth century, Butte was home to the world's largest copper-mining operation, run by the Anaconda Copper Mining Company, a giant of industry. Butte began as a mining camp, with the first strike of gold along Silver Bow Creek in 1864. A rush of hopeful miners and merchants followed in pursuit first of gold and then silver. By 1867 the Butte City townsite had been laid out. The gold was soon exhausted, and by the mid-1870s silver mining was the primary focus of economic productivity.[1]

Butte's future, however, lay not in gold and silver but in the massive deposits of copper beneath.[2] Copper mining and smelting are labor-intensive processes that require both technical know-how and capital investment to be successful. It was not until the 1880s, when the generation and harnessing of electricity launched what came to be known as the Second Industrial Revolution, that copper, an excellent conductor

Beginning in the 1880s, jobs in the copper mines began attracting immigrants to Butte. The new arrivals settled in ethnic neighborhoods, including Dublin Gulch (shown here in about 1910), where they could speak their native languages and maintain cultural ties to their homelands.

of electricity, became an important commodity on the world market as the technological possibilities of electrification began to be realized.[3] With the discovery of rich copper deposits, the arrival of the Northern Pacific Railroad, and investments in mining and smelting technology by a few bold entrepreneurs, Butte began to boom. Initially a magnet for a transient workforce of young men, Butte soon was home to increasing numbers of women and children.[4]

Before long, nearly five thousand miners were bringing Butte's riches to the surface.[5] The air was thick with smoke from smelting operations. Dozens of gallows frames—massive structures housing the hoists that carried men and material to and from the surface—marked the entrances to Butte's labyrinth of underground mines. As the kings of the copper industry battled over control of the Butte mines and Montana state politics, working men and women built a town, a community, and a way of life on harsh terrain. Given the dangers of underground mining, miners moved swiftly to unionize. In 1878 the Butte Miners' Union was founded to demand wage increases, shorter work days, and improved working conditions. In the ensuing years, Butte would earn the moniker "Gibraltar of Unionism" in recognition of its fierce commitment to organized labor.[6]

Despite the tough working and living conditions, the promise of steady work and union wages continued to lure new immigrants to Butte well into the first decades of the twentieth century. Cornish and Irish immigrants dominated the first wave of migration to Butte. By the turn of the century, Irish comprised 25 percent of Butte's burgeoning population.[7] They were followed by Italians, Finns, Swedes, Serbians, Croatians, Slovenians, Montenegrins, Syrians, and Lebanese. New arrivals gravitated to their familiar ethnic communities, where they not only worked together underground but also created strong neighborhoods—Finntown, Hungry Hill, Dublin Gulch, Stringtown, Corktown, Butchertown, Dogtown, Centerville, Meaderville, McQueen Addition, Walkerville, the Cabbage Path, the Flats—where they could speak their native language, buy and prepare familiar foods, and maintain ties to their homelands through native-language newspapers, social clubs, and fraternal organizations.[8] Richard O'Malley describes the polyphony of early Butte: "Talk English at school. Talk Czech, Italian, Yugoslav, Serb, Finn, Swede, Norwegian at home. The old folks don't talk English so good, grandma don't know a word ain't it funny I wish grandpa would talk something besides Gaelic he's been here five years now. Let 'em alone, they're old, they're set in their ways and what's wrong with Gaelic, Finn, Yugoslav, any of them?"[9]

As new arrivals came to Butte and the number of families grew, so did the accompanying social, cultural, religious, and educational institutions. Irish immigrants established one of Butte's first neighborhoods, Dublin Gulch, nestled on the Hill northeast of the Uptown business district and surrounded by underground mines. By the time Butte became an incorporated city in 1879, its first Catholic church, St. Patrick's, had opened its doors, with a school soon to follow. St. Patrick's Parish had a congregation of seven thousand members by 1889, and by 1901 Butte had five Catholic parishes with combined memberships of over twenty-five thousand.[10] While the Catholic presence was certainly strong, Butte was home to diverse faith communities. By 1900, eight Methodist, three Presbyterian, and two Episcopal churches, along with a B'Nai Israel congregation and Baptist, German Evangelical Lutheran, and Seventh-day Adventist churches, a Church of the Latter-day Saints, a Church of Christ, Scientist, two Pentecostal missions, and a Salvation Army headquarters, had been established in Butte.[11]

The Italian neighborhood of Meaderville began to be settled in 1878 by immigrants from northern Italy, and it was well established by 1890. Residents founded Butte's Cristoforo Colombo Society in 1890, which is still in existence today.[12] Society dues were used to help support the families of members who became ill or injured and unable to work.[13] The Meaderville Bakery, opened by the Sconfienza family in 1890, became a local institution, along with the restaurants, grocery stores, and barbershops through which the familiar aromas and sounds of Italy flowed.

Extending from Meaderville on the northeast edge of Butte's mining district lay the McQueen Addition. The neighborhood was initially established in 1891 and settled primarily by immigrants from Slovenia, Croatia, and Austria along with a mix of Finnish, Swedish, English, Norwegian, Italian, and German immigrants. It was a neighborhood of modest, single-family homes, many with chickens, pigs, and smokehouses in the backyards.[14]

In the late 1870s, a number of Jewish families, mostly Russian immigrants, came to Butte from the Deer Lodge Valley and established a significant niche in the local economy. They organized the B'Nai Israel temple, which was housed first in the Carpenters' Union Hall and then in the Mountain View Methodist Church, until a permanent temple was constructed in 1903.[15]

The turn of the twentieth century saw an influx of Finnish as well as southern European immigrants to the city. Finns were coming west from the copper mines of Michigan, bringing with them their experience in underground mining and hopes for higher wages. They established a tight-knit community just east of Uptown Butte, with their own boardinghouses, churches, bars, shops, and saunas.

In the first years of the new century, immigrants from a global diaspora continued to make their way to Butte. Soon the city was home to a range of institutions that supported collective ethnic identity, nurtured intergenerational ties, and eased the transition to life in the United States. Among them were the Scandinavian Fraternity (which established the Scandinavian Hall), the Narodni Dom (Slovenian American Hall), the Finn Hall, the Ancient Order of Hibernians, the

Immigrants from northern Italy began settling in Meaderville by 1878, and the neighborhood was well established by 1890. Residents bought familiar Italian foods at Ciabattari and Son Meaderville Grocery (above, 1923) operated by Michael Ciabattari and his son, Tom.

The Bart and Michael Ciabattari families pose in front of their Meaderville home circa 1910. Bart's family, on the left, includes, from left: Rose, wife Mary, Medette, Eatolo (later nicknamed Speets), and Bart. On the right, Michael's family includes, from left: Tom, wife Margarita, Ines, Michael, and Vincent.

Hebrew Benevolent Society, the William Tell Benevolent Society, and the Cornish Order of the Sons of St. George. By 1900 Butte had over forty fraternal and benevolent organizations and another forty trade and labor unions.[16]

Chinese immigrants who had followed the gold rush to Montana began to settle in Butte as early as 1868. Some established hand laundries, apothecary businesses, tailor shops, noodle parlors, and restaurant businesses in Uptown Butte, and others worked in domestic service

Chinese immigrants who had followed the gold rush to Montana began to settle in Butte as early as 1868. Quong Pock Huie (left), the son of physician and surgeon Huie Pock, worked in his father's mercantile on the edge of Butte's Chinatown at the turn of the century. The store also housed the doctor's office. The other young man is not identified.

and started produce gardens south of town. Butte's Chinese population, which peaked in the 1890s, faced virulent discrimination at the turn of the century as Butte boardinghouses advertised "white only" hiring practices, and city and state ordinances were passed that levied harsh taxes and licensing charges on Chinese businesses.[17]

African Americans migrating north and west in the post-Reconstruction years began to arrive in Butte as early as the 1890s, with the main influx occurring in the early 1900s. Black-owned newspapers, such as the *New Age,* edited by John Duncan, encouraged African American migration with the promise of economic opportunity in Butte. However, the prevailing racism of the times cut short those opportunities. African Americans who came to Butte were successful in finding jobs, but the employment they found was often limited to service work.[18] For Chinese and African Americans alike, discriminatory hiring practices ensured that better-paying jobs, such as those in the mines, were not open to them.

A Place to Raise Children

Butte's population was doubling every few years, and new arrivals were putting down roots and raising children. The security of children and families was a priority for Butte's laborers. Given the dangers of hard-rock mining, early union efforts focused not only on wages but also on benefits for widows and children in the event of injury and death.[19] As men labored underground, women dominated the service industries, catering to the feeding and clothing of this behemoth workforce. Women workers in Butte quickly followed the lead of the miners' unions and began to organize. In 1890 a group of working women formed the Butte Women's Protective Union (WPU). The WPU operated as a community-based social service and action organization, concerned with improving the well-being of all women and recognizing women's rights and responsibilities as workers, women, and mothers. The WPU was well aware that many women were juggling the responsibilities of working and raising children, and the union sought not only fair wages and safe working conditions but also social and health insurance for women workers and their families.[20]

The challenges of child rearing in America at the turn of the century were daunting. Overall, children were often poorly housed, clothed, and fed. Twenty percent of children did not live to celebrate their fifth birthday, and 50 percent of infant mortality occurred in the first year of life.[21] In addition to problems of prematurity and injury at birth, respiratory illnesses and severe diarrhea—often referred to as cholera infantum—struck newborns and infants. Parents, midwives, and doctors were often helpless to intervene. In Butte, air laced with arsenic from the copper smelters, coupled with poor sanitation and living conditions, exacerbated newborns' struggles for survival. Turn-of-the-century attention to public health resulted in improved record keeping regarding child birth and registry of children's deaths. The Silver Bow County coroner's records circa 1900 reveal the stark realities of infant mortality and the struggles for survival that belied the bravado of Butte. Some entries report a diagnosis of cholera infantum, while others simply state "delicate since birth." Ann Pentilla was born in Butte in 1907; she was the eldest of four girls. Ann remembered her mother's experience: "She lost two babies. They were blue babies. They lost a lot of children [in Butte]. I remember the midwife putting the child in the oven at a certain temperature in a blanket to keep it warm, but it didn't survive."[22]

Deaths of infants were daily occurrences as were deaths of toddlers as a result of accidents and injuries at home and in the streets. Reports of the county coroner documented the occasional discovery of bodies of infants found in mine shafts. One can only imagine the desperate circumstances behind these terse words: "Inquest—Unknown Infant—2 Oct 1902—found in bottom of mine shaft known as Peter mine located about five miles S. of City of Butte. No info on parentage or who put infant in shaft."[23]

Physician-assisted births were replacing midwifery, and professionals across the country were publishing advice pamphlets on the care and rearing of infants and toddlers. However, working-class women in Butte and elsewhere still relied largely on the assistance of midwives and knowledge passed along through generations of women. Midwives not only would assist in the delivery but might also support new mothers for a week or two afterward, helping with cooking, washing, and childcare. Immigrant women, such as Ann Pentilla's mother, also drew on traditions they brought with them when it came to infant care: "When we were infants, my mother used to wrap us up like mummies every night, with our hands to our sides and our feet together. We wouldn't go to sleep until she wrapped us. I think it was up to six months. She said if we weren't wrapped, we were restless. That was a tradition in Europe so that the children's limbs would be straight. We all grew up straight, the four of us, tall and straight."[24]

Growing attention to maternal and child health at the turn of the century also offered more hopeful outcomes for newborns. For example, on November 3, 1901, an Irish immigrant mining family welcomed Montana's first recorded triplets into its home. The children, two girls and a boy, were born at home with support of a Butte doctor, and the newborns were feted with gifts from the Butte community, including a ten-dollar savings account deposit for each made to the State Savings

The challenges of child rearing at the turn of the century were daunting. Overall, children were often poorly housed, clothed, and fed. These children were photographed in the backyards of houses on the 1100 block of East Broadway for a 1908–1912 report on the working and living conditions of Silver Bow County miners and their families.

Bank of Butte by the Butte Women's Club. So taken was the community with the threesome that in 1903 state legislator Guy Stapleton of Butte introduced a bill to provide a fund of three thousand dollars for their future education. According to the *Butte Miner*, the law would "provide for the education of the tiny mites, who are still in the blissful state of babyhood, all oblivious to the great public interest that is being taken with them, as yet free from all the cares that will weigh upon them as well as upon the rest of humanity, as to the grave problems of this life."[25]

Public health campaigns promoting improved home sanitation, safer feeding practices, and milk pasteurization, along with development of public water and sewer systems, contributed to a decrease in infant mortality around the country by 1910.[26] However, a Silver Bow County Board of Health investigation into housing and sanitation in Butte, conducted between 1908 and 1912 to find out why tuberculosis rates were inordinately high, documented the poor living conditions that continued to plague many families.[27]

Time for School

Education mattered to Butte residents. In the winter of 1866, the mining camp established its first school with one teacher and about a dozen students who met daily in a log cabin on East Broadway Street for music, calisthenics, and spelling lessons. Parents paid for books, and the teacher was paid by subscription. A single school and teacher served Butte for a decade, until the town, and the school system, began to boom. By 1884 the Mining City not only had three hundred mines in operation but also had established its first high school. In 1886 the first graduating class of Butte High School held commencement ceremonies in the Miners' Union Hall.[28]

As diverse ethnic neighborhoods came to life around the city's many underground mines, elementary schools soon followed. Adams School opened in 1885, followed in close succession by Monroe, Blaine, Lincoln, and Garfield schools. By 1886 Butte's public school system employed twenty teachers. By 1892 Butte had fourteen schools in operation. Butte High School was proud to award diplomas to ten graduates that year. In 1893 St. Patrick's Parish, home to Butte's first Catholic elementary school, established a high school as well.[29]

Butte's workforce was planting roots, and its neighborhoods and numbers of children were growing. School construction and expansion were ongoing activities in the early 1900s. Between 1900 and 1905, the Emerson, Sacred Heart, Sherman, Jefferson, Harrison, Holy Savior, St. Mary's, Franklin, and McKinley schools were built. Holy Savior Church and School opened as a Jesuit mission in the McQueen neighborhood in 1902. Franklin School opened in this working-class neighborhood the following year; it also housed a nursery for the children of working parents that continued until the 1940s. By 1904 the Butte Public School District employed two hundred teachers to serve an enrollment of eight thousand students.[30]

The leadership of Butte's Catholic schools saw the need for a centrally located high school to serve students from all of the city's parish-based elementary schools. In 1908 Central High School, a coeducational institution, opened, replacing the high schools previously established at St. Patrick, St. Lawrence O'Toole, and Sacred Heart parishes. One hundred and seventy students registered on the first day of classes. By 1908 Butte was home to forty-seven churches, twenty public schools, and seven parochial schools.[31]

Butte and the State of Montana were national leaders in public education. For example, the Montana legislature passed a stringent compulsory education law in 1902 that included harsh consequences for truancy and called for the establishment of industrial schools for the detention of habitual truants in cities with twenty-five thousand or more residents.[32] The Butte Industrial School, with capacity for forty students, opened in November 1903 with the mission to "reform the wayward and save the lost" so that Butte children did not grow up in "idleness, ignorance, or crime."[33] The school was touted as the only one of its kind west of Chicago. Butte also demonstrated its commitment to progressive education by establishing the state's first junior high school, serving both boys and girls, in 1915.[34]

Celebrating the New Century

In order to survive on Butte's tough terrain, residents not only worked hard but played hard. Young and old alike found escape from the rigors of mining life in dance halls, theaters, ball fields, and skating rinks. Butte residents were swept away by the national roller-skating craze at the turn of the century. Hundreds of skaters glided to the music of a brass band along the sleek maple floors of the Byrne Roller Rink. The expansive facility also served as an auditorium for political rallies and celebrity shows and as a "big tent" for Christian revivalist gatherings.[35] The Holland Roller Rink, built in 1905, was later converted to an ice rink and was a popular spot through the 1930s. As Tubie Johnson recalled: "We sure had a lot of fun playing hockey at the Holland Rink. All the kids rolled up *Life* magazines around their lower legs to use as protection when they got hit with the puck. We had no other type of padding or helmets to use. All we had was a stick."[36]

From its early days, Butte was a die-hard sports town. Butte children grew up in a world as dominated by the rivalries of high school and Independent League football, the brash blows of boxing, and the joys of sandlot and league baseball as by mining. Irish competed in Gaelic football, while Meaderville's Italians enjoyed games of bocce. Miners shifted from camaraderie underground to competition above as they tested their mettle in rock drilling and tug-of-war competitions with their children cheering them on. Professional boxing was a Butte favorite, and children as well as adults rallied around local heroes as they came up against reigning champions. Inspired by the physical prowess of local boxers such as Jack Munroe, Buddy King, and Spider Kelly, Butte boys filled boxing clubs around the city.[37]

Children invented their own competitions, from high-speed sled races down Butte's steep hillsides to fiercely competitive baseball and football games between rival neighborhood teams. While formal parks and playgrounds were scarce, gangs of children took to the streets and mine yards, creating their own play spaces. Clad in their denim overalls, boys and girls joined their neighborhood gangs for a game of marbles or Ante I Over, and when the brief heat of summer arrived, they headed to Bell Creek to swim.

Butte residents enjoyed a rich cultural life as well. By 1900 Butte had four theaters and the Grand Opera House. Plays, acrobatics, musical performances, vaudeville shows, Italian opera, and magic shows captured the public imagination. It was not long before children were being recognized and courted as consumers of entertainment and regular customers for Saturday matinees. The Broadway Theater, with its fire escape leading to a skylight above the second balcony, was a favorite attraction for the more audacious. Young risk takers willing to clamber to the skylight, pry it open, and drop ten feet to the balcony could enjoy the show for free.[38]

Butte's true centerpiece for celebration was Columbia Gardens, which made its debut in June 1899. Columbia Gardens was an elegant park nestled in a protected fold of the rugged mountains east of town. It featured a lake, zoo, dance pavilion, arcade, and amusement park complete with roller coaster and carousel as well as vast gardens, picnic areas, and playgrounds. Funded by copper magnate William A. Clark and managed by the Clark-owned Butte Street Railway Company, the

In 1899 copper magnate William A. Clark created Columbia Gardens, an amusement park east of Butte that offered miners and their families a magical place to escape from the rigors of daily life. Here, visitors enjoy the swings of the upper playground circa 1900. Beyond them, people crowd the porches of the pavilion (center). The outside of the ballpark stands can be seen in the background (right).

Gardens offered miners and their families a magical place to escape from the rigors of daily life. From the start, Clark treated Butte children as special guests of Columbia Gardens, hosting regular events that placed them center stage.[39]

Hopeful Dreams and Harsh Realities

On June 13, 1900, mining families celebrated the twenty-second anniversary of Miners' Union Day, honoring the founding of the union in 1878. Five thousand mine, mill, and smelter workers marched through Butte to the beat of the Boston & Montana Band while loved ones lined the streets. The crowd cheered union president Michael McCormick as he announced that Butte mine owners had agreed to union demands for an eight-hour day.[40] Butte's population had reached sixty-two thousand.[41] Eighty-eight percent of the population was under age twenty-five.[42] The Butte mines were soon producing one-third of the nation's copper; its mining workforce was twelve thousand strong and earning "the world's largest" payroll of $1.5 million a month.[43]

Women's work was largely dedicated to feeding, cleaning, teaching, and healing this human engine of mining. Children made their contributions as well. State labor laws required young people to be sixteen years old before gaining employment in the mines, but documentation

Kids tagged along as the Butte Mine Band marched in the annual Miners' Union Day parade circa 1900.

of age left plenty of room for error and exaggeration. Beyond the mines, many children contributed to the family and community economy by selling newspapers, working in family-run stores and domestic service, packing miners' lunch-buckets, and delivering groceries.

Population and payroll figures provide a glimpse into one dimension of early Butte, but they do little to reveal the human dimension. The copper mines held hope for a better future for new immigrants, their families back home, and the new families they were forging. For some, the grueling work in the mines brought a modicum of comfort and security. For others, life in Butte wrought desperation, tragedy, and death. In 1903, for example, all mining operations were shut down for nearly two months, affecting twenty thousand wage earners in Butte and four-fifths of the wage earners in the state, as corporate power brokers vied for control of the copper market.[44] In 1906 mining operations were dramatically cut back in an effort to squelch union activism.[45] Some families survived these challenging times with the support of neighbors, kin, and public relief. For others, charity organizations offered basic support. In response to widespread poverty in early Butte, the Associated Charities sponsored a soup kitchen and solicited donations of coal. By the end of 1904, the soup kitchen had served more than thirteen thousand meals.[46] In July 1906 the Salvation Army established a facility to provide shelter for homeless and destitute families.

Mining was notoriously dangerous work, and Butte families knew well the sounds of sirens and bells signaling an accident in the mines. As Richard O'Malley describes:

> Nine bells means trouble in a mine and everybody goes into
> action. They rang them in sets of three and everyone on the
> surface knew that something bad had happened down below.
> Whoever rang them would ring nine bells, and then ring the
> station call. The way the calls went, you'd ring one and one for
> the 100-foot level, two and two for the 200-foot level, on up to
> four and four for the 400-foot. Then it could be five and one
> for the five hundred, and so on. They rang by fours. When we
> were up around the mines, we used to listen to see if anyone
> was ringing nine bells. They called them bells, but it was really
> a great big buzzer that you could hear all around the mine
> yard.[47]

Injuries wrought by a "fall of ground"—when massive slabs of rock gave way in an underground tunnel; premature explosion of dynamite; and illnesses such as tuberculosis, pneumonia, and miner's consumption ("miner's con") claimed lives every day in Butte.[48] Generally only accidents resulting in multiple deaths were deemed newsworthy. The 1913 Leonard Mine accident warranted such attention. On April 24 a hoist carrying fourteen men underground went out of control, sending the miners plummeting 1,500 feet and killing five of them. Four men were crushed to death, and another was killed by flying steel when a cable disintegrated. The *Butte Miner* reporter captured an intimate perspective on the tragedy. Mary H. Adams and T. J. Pascoe, one of the deceased, had wed a mere eleven months earlier. The young couple were new parents of an infant son.

> After their marriage the couple moved to a bungalow in the McQueen Addition. They had planned so much for the summer and were improving their home every day. . . . Mrs. Adams [mother of the widow] and other women did the household duties during the afternoon and cared for the little fellow. He appeared to be the young mother's only comfort as she lay in bed and stroked his head. He slept and dug his tiny fists into his eyes and cried once for more food. The mother wept softly and kept her grief to herself. Pascoe was born in England 26 years ago. His parents died when he was an infant and he was reared by relatives, several of whom survive him. He had been a resident of Butte for four years.[49]

The account in the *Butte Miner* offered poignant details of the families of other victims:

> Andrew Bartell (deceased) was born in Finland 41 years ago and came to America when but a young man. He had been a resident of Butte for 22 years and had worked continuously for 11 years at the Leonard mine. He is survived by a wife and four children living at 1121 Gallatin Street. The eldest is a girl 13 years of age and the others are 11, 8 and 7 years old respectively.
> Nicholas Treglown had been in Butte but a comparatively short time. He is survived by his wife and three-year-old daughter. With his family, he lived at 2101 Ash Street. When news of the accident reached the Treglown home the little girl was playing just outside the door. Realization of its import did not come to her. She played about the house all afternoon, noting her mother's tears with wonderment, and when she saw the men coming off shift from other mines she called repeatedly, "Daddy, where's my Daddy?"[50]

Tragedy visited Meaderville's Leonard Mine (above) in 1913 when a hoist carrying fourteen men careened out of control, sending the miners plummeting 1,500 feet. Five of them died, leaving widows and fatherless children.

Miners' deaths and injuries left many families in precarious circumstances. It was a truism in Butte that miners were lucky to live past forty. Michael Patrick "Packey" Buckley recalled his mother running a boardinghouse to keep the family afloat after his father was disabled.

> She had to [start the boardinghouse]. . . . My father couldn't work. He had miner's con. He died when I was in the sixth grade. You know what they called St. Mary's Parish, don't you? The parish of widows. They were all widows. Just for the hell of it, if you ever go by St. Patrick's Cemetery, go in and see the miners. Do you know what the average age is on the cross on the burial? Thirty-seven years old. And when you look back, a lot of them died from miner's con. But a lot of them died from pneumonia. They would come home on open streetcars, and [they had] no change rooms. They could get pneumonia and die, and a lot of them died from cancer, which we didn't know much about in those days.[51]

Young widows struggled to provide for their children and counted on the paid and unpaid labors of their children to help make ends meet.

Older residents recalled boys seeking work in the mines shy of their sixteenth birthdays after the boys' fathers had been injured or killed and responsibility for the family fell on their young shoulders. In his book *The Butte Irish*, historian David Emmons writes of the plight of widows and children in Butte:

> The mines created more Irish widows—fifty to one hundred per year from accidents alone—than Irish fortunes. Census statistics tell a part of the story. In 1900 there were 153 Irish widows under fifty years of age with a combined total of 392 children living at home; in 1910 the figures were 434 and 1,117. A closer look at what these numbers meant can be had by considering the 100 block of East La Platta Street in 1910. There were ten homes on the block, eight of them occupied by Irish widows. The women ranged in age from thirty-two to fifty-five; six had been born in Ireland, two in Michigan of Irish parents. Four of them rented rooms to single miners; three had working children; one sold milk and eggs; and two were without visible means of support. A combined total of forty-eight children had been born to the eight; thirty-four of them were still living, and thirty-two of those, ranging in age from two years to twenty-four, were living at home.[52]

Widows engaged in a vast array of informal labor and made subsistence livings as midwives, cooks, and domestic servants. Small widows' pensions, funded first through the county and later through the State, provided them a flimsy safety net. The Montana legislature approved a mothers' pension program in 1915, which provided aid to widows or mothers whose husbands could not support their families. Aid was limited to children fourteen and under, and it provided a maximum allowance of ten dollars a month for the first child with decreasing amounts for additional children.[53]

Prior to 1915, poor women and children were largely dependent on the Silver Bow County poor fund. The brief entries in the notebooks of county investigators shed light on the difficult conditions of widows and children, the meager assistance available to them, and the assessments made of their worthiness to receive aid.

> Mrs. P.D. 3/18/09—Age 44 years. Husband died 1 year ago. Left no money no insurance. 5 children oldest girl 19 yrs. Married cannot help them. 1–16–15–10 & 6 yrs. Boy of 16 is delicate not able to work or go to school. They own a little

3 room shack. Works herself when she can get it. She cannot go out to work as 6 year old one is sick. This seems to
be a deserving case. She got relations but gets no help from
them. . . .

Mrs. D. H. 5/18/09 Age 34 years old. 3 children ages 11, 4, and
2 yrs. Husband dead left no money, no insurance. She got
no relations that could help her any. Youngest child is sickly.
She got a nice clean house. Paying $10 rent. She seems to be a
rustler she packs old timbers from the mines, saws and splits
them herself. I seen some chickens here not many. I think she
might get along with a little less. This women is deserving. . . .

Mrs. W. C. 10/27/09—Got 7 children, ages from 15 years
down to 2 years. 5 going to school, 2 sell papers Saturdays
and Sunday. 2 little ones stay home. Husband . . . got miner's
consumption for over two years. She owns two houses 1–2
room not rented, 4 room lives there herself and children. This
is a nice tidy house, this woman would go out washing sooner
than come to the county but children too young to leave them
alone. Husband in good standing in M. union. She says if
she got some clothing and shoes for children she would not
bother anymore. Nov. 15th 1 child died with diphtheria.[54]

Meager support helped many families survive, but harsh conditions
defined daily life.

Children's Progress

Children played central roles in the social, economic, and cultural life
of Butte, and, reflecting Progressive Era efforts around the country,
considerable adult interest and energy was devoted to the oversight,
organization, and engagement of young people. Both public officials
and concerned citizens worried about the dangers of children on urban
streets and sought to intercede. Butte's first humane officer, P. J. Gilligan, who was responsible for investigation into the safety and welfare
of children, began his duties in 1904. Judge Michael Donlan oversaw a
weekly parade of young delinquents in his courtroom for several years
prior to the establishment of a formal youth court system in Montana in 1911. Organizations such as women's clubs and the Women's
Christian Temperance Union (WCTU) also took an active interest in
the lives of Butte children. For example, a curious mix of community

business leaders and WCTU activists joined forces to establish the Butte Newsboys Club in 1903. Newsboys were ever-present on Butte street corners, hawking the city's myriad daily papers and defending their turf. Concerned for the boys' moral and social well-being, club organizers brought them together in a self-governing system whereby the boys themselves enforced a strict code of discipline and order on members.[55]

W. A. Clark was clearly among those adults who paid close attention to the interests and activities of Butte children. His efforts to promote Arbor Day as a way to endear himself to the children and families of Butte offer a case in point. In 1901 Columbia Gardens was the site of Butte's first Arbor Day activities for the city's schoolchildren, and the event grew each year. In May 1906 Clark provided thirty thousand free trolley tickets to transport children to Columbia Gardens to take part in Arbor Day ceremonies. In 1907 President Theodore Roosevelt declared April 16 as Arbor Day nationwide, and governor Joseph K. Toole issued a proclamation recognizing the date in Montana. Clark and his supporters, including Butte's superintendent of schools, took issue with the date given that it was far too early in the spring for successful tree planting in Butte. They lobbied the governor for a change of date for Arbor Day in Silver Bow County to later in May so that the thousands of young participants could enjoy better weather. The request was denied, but Clark was undaunted. He initiated Children's Day at Columbia Gardens in May 1907. Ten thousand children took part in the inaugural event, which included free trolley rides, organized games and contests, and free use of the amusement park rides.[56]

William A. Clark endeared himself to Butte families, and especially its children, by providing youngsters with free days at Columbia Gardens. Here, he posed (left) with a group of boys and girls circa 1915.

Butte residents made concerted efforts to encourage young people's civic participation. For example, the city's first Boy Scout troop was founded in 1910.[57] The East Side Athletic Club, offering a needed venue for youth sports leagues, opened in 1910.[58] By 1912 Girl Scouts had organized, and in 1915 Butte saw its first Camp Fire Girls troop.[59] Religious and cultural organizations also focused efforts on organized activities for young people. For example, in 1913, Butte's Jewish community organized the Junior Auxiliary of the Temple, and the Gaelic League began offering courses in Gaelic language and dances to the children of the city's Irish immigrants.[60] Free Chautauquas—community-based cultural and educational gatherings—targeting audiences of children and youth were organized at Columbia Gardens. A favorite featured entertainment by Bronte, a Scotch Collie that held the title of "the World's Smartest Dog."[61]

Adults were recognizing children as consumers of culture and took pains to protect their moral, intellectual, and social development. In March 1913 Butte schoolchildren were the captive audience for a motion picture on how to avoid the "perils of the street." The Orpheum Theater provided every school-age child in the city with a free ticket for a designated show time.[62] The Butte Public Library launched its first "Children's Hour" in 1914.[63] And Butte parents and teachers debated whether dance classes in the public schools constituted a "social evil" or a legitimate part of the physical education curriculum.[64]

Little tykes were also the focus of increased public attention. Child advocates in Butte were inspired by reports of New York City's Better Babies Campaign that sought to reduce infant mortality by having public health nurses train new mothers in baby care and early childhood development. In 1914 Butte hosted its first annual "Beautiful Baby" show held under auspices of Shortridge Christian Memorial Church. According to a news report of the event, "Every mother present knows that her little one was by far the most beautiful one in the contest, but beauty alone could not win. The measurement of each little chest, girth, size and shape of head, complexion, health, and numerous other facts were taken into account."[65] Butte Women's Council soon began hosting an annual event promoting free weighing, measuring, and basic health examinations for all children under age six. By 1917 Montana's State Board of Health, established in 1901, had also instituted programs to better protect the health of Montana children.[66]

Fighting, Fire, and Fear

The hopeful focus on healthy babies, however, was tempered by more global concerns of war. As the nation faced the prospect of entry into war in 1917, tensions ran high in Butte. According to historian Howard Zinn, World War I was not a "people's war."[67] In 1917 the Selective Service Act was passed authorizing the conscription of soldiers, and a national public-relations campaign was launched to garner support for the United States' entry into the war. The specter of empire building and the military draft heightened class divisions across the country as poor and working-class men questioned why they were fighting the capitalists' battle.[68] These tensions played out in Butte as well. While political factions within the miners' union were engaged in internal struggles, corporate interests were eager to squelch radical labor activism and class-based solidarity. The ire of Butte miners over the discriminatory "rustling card" system—which the Anaconda Company had instituted as a means of screening out workers who were deemed to have strong union sympathies and "undemocratic" leanings—was also running high, as was resistance to the military draft. Moreover, Butte's strong Irish community was actively leveraging solidarity and support for the cause of Irish independence and had little sympathy for the plight of England's unstable empire.[69]

The volatile environment in Butte prompted Governor Samuel V. Stewart to declare martial law and call for federal troops to be dispatched to the Mining City in August 1917.[70] While adults might have responded with resentment or relief, children were curious. Some recalled boardinghouses transformed into barracks and the uniformed presence in the streets. Students in Sister Mary Xavier Davey's chemistry lab got front-row seats when the National Guard set up a post right outside St. Patrick's School. Sister Mary Xavier defended the rights of miners but also demanded that students respect the militia. As a gesture of goodwill, she had her students prepare coffee in the chemistry lab and serve the troops.[71]

In the midst of this already charged context, Butte experienced its worst mining disaster—a cataclysmic fire at the Granite Mountain Mine that claimed 168 lives and injured hundreds more in June 1917.[72] Some of the miners died instantly, and others were trapped underground for days as families and loved ones held anxious vigils in the dim hope of rescues. As Michael Punke described in his book *Fire and Brimstone*, family members of the missing miners made their way through Butte's many mortuaries, tackling the grim task of trying to identify loved ones among the rows of unidentified bodies: "In some families, circumstance required mere children to make the awful rounds. A Polish boy, 'perhaps seven years old,' showed up at one of the hospitals and asked the nurse in charge, 'Is my papa here?' He had already walked to all of the other hospitals and funeral homes. 'Mama is sick in bed and couldn't come, so I'm looking for him,' explained the boy. 'We are afraid he was killed.' The hospital could say only that the boy's father had not been admitted."[73]

Fifty-eight married men died in the fire, leaving wives and children behind. Over eighty children lost their fathers in the disaster. Miraculously, twenty-five men survived for days underground and were eventually rescued, thanks to the actions of Manus Duggan, a nipper for the North Butte Mining Company.[74] Duggan's quick-thinking effort to build a bulkhead that created a space of breathable air kept most of his group alive until rescuers reached them. Manus Duggan himself, however, did not survive.

Duggan's wife, Madge, was pregnant at the time. On June 14, six days after the start of the fire, Duggan's body was lifted from the depths. In his pocket was a handwritten note: "To my dear wife and mother: It breaks my heart to be taken from you so suddenly and unexpectedly, but think not of me, for if death comes it will be in a sleep without suffering. I ask forgiveness for any suffering or pain I have ever caused. Madge, dear, the place [house he had built] is for you and the child."[75]

Madge Duggan was heartbroken. She had met Manus when he was a young miner living in her mother's boardinghouse in 1915. Madge described him as "the finest looking man who ever walked the earth. I was crazy about him from the time I met him when I was 11 years old."[76] With the baby due, Manus had offered to stay home from his afternoon shift to be with Madge on that fateful day. She urged him to go to work as they needed his wages to pay for the home they were building. She awoke not to Manus's return but to the news of the disaster. When Manus died, Madge's grief was compounded by anxiety as the baby she was carrying went still and did not enter the world for another month.[77]

Madge gave birth to a healthy baby girl on July 7, 1917, and named the baby after her husband. Madge was fortunate to have a strong extended family to help complete the house Manus was building and to help her raise her infant daughter. As Michael Punke described, others faced further hardship. Henry Bennetts had recently arrived in Butte with his wife and six young children, hoping to make a living in the mines. His widow faced dim prospects, with no savings and no family support. Maurice Fitzharris had lost his wife and was raising three small children on his own. Hoping to work his way to shift boss, Fitzharris had taken a job at the Speculator Mine just days before the fatal fire. His children were orphaned as a result of the fire.[78]

The fire sparked outrage among Butte's miners, and within days they were on strike. The murder of union organizer Frank Little in August 1917 brought labor tensions to the tipping point, and Butte residents found themselves under guard by federal troops sent in to quell unrest. Butte women, however, expressed more concern for the desperate economic conditions brought on by the strike and exacerbated by skyrocketing wartime food prices. Feeding their children was their primary concern, and they began to organize. Some wrote of their plight to newly elected congresswoman Jeannette Rankin seeking her intervention so that the innocent children of Butte would not be left to suffer. Others took direct action, organizing the Butte Housewives' League to combat high food prices.[79]

World War I and its aftermath produced chilling effects for many people in Butte, in Montana, and throughout the country. Those who voiced their opposition to war or who expressed virtually any form of dissent were targeted as "anti-American." Councils of Defense were established at state and local levels across the country to promote the war effort and keep watch on those citizens who did not wholeheartedly support it. In 1918, as a result of the determined efforts of the Montana Council of Defense, the state passed the Montana Sedition Act, declaring it a crime for any person to "utter, print, write or publish any disloyal, profane, violent, scurrilous, contemptuous, slurring or abusive language about any form of government of the United States."[80] The new law became the model for the National Sedition Act passed later that year. Seventy-nine Montanans were convicted of sedition, mostly for causal comments that were perceived to be pro-German or anti-American.[81] The act resulted in widespread violations of civil liberties and fostered anti-immigrant sentiments.[82]

The state law provided the Montana Council of Defense with extraordinary powers to pass "orders" that carried the weight of law. Those orders were used in curious ways. For example, Order Number One expressly prohibited parades and processions not authorized by the governor. The order was aimed at stopping Butte's St. Patrick's Day parade out of concern that it would turn into an antiwar demonstration. Orders were also passed banning books that made positive reference to Germans and Germany and the teaching of German language in schools.[83]

By the time the 1918 school year had started, wartime anxieties were beginning to be overshadowed by fears of Spanish influenza. As John Astle described, "When schools opened in Butte in September, little girls on the playground were jumping rope to a new song that had spread across the nation":

> I had a little bird
> And its name was Enza
> I opened the window
> And—in-flew-Enza.[84]

As a result of the epidemic, schools were closed from October to mid-December 1918, and Washington School was converted to an emergency hospital. Students had to attend school on Saturdays and holidays once classes resumed in order to make up the lost time. Herb

Wendel was just a boy when the epidemic hit. He and five members of his family were taken ill. "I laid there in the front room in the big folding bed and looked out the window. I could see in the Catholic Cemetery three or four funerals in there at one time. It was really a terrible, terrible situation."[85]

Nine members of Waldemar Kaiyala's family contracted the flu.

> Besides my parents, seven children contacted the flu, although not all of them were sick at one time. Everyone in my family survived. My father went to see the Finnish doctor, a Dr. Pitkanen. He said the only remedy he could suggest would be whiskey. The youngest was near death, so my father poured whiskey into his mouth, causing him to vomit and clear the congestion in his chest. Many people died each day. Friends were not allowed to attend the funerals. Our closest friends, a father, mother, and a baby, all died from one family.[86]

City health officials reported 3,500 influenza cases and 305 deaths in October 1918 alone.[87] On Christmas Eve 1918, Butte's humane officer, P. J. Gilligan, made a public plea for "big-hearted, generous, responsible persons to provide homes for orphaned children who lost their parents in the influenza epidemic."[88]

Despite the influenza crisis, Butte children remembered the eleventh hour of the eleventh day of the eleventh month of 1918 when the armistice between Germany and the United States and its allies was signed, bringing an end to World War I. Jule McHugh, who was twelve years old at the time, recalled:

> All the church bells rang, and the mine whistles blew at 11 o'clock on November 11. We didn't know too much about the war—we sure did later—but when all the excitement started, we were out in front sleigh riding. Helen was in the big dishpan, I was on the breadboard, and Lil was on the drawer of the sewing machine (on its side). We hollered, etc., but went right on riding. Tom and all the boys headed for the *Post* and the *Standard* to sell the extras. It was a money day. There was no radio for bulletins, so people had to buy the papers.[89]

Perdita Duncan, daughter of *New Age* editor John Duncan, recalled that her father took her and her brother and sister into the streets of Butte that cold November night. Her father wanted to impress upon the children that "this bloody war had been fought to preserve democracy." He wanted them to remember the date. Perdita remembered the date and the night, with the mine whistles blowing and newsboys hawking special editions on the street corners.[90]

In the repressive climate that followed World War I, immigrants in Butte and across the country faced heightened scrutiny and pressure for "Americanization." Some families pushed their children to learn only English and discouraged them from speaking their ancestral languages. Parents flocked to newly organized Americanization and citizenship classes. Butte's first Citizen School, a night school for adults inaugurated in January 1919, offered instruction in English followed by courses in civics. Schoolchildren were encouraged to bring flyers home to their foreign-born parents. The sessions, open to both men and women, cost one dollar per year, and 150 students registered the first night. By the end of January 1919, there were 344 students.[91]

Aili Goldberg's mother, a Finnish immigrant, was one of the students. Aili recalled: "I went to school with Mother all the time to get her citizen papers. . . . She did have to learn a certain amount of history. . . . I learned more history and more civics than I did when I was in school, I guess because the teacher just had to repeat and repeat and repeat. . . . I just thought it was really something. It was like the League of Nations here."[92]

In contrast to this growing emphasis on Americanization, Butte's working-class Irish community held to its strong political and cultural roots.[93] St. Mary's Church was a center of social, religious, and political life for the residents of Butte's Dublin Gulch, Corktown, and Hungry Hill. From the 1910s through the 1920s, faith melded seamlessly with the cause of Irish freedom under the influential guidance of Father Michael Hannan. Father Hannan deftly blended his commitment to Irish nationalism with his deep Catholic faith and encouraged his

School Childrens Welcome to the President of the Irish Re

parishioners, including children, to do the same. For example, St. Mary's schoolchildren thronged the courthouse steps of Butte dressed in their Sunday best to greet Irish independence leader and future president of the Irish Republic Eamon de Valera on his visit to Butte in 1919.[94]

The post–World War I era also brought a downturn in copper production in Butte, and the Anaconda Company responded with a dollar-a-day reduction in wages. When miners organized a strike in protest to the wage cut, they were met once again with the power of federal troops enforcing corporate will. Families faced tough economic conditions, but Butte children also enjoyed some welcome diversions. In 1919 the Butte YMCA opened its new six-story facility complete with an indoor swimming pool, with times set aside for free recreational swimming and lessons for kids.[95] In the summer of 1920, Kid Wiley, the Human Fly, made an appearance in Butte. The nineteen-year-old Wiley awed youngsters by scaling the six-story Hennessy Building and smoking a cigarette the entire way. Soon spirited children all over the city were testing their abilities to "stick" to brick walls, sheds, fences, clotheslines, and gallows frames. A reporter for the *Butte Miner* found two young protégés training for their own feat:

> Two urchins of the age that delights in the tin-canning of
> homeless dogs were lying flat on their backs, shoes and stock-
> ings removed, working their fingers and toes as if practicing

In the repressive climate that followed World War I, immigrants in Butte faced heightened pressure to become "Americanized," but that did not prevent the Irish community from welcoming Eamon de Valera, Irish independence leader and future president of the Irish Republic, on his visit to Butte in 1919.

to fight a tom cat with its own weapons. Their faces wore a rapt expression as though their minds were set on a weighty enterprise.

"What are you kids doing barefooted on a day like this?" asked a "grownup" who had been watching them.

"We're learning to be human flies," said one of the kids sheepishly.

"Well, but what's the idea?"

"We're exercisin' our toes and fingers so we can hold on," was the answer.

"When we get through we're goin' over to hang by our hands on Jimmy's mudder's clos' line."

The reporter warned: "If some of Butte's future statesmen splatter themselves over the cement sidewalks while trying to negotiate the top of some tall building, Kid Wiley, the human fly, will have something to answer for."[96]

Children and the Roaring Twenties

The 1920s marked a dynamic time in America as consumer culture expanded, radios and movies became part of social life, and many families enjoyed greater prosperity. More youngsters were attending and graduating from high school than ever before, and literacy rates were on the rise. Children were coming to be seen as consumers in their own right—a ready market for Lincoln Logs, Erector sets, crayons, or the latest book in the Bobbsey Twins or Hardy Boys series.[97]

For Butte's mining families, however, dreams of prosperity were elusive. Copper prices remained low, and corporate interests were looking to invest in rich ore deposits and cheaper labor beyond U.S. borders. Anaconda Company officials made the decision to suspend all mining operations in Butte from April 1921 to January 1922.

Some families left Butte during the shutdown, and others struggled to hold body and soul of family and community together. The Joshers' Club, a charitable organization comprised of prominent local businessmen, delivered a record four thousand Christmas food baskets to needy families in 1921.[98] The Butte Women's Council organized a relief program that provided a pint of milk a day for the city's needy children. As the *Butte Miner* reported, "Scores of little folks in the Butte schools, victims of malnutrition—some of them underfed, others lacking the food that goes to develop sturdy boys and girls, will soon be helped to find the highway to health through the free milk fund established by the Butte Women's Council."[99]

More and more women sought work outside the home to support their families. In 1921 Butte's Salvation Army opened a nursery so that mothers could have a safe place for their small children while they were at work.[100] The Butte Public School District was also forced to lay off forty-one teachers, and the Butte Industrial School, which housed truant and otherwise "incorrigible" youth, could not afford to keep operating.[101]

The opening of the East Side Neighborhood House in the fall of 1920 brought welcome diversion for many children of Butte. Modeled on the settlement houses of the nation's urban centers and organized through the National Board of the Presbyterian Church, the Neighborhood House offered a center for recreational and educational activities and a meeting place for a variety of social organizations.[102] As a 1921 feature story in the *Butte Miner* described, the Neighborhood House quickly "won the hearts of the kiddies" with its pool table, library and reading room, needlepoint classes, and checkers tournaments. Kindergarteners enjoyed arts and crafts, and teens had a place for clubs, parties, and dances. It provided a meeting place for Boy Scouts, Girl Scouts, and Camp Fire troops. Older youth could also participate in governance as delegates to the house council. Hundreds of children took part in Neighborhood House activities.[103]

Despite the adversity, 22,000 kids and adults gathered at Columbia Gardens in July 1922 to celebrate Miners' Field Day with races, competitions, and picnics.[104] A record crowd of nearly 10,000 filled the new grandstand at Clark Park to watch the Clarks defeat the Anodes. And when September arrived, 9,500 children headed back to Butte's public elementary schools. Butte High School enrolled 1,428 students that year, an increase over 1921, which the *Butte Miner* proudly announced as evidence that "modern children need higher education."[105]

Organizations dedicated to youth development and civic participation were also expanding. The Sunday *Butte Miner* featured a children's page, advice columns addressing the rearing of "modern" children, and regular features highlighting the activities of Butte's numerous Boy and Girl Scout troops. Boy Scouts earned high praise for their work in building "future citizens": "The Scout organization is skillfully planned to adapt and apply the 'gang' spirit that is characteristic of every real boy. It eliminates the development of such spirits as are unruly and uncouth and uses the better side to bring out team play, co-operation, and the manliness that grows into useful citizenship."[106]

Diverse community groups envisioned ways to engage young people in civic action and provide organized outlets for recreation. For example, Alma Higgins, founding president of Butte's Rocky Mountain Garden Club, sought to cultivate an interest in gardening and community forestry among Butte's school-children. Beginning in 1922, Higgins initiated school-based programs in which grade-school children learned about bulb planting in the fall and competed for prizes at the spring flower show. Higgins involved Boy and Girl Scout troops in community beautification campaigns, and she led a collaborative rose planting initiative involving the Butte public schools and members of the Garden Club. In 1927 schoolchildren purchased and planted 1,500 rose bushes at twenty-five cents each, and by 1928 they were purchasing and planting 2,500 bushes. The Garden Club provided lessons in rose cultivation and offered prizes for the best roses grown by children and the best essay written about their experiences of gardening.[107]

The growing numbers of children attending public schools also provoked public health concerns. The Progressive Era attention to children's health continued into the 1920s with ongoing efforts for State intervention in support of children's well-being. When the vaccine for smallpox became available, health officials called for compulsory vaccination of schoolchildren while anti-vaccination groups, citing inflammatory publications such as C. M Higgins's 1920 treatise *Horrors of Vaccination Exposed and Illustrated,* voiced their resistance.[108] In Montana, the State Board of Health issued an order making vaccination of schoolchildren compulsory in November 1923, and beginning in January 1924 Butte's public schools were to require certification of vaccination for all of their students.[109] Massive free vaccination campaigns were launched, schools were required to submit certificates of student vaccination to the superintendent of schools, and teachers were warned not to debate with parents over the merits of vaccination.

Concerned Butte parents organized in opposition to the vaccination mandate and sued the State Board of Health for exceeding its authority. The case made front-page news as it went to court in January 1924. A nine-year-old girl who had been vaccinated was brought to court to present her arm, swollen to three times its normal size, to the judge. Another witness testified that vaccination had cost his brother his life. On January 20, 1924, Judge W. E. Carroll ruled in favor of the anti-vaccination group, stating that the State Board of Health had exceeded the bounds of its authority in making the vaccinations compulsory.[110]

Radio came to the Mining City when KGIR began broadcasting in February 1929. By the 1930s, all these children posing on the Silver Bow County Courthouse steps belonged to "Cousin Carl (Clark Kellett) and his KGIR Happy Hour Kids Program."

Things Fall Apart

The Butte community entered 1929 on a positive note. Radio came to the Mining City when KGIR radio began broadcasting in February 1929, marking the start of a new era of communication and social life.[111] Butte schools were closed on March 4, 1929, so that children could hear President Herbert Hoover take the oath of office and deliver his inaugural address.[112] The Broadway Theater hosted an enraptured audience of schoolchildren for the broadcast. The comedy of *Amos 'n Andy* soon became weekly family entertainment, and neighborhood children flocked to the homes of friends whose families had radios to gather around. For Christmas 1929 Butte's Kiwanis Club donated a radio to the East Side Neighborhood House, which drew an enthusiastic cadre of young listeners.[113]

But 1929 did not end well. The Roaring Twenties came to a crashing close as the collapse of the stock market sent shockwaves around the globe and signaled the beginning of a nearly decade-long economic depression. Some Butte residents were blissfully unaware of the first jolts of economic disaster. On November 2, 1929, the front page of the *Butte Miner* featured the annual football clash of Butte Central and Butte High schools at Clark Park, with the winner advancing to the state championship game.[114] Rooters from both squads paraded through Uptown Butte as the Butte High marching band entertained the crowd. Butte residents had weathered so many twists and turns of economic fate over the years that the early ripple effects of the national economic downturn did not seem to be of particular consequence. However, by late November county commissioners were taking note of the growing numbers of Butte residents seeking relief, and the Salvation Army had a record number of needy children participate in its 1929 Christmas celebration.

By the early 1930s, the Great Depression hit hard across the country. Between 1929 and 1933, the gross national product dropped 25 percent, and national unemployment soared to 25 percent.[115] Factories were idled, and farmers were destroying crops they could not sell. Nearly 30 percent of the men, women, and children in the United States had no income at all, and hunger was widespread.[116] Secretary of Labor Frances Perkins reported in 1933 that one in five preschool and school-children suffered from malnutrition.[117] The economic crisis forced children out of school as loss of tax revenues resulted in school closures and teacher layoffs. Hunger, lack of shoes and clothing, and efforts to find work kept other children at home.[118]

Butte families struggled as the price of copper dropped from eighteen cents a pound in 1929 to five cents a pound in 1933. Employment in the mines dropped by 84 percent over that time period, and families turned first to charities and then to the State of Montana for relief. By 1931 Butte and Silver Bow County had nearly six thousand residents on relief, and it was using the lion's share of Montana's child welfare and mothers' pension resources. The State's mothers' pension funds were cut by 20 percent in 1933, exacerbating the struggles of children and families.[119] Butte's Junior Service League, a charitable organization founded by "prominent young women" of Butte in 1931, took up the cause of the city's needy youngsters.[120] Working in conjunction with the East Side Neighborhood House, the League hosted a Christmas party for poor children of the East Side and then worked in cooperation with a local dairy to provide a daily snack of milk and graham crackers for children. Unfortunately, the East Side Neighborhood House itself was forced to close its doors in late 1932. The Junior Service League continued its efforts in conjunction with the Silver Bow Emergency Relief Association.[121]

When President Franklin D. Roosevelt took office in 1933, he witnessed "one-third of a nation ill-housed, ill-clad, and ill-nourished."[122] His administration took swift action to bring relief and economic stability. The U.S. Congress authorized the Federal Emergency Relief Act (FERA) in May 1933 to provide direct aid to states for the poor and unemployed. The National Industrial Recovery Act, passed in June 1933, provided support for public works programs to address widespread unemployment. Forty percent of those on public relief across the nation were children. FERA provided for some basic material needs such as shoes and clothing, and public works programs established nursery schools to support children and employ teachers.[123]

Children were keenly aware of their families' dire straits. Youngsters around the country began writing to First Lady Eleanor Roosevelt seeking her help. One nine-year-old wrote, "My mother cryes because maybe we'll lose the store. . . . I'm always sorry, because I am still very young and can't help out." Others wrote with appeals for small loans—and solemn promises to repay them—to buy clothing, household necessities, or a small Christmas gift for their siblings.[124]

Individual states needed to pass legislation in order to take advantage of FERA and the National Industrial Recovery Act funds and programs. Montana governor Frank H. Cooney called a special session of the legislature in November 1933. In his opening address, Cooney described the widespread unemployment, economic stagnation, and drought that plagued the state. He called on legislators to take action that would allow Montana access to federal dollars and recovery programs.[125] Soon thereafter, Montanans joined the millions of Americans already on the relief rolls.

The *Eye Opener*, Butte's pro-labor newspaper, described Butte in 1935 as a "poor city atop the richest hill on earth."[126] More than eight thousand people in Butte were unemployed—the second highest percentage of people on relief in the country—and, thanks to FERA, nearly half of the families in Butte were receiving relief.[127] By the end of 1935, six thousand people were employed through Works Progress Administration (WPA) programs in Butte.[128] Many Butte women went to work in WPA sewing rooms, cutting and sewing garments for needy men, women, and children across the state. The city received over one million dollars in FERA and WPA funds that year, and the county spent an additional one hundred thousand dollars on poor relief and widows' pensions.[129] The WPA funded public work on construction of streets, sidewalks, and a city sewer system, and for the first time many Butte families had access to indoor plumbing.

Hardships of childhood during those years remained firmly fixed in people's memories. John T. Shea and his siblings benefited from WPA sewing-room products, FERA meat distribution, and his mother's resourcefulness.

We had clothes that were made down there right behind the Masonic Temple, and the girls all wore the same kinds of dresses, and the guys all wore the same blue suits and overalls. I never remember being hungry even during the Depression. My mom was a hell of a cook. . . . My mother made bread, we had rice and flour, and, I'll never forget it, Lion's Syrup. It had a picture of a lion on it. It was green. That's what we had was Lion's Syrup. We'd come home from school, and my mom would give us a piece of bread with syrup on it to do you over for supper. We didn't have everything when we were growing up, but we were well fed. . . .

Centerville, that's where I lived. Walkerville is up above that. The WPA had the meat up there, and I pulled the little red wagon, and my mother and my sister and I would go up there, and we'd get the meat. But you had no refrigerators, so you had a brine barrel. That's where the meat went. And you reach in there, and if your hands were cut or had nicks in them, boy, it burnt. It'd sting the hell out of ya. And I told my dad, "Boy, that's tough on your hands." He said, "That's what the bare-knuckled boxers do. They stick their hands in that brine. It'll toughen you up. Don't let it bother you." Okay, then down . . . on the corner of Mercury, that's where you got the overalls and the shoes and the shirts and all the rest of it.[130]

Vadis Stratton was five years old at the start of the Depression.

I didn't realize we were poor. My mother raised chickens and planted a big garden. We never went hungry. My father found work on the WPA at Hansen Packing Company. They killed livestock, and he found work there. He was laid off from the mines at the time. He got a pension from the government because he was in three wars, but they stopped the pension during the Depression. . . . We burned coal. My dad would go get wood up in the forest, but it didn't hold the fire, so we burned coal. We lived a couple of blocks from the roundhouse, and we'd go over there at night and take a gunnysack and the little wagon. I was little and just went along in the wagon. My mother would bundle me all up because it was cold. We'd go over there, and if we got a sack of coal, we thought we were rich. The watchmen turned the other way when the women and children came over. They came with baby buggies and everything to get coal. And the watchmen turned their backs and let them take it.[131]

Joe Roberts remembered the spirit of generosity among his parents and grandparents.

> They survived by loving each other and helping. Anything
> you needed if somebody else had it, it was yours. We'd have
> dinners together. In my own home, we had Grandma Roberts
> and Grandpa Roberts, my father and mother, and we had
> a table about five feet in diameter, but we had two or three
> leaves for it, and I can remember we could have up to fifteen,
> twenty, thirty people every Sunday for dinner because they
> didn't have any place to eat. We had them stay with us. Any-
> thing you had you would give to somebody else. It didn't make
> any difference. And we had at that time what you called hobos
> and the bums and everything. Well, I can remember them
> lining up outside of our back door, and Mom would be fixing
> them whatever she had in the house to make sure they didn't
> leave hungry.[132]

Helen Evankovich remembered going to the VFW Hall and Jefferson School to get clothes and food: "We'd get food baskets to take
home. Surplus food. You knew that your folks and a lot of folks weren't
working. And that's where you got something to eat and got clothes,
particularly in the wintertime. I remember going down and getting
food and heavy coats and galoshes."[133]

Lula Martinez's mother would make big pots of beans and soup to
feed all of the kids in her East Side neighborhood. Lula and her friends
all attended Grant School. As Lula described it, "The kids would fight
together, eat together, and go to school together." Other mothers would
send their kids to play with Lula and her siblings because they knew
Lula's mother would feed them. Lula was eager to help her family. She
lied about her age in order to get a job with the National Youth Administration, a New Deal program targeting high school– and college-age
youth ages sixteen to twenty-five whose families were on relief. Participants earned a small income (six to forty dollars per month) for
work-study projects in schools and libraries. Lula's stepfather was
employed through the WPA. Lula never received her own paycheck;
her wages were included in her stepfather's check, a practice she never
understood.[134]

Radio and movies brought eagerly awaited distraction to Butte
children during the lean years. The Lone Ranger rode onto the scene in
1933 with his familiar charge "Hi-ho, Silver! Away!" drawing millions of
listeners around the country each week. Special Saturday morning pro-
gramming for children featuring the adventures of Tarzan and Flash

Gordon captured a loyal radio following. The special treat of a Saturday matinee transported children from the realities of everyday life to new realms of adventure. They could escape into the worlds of their favorite superheroes, ride the plains of the Wild West, or celebrate the rags-to-riches story of Little Orphan Annie.[135]

The height of the Great Depression was also a time of labor activism as unions demanded recognition and representation. A wave of strikes throughout the country pointed to the urgent need for labor reform legislation. Butte was again a site of labor struggle as the community endured a long, and at times violent, strike that ran from May to September 1934. While the miners' union claimed the right to organize, the Anaconda Company–owned newspapers vilified miners' actions and dismissed their demands.

Tempers were running high by June, and the miners' union and labor newspapers were posting lists of scab workers who crossed the picket lines to work. Daily front-page news reports detailed "violent acts of rowdyism" by local mobs made up not only of miners but also of women and children, who were accused of harassing the families of men who crossed the picket line. Crowds numbering in the hundreds were reported to be roaming the streets, hurling rocks at mine watchmen, and "serenading" at the homes of men who were working "behind the fence" during the strike. Striking miners were accused of setting fires, tossing lit sticks of dynamite into mine yards, and throwing acid on mine watchmen.[136]

The *Montana Standard* offered grueling details of "serenades" in which crowds would surround the homes of men accused of being "scabs" and "strike terror to women and children" who were "left cowering in darkened rooms."[137] Childhood memories of the strike remained fixed in people's minds. Some told stories of the "scabs" who went "behind the fence," and others still whispered when speaking of relatives or neighbors whose names were posted on "scab lists." Two older men who were youngsters during the strike recalled:

> We lived near the Hill. It used to be all lit up, but during the strike, it was all pitch black. All you could see was big spotlights, shooting around like during the war.
> And they'd have guards, oh, you bet, and when the strike started, they'd bring in railroad cars, Pullman cars. They'd bring everything in—all the food. . . . Everybody behind the fence was well taken care of. Scab laborers just stayed there. And the railroad cars would be there with all the food and booze and everything.[138]

Miners achieved a significant victory as a result of the strike. The International Union of Mine, Mill, and Smelter Workers won recognition, a closed shop, and a contract from the Anaconda Company providing for a minimum salary of $4.75 per day and a 50-cent-per-day wage increase for all classes of workers.[139] However, miners were called back to work on a part-time basis, and with food prices increasing by 40 percent since 1933, families were still relying on public relief to get by.[140]

Economic recovery came slowly. By the late 1930s, the number of persons on relief in Butte was dropping, and the city had weathered the worst of the Depression. With the passage of the Federal Social Security Act in 1935, federal, state, and county funds could be directed toward modest financial support for the children of poor families through the Aid to Dependent Children (ADC) program. By 1937, 392 children from 175 families in Butte were receiving ADC support.[141]

New Deal public works projects provided some direct benefits for Butte youngsters. For example, the new Butte High School building opened in 1938.[142] Butte children were delighted with the construction of the Broadway Rink, installed on top of mine tailings that had been leveled years earlier for temporary barracks when Butte was under martial law.[143] The WPA also sponsored and staffed nursery schools at the Blaine, Franklin, and Greeley schools. The Junior Service League lent its support, organizing Christmas parties at each throughout the Depression. The WPA Division of Recreation sponsored a variety of music, dance, art, and crafts classes for children.[144] Butte's winter sports enthusiasts were thrilled by the construction of Butte's first ski jump, a WPA project completed in 1937.[145] WPA funding also went into improving public parks and access roads in the forests surrounding Butte.

WPA programs focused both on youth and adult sports leagues as well as on family activities. Butte youth occasionally benefited from talented teachers and coaches whose salaries were paid through the WPA. John Mazzola recalled joining the Grant School track team around 1938:

> I was in seventh grade. . . . We had good coaches [at Grant School]. These coaches were paid by the WPA. We had a coach, his name was Hi Brown. He was a black man. He and his brother Bruce Brown, they were Olympic athletes— Olympic athletes. They ran with Jesse Owens in the Berlin Olympics. And he was our track coach, and he couldn't make a living, and all he could do was make sixty dollars a month like everybody else. So they made him a coach, realizing he was an athlete. He coached us in football, basketball, track,

everything. He was a wonderful, wonderful, wonderful human being. One of my best friends in the whole world.[146]

The 1930s also saw increased support of organized activities for children and youth by private groups such as the Catholic Youth Organization, which sponsored sports and social programs for children in Butte's Catholic schools, and the Knights of Columbus, which sponsored boys' boxing and basketball leagues.

By 1939 Butte's population was 49,000, significantly lower than in 1930, but the community looked to the future with pride.[147] As a 1939 Butte economic survey noted, Butte had a high literacy rate and high enrollment in both public and Catholic schools. Ninety percent of Butte households had radios by 1939, and Superman, Jack Benny, Bob Hope, and The Shadow were weekly visitors in nearly every home.[148] The city itself had experienced a makeover, with nearly four million federal dollars invested in community development projects, including seven parks with playing fields, baseball diamonds, and tennis courts.[149]

Coming of Age in Wartime

Butte residents entered the 1940s with a renewed sense of hope. The realities of war in Europe seemed distant from lives in Butte even as they enhanced the market for copper. Although some WPA projects, such as the sewing rooms, continued until the early 1940s, residents were coming to believe that the hard years were behind them. Butte was getting back on its feet and ready to celebrate. Thousands of Butte residents turned out for the annual Fourth of July parade in 1941, where they witnessed the first float ever entered by the Meaderville Fire Department.[150] Butte's YMCA had become a weekly gathering place for children throughout the city, who bravely crossed the borders of their familiar neighborhoods and traipsed across town to take part in bowling leagues, swimming lessons, and boxing matches.[151]

Life for many young people in Butte changed profoundly after December 7, 1941. Shirley Trevena recalled that day:

> I can remember where I was when Pearl Harbor happened. My dad took us all out in the car to get a Christmas tree, and we heard the news that Pearl Harbor had been bombed. All of us kids started crying. We were all crying in the back seat. It was too weird to believe that we were attacked and that we were at war. I think it was a real hard time, and it was a real patriotic time. I think it was different from so many of the wars we have had since then because you got a real strong

sense of your country and your loyalty and patriotism. I think even though it was very bad, it was very good. People knew that they were working making things for the war, and you knew that you had to sacrifice. You didn't have all the things you usually had, and they were a sacrifice for your country. It lasted a long time. I think I was in the eighth grade when the war started. Before that, you are not too much aware of what's happening in the world, and then you realize that you are watching history being made. And my dad did very well after that war started. The economy was booming, and all the people that were brought in to work the mines, that was a big boost to our city. It was a bad way to get it, but it was a boost.[152]

World War II disrupted family life across the country as 16 million men and women joined the military.[153] Fifty-seven thousand Montana men and women served in World War II, nearly 10 percent of the state's population.[154] Over 2,400 Butte mine workers served in the armed forces during the course of the war; another 3,500 contributed to the war effort through their work in the mines.[155] Given the need for copper as a strategic metal, miners were exempt from military service.[156] As articles in the *Copper Commando*, the official newspaper of the Victory-Labor Management committees of the Butte, Anaconda, and Great Falls mining and smelting operations, described, war "has an insatiable appetite for copper."[157] Six hundred pounds of copper went into the construction of a single tank. One ton of copper was required for every P-38 fighter plane, and the army's Signal Corps needed five thousand tons of copper per month for radio, telegraph, and telephone equipment. The Medical Department required an additional 375,000 pounds of copper each month.[158] Miners gave their all to meet the overwhelming demand for copper. However, as part of wartime policy, miners' wages were frozen. When the Miners' Union protested, members were criticized for their lack of patriotism.[159]

Wartime created opportunities for young people to serve their country and assert their independence. John Mazzola was in high school when the United States entered World War II.

The Second World War came along, and the four of us [John and his brothers] went in the service. My brother Tony was drafted in 1941. He went to the Solomon Islands, New Guinea, the Philippines, Okinawa, and all that. . . . The day after Pearl Harbor, my other two brothers, Joe and Sam, went up to the recruiting at the old post office, and they enlisted. I tried to enlist, but I was only sixteen. They got in separate lines, and one went in the navy and one in the army. That was it. So, the recruiting guy said you have to wait until you're seventeen, and even then you have to have your mother and dad's permission to join.

I went to Butte High School. I was supposed to graduate. In those days, the high school had two classes; they'd graduate in January and in June. I was supposed to graduate in '43, but in February of '43 I got patriotic. I thought, well, this war is going to be over. I want to help my brothers, and I want to help my country, too. So I became seventeen, and I went up and enlisted.[160]

During World War II, children of all ages were expected to contribute to national defense efforts. Butte kids searched neighborhood yards, alleys, and empty lots, looking for all kinds of scrap iron, steel, copper, and rubber. This group of "scrap detectives" posed with their finds in October 1942.

Children of all ages were expected to contribute to national defense. As the 1943 publication *Your Children in Wartime* instructed the nation's youngsters, "You are enlisted for the duration of the war as citizen soldiers. This is a total war, nobody is left out, and that counts you in, of course."[161] Butte children joined in the nationwide war effort by both selling and buying war bonds and Victory Stamps. The bonds provided funding for military operations in wartime and yielded 2.9 percent interest after ten years. Stamps could be purchased for as little as ten cents each as a means of saving toward a bond. Children could buy the stamps and paste them in a savings booklet until they saved the $18.75 needed to purchase a $25.00 bond. Some war bonds posters featured characters such as Mickey Mouse, Captain Marvel Junior, and Popeye encouraging American youngsters to fulfill their patriotic duty.[162]

Little red wagons were put into military service as children gathered and hauled scrap metal for drives being coordinated nationwide. As Edward Jursnich remembered:

The whole community participated in combing and scouring the neighborhood yards, alleys, and empty lots, looking for all kinds of scrap iron, steel, copper, and rubber. The East Side contributed to a huge scrap pile at least thirty feet high and probably just as wide on the upper playground east of Atlantic Street. . . . All the junk eventually was hauled away for recycling and used in the manufacture of guns, tanks, warships, and airplanes in the war against Germany and Japan. There were special paper, copper, and rubber drives to support the war effort. My mother saved cooking grease, which was used in the manufacture of munitions.[163]

Wartime rationing also became fixed in childhood memories, and images of war permeated children's play and preoccupations, as Shirley Trevena and Kay Antonetti recalled:

During the war, we were on ration coupons—sugar, coffee, nylon stockings, gas. And my dad brought some meat home, and it was very good-looking hamburger, rich and red. Anyway, he cooked it that night. And then he let out a big "neigh." It was horsemeat.

I remember the butter. You couldn't get [real] butter. My mother had to mix the oleo. You'd put a little tablet pill in it. It was like a pound of butter, only it looked like lard. That's probably what it was. And there was a little yellow-red pill, and you'd put that in and stir it and stir it until it would turn yellow. Everybody ate it. . . .

We used to play that we were army nurses, and the bikes were our ambulances. And we had a hospital set up in our garage. And, oh, my God, we'd ring the sirens and go get the patients and just have a wonderful time.

I wanted to join the [Cadet Nurses Corps], the young girls who wanted to be nurses, but I was too young for that, so I wrote letters. I wrote tons of letters. I thought I wrote to everybody in the country. Some of my dad's customers went into the war. I had their addresses, and I wrote to them while they were overseas.[164]

Shirley Trevena and Kay Antonetti were among the many Butte girls who dreamed of becoming nurses. Girls played with Army Nurse paper dolls, imagined heroic missions, and watched their older sisters join the Cadet Nurses Corps, a federally sponsored program begun in 1942. A national campaign touted the importance—and glamour—of the job. The St. James School of Nursing, which was established by the Sisters of Charity of Leavenworth in conjunction with St. James Hospital in 1906, became a key site for training Montana women. The program in Butte graduated an average of twenty to twenty-five nurses a year between 1942 and 1949, and it contributed 140 nurses to the Corps.[165]

A joint committee of Anaconda Company employees and mining union members launched a newspaper, the *Copper Commando,* in 1942 to promote the role of copper and copper-mining operations in the war effort. The *Copper Commando* also recognized family-level contributions in Platter Chatter, a column of household tips and low-cost recipes to help homemakers respond to wartime shortages. This photograph of Joan Glynn and her children accompanied one of the columns.

The Anaconda Company Victory Labor-Management committees enthusiastically promoted the key role of miners and their families in waging the war. Weekly flyers, distributed to miners with their paychecks, encouraged them to participate in war-bond drives. Nearly every *Copper Commando* issue featured photos of children doing their patriotic duties as well—saluting the flag, emulating a sailor in pint-size navy attire, or putting coins in their "war savings stamp" piggy banks. Mothers and children were sometimes featured together alongside articles offering meal-planning ideas that dealt with the challenges of war-time food rationing.

The entire November 24, 1944, issue of the *Copper Commando* was dedicated to the McQueen Addition, a Butte neighborhood populated almost in its entirety by mining families. While giving a brief nod to the neighborhood's strong immigrant roots, the article insisted that the residents were "all Americans." The children were described as bright, cheerful, clean-cut, nice-looking, and respectful youngsters. McQueen as a whole was praised for both its sense of community pride and its dedication to those in the armed forces:

McQueen does not forget its own. The people have pulled together all during the war to keep the community shipshape. No one in McQueen has forgotten that their sons and brothers and friends must come back to a better McQueen than they left. Probably that accounts for the number of folks you see fixing gardens, trimming lawns, painting fences, and doing the general tidying up that is the pleasure and privilege of the American homeowner.[166]

Postwar Promises and Problems

Butte families joined the nation in celebrating the end of the war on August 14, 1945.[167] Word of Japan's surrender reached Butte about 5:00 P.M. on August 14. "Immediately car horns were honking, people were shouting, and the roar of the crowd in Uptown Butte was near deafening. Tears of joy were streaming down many faces."[168] As Kay Antonetti recounted, "On VJ-Day everybody was out in the streets, you know, with confetti and horns honking and horns like for New Year's Eve, and everybody happy—just like you see in the pictures, with everybody hugging each other and dancing and just a wonderful time."[169] Bill Hitchcock and Oakie O'Connor were juniors in high school at the time. Bill celebrated at a street dance in Uptown Butte that lasted until the wee hours. Oakie headed to Meaderville where, he recalled, "I think I got four hundred kisses that night. People were the happiest I'd ever seen them."[170]

But postwar promises of prosperity were short-lived in Butte as men returned to the mines only to find fewer jobs and frozen wages. A brief but violent strike in April 1946 polarized the community. News accounts lambasted the impropriety of women's involvement in the strike and the troubles caused by "young hoodlums" as they joined men in the streets to support the strike and expose scab laborers. Headlines in the April 15 *Montana Standard* blared: "Mobs wreck dozen Butte homes. Pictures reveal wanton destruction. More than ten homes wrecked by apparently organized gangs of terrorists reveal the unparalleled destruction when mobs roamed the streets of Butte and vicinity Saturday night and early Sunday. Orgy uncontrolled in wild night of terror, lawlessness. Boy wounded. Houses wrecked and hacked by roving bands of hoodlums. Windows broken, furniture tossed out."[171]

The violence that accompanied the 1946 strike is firmly fixed in local memory and recounted with a mix of bravado and shame. Several homes of salaried employees of the mines were damaged. With the men working "behind the fence," it was once again women and children who suffered the brunt of the attacks. According to news reports, a sixteen-year-old boy suffered a gunshot wound to the back in one night of mob violence.[172] Some youngsters reported that they had been paid by adults to perform acts of violence. One woman claimed that a mob surrounded her house and proceeded to club her rabbits to death, wring necks of chickens, and swing a puppy against the wall.[173] Images of one home, severely damaged by the "serenading" mob, offered grim documentation on the front page of the *Montana Standard*.[174]

Those who experienced the strike as youngsters held on to powerful memories. Tom Holter remembered the damage done to a neighbor's home in McQueen. Tom's father, a strong union supporter, did not condone the violence. Instead, he took young Tom for a walk to bear witness to the violence. They watched the crowd that had surrounded one house and saw a woman come out on the porch. Tom recalled, "I think she had a gun. . . . She came out, and she threatened if they didn't get away she was going to start shooting. I felt kind of sorry for her because it wasn't her fault, you know."[175]

Many Butte youngsters experienced the conflict and confusion of the strike in more subtle ways. As one woman, whose father had a non-union, salaried job, recalled:

> My dad would go and he would stay [behind the fence] because he was salaried. I can remember this girl who lived near us. She couldn't play with me. It was 1946. She could not have a thing to do with me. She has since become my good friend, but at the time she wasn't allowed to play with me. . . . In later years, people understood that management had to

Violence accompanied the 1946 strike, and dozens of homes were damaged when angry mobs roamed the neighborhoods.

While labor politics and strike economics created a powerful divide among Butte residents, all could agree on the spirit and talent of the Butte High School marching band. Under the leadership of Henry Schiesser, the 140-piece band, with its intricate choreography, sophisticated musical arrangements, and sharp costumes, was peerless in the state. Butte residents turned out by the thousands to see the band perform at ball games, parades, and other public venues. Here, the band marches up North Main Street in Uptown Butte in 1939.

cross the line to keep up the maintenance on the mines so miners could go back to work when the mines reopened. But in my dad's time, it wasn't like that. Anybody who crossed the line was a scab. I hate that word, "scab." I just hate it. It gives me the willies still.[176]

It could be argued that Butte's young people played a key role in healing the wounds of a community torn apart by the strike. While labor politics and strike economics forged a powerful divide among Butte residents, all could agree on the spirit and talent of the Butte High School marching band. Under the indomitable leadership of

Henry Schiesser, the 140-piece band, with its intricate choreography, sophisticated musical arrangements, and sharp costumes, was peerless in the state. Butte residents turned out by the thousands to see the band perform at ball games, parades, and other public venues. The members were the pride of Butte as they departed by train to march as the Honor Band in the 1948 Tournament of Roses parade in Pasadena. They dazzled Harry Truman with a fifteen-minute concert on his presidential campaign whistle-stop in Butte in June 1948. Their musical prowess earned them official praise from Senator Mike Mansfield, published in the *Congressional Record*.[177]

Bidding Farewell

New directions in postwar mining development resulted in profound physical and social transformations in Butte. In 1947 Con Kelley, president of the Anaconda Company, announced plans for the Greater Butte Project, which introduced a technology known as block caving to maximize output of underground mines. In a speech at the Finlen Hotel, Kelly heralded the project as the "third great period of mining in Butte." He told the audience that the project "not only means great industrial activity for Butte and a period of community longevity that will extend beyond the mortal expectancy of anyone present in this room, but it should also be the dawn of an era of a greater, finer city."[178] The Greater Butte Project moved forward in the early 1950s, but block caving was soon overshadowed by plans to move from underground to open-pit mining. In 1955 the Anaconda Company launched the Berkeley Pit, an open-pit mining operation, to wrest lower-grade ore from the Butte Hill.

At first, the Berkeley Pit signaled hope for Butte's future. Not long after the start of open-pit mining, the miners' union and the Anaconda Company signed a three-year labor contract, which gave Butte families a sense of stability even as the character of mining and the community itself was changing around them. Butte was featured in a 1956 *Time* magazine article that touted it as a "model" company town and praised the progressive role of the Anaconda Company in providing for workers and their families: "In quick succession Anaconda backed a housing program that provided homes for 650 families . . . invested in a hospital, a civic auditorium, and a $400,000 club where C.I.O. miners were soon bowling and drinking beer with the once-hated 'sixth floor boys,' i.e., Anaconda executives. . . . Today, in the town John Gunther once called 'the only electric lit cemetery in the U.S.' signs in merchants' windows proclaim, 'Butte is my home, I like it.'"[179]

Buoyed by anticipated industrial expansion, the Butte Public School District called for a bond issue to repair and modernize city schools in 1956.[180] Anaconda Company executives were reporting that upwards of twenty-five hundred more miners would be needed when the open-pit operations were in full swing.[181] School officials believed that could translate into an increase of three thousand students.[182]

The over-optimism of such predictions became apparent as the effects of copper production from Anaconda Company holdings in northern Chile began to exert an influence on Butte. For thirty years, the Anaconda Company had effectively managed its mining operations in Butte and Chuquicamata, Chile, to corporate advantage. In the late 1950s, the company's newest and potentially richest Chilean ore deposit, El Salvador, was about to be mined.[183] El Salvador would be the economic savior for the Anaconda Company but Judas for the people of Butte.

In 1959 the Butte Miners' Union was again negotiating a three-year contract and seeking substantial increases in wages and pensions. Meanwhile, the Anaconda Company began producing copper from the El Salvador Mine in May 1959. Labor negotiations in Butte ground to a halt, and in August 1959 the Butte miners prepared to strike. Minutes before midnight on August 17, 1959, a powerful earthquake struck Yellowstone National Park, and its seismic effects shook Butte, 150 miles away. The next day, Butte miners went on strike.

For many Butte residents, memories of the 1959 strike were fused with those of the earthquake. Danette Harrington, daughter of a hoisting engineer in the mines, was sleeping on the front porch of her family home when the earthquake hit.

My brother and I never slept in the home in the summertime. I had a little front porch and a rollaway bed with a little
nightstand and radio. So, the night of the earthquake, it was
right after we had gone to bed. My mother had a sewing
machine in the front room with a tea service on it that had
been a wedding present. I could hear that tea service rattling.
I thought, "What is going on?" I had a dog named Smoky,
and he slept under my bed. I thought he was scratching and
making my bed shake. All of a sudden my mother got up, and
she was panicking, saying, "It's an earthquake." . . . My father
was underground when that happened, and they had to stay
until they got the men up, and I can remember that he was
totally shattered because of the fear of taking the men from
the 4,000-foot level to the 2,000-foot level with the chipping

engine and then from the 2,000-foot to the surface with the main engine. The fellows down at the chipping engine had to stay there to make sure they got the men out.[184]

The 1959 strike started with a bang, lasted six months, and devastated Butte's labor community. Some described it as the strike that broke the backs of Butte's unions. Rumors spread that the Anaconda Company planned to close the Butte operations completely due to high operating costs. Some miners left town in search of work elsewhere. Grown-up worries preoccupied Butte's children. Bonnie Stefanic was in grade school during the 1959 strike.

> The '59 strike was awful, really scary. My dad and mom, they always saved money. . . . And my dad, he'd run around and do whatever work he could do for somebody else under the table—fix cars, put on a roof, sometimes for free. . . . Some days we'd be eating beans. Christmas was sad, not so much because we didn't have money, but it was the fear. What is it going to be like next Christmas? I remember thinking this could be real awful. It could be the end of our families. We might have to go back to Yugoslavia. As a kid, I thought that was sort of neat. My family felt forced by the union. The workers didn't want that strike. I remember the talk in the living room with names of union men coming up: "So and so is just worried about paying off his truck." "The Company bought him." "He's a Company man." There was terrible suspicion and fear. I was afraid when they'd say things like "gonna burn the Hill."[185]

Bonnie's fears were echoed through others' childhood memories. Some recalled fear and uncertainty taking a greater toll than material hardship. They remembered the tensions between their parents when their mothers went to work and became the primary breadwinners. Many felt the absence of fathers who sought work elsewhere during the strike. They said goodbye to relatives and friends who gave up the struggle and left Butte for good. Some described the silence as ore trains stopped running as well as the taste of commodities such as the cornmeal and powdered eggs that were distributed to families on strike and that became a part of every meal. And many treasured the special memories of holiday potluck dinners where families shared generously with one another, bringing not only food but also clothing to trade.

By Christmas 1959 the strike had lasted four months. Full-page ads appeared in the *Butte Daily Post* sponsored by a coalition of business leaders, ministers, doctors, and school personnel, urging the unions and the Anaconda Company to negotiate a settlement so that miners could be back to work by Christmas.[186] But the end was not in sight. In January 1960 an emergency aid committee began to organize food and clothing drives to respond to the growing needs of mining families.[187] By the end of January, the county's relief coffers were empty, and Aid to Dependent Children rolls were soaring.[188] Volunteer groups redoubled their food and clothing distribution efforts and began to organize a school-lunch program. The emergency aid committee was fielding four hundred requests for assistance per day by early February 1960.[189] Parent-teacher associations, churches, and service clubs joined forces to provide lunches for schoolchildren. The Longfellow School recreation center was transformed into a makeshift kitchen and staging center as volunteers packed upwards of six hundred lunches a day.[190] Donations of meat and potatoes came in from throughout the state. The Campaign for the Needy sent telegrams to its representatives in Washington, D.C., asking federal aid for Butte families.[191]

By February 4, 1960, the school-lunch operation had outgrown Longfellow School and was moved to the Butte Civic Center, where volunteers prepared nearly nine hundred lunches a day.[192] Girls in home economics classes at Butte Central High School received instruction on how to prepare dishes with commodities that disguised the taste of the infamous cornmeal and powdered eggs. Student groups and local merchants joined forces in food drives. Local theaters offered free movie admission two nights a week with a donation of food. Local bakeries and dairies donated bread and milk.[193] On February 12, 1960, the unions and the Anaconda Company negotiated a settlement of the strike. A special issue of the *Montana Standard*—the first special issue since the end of World War II—announced the good news. Church bells rang throughout the "thankful city" whose "load of dread and despair had lifted."[194]

But Butte never recovered from the 1959 strike. Miners went back to work in 1960 for five cents less per hour than they were making before the strike. The long-awaited end of the strike was accompanied by sobering news—the Anaconda Company planned to close the Anselmo and Emma mines and cut back the size of the mining workforce. Seven hundred miners were out of work as a result of the closures.[195] While the *Montana Standard* ran the upbeat headline "Friday is Payday Again" on February 25, 1960, the grim reality was a loss of seventeen million dollars in payroll over the six months of the strike.[196] Butte's population continued to decline. Schools, churches, and businesses closed. Franklin School, serving Meaderville and McQueen for decades, was closed due to damages leveled by the 1959 Yellowstone earthquake. Many were left to wonder about mining's precarious future.

Open-pit mining, along with modest underground operations, continued in Butte through the 1970s, but as the Berkeley Pit operation expanded, the mine consumed several of the close-knit ethnic neighborhoods that had come to define the city. Starting in the late 1950s, the Anaconda Company had begun to buy up homes in Dublin Gulch in order to expand the Pit.[197] The Anaconda Company's ownership of the land beneath the neighborhoods and right of eminent domain left residents with few options but to accept the price offered for their homes and resettle. In 1960 the company announced plans to expand eastward toward Meaderville.[198] As Joan Filpula described, "By the mid-1960s, the area was gobbled up by the mining industry."[199] McQueen and East Butte residents faced similar fates as expansion of open-pit mining continued throughout the 1960s and early 1970s.

Dolores Kangas and her family relocated from McQueen to the Flats as a result of the shift to open-pit mining: "Well, we just decided to go live on the Flats. My folks found this house on Stuart Street. It was after that that they started tearing everything out. McQueen, Meaderville, they just wiped it all out. A lot of McQueen people— I don't think they were too happy about it. That was their home for years and years. I don't think a lot of them liked going, but they had no choice."[200]

Those who moved to new neighborhoods on the Flats found themselves living on foreign terrain and removed from the familiar contours and camaraderie of their communities. Those who held dear to their homes for as long as they could found their walls and windows cracking around them as daily dynamic blasts rocked the neighborhood and reminded residents of the inevitability of their departure. As a former resident of East Butte described:

> From East Butte to Meaderville to McQueen, they are part
> of the Pit now. Other people get displaced by renewal projects
> or whatever, but at least they can go back to the physical place.
> They can say, "This used to be my home." Even if it's a differ-
> ent building, they can still stand on the spot. But not Butte:
> it's eaten up. The ground isn't there anymore. It's hard to orient
> yourself to where things used to be. Those moves were hard on
> people.[201]

The last Mass at St. Helena's Church, heart of Meaderville's Italian community, was celebrated on February 27, 1966.[202] The church building was later moved to the grounds of Butte's World Museum of Mining. The destruction of the McQueen Addition and the East Side played out more slowly, into the 1970s, as residents accepted Anaconda Company

McQueen's Holy Savior School disappears under a truckload of overburden from the Berkeley Pit, which ate up McQueen, Meaderville, and most of the east side of Butte before the Anaconda Company discontinued mining operations in 1982.

offers to buy or move their homes. Sacred Heart School, serving Butte's East Side, was closed in 1967 and the church in 1970. Grant School was destroyed to make room for mining in 1975. McQueen's demise was dramatically marked by the burial of Holy Savior Church under tons of rock excavated from the Berkeley Pit in the summer of 1979.

While mining operations in Butte continued into the twenty-first century on ever more modest scales, children who came of age in the 1950s were the last generation for whom mining defined reality as it had powerfully done for tens of thousands of children for over a half century.

CHAPTER TWO

Mining Childhood

As far as the mines were concerned, it was something we were born and raised around, so we were used to it. We'd play back up there by the old claims, and we knew where they were, and we stayed away from them. But it was nothing for us to go sledding down in the winter. The ore dumps were great for sledding. Well, not with a sled either but on your rear end or on a little piece of cardboard. My mother would say, "Why don't you stay off those damn, dirty ore dumps" because when they get wet, they're kind of smelly, you know?

—Butte resident

BUTTE CHILDREN grew up with a keen awareness of the labors and landscape of copper production. Children negotiated the hilly terrain of their ethnic neighborhoods, precariously perched alongside dozens of gallows frames, those massive structures that marked the entrances to underground mines. At home and in their neighborhoods, children were keen observers of and active participants in cultural life. They bore witness to the myriad ways in which mines and mining shaped the intimacies of family life and punctuated the local landscape. They were socialized early to the boundaries of belonging and difference that marked the community along neighborhood, class, ethnic, and labor-management lines, and their accounts provide windows into children's understandings of mining life, attachments to home and neighborhood, ethnic identification, sense of belonging, and spirited community participation. They also illuminate some of the strife and struggle in children's lives and the hurts hidden beneath Butte's surface.

Rhythms of Life

The sights, sounds, and smells of mining infiltrated the lives of Butte's working-class children. They knew the tone of bells that signaled danger

Butte children grew up with a keen awareness of the labors and landscape of copper production. Photographer N. A. Forsyth caught these three youngsters on an outing circa 1909.

and death underground. The rumble of ore trains reverberated beneath their beds. The constant fans and whistles of the mine yards were noticed more in their absence than their presence—their eerie silence accompanying a strike or shutdown in the mines. John Sheehy, son of an underground miner, was born in 1918 and raised in Uptown Butte, his family home surrounded by the Original, Stewart, and Anselmo mines. The sights and sounds of mining remained a vivid part of John's childhood memories.

> There was always a background of industrial noise. The several
> gallows frames were always at work, whirring away as they
> paid out or recovered the cables up over the idlers and sheave
> wheels and up and down the shafts, some for half a mile or
> more in depth. The trains rattled back and forth, and they
> were so heavy that they caused a rumble around them. . . .
> Each mine blew its work whistles at the beginning and end

of each shift and for lunch periods, day and night, so that we always knew the approximate time without a watch. . . .

When you see pictures of old Butte, every time you see a smokestack there was a forge below the smokestack. So if you see seven smokestacks outside of a building, there were seven forges down below that the blacksmiths worked at. And the purpose was to sharpen the bits that they used down below in the mines. They brought them up every day, and they resharp-ened them in the shops. And that's why they had so many smokestacks running. With all the mines, they had to keep the tools up. . . .

Those tools, they called them "buzzies." They were actu-ally jackhammers, and they worked off compressed air. They were not electric or gas. And that compressed air came to each mine through a network of pipes. Those pipes were a foot in diameter. . . . I could walk on them, so they were quite large pipes. And where they came to a mine, there was a junction that took an offshoot to the mine from the main line. And they built a box around that—fairly high—half the size of this room. And they were warm. The heat of the compressed air would raise the temperature in that box. They called them "hot boxes."

Near where we lived on 621 North Montana Street, the Butte, Anaconda & Pacific Railroad ran right next to our house. There was a tunnel that ran right underneath Montana Street for the train to pass on to go on up the Hill. . . . [I remember] the first time Rita [my fiancée] came to our house. I brought her home so the folks could see her. We were sitting in the living room, and the train passed underneath. The house was shaking, and we were talking normally, and poor Rita over there, she thought there was an earthquake or something. There was the song in later years called "A River Runs through the Middle of the House." Well, the railroad really ran through the middle of our house. We were that close.[1]

Elinore Sterrett Shields Penrose was born in Butte in 1913. As a young girl, she and her family lived north of the Anselmo Mine. Her father, who sold real estate, believed that Butte was going to develop on the Hill north of the mines. He built a cement-block house north of town that provided Elinore and her siblings a bird's-eye view of the mines: "We lived near the Anselmo Mine, which was just about as close to the city as any of them. When we were coming home from school, we'd go by [the Anselmo], and about then the bell would ring, the four o'clock shift would come on, and the others would come out. Then there was a special sound when there had been an accident, and the women from the neighborhood, if they had a man on that shift, would be pretty scared."[2]

Elinore's childhood memories captured the provocative images of mines and mining.

> We had a sleeping porch upstairs. It was a two-story house, and my father was a fresh-air bug. The sleeping porch faced the mountains, and it had great big screen windows, and for many years the whole family would sleep out there. They would take the carts out of the mines and dump them into big ore wagons. They had great horse-drawn wagons. From the sleeping porch, I can remember, early in the morning on a snowy morning, watching the fellows that drove these wagons up to the mines above our house to pick up the ore. It was so cold that they didn't ride. They walked, and they'd be slapping themselves and keeping the horses going. A lot of that sort of ore from the smaller mines went down to the Pittsmont Smelter. They smelted the ore, and they had huge fires in the furnaces. Now, I am not positive how they got the copper out of the ore, but there was a lot of slag that is not copper but is just waste. From our house, we could see a great wall—it was probably forty feet high—that had grown from the Pittsmont Smelter. And there on top of that wall was a track, and the little pots of melted slag would come on top of that wall, and on a very cold, wintry night, you'd see the red-hot slag run over the edge. But it has done terrible things, too. Dad told about one fellow he knew: it was very cold, and the slag had a crust on it, and the fellow couldn't get it to dump, so he got on top there with a shovel, and he went clear through with loss of his legs.[3]

The rhythms of mining formed the backbeat of community, and children as well as adults could tell the time of day by the mine whistles. Children invented their own names, such as "hooters," for the whistles that marked the shift changes in the mines. Many families geared their lives around shift work, constantly accommodating the family schedule as mine workers rotated among day, afternoon, and graveyard shifts. When there was a strike, there was silence, no "hooters" by which to measure time. One daughter of a miner spoke of a visitor asking how her family could stand living so close to the mines with the constant noise of the engines and bells. She recalled, "It never bothered us. The only time they ever bothered us was when they stopped. Nobody could sleep. It was horrible. Funny how it shapes your life."[4]

Youngsters registered the subtleties of their surroundings as they absorbed the details of mining life. Lula Martinez and Frank Carden grew up on Butte's East Side, where mining carved the contours of their childhood terrain. Lula's family lived on East Galena Street.

> We were all surrounded by copper dumps. Waste dumps . . .
> but then we called them the copper dumps. And the ore bins
> were a little ways down from where we used to live, where
> a little car used to come from the Belmont Mine and dump
> the waste or the ore into the bin, and we could hear that at
> night. . . . And then at six o'clock in the morning, there was a
> train that came with cars, and they would dump the ore from
> the bins . . . load it onto the train cars, and the train would pull
> it away. And it would whistle while it went.[5]

For Frank the mine dumps served as his playground.

> In the neighborhood, there were numerous mine dumps,
> which were the despair of our mothers who had to wash the
> dirty clothes we got playing on them by hand. No electric
> washers in those days. You could find some of the funniest dirt
> on the dumps, all of it taken up from the bowels of the earth.
> No one knew what it contained, but it never seemed to hurt
> anyone. I remember a light-yellow dirt, which if wet by rain
> or snow would stick to you and your clothes and your shoes
> like glue. If you came home with this on you, you would really
> get bawled out and maybe a few licks of the razor strap in the
> bargain.[6]

Patricia was raised in Walkerville, a small community immediately north of Uptown Butte. She grew up playing on an old ore dump that she and her friends dubbed the "Rising Star." She vividly recalled the sound of the cages carrying miners underground being lowered down the shaft, the cranking of the wheel in the gallows frames, and the reverberation of the ore trains. For Patricia, though, it was the smell rather than sound of shift change in the mines that is fixed in her memory. "I can remember the miners coming home. They walked home. They didn't have cars. If it was shift change and the miners were coming home, there was that medicinal smell from when they came up from the dries [miners' changing room] where they'd take a shower. They must have all used the same kind of soap. They all had this medicinal smell. And they always carried their buckets under their arms, and they always had that tired look."[7]

Other children recalled the anticipation of shift change, when the Hill was thick with miners carrying their lunch-buckets. Young news-boys knew it was time to hustle to their street corners with the daily papers as miners were returning to town. Miners were their best cus-tomers. Bucket girls, who worked in boardinghouses preparing lunches to be carried underground, had the timing and tastes of the miners indelibly marked in their memories. Some youngsters would hurry to the mine yard entrance at shift change to ask miners for fruit from their lunch-buckets. Some waited outside the dries or at the corner bus stop to walk home hand-in-hand with their fathers. Others would eagerly await their chance to rummage through their fathers' lunch-buckets in search of a leftover treat. As Danette Harrington and Linda Raiha, two Butte women who grew up in mining families, recounted:

[Linda] My father always brought me something out of his lunch-bucket, always saved something.

[Danette] Yeah, it was wonderful, wasn't it?

In a community devoid of grass and trees, ore dumps often served as playgrounds. They were well suited for sledding and such other activities as digging one's own mine, the pursuit of the "Young Prospectors" in this circa 1909 image.

The miners carried their lunches in buckets like the ones held by these men standing in the hoist that will lower them to their worksites in the depths of the mine. Children waited for their fathers at the end of the shift to see what had been saved for them from their dads' lunches.

[Linda] And it might be half a [cookie], a piece of an orange slice. It didn't matter.

[Danette] And as soon as he came in the door and put the bucket down, I would be there to see what I got.

[Linda] And we used to fight because the first one there would be the one who got it.

[Danette] No, see, I didn't have to fight because my brother wasn't there with his eye on the bucket like I was.

[Linda] I can remember with my dad we would just walk right down to the mine yard and wait for him. We'd walk to the street where the dries were and wait for him to come out of the dries.[8]

Children were also well aware of the sounds that signaled the imminent toll of death and disaster in the mines. Few mining families escaped loss of a loved one or close friend to the mines. Children knew the realities behind the euphemisms of mining. Frank, Richard O'Malley's childhood friend in *Mile High, Mile Deep*, bluntly described the death of their neighbor, Old Man Powers, at the Orphan Girl Mine: "A fall of rock. That's what they always say when about a ton of ore hits you in the head."[9] Children recalled both the sounds of disaster and the responses. Their mothers would get together and go to the houses of the injured men to stay with their families while the wives of the injured held vigil at hospital bedsides. When deaths occurred, neighborhood women helped with funeral arrangements and were there for support in the hard days that followed.

John Sheehy described the toll that mine accidents took on families and the many widows in his neighborhood who struggled to support their young families.

> There were so many widows around. It's hard to explain to people, but those mines were killing one a day, I think. And there were all those widows living in our neighborhood. Right next door to us was Mrs. Bennett, who had three husbands. She had a man named Sullivan, a man named Burns, and a man named Bennett. All three, she was widowed three times, and with different children from each of them. And there was Mrs. Hanley, down on Boardman Street. And Mrs. O'Neil, who my mother hired to help clean the house. And Mrs. Murphy, who lived two houses up from us. How they lived I don't know except that the kids would sell papers. That was common in those days.[10]

Ann Pentilla told a similar story of struggle.

> When there was a mine accident, if the man was killed, it was sure hard on the woman. She had to go out and scrub floors. That's about the only thing she could do to raise her family. It was really hard. There was one woman who had twenty children. Her husband died when the children were very young. She was a midwife, and she rustled [railroad] ties, and she had a cow, and she baked bread, and she used to take in washing, and then the children would deliver the washing. That's how she raised her children.[11]

Knowing Your Place

The machinations of mining shaped children's lives in both mundane and profound ways, but the stark rhythms of mining were tempered as they flowed and filtered through Butte's diverse neighborhoods. Many Butte children grew up with a deep attachment to their neighborhood, a strong sense of ethnic identity, and a curiosity about the social and geographic boundaries that shaped their lives. As Nancy Klapan described: "You grew up knowing the ethnic distinction of Butte neighborhoods. The East Side was always Austrian and Serbian, and the Irish were uptown a little ways, but they were all very distinct. And if you lived on the East Side, everybody knew, and you lived up above Park Street, you were Finnish, or you wouldn't be living there. Meaderville was off by itself, and it was very strong Italian. And the whole town was very strong Catholic from the Irish."[12]

Children came to know their neighbors and neighborhoods on their own terms. They absorbed the experiences of family and neighborhood life, observed the adults around them, tried to make sense of spoken and unspoken rules, and created their own understandings of place. For some children, a sense of cultural identity instilled in their families was further nurtured through ethnic neighborhood ties. Others witnessed and negotiated ethnic differences in their families and neighborhoods.

"This was my First Communion picture in front of the statue of St. Helena at St. Helena's Church in Meaderville," recalled Andrea Ciabattari McCormick. Pictured from left are Ernestine Sheehan, Andrea Ciabattari, Mary Ann Jones, Martin "Tino" Grosso (whose father ran the Aro Café), Jerry Brown, and Danny Horgan. Father James Gannon was St. Helena's pastor and performed the Mass that day, October 25, 1959.

Bessie Toy Sherman came to the United States from England in July 1895. She recalled that "the day we landed in New York City was very exciting for me, for on that July nineteenth, I celebrated my ninth birthday." Bessie's father had come to Butte first and rented a house in Centerville, a neighborhood north of Uptown Butte and surrounded by the Mountain Con, Mountain View, Diamond, Moonlight, Raven, and Buffalo mines. The clapboard houses of Centerville appeared to cling to the hillside. In the early 1900s, the residents were largely Irish and Cornish immigrants. According to Bessie, "We came directly to him from New York, and the first thing I wanted to know was where I could go to pick some flowers. I had brought my flower basket with me. My dad was sorry to tell me there were no flowers growing wild anywhere. I soon found out that there wasn't even a blade of grass to be seen."[13]

Toxic fumes from Butte's numerous smelters had left Butte largely barren of natural beauty, but Bessie adjusted readily to her new home: "In Centerville I attended the Trinity Methodist Church and was enrolled in the Blaine School. The big attraction for me in Centerville was the cable car, which went from town, through Centerville, to Walkerville. I managed to get to Main Street to see it at every possible opportunity. Another fun thing that I remember is when several of us would run over to Pat Mullen's boardinghouse and stop at the window of the cook's kitchen. He would always hand us some biscuits, and we would thank him and run off delighted."[14]

After Bessie's family had lived in Centerville for a year, her father got a job at the Leonard Mine, and they moved to Meaderville. Meaderville was home to Italian markets, restaurants, and bars, and, for many years, wide-open gambling. It was also home to mines, mine dumps, and smelter operations, which residents referred to as "stink pots."[15] Smelter smoke left a dense cloud over the neighborhood and took its toll on residents' health as well. According to Butte writer William A. Burke, "In winter mothers would have to take their kids to school and call for them again comin' home, for they would never find their way along in the smoke. They would wrap big shawls and 'fascinators' around the kids' heads, so they wouldn't inhale that sulfur. There wasn't a blade of grass or a tree in the town that the smoke didn't kill. The old-timers had to be hardy devils to stand it all, and at that half the town was barking their lungs out with the asthma."[16]

But Bessie was undeterred: "We liked it there. I was very happy because at the back of our house on Main Street there was a creek of clear water in which we could wade in the summer and go ice-skating in the winter. The tunnel mountain on the East Ridge was covered with sunflowers in the summer, and we called it our Sunflower Mountain. Now I could pick flowers and see grass."[17]

Marie Butori also grew up in Meaderville and shared Bessie's love for the neighborhood.

The Italians lived in Meaderville, and you knew everybody and everybody knew you. And in North Meaderville the English people settled, and they were really nice people. They were the ones that taught us how to make the pasties, especially Mrs. Pierce. She was a great person during that time, and she made pasties, and she worked on the elections, and we all got to know her.

Up above North Meaderville was the McQueen Addition, and the Croatians and the Yugoslavians and Austrians lived up there. And so we heard about all the different cultures, and we learned to get all the different food from the different cultures in this area and in Meaderville. The Irish lived up in Dublin Gulch, and they were a very different part of town than we were, and they usually just made stew and potatoes. People didn't have any money and all the things we have today, and it was really, really hard living, but everybody was satisfied.[18]

Meaderville was settled primarily by immigrants from central and northern Italy. Many families raised pigs, chickens, and rabbits and cultivated bountiful vegetable gardens alongside their modest homes. Single-family homes were intermingled with boardinghouses noted for their fine cuisine and home-style hospitality. Homemade wine was a mealtime staple. The Ciabattari and Son Meaderville Grocery, Meaderville Mercantile, Sconfienza's Meaderville Bakery, and Guidi Brothers grocery and meat market kept residents supplied with the familiar flavors of Italy.[19] St. Helena's Church served the neighborhood's many Catholic families.

Meaderville's institutions made an impression on young Marie.

There were the Guidi brothers, and they were really Italian, and . . . they had *salcina*. It was some kind of fish. They salted it, and they spread it out, and you could only get it from them. It was just like the shape of a fish and really hard, and you'd salt it. My mom used to boil it and cook it, and it was really good. And they made thick, thick blood sausage. It had raisins in it and a lot of stuff in it, and it was big like that [hands about six inches apart]. It was called blood sausage, and you cut it. Mmm, it was good. They were the only ones who really made it at that time. They had everything. They had real Italian olives, you know, big ones—kind of shriveled, tasted really good. There were two brothers [Dominic and Alfredo], and Alfredo used to come around and get the orders, so he was at our house every Saturday. He was part of the family.

Most of the people there were Catholic, and so we had the Catholic church, St. Helena's, and the choir. We had Pochie, Pochanelli was his name. He was a singer. He had lost a leg in the mines, and so he'd climb up those steep steps with the stump and his other leg, and he would sing at the Masses every Sunday. He had a beautiful voice. . . . When we didn't have anybody to play the piano, Mrs. Cooney, who lived in McQueen with the Austrians, would come down

PASTIES

Have you ever eaten pasties? They're a half of a pie plate, and you cut out a round piece of pie crust, and you put in onions and potatoes and meat. Some put turnips in. You get them half full, and then you turn it over and make a nice little crimped edge and cut little slits in the top. When you were all ready, you put a little water in there so that you had sort of a gravy forming inside. That was a very famous thing for the miners because they were just the right size to fill the main part of their lunch pail.

—Elinore Sterrett Shields Penrose[20]

and play the organ for us in our church so we could have Mass. People were devout Catholics.[21]

St. Helena's Church in Meaderville became identified as Butte's Italian parish. While the church contributed to a sense of belonging among the city's Italian Catholics, it also caused confusion at times for children growing up in Italian families outside Meaderville. For example, Bernice Favilla Maki grew up in an Italian family in McQueen, an ethnically mixed neighborhood adjacent to Meaderville. As Bernice recalled, "It was really puzzling for me as a child growing up. I could not understand why as a kid I had to go to St. Helena's in Meaderville when Holy Savior Church was only a block away from my house in McQueen. It was only later on did I realize why as an Italian I had to go to St. Helena's rather than Holy Savior, because it was the proper thing to do."[22]

Lucille Martinesso Sheehan (left) and friend Columbine "Bina" Fontana Mazzola, Meaderville, circa 1925

Lucille Martinesso Sheehan was also a Meaderville girl. Her parents emigrated from Italy in 1906, making their way straight to Butte, where her father went to work in the mines. As with many families of Meaderville, mining culture mixed readily with Italian culture in the Martinesso home. Her father made wine each fall, storing it in the dirt cellar of their home. She grew up with wine as a part of mealtimes, preferring a glass of wine and water to milk with her supper. Her parents were also avid gardeners, and they maintained a small subsistence farm at the family home. Despite Butte's reputation as an inhospitable place for crops, the Martinesso garden flourished. The home's south-facing windows were ideal for tomatoes and a year-round supply of herbs. The family also raised rabbits. Lucille's mother worked magic in the kitchen with her culinary talents.

> Mother was a marvelous cook. A main dish was polenta—polenta and chicken. Then you'd have like a cacciatore chicken and mushrooms, and then you'd have all that gravy on it. Oh, it's so good. . . . The Italians really celebrate your feast day rather than different holidays. Mine is St. Lucy, and she is the patron saint of the eyes. Whatever I'd like, Mom would make it. We'd have a nice dinner, and, oh, it was so festive, really wonderful. And Mom was such a good cook. Most Italians were. They'd use a lot of tomatoes and lots of spices.[23]

Lucille's father died at age fifty as a result of miner's consumption. Her mother used her culinary skills to help support the family. As Lucille recalled, some of Meaderville's fine Italian cooks would serve meals in their homes to paying guests. For example, Pete and Clem Madlena began running an eatery out of their home in the 1920s, featuring home-cooked chicken, ravioli, and spaghetti.[24]

> A lot of people, they would serve these dinners in the home, the Italian dinners. Oh, and they were really good. . . . And people, like some of the ACM people, would call and make a reservation. Con Kelley would come to Mrs. Madlena's for dinner. And there would be, oh, say about fifteen, twenty people, and they'd have a regular Italian dinner. It was catered in their home. It was really nice. My mother used to help Mrs. Madlena. She was our neighbor, and she did a lot of that.[25]

Tom Holter's grandfather and later his uncle ran Ciabattari and Son Meaderville Grocery, where Tom worked as a boy. One of the perks of the job was picking up bread orders from the Meaderville Bakery.

> Meaderville Bakery made the best bread and breadsticks. A lot of times customers would order the bread and breadsticks through my uncle, and on his deliveries he'd go to the Meaderville Bakery. Sometimes I was with him or my aunt would send me down there to pick up the orders that they were going to deliver. They probably gave it to him for a lower price, so he'd make a cent or two on it. I was always glad to go down if [Mr. Sconfienza] wasn't there. He was a crabby old bugger. If he wasn't there and I'd go down there, his wife always gave me a little bit of a treat. She couldn't do it when he was there. I tried to time myself if she was there, and I'd try to go down there when he wasn't there. She'd give me maybe a little piece of cheese and salami and a breadstick, something like that. . . . I also remember the Guidi Brothers sausage and salami. For the longest time when I was a little kid, they had Guidi Brothers sausage and salami. I always thought that was their names. Sausage and Salami. And they made sausage and salami that were, oh, unbelievable.[26]

Tom was born in Meaderville but grew up in McQueen. Tom remembered both the ethnic ties and the tensions among Butte residents and the labels marking identity and difference.

Well, see now, in McQueen, McQueen was a lot of Austrians. Bohunks. We had names for everybody. We were the wops, and they were the bohunks, and, of course, Meaderville was mostly Italians. McQueen was mostly Austrian. And East Butte was kind of a separation. Well, my wife's family lived in East Butte. Her dad was Austrian, and her mother was Irish. Now, can you imagine in 1953 an Italian kid from McQueen going with an Irish girl? Can you imagine that Irish family? I wasn't really accepted too much when we first started going together.[27]

Ethnic identity and difference were only part of the story in Butte. Nicknames were also part of local culture, and once attached in childhood, they stuck throughout a lifetime. The stories behind the nicknames might be lost, but the names endured.

There was a guy—we called him Temporary Pete—and his mother made wine. We'd get wine from Temporary Pete's mother. I don't know how he ever got that name. Like I say, my uncle's name was Sousa, and then there was Fatty, that was his nickname, Fatty Maffei. And then Gianino, his name was Sparky, and his brother was Babe. They had names like that in Meaderville. And in Meaderville everybody has names—I can name names—I was Bull, and there was Boo, Jibby Eyes, Bones, Baffer, King, Oly, Lefty, Legs, Greek, Chip, Pal, Spike. I only know them by these names. Spike Pelletier, he married my wife's sister. And his brother was The Duck. I still call him The Duck. That's still how he writes it when he writes me Christmas cards—The Duck. That's how it was.[28]

Ann Pentilla grew up in the Boulevard area on South Montana Street, which was home to many southern European immigrants, particularly Croatians. Her parents were Croatian. They had immigrated from Yugoslavia and changed their last name in the process, fearing prejudice against people with names ending in "ich." Hers was a tight-knit community "where everyone helped one another." Ann had fond memories of wedding anniversary celebrations in which neighbors would get together, go house to house collecting money,

Andrea Ciabattari from McQueen-Meaderville, 1955

and throw a party for the couple. Children were always part of the festivities that included dinner and dancing into the night.[29]

Like many in her neighborhood, Ann's family had a big vegetable garden, a smokehouse, and a root cellar where they put away provisions for the winter.

> In the wintertime, our dad used to get all set. We used to buy maybe twenty sacks of spuds. And then he would make his own sauerkraut—about two or three fifty-gallon barrels. Sometimes we'd raise a pig and then cure it and smoke it. . . . My dad used to go to the Metropolitan Market, and he'd buy a whole hog for about fifteen dollars. He would cut the meat in pieces and put it in a brine. We'd hang the meat on hooks out on the clothesline and have it dried. Then he'd smoke it. He had a certain kind of wood he used for the smoking, and he had a real huge smokehouse. That would be our food for the winter—sauerkraut and smoked meat. We had a basement that was all dirt. It was real damp down there. We used to have to stamp down the sauerkraut in the barrels with our feet, stamp it until all the juice came out. It would have to be solid. If not, it would get mushy and spoil. It would keep all winter. They used to do that with turnips, too, if they made wine. They would take what was left of the grapes, after the wine, mix that with whole turnips, and put it in a barrel, and that would sour. They had a certain kind of cutter that you used to cut it. It looked just like spaghetti when you cut it. Oh, it was the best tasting stuff.[30]

While smokehouses and sausage making were familiar parts of family life for some children, others grew up with a curiosity about the social practices of their neighbors. Vadis Stratton spent her childhood on Walnut Street in the Race Track neighborhood, where, as she described, "there were a lot of Austrians." Vadis was not exposed to a strong sense of ethnicity and religion in her family, and she loved being part of neighbors' activities. She was both drawn to and, at times, repelled by the sights, sounds, and smells in her neighborhood.

> They used to have big Austrian weddings, and we were invited to the weddings. And they had the best fried chicken and homemade *povatica*. I just loved that. The neighbors next door, in the fall, would buy a couple of pigs, and they had this big framework, and they'd hoist the pigs up on there, and they'd

stick 'em in the throat, and the women would catch the blood. They had to stir it all the time. They'd make blood sausage. And I used to watch them. I really never got over it. I was fascinated by it. I had to see everything. But I don't like to see things killed.[31]

Butte's East Side may have been the city's most ethnically diverse neighborhood.[32] Grant School, Sacred Heart Parish and School, and the East Side Neighborhood House were community institutions. Some described it as a tough neighborhood where children grew up learning to defend themselves or run fast. Others remembered it as a neighborhood infused with a spirit of cooperation forged from struggle.[33] Lula Martinez grew up on Butte's East Side. Her family was Mexican, and her parents had migrated north from Texas following her father's work building the railroad.

> When they finished on the railroad, they finished somewhere close to Butte, so they stayed here, and he went to work in a mine. But he didn't work a year before he was killed in a mine. My mother had five children when he got killed, . . . so she stayed. But my mother couldn't read or write English. She was only Spanish. She remarried in a year, another Mexican from Mexico who couldn't read or write English, and had more family. Then he died from the result of the mine also. She stayed, raised her children here. I suppose one of the reasons why she stayed was because of the fact that she couldn't move. With eleven children, you don't. . . .
>
> [In our neighborhood] we were surrounded by different nationalities. We had Vankoviches and Joseviches and Biviches, and we had Serbians, and we had Chinese. We had *italianos, españolas,* and Mexican people. We had the whole United Nations around on the East Side.[34]

John Mazzola grew up on Butte's East Side as well. He was the fourth of five children, born at home on East Park Street. John's father emigrated from Italy at the age of ten. An uncle helped his father get as far as St. Louis, and then his father went to work as a water boy on the railroad, making his way over the years to Livingston, Montana. Once in Livingston, he learned of the mines and the possibility of better wages in Butte and decided to try his luck. There he met John's mother, one of fifteen children of an Italian immigrant family. John's maternal grandparents ran a boardinghouse on East Park Street.

John's was one of a handful of Italian families who lived on the East Side, and John grew up with a keen understanding of the cultural geography surrounding him.

> Up above us there was a place called Dublin Gulch, where people of Irish descent lived. West of Dublin Gulch was a place called Hub Addition—mostly English; then Centerville, mostly Irish; then up here was Finntown—Scandinavians mixed up with a few Chinese, a few blacks, Armenians, Turks, Chinese, Serbs, and the other side of the Serbs. They all spoke the same language, but they didn't like each other—the Serbs and on the other side the Croats. The Croats were Catholic, and the Serbs were Serbian Orthodox. They spoke the same language, cooked the same food, everything. In the Old Country, they didn't like each other, but here they did. They got along wonderful. Down south of here was a place they called Parrot Flats that was a mixture of everything, too.[35]

After his grandfather died, John's grandmother lived next door to John's family, and John often served as her guide and interpreter in Uptown Butte.

In Butte single men often lived in boardinghouses, which were frequently run by the widows of men killed in mining accidents. This boardinghouse pictured circa 1900 is a railroad section house whose residents included children and pets.

My grandmother couldn't speak English. She came here as a young girl with her husband, had all of her kids here in this country. She could speak four or five European languages, but she couldn't speak English. When I was a kid, I used to take her Uptown to go shopping, and she would tell me what she wanted. She pointed at the [merchandise], like peaches, spinach over here, string beans over here. That was the way she did things.[36]

John's grandmother passed along a love of music to his mother. His mother was a strong woman, full of spirit, who loved to sing grand opera. His grandmother worked hard to instill that love of opera in John as well.

My mother could play a little bit of everything.... We had a bunch of old, beat-up instruments. In our house, we had a mandolin, a banjo, a guitar, and a thing they called a xylophone. They'd get together, the older folks, my mother and aunts and uncles and all that. They'd all sing and play. My grandmother lived right next door to us, and when all the kids were out playing marbles and having fun, once a week we had to go to her house and listen to Italian opera. I hated it, but I thank God that she taught me that because I love it now. She sold me to it. I was the smallest of the boys, and I'd have to roll the Victrola, you know, wind it, and then she'd go through the *mutetto*, they called it in Italian, the pantomime.... We'd go over to listen to opera, and she'd make some kind of little cookies, and we'd have tea. I'll never forget, when I went in the army, in 1943, big cities would have opera, and we'd to go to town, and GIs could go to the opera free. I would go and take my buddies with me, and I'd do all the interpreting. I'd sit there and tell them all about the opera, and they loved it. I knew about it, that was part of my culture, part of raising kids.[37]

Although he learned the fundamentals of opera, John only learned bits and pieces of Italian from his grandmother. His father wanted the children to be "all American," and that meant English speaking. At the same time, John's father kept Italian traditions alive. Despite the challenges posed by the Pittsmont Smelter, which left its clouds of toxic fumes over the neighborhood, John's father kept a vegetable garden and grew flowers for his mother. His mother would buy two or three lugs of peaches each summer for canning, and every fall his parents would buy grapes to make wine.

Most of the people on the East Side made their own wine. You could buy a ton of grapes for fifty dollars. And, there again, they'd bring them to your door. The railroad would bring them in, and they would deliver them to your door in twenty-pound lugs. Concord grapes—they made a wine they called "dago red," and it was good wine. Today's wine is full of chemicals and stuff.

We'd have wine on the table, a little pitcher of wine. My dad would have a glass of wine, my mother would have a glass of wine, my older brother would have a glass of wine. I could have one if I wanted. My friends would come and eat with us sometimes, and, boy, they loved it. Then we'd save all of the mash from the wine, and some of these older people, Croats, they'd come by, and we'd give it to them, and they'd make what they called grappo [a liquor distilled from muscatel grapes].[38]

John attended Grant School and Holy Savior Church. He recalled the close ties among the children of his ethnically diverse neighborhood.

[We] got along very well. Later on when I was a little older, they started football leagues. They had Hub Addition, Engle-wood, McQueen Addition, Meaderville, and they had baseball games and football games. They got along good. We had block fights, too, you know. We'd meet the kids from Dublin Gulch and fight with them. [We'd have] fistfights. But there was no animosity. Nobody kicked anybody or anything like that. We were clean fighters.[39]

Through street games, school activities, and sports leagues, groups of youngsters forged enduring bonds of friendship. As John described, youth "gangs" might defend neighborhood turf, but they also employed basic rules of respect.[40]

Butte experienced a significant wave of Finnish immigration in the early 1900s, and Finns established their own enclave, Finntown, just east of the central business district along East Broadway and East Park streets. Maki's Grocery Store was a local institution, and many Finntown families weathered the strikes and the Great Depression thanks to the willingness of Alex Maki to sell groceries on credit. Ray Wayrenen grew up in Finntown and described the neighbor-hood: "The Finns had their boardinghouses: the Broadway, Tuomala's on East Granite, Kingston House, Central House on East Broadway,

Finntown and the Neversweat Mine, 1939

Suominen's on Covert, and the Clarence on East Park. There were also the saunas. The most notable was Isa Matti [Father Matt's] on Faucett Street. The Finns had the Finn Hall in the 300 block of North Wyoming and Finn Swede Hall on East Galena. There were dances and plays and programs there."[41]

As a child, Ray made regular trips to the Broadway Bar to fetch a bucket of beer for his father.

> My father was a miner, but he wasn't much to spend time in the saloons. He enjoyed a few glasses of beer at home when he returned from work, so he used to give me his miner's bucket—which was called a pie can—and twenty-five cents to go across the street to the Broadway to get a "bucket of beer." Now, the Broadway at that time was run by a big guy (over six feet and 250 pounds) by the name of Victor Kontola, so he was called Condo Vic. Anyway, I'd come in with Pa's bucket and a quarter, and Vic would say to me—regardless of how busy he was, and the Broadway was always busy—"Let's arm wrestle to see who buys the bucket of beer." So, here I am in my early teens—talk about selling beer to juveniles—I'd say,

"Okay." I'd have to stand on the bar rail to do my best arm wrestling while everyone is watching me take on big Condo Vic arm wrestling. Naturally, Condo Vic would win. But every once in a while, he'd let me win, so he'd say to me, "You won. You get the old man's beer. What ya gonna do with da twenty-five cents?" This, of course, was like a kickback. So, what do I do with the quarter? I buy a package of gum, a candy bar, and put fifteen cents in my pocket.[42]

Ray's childhood memories were also marked by the enduring presence of militia that kept miners under surveillance over extended periods of time in the 1910s and 1920s.

Our fathers were able to work in the mines when the Anaconda Company wanted them. Sometimes Anaconda closed the mines and had the National Guard protect their property. They even had machine guns. I remember one time in 1919 or 1920 when a Finn fellow came running off the hill on East Broadway with blood running down his neck from a bullet wound. During World War I, soldiers were quartered in the "Big Ship" [boardinghouse] in the 200 block of East Broadway. I remember the old barracks behind the Moonlight Mine. Then later the barracks were built on the north side of the 800 block of East Broadway, and soldiers moved there.[43]

John Onkalo also grew up in Finntown when it was "teeming with people."

It seemed like all families had kids. There were kids all over. In fact, the houses were almost skin to skin, and, boy, there was kids all over in the neighborhood. You knew everybody, and you knew who lived here and who lived there. If you wanted to see somebody, it wasn't like now. . . . In those days, if you wanted to see somebody, you'd go in front of his house and you'd call him. Either he or somebody would open the door and answer you. There sure was a lot of kids. Kids all over the place.[44]

Aili Goldberg's father, a Finnish immigrant, had died in a mining accident in Michigan when Aili, the youngest of three children, was three months old. Her mother could not support the family on the meager widow's benefit from the Michigan mines. She moved her children to Butte in the hopes of a better future and settled in Finntown. Aili's mother began cooking at the Clarence boardinghouse on the corner of East Park and Ohio streets, and the family lived in a rooming house across the street. Aili recalled:

> It was very interesting living on the East Side. There wasn't a blade of grass there. Nobody had a piece of lawn or anything. You just lived with the old mine dumps for a backyard up there. . . . Mother cooked all the time. And wherever Mother worked, why, we would have our meals there, because that's one thing—she wanted to be sure that we had a hot meal, being she was gone all day. Now, the Clarence boardinghouse . . . it also had a rooming house. It had a barbershop, and it had a bar all in this one building. And that's true with some other boardinghouses, too. [With others] the rooms were directly across the street. I know of four boardinghouses that had rooms right upstairs.
>
> . . . The Finnish boardinghouses all served the men that would come off shift at two o'clock [in the morning]. Now, they were the only boardinghouses that fed the men on the two o'clock shift coming off. They could come in and have a lunch before they went to bed. The Belmont House was run by Finnish people. Their clientele was some Finnish but kind of mixed. There was Irish, and there was Serbians, and there was English, and there was a little bit of everything. The East Side was predominantly Finnish, Irish, and Serbian. . . . Broadway was on the Mannheim [trolley] Line, and they said it was like a fish because it had Finns on both sides.
>
> We ate with Mrs. Jackson in the Belmont House, which was right across the street from the Silver Lake. Mrs. Jackson was very good-hearted. She wanted us to eat our meals there, and there was no charge. And this is the way most of them were. . . . It was family style. Your breakfast was short-order, just like anything else. You ordered anything you want. But your noon meal, it was potatoes, and it would have stew. There was always one fried meat at noontime. But us children never ate at the table with the men. There was a little table on the side, and we would always sit there. And we always managed to come either before their busy time or after it had kind of slowed up. When we were smaller, we didn't want to be underfoot. . . . Lots of mothers worked, and a lot of women had their children [eat at the boardinghouses]. I liked the atmosphere of a boardinghouse. Guess it was different for a girl, maybe, because the men were very generous, and I was little, and it would be payday, and it was always a quarter or

it was fifty cents. And come the holidays they always had a little package for you. . . . Sunday, men were dressed up in their suits and white shirts, and they sat outside talking, reading the papers, and stuff.

At Riipi's [boardinghouse] Sunday was a big thing. Your Sunday dinner was quite a specialty at Riipi's. We had everybody. Dr. Crouse was one of our very best customers on a Sunday. It wouldn't be slumming because there was no slumming done there, but we had a cross-section of people. There were those that was wealthy, and yet they really did put out a real fancy dinner. . . . Chicken would always be, and there was always all you wanted to eat. And there was mashed potatoes, and there was roast, and there was your ice cream and your cake and fruit, and all the milk you wanted and all the buttermilk you wanted, and all the bread and the butter.[45]

Aili enjoyed the youth activities and entertainment offered through the Finnish Hall, located near her home. The Hall was also a favorite spot of members of the Industrial Workers of the World labor union, who provided Aili with some early political education.

We had what we called Finnish Hall, which was a cross-section again of Finnish people. You either belonged to a church or you belonged to this group of people. And we always called them Wobblies, my mother did. They were IWW, Industrial Workers of the World. They would have big doings always for Christmas. There would always be a Christmas play for children and a dance afterwards, and then there were presents for all the children. Mother never approved of it too much. . . . She'd let us go to the plays because all the plays were in Finnish. . . . The one I remember best of all was the show of the Volga Boatmen. . . . You know, there's always been such a conflict with the Finnish and the Russians. It was actually about the Russians. They were the "Reds." Mother didn't think it was something we should go to, but it was very well put on, and the actors, I thought, were very, very good. As a child, I thought it was really quite wonderful. It was where the lower-class people were almost like slaves. They had little or nothing. They were being domineered by the Russian people. [The plays] would invariably be political. Oh, I saw a few, I guess, that were kind of, maybe, a little bit of a love story, but I think in the background always there was this political conflict. . . . I would say the majority of the [Finnish] people were Wobbly supporters. The Finnish Hall was very socialistic. . . . My brother called them the Wobblies. . . . He didn't like it either. The only thing was they accepted us kids fine because there was no father on our part to interfere with anything or what their feelings were. Mother didn't approve, and they knew Mother didn't approve but didn't care.[46]

Thelma Karki Point Hjelvik was born to Finnish immigrant parents in Butte and grew up in the shadow of the Finnish Hall. Her parents, she recalled, "were caretakers of the old Finnish Hall for a short period of time. . . . This hall was the center of Finnish culture and entertainment. There was a dance floor and a stage. Numerous plays were put on, and the men had a gymnastics team. Dressed in white trousers, undershirts, and red sashes, they performed acrobatics, made pyramids, etc. There were no babysitters in those days. The children came to the dances and when they got sleepy would lie down on the chairs along the wall among the coats of the dancers."[47]

Butte's large Irish community dominated much of the Butte Hill. Dublin Gulch, Corktown, and the Hungry Hill comprised tight-knit Irish neighborhoods that extended north and east of Uptown Butte and along Anaconda Road. Children grew up steeped in Irish culture, politics, and history. St. Mary's Parish, established in 1903, was a centerpiece of these Irish neighborhoods and the second home to many mining families. On Sunday mornings, the vestibule of the church would be filled with miners' lunch-buckets. [48] St. Mary's School offered Gaelic language and Irish history classes. Children kept up the practices of old Irish traditions and participated in the creation of new ones. As Vince Dowling remembered, on St. Stephen's Day, the day after Christmas, "Kids in the neighborhood would form a group and go sing songs at all the homes in the area. It was a sign of good luck if we came to your home and sang the 'wren bird song.' The neighbors always appreciated our efforts and would give us nickels and dimes."[49] At Easter children showed their solidarity to the cause of Irish independence by wearing Easter lilies. As Father Sarsfield O'Sullivan recalled, "All the kids in the neighborhood went to church the day after Easter wearing a cardboard Easter lily. . . . The lily was a tribute to the 1916 Easter Rebellion in Ireland. It was the way the Butte Irish showed their appreciation for the efforts of the rebels of 1916."[50]

Catherine Hoy grew up in an Irish Catholic home on Anaconda Road with her parents, siblings, and grandmother. Her Irish grandmother was a great storyteller.

Irish children kept up the ethnic traditions of their parents. The 1927 Boys Central High School annual included this photograph of Irish step dancers (top, left to right) W. McCarthy, A. Groo, D. Sullivan, T. Lally, R. Sullivan, and C. Slatt, and (bottom) J. Church, W. McGowan, A. Slatt, R. Grace, and G. Norton.

> This aged grandmother of mine, she would gather most of the kids from around the neighborhood. They'd come in, and she'd tell them ghost stories about the banshees and the Little People and all that. She'd sit there for hours and tell us all those stories. Then the kids were too scared to go home, so my mother and my oldest brother would have to take the kids home. . . . Well, then the kids would have nightmares during the night.[51]

John Sheehy grew up in the embrace of an Irish immigrant family and community on Butte's north side.

> We lived about a block from the Original Mine, two blocks from the Stewart Mine, and to the west about a quarter of a mile from the Anselmo. At that time, in those years, all that area was fully populated and crowded with houses and people.
>   My father and mother both came from Ireland. My father came from County Kerry and my mother from County Cork. They met in Butte, where my father was miner and mother, I think, was a bucket girl. My father lived in a boardinghouse

run by a Mrs. O'Neil. I am told that Mrs. O'Neil encouraged the romance that brought them together.

John's family home was a hub of Irish family connection and culture.

My earliest memories are of my father and mother going back and forth among the Irish families, visiting each other and mostly talking about the Old Country. . . . At our house at night, it was a great gathering place for women, Irish women. They'd come in their shawls. They always wore shawls. They'd sit in the kitchen around the fire—we didn't have gas at that time [and] people burned coal and wood—and just talk about the Old Country. They were great for reciting poetry. There was a little niche behind our kitchen stove where [my brother Ed] could kind of hide himself and listen to the old folks. And from that he learned all kinds of Irish poems. From the top to the bottom, he could recite them. In his later years, he always remembered those poems.

And there were always letters from Ireland. They would be referred to and talked about. We used to receive what they would call "letters edged in black." That announced from Ireland the death of somebody back there to the family. . . . My father received the news of the death of his mother some time in the 1930s. And news came as a letter edged in black, so they knew as soon as they saw the letter that there had been a death in the Old Country, as they called it.[52]

Together these families built a strong community, weathered hardship, and found reasons to celebrate. Jule Harrington McHugh was born in Dublin Gulch in 1906, the eighth of the ten children of Mary and Pat Harrington. Her family home was a hub of social life.

All the "greenhorns" from Ireland would come, and almost every night was like a "shindig." Jim Rafter would play jigs and reels on his fiddle, and they would have square dances. Belle and Eva were great dancers. They would get a bucket of beer for the men and a bottle of Iron Brew for the women. It was like Coke or root beer. And the house would be jumping with a good time. . . . Growing up in the Gulch in my time . . . was memorable. . . . God knows, it wasn't beautiful, surrounded by the mines, . . . but we had something else. We had neighbors who were all caring for each other. We didn't have money. Somehow it didn't seem like we ever needed it in the Gulch.

There were so many things—we always had something to do—but we had time, and our families could always dump a shift to go to a friend's funeral.[53]

A strong sense of community prevailed in Dublin Gulch, even as the neighborhood diminished in size in the post–World War II years. Danette Harrington and her brother grew up in the same Dublin Gulch home where her father and his ten brothers and sisters were raised.

Danette Harrington in her Dublin Gulch backyard, 1950

At one point, when my parents were young, there were over a hundred homes in Dublin Gulch. When I grew up, there were only eleven families left in the Gulch. It was like a family of eleven families. Everybody just went in and out of everyone's home, and nobody had to knock. We all had telephones, but no one really used them. We knew everybody, and the kids were basically about the same age. The families spent a lot of time visiting. We all took vacations at the same time with the exception of one family. They used to go to Elkhorn, and the rest of us went to Pipestone [Hot Springs]. We all got the same cabins, and we all went to Pipestone at the same time.[54]

Uptown Butte's Irish community was also home to young Packey Buckley, who was born in a boardinghouse at 526 North Wyoming Street in 1914. He was one of six children, all born at home. Like many young Butte residents, he and his siblings grew up surrounded by an extended family of miners. As Packey remembered:

You had the Irish boarders that came from Ireland. They were told, "Don't stop in America, go straight to Butte," with a shipping tag on them: "Ship to Mary Buckley, 526 N. Wyoming." . . . They weren't boarders. They were just like family. I want to tell you that when my mother prepared supper and you and I were a boarder and something came out on the plate [and you didn't eat it], she would ask, "Patrick or John, what was the matter with it?" And if you said that you just did not care for that, you never got it again. Just like a family, just like a family home.

There were seventeen rooms in the house with two men to each room, so that is thirty-four. I would say she had another fifteen on the outside [men who came just for meals], so

I would say [the boardinghouse served] in the vicinity of fifty miners. . . . Three meals a day if you slept in the house, and it was nine dollars a week. And if you stayed in another house and came for three meals and a bucket, it was seven dollars a week. . . . [My mother] would have people make beds, she would have people wash dishes, she would have people wait on tables, but nobody touched the stove, nobody. She did all the cooking.

In the seventeen rooms, there were one, two, three, four, five, six, seven rooms upstairs, and then downstairs there were two single beds in each room. My mother and Ellen slept down on the main floor where there was the kitchen, dining room, and front room and two bedrooms, and us boys slept in the basement. . . . My mother had to [start the boardinghouse]. . . . My father couldn't work. He had miner's con. He died when I was in the sixth grade.[55]

Vacationing at Pipestone Hot Springs in 1931 are (standing from left) Stella Lazarri Favero, Margaret Grosso, Mary Martinesso Ciabattari, Amelia Gross, and (seated) Violet Michelotti Botton.

Many Butte children, like Packey Buckley and Aili Goldberg, were raised in and around boardinghouses and grew up observing the habits of miners. Their family homes were 24-7 machines of cooking, cleaning, and feeding. Children sometimes slept in far-flung nooks and crannies as beds and bedrooms were precious commodities. Some recall boarders giving them an occasional gift or a tip for running an errand. Others report pilfering a bit of whiskey from a miner's private stash while he was on shift. The common memory, however, is of the respect with which boardinghouse residents treated women and children alike. For example, Collette Tarrant's grandmother ran the Hazel Block, a Finntown boardinghouse. As a little girl, Collette would walk to the boardinghouse to spend the day with her grandmother. The boardinghouse loomed large in her memory:

It was about four stories high. There had to be eighty or ninety rooms. In the Hazel Block, it was all single men. They were all what they called transit workers. They worked in the mines. When you would come into the Hazel Block, you would come up the stairs, and you would walk into a great big meeting room and card room. They had chairs set up along the walls and spittoons because they all chewed tobacco, so they had big brass spittoons. Then they had this great big card table at the end, and that's where the men would play cards. The basement is where they did the cooking, and they had the eating room where the men ate at long tables, probably like they had in the service. Over on the side, they had this long table where they put the bread, butter, sugar, cream, and the desserts. They would have cakes and pies. Oh, it was like walking into bakery. It was, well, for a little kid, it was like Christmas with all the cupcakes, cakes, pies, and cookies. I remember I used to go in and sit in the kitchen on a stool, and the cook used to let me sit there. They would have a great big copper pot, and they would be cooking stews, or they would be cooking potatoes, or they would be cooking spaghetti or whatever was for dinner that night.

I would go over and stay with my grandmother. Oh, I loved to run up those halls. I had a great imagination, like all kids. . . . I was a princess, and I was running away from the knight. When you go in and go up these stairs, there were these two swinging doors. And you come in, and there would be this great big room, and right along here would be all these chairs and rocking chairs where the miners would sit and gossip and talk. And I would go down the line, and, geez, I would get nickels and dimes, and, heck, I would walk out with two or three dollars.[56]

By the early 1900s, Butte was home to a Jewish community of about five hundred people. They established an economic niche in Butte as jewelers, tailors, restaurant and grocery store owners, and clothing and furniture merchants. Henry Jacobs, a businessman and prominent member of the Jewish community, became Butte's first mayor. Writer Myron Brinig, the son of Jewish immigrants from Romania, grew up in Butte, the youngest of eight children. His father ran a men's clothing store on East Park Street, where Myron spent much of his childhood. Brinig drew on his memories of childhood in Butte and the hours spent in his father's shop in writing his first novel, *Singermann*:

The clothing stores of the Jewish merchants were on East Park Street. They caught customers with traps of words, and they were constantly dragging miners inside to sell them shoes, socks, suits of ribbed underwear, and maybe a suitcase to go away with. East Park was a beehive with its Jewish stores, its Greek restaurants, and its Irish saloons with swinging doors. . . . In his shop on South Montana Street, Rabbi Lachter sold kosher beef and butchered chickens on Saturday night. The room back of the shop was where he took the chicken and slit its throat with a sharp-edged blade. Some said it was the same blade he used for circumcision—but they may have been talking for drama.[57]

Dorothy Martin's family was part of Butte's Jewish community. Her maternal Grandfather Rosenstein and her Uncle Isador were both tailors. Her uncle started his own business in Butte when he was a mere fourteen years old. Dorothy's family also ran Rosenstein's Confectionary in Uptown Butte. After her grandparents died, Dorothy, her mother, and two uncles moved into the former rooming house located over the confectionary, and they converted it into their family home.

They remodeled it. It was great—Rosenstein's Confectionary, on Hamilton and Broadway. We each had our own room, and the bathroom was down at the end of the hall. And the kitchen. Then we had a living room and a great big dining room. A lot of people were upset that mother was moving me—I was an only child—up into the rough part of the city. . . . About the time we moved, they were breaking up the red-light district. I was in the first grade. There were not many children living in the business district. The Hamilton Block, across the street, was always filled. And, of course, some prostitutes started moving into the area. And that's what people objected to. And then there was a bar on the side street there. I can still hear "Roll Out the Barrels." They played it all night long, I think. I played on the street, right down on the sidewalk, a lot. Or in the store. And I had a dog. The dog was close to me. He was right there. When I first got him, he was so tiny I used to carry him in a cigar box. That was his name. We called him "Tiny." When I went away to college, he was still alive. He stayed in the store, and my uncle was just crazy about him and took care of him all the time. Somehow he got out on the street and was hit by a car and killed, so they wrote this big article in the paper about the tiniest dog. Everybody in Butte knew Tiny because I carried him in a box wherever I went.[58]

In Sickness and Health

Many Butte children grew up under challenging circumstances. Parents often struggled to keep houses warm and children adequately fed and dressed during Butte's long, harsh winters. Toxic waste from the mines exacerbated the difficulties of keeping children healthy, and many families lacked the resources for basic health care. They relied instead on health practices and home remedies passed down through their families. Betty Henderson's mother had a standard cure-all for any number of illnesses: "My mother would dry up some onions and make a poultice out of onions and eucalyptus, and then they'd make a bag out of a rag and pin it on you."[59]

John Mazzola's mother would give the children hot wine when they showed symptoms of a cold or flu, then she would rub their chests with olive oil and turpentine. John remembered, "It would take the hide right off you, but it sure cured the cold."[60] Vadis Stratton's mother made her own cough syrup: "We had a wood stove, and my mother used to take a pie plate, cut an onion in half, put it face down, let it simmer on the back of the stove, and let it make a syrup. And then she'd put in a little sugar, and that was cough syrup. It was good tasting."[61]

In Ann Pentilla's household, children and adults had wine with meals. "That was more for health than to be drinking," Ann recalled. "We had whiskey, too. We drank whiskey in the morning and wine in the evening. . . . It kept you healthy." Ann's mother used a variety of home remedies when one of the children was ill.

> For flu and cold, you put turpentine on your chest with some lard. Melt the lard and turpentine and put it on your chest—talk about burn. We used onion syrup for coughs. You chop the onion up and fry it, mix it with sugar and water, and make syrup of it. We used to boil wine and drink the wine, then crawl into bed. You'd sweat it out and be well the next day. Flaxseed was used to put on the outside of your throat for sore throats. It was boiled like a mush and placed on a cloth. It was supposed to be a poultice. It would draw out the soreness.
>
> We used garlic in everything. In fact, my mother cooked a lot with garlic. My mother flavored everything with garlic. And now everybody uses it, but in those days just the Slavics and Italians used garlic. My mother made blood sausage and put a lot of garlic in it. And that would be our lunch. Well, when we'd go back to school after lunch, it would be pretty potent.[62]

Children in a Hard-Working, Hard-Drinking Town

Many Butte children grew up with a strong sense of belonging shaped by the rhythms of mining, infused with cultural identity, and grounded in the familiar space of their neighborhoods. Children witnessed the habits and rituals of adults as they negotiated work and family obligations. They also struggled to make sense of conflict and tensions that, at times, violated family safety, threatened friendships, and ruptured community relations. Hardships and hurts challenged the innocence of childhood, and children bore the burdens of conflict and violence.

For some children, paydays at the mines produced a poignant and problematic pattern in family life as miners carried out the custom of cashing their paychecks at one of Butte's many bars. For decades, miners got their paychecks every Friday from the pay offices on the corner of Quartz and Main. Women might be there, too, hoping to secure their husbands' paychecks before they were cashed in a local bar. When those efforts failed, they might resort to sending one of their children into the bar to try to persuade Dad to hand over what money he had left.[63]

Waldemar Kailaya was raised in Finntown, one of ten children of Jacob and Susanna Kaiyala, who had come to Butte from Finland by way of the mines in Michigan. Waldemar wrote in his memoir of childhood: "There were four Finnish saloons located around Finntown. Two were located on East Broadway and the other two on East Park St. These were a great impact on many families, my own among them. I always had to meet my father at the pay office on payday; otherwise he would stop at the saloon and lose his weekly pay. At one time, he lost his full month's wages when I was not there to meet him. That caused a great hardship for a large family like ours."[64]

Bars acquired legendary status in Butte, with the culture of mining often described as virtually inseparable from the culture of drinking. Pints and shots at the end of a shift soothed the harshness of the work and fueled the camaraderie of the workers. Many children looked forward to payday and the chance to stop by the neighborhood bar. Miners were often in a generous mood, pop flowed as freely as beer, and kids traded pennies, nickels, and dimes for "pick candy." Many Butte youngsters grew up with a child's-eye view of bars and drinking as part and parcel of family and work life. As Laurie Ugrin described:

> Every Friday night was payday. The miners would cash their
> paychecks and go to the bar. They bought a beer and got a
> shot for free. My dad would sometimes be coming home late
> on Fridays. He used to go out every Saturday night, too, but
> I don't think my mom minded. That was our time together—
> Mom and the kids. Dad spent Sunday afternoons at Charley
> Judd's New Deal Bar, and he was always home for supper.
> Sometimes after we left 5:00 Mass on Sunday we'd swing by
> the bar and pick him up if he hadn't left yet.[65]

However, when labor-management conflict flared and the possibility of a strike or layoff loomed, tensions fueled drinking and vice versa in many homes. Bonnie Stefanic grew up in a mining family. Her father and several members of her extended family worked in the mines. Bonnie recalled the heated union discussions in her home among her father and uncles as they pieced together information, reported rumors of impending layoffs, and fueled one another's fears. Bonnie would take up her strategic spot in a corner of the dining room, out of view of her father and uncles in the living room and her mother and aunts in the kitchen.

They'd start to worry about layoffs, and there'd be more drinking, more arguments. I remember there'd been a strike threat about 1956 or '57, and that was when the Company brought the West Virginians in [as replacement workers]. Once that happened, then it was, "The Company is going to try and break our union. They aren't going to pay us what we deserve. They are going to try to get rid of us." There was the fear that they were going to lay off everybody and even shut the mines down for a couple of years, then bring in all of these people from outside who don't know any better to go through everything we did. Only we'll have lost our homes, our history, and all that stuff.

The idea was that this was their home, everything they'd worked for, from the union to Columbia Gardens, the baseball leagues, all of those things. The idea of moving was terrifying. There was so much fear that rotated around the threat of a strike. It caused all kinds of family problems. Domestic problems were common. The man would be scared and start drinking too much, and he would get violent. . . . At least in East Butte, it was common that the men drank heavily, and the women didn't hardly drink at all. The women were busy. They were working, and they were resentful and angry and scared. So when this stuff started coming down, what I remember is the women being real secretive, whispering a lot. The men would be in the front room and the women in the kitchen. They'd be working, and they'd visit in whispering tones. Even when they talked to us kids, it would be in a whispering tone. We had to be quiet. We couldn't irritate any of the men. It was like walking on eggshells, and it got worse and worse before the strikes. Then once the strike happened, it meant the men would be out of work, and that meant they drank all day long. There was no money. The woman was angry, and the guy was angry, and it was an ugly, violent cycle.[66]

Some children faced the chaos of violence and alcoholism on the home front as the dangers and uncertainties of life took their toll on their parents. Aili Goldberg described her mother's reaction to seeing a co-worker at the boardinghouse with a black eye. "We stayed in a rooming house across the street. There was a Finnish lady, and Mother saw her, and Mother said, 'What did you do? Fall down the stairs? Or did you get pushed by a cow?' Well, you know, there were no cows here in Butte on the streets, but her husband had beat her. So, that was Mother's first experience, and she just couldn't believe it. Of course, drinking and stuff was quite wide open."[67]

As John Sheehy recalled, families were poor, and miners' salaries did not go far. Too often, alcohol exacerbated those tough financial conditions.

> Very few had bank accounts. They probably kept their money
> in a tobacco can. They'd cash their check and take the
> money home. And, hopefully, they didn't stop at a bar on
> the way. There was a lot of alcoholism. We knew that there
> were women in our neighborhood being beaten by their
> husbands. They didn't talk about it as a gossip sort of thing,
> but they were aware. And you could see it in the kids. They
> were different somehow. The kids themselves were affected in
> a sad way. I remember one family was particularly bad. Mr. C.
> would regularly beat his wife. He would come home drunk.
> There was a lot of alcoholism.[68]

For the most part, violence was a painful subject that few people addressed directly when revisiting memories of childhood. The references were more oblique—a sense of awareness and concern rather than detailed depiction. On occasion, the trauma of violence in a child's life was thrust dramatically before the public eye, as happened in the case of young John Isakson. The March 30, 1923, *Butte Miner* story reported "Boy Cries as He Describes Death of Step-Father":

> Early in the morning in the Daly-Shea undertaking parlors
> John Isakson, 15 year old step son of Nick Kumpula, gazed
> upon the dead body of his stepfather, and although the boy's
> lips trembled as he spoke, he answered all questions relative to
> the tragedy in a little house in the rear of 358 ½ East Granite
> Street that ended when he fired a shot that almost instantly
> killed his stepfather. His replies were given in a firm, steady
> voice, ending invariably with the explanation, "I shot him to
> save my mother and sister." . . . Suddenly he started to cry, and

between sobs he told his mother and sister that he was sorry his stepfather was dead. "I didn't mean to kill him," he finished. "I just wanted to take care of you."[69]

According to the news account, young John had been awakened in the middle of the night by the sound of someone trying to break through the door of the family home. As John started toward the stairs to investigate, the door gave way. His stepfather barged in, shouting at John to keep back or he would kill them all. John heard his mother and eleven-year-old sister screaming as his stepfather charged toward the stairs, one hand behind his back. In a second's glance, John caught a glimpse of a knife blade in his stepfather's grip. John grabbed his .22 rifle and fired a shot as his stepfather charged for him, shouting, "That's only one shot, kid." Having spent the only bullet in the gun, John, in desperation, took the barrel, shoved it into Nick Kumpula's chest, and knocked him down the stairs, where he crumpled and lay still.[70]

John's mother, Anna Kumpula, spoke words of comfort and grief in Finnish to her son as she tried to grasp the enormity of the situation. Finding her words, she told authorities of her husband's relentless violence and abuse in recent months. She had told him to leave, but he repeatedly returned, threatening her and the children and victimizing them with his violent rages. Neighbors corroborated her story and expressed their empathy for John and what they saw as his justifiable actions.[71]

For some children, violence was an unspoken part of family life, kept behind closed doors. Some families experienced outbursts of violence seemingly fueled by the stresses, uncertainties, and dangers of mining itself. And on occasion children bore witness to and the brunt of violence against neighbors as the tensions of strikes divided the community into "us" and "them."

"Us" and "Them": Negotiating Belonging and Difference

Butte children learned to negotiate the complexities of belonging and difference in their families, neighborhoods, and schools. Many miners' children grew up with a consciousness of class differences, aware of who were "in the same boat" and who lived in a different social and economic reality, relatively unaffected by the vagaries of mining. Some children of miners distinguished their families from the "high mucky mucks" or "big shots" of the mines, taking pride in their working-class neighborhoods. Others became more aware of class differences once they entered high school and encountered young people from other neighborhoods who sported new clothes, had access to cars, and had traveled beyond

Butte. Many people who grew up in mining families spoke of getting through hard times by counting on relatives, friends, and neighbors who understood and shared their hardships. As Catherine Hoy remembered about her childhood in Dublin Gulch and along Anaconda Road:

> Everybody was pretty much the same sort of people and [had] the same way of living because they had a certain income, and they didn't go beyond it. They lived within their income. They didn't try to outdo one another. If you did, you got in trouble. The kids wouldn't associate. If they thought you were a little richer than they were, they wouldn't associate with you. They'd think, "What the heck, she's too rich for me."[72]

Catherine was well aware that hers was a world apart from Butte's West Side, home to many of the city's more well-to-do families. "They knew their place and we knew ours. That's all there was to it." However, she held clear memories of the handful of mine bosses who lived on the Anaconda Company properties at the end of Anaconda Road.

> It was nothing to see their big cars drive up. Their big limousines and stuff like that. I remember the first time they had an automobile go up and down Anaconda Road. . . . It was an open car. And us kids, we would walk down, I'd say, two or three miles to get a ride. We would walk down Anaconda Road for maybe two or three miles to ride up to his [the mine superintendent's] house, which was on the top of Anaconda Road. And we would ride up there in order to get the ride. And then we'd have to walk home. But there was from eight to ten kids in this open car at one time getting this ride up and down Anaconda Road.[73]

While Catherine described class differences as simply "the way things were," she also justified "petty stealing" from the mines as one way kids dealt with those differences.

> Well, you know, in order to get money for the Fourth of July . . . for the Gardens and stuff like that, we would go up to the mines and steal their copper. And we'd steal their iron, take the wheels off the little cars, little ore cars, and sell them. We got about seventy-five cents for a wheel. A junkman would come around about once a week, and he'd buy it up. Sometimes we'd have about five or six dollars worth of copper or wheels and so forth. There was always mischief we could get into. Not like

[vandalism]—it is not destruction or destroying property. We didn't do things like that. We did a lot of petty stealing.[74]

However, the strife and struggles of economic hard times brought differences of "us" and "them" to the fore. Strikes were particularly charged periods that brought differences between union and Company sympathies to the surface in memorable ways. Children took cues from parents, teachers, friends, and schoolmates in learning to make sense of divisiveness. For example, Kay Antonetti grew up with strikes as a fact of life:

> Well, I remember the strikes. My dad was good, you know. He and my mother were both very charismatic. And I remember one of my friends in my class when I was a freshman at Central—I am still a friend of hers now—her dad had an upper job in the ACM. So when they would go on strike, he stayed behind the fence and was a scab. And that strike, our freshman year, it was when they threw the pianos out the window. And I know my dad said, "You be nice to her. Her dad has a nice, important job, and if he doesn't do what he is doing, he would lose his job. They're nice people. . . . Don't you ever criticize anybody because you don't know what it's like to walk in their shoes." I remember driving around on East Park by the houses where they'd thrown things through the window, and I remember it was a scary time.[75]

The strikes of 1934 and 1946, in particular, stand out in childhood memories. John T. Shea vividly recalled the 1934 strike when the Company brought in scab laborers to work "behind the fence." He and his friends headed to the mine yards, ready to fight the men who had taken over their fathers' jobs. "We used to practice our pitchin' arms throwing rocks at those scabs behind the fence. They'd walk to work with paper bags over their heads, and we'd run alongside to get a peek at their faces, but lots of 'em you could recognize just by their shoes."[76]

Some children found the division of "us" and "them" confounding, and they struggled to grasp their parent's hostility toward those who went "behind the fence" during a strike. Betty Matesich's childhood memory of the 1934 strike illustrated her confusion and hurt.

> We lived right next to the Stewart Mine. And behind the fence were what we found out later were scabs. In my mind, they were very, very nice men. And they always gave us an orange and a Hershey bar and a bar of Palmolive soap. And

when my father came home, he said, "Where did you get the soap, Betty?" And I said, "These nice men gave it to me behind that fence at the mine." So, he put all the soap in a sack, and he said, "Now, I want you to throw this back at those men." And I threw the soap and cried.[77]

Marie Butori grew up in a family of seven. Her father ran a gas station next to the family home. Marie remembered the violence of the 1946 strike that resulted in damage to homes of workers accused of being scabs. She vividly recalled her confusion of being caught in the middle when trying to do a good deed for her neighbor:

I got in trouble myself 'cause we lived right next door to the foreman and assistant foreman of the ACM, and they had big family houses there. We had a house and gas station next to them. So, Mrs. Hagen [wife of the foreman] one day said to me, "Marie, I don't have some stuff I need at the store so will you go?" So I went to the grocery store, and I brought her home some groceries, and my dad came home and said to my mother, "Your daughter is going to get herself killed if she doesn't knock it off." He said, "Do you know she went to the store for Mrs. Hagen?" And Mom said, "No," and I said, "Yes, and she gave me two dollars." It was hard to get two dollars, but I never went any more, I'm telling ya.[78]

Some youngsters struggled to make sense of changing alliances as their fathers moved from union jobs to salaried positions as "Company men" who had to "stay behind the fence" and keep the pumps dewatering the mine operating during a strike. With the change in job came a shift in perceived "us" and "them" loyalties, and parents took measures to protect children from possible repercussions. As one youngster recalled:

When Dad knew there was going to be a strike, he'd put us on the train to . . . go and live with my grandmother until the strike was over because he would have to stay at the mine and not even come out. They ate, slept, and everything there until the strike was over. . . . It was dangerous. In those days, they weren't just being nice with picket lines. They were throwing rocks. And miners' homes, if they knew that the "Company men" were at the mine and their family was home alone, there was a lot of destruction done to people's houses and that kind of thing. So he would put us on the train so that we'd be gone, and he'd stay there until the strike was over.

When I was older and then things weren't quite so violent, in my teen years, we would just stay here, and my dad would just stay at the mines. And the people went without. I mean, sometimes they were on strike for nine months to a year and a half with no paychecks. And those were hard times for people. But I was always the "Company man's daughter," who, probably if I would've known what was going on a little better, I might've been a little more nervous.[79]

Another woman described a painful grade-school memory when a teacher asked the class for a show of hands if their fathers were on strike. "My dad had just moved from union job to salaried job. I raised my hand. I was still identifying with my dad being on strike, even though now he had to cross the picket line. A boy in the class yelled at me, 'Your dad is a boss.' It was humiliating. I tried to defend myself, saying my dad was taking a lot of risks crossing the line and that my family was affected, too. The boy yelled back, 'Scab. He crossed the line. Scab.' It was mortifying."[80]

Helen McGregor's father was employed as a veterinarian for the Anaconda Company. Up until the strike of 1946, no one said anything to her father regarding his status during a strike and his role in caring for the horses that worked underground. During long strikes, her father took the horses from the mines and out to pasture. But in the 1946 strike, she recalled, things were different. After that strike, children whose families were divided along labor-management lines would call each other names. The 1946 strike was also the first time that anything was said to Helen's father when he went on the Hill to work during the strike. Helen recalled, "He had known practically everyone. He used to take care of the widows' cows."[81]

Tom Holter recalled the tensions of the 1946 strike as well.

Our next door neighbor in McQueen, Phil Trythall—everybody in McQueen had a name, his was Greasy—he was a boss for the Anaconda Company. He walked out. He walked out. He didn't stay in for the strike. And he got blackballed. His son and I were really close friends. Young Phil. We were like a month and eighteen days apart. And I can remember his dad, he wouldn't stay in like most of the bosses. He got blackballed. And the guy who lived across the street from us, Hank Matule, he did the same thing. Hank, he moved. His daughter Marcella was in my class. I was sorry to see them move. She was beautiful. She was the prettiest girl in the class.[82]

Sarah Massey was five years old at the start of the 1946 strike. Her father was a supervisor with responsibility for keeping the pumps going. Her family home was violently vandalized in the late night hours of Friday, April 12. In June 2011 Sarah wrote an account of that terrifying weekend, which she donated to the Butte-Silver Bow Public Archives.

The first sign of trouble came in the middle of the night when a rock was thrown through our living-room window. My sister Ruth was awakened by the sound of the breaking glass. Ruth and I were sleeping in our upstairs bedroom; mother was asleep downstairs. Mother hollered for Ruth to come downstairs, bring Sarah, and don't turn on any light. I remember being awakened by sounds I did not understand. My mother was yelling. I heard glass breaking and the sound of rock hitting the side of our house. It was very dark, and I did not know where I was or what was happening. Ruth and I were on the floor behind the kitchen stove covered in a blanket. We were both crying. I was five years old; Ruth was fourteen.

Our dad was not home. He was a supervisor in the mines and had been told to stay at the mine during the strike to keep the pumps going so that the mines did not flood. Later I was told that the supervisors had to cross the picket lines to get into the mines, and this angered the union, which, in turn, led to widespread mob violence throughout the city and the vandalizing of more than a dozen homes.

When the angry crowd assaulted our house, our mother tried a number of times to get help from the police, and when she was finally able to talk to them on the phone, she pleaded with them to come to our house. Initially, they did not respond. I was told that the police finally did come to our house later that morning, but when they drove into the alley at the back of our house, the crowd ran around to the front. And when the police drove down the street in front of our house, the crowd ran to the alley. After driving back and forth several times and without being able to control the angry mob, the police told my mother to leave the house immediately. Then the police drove away, leaving my mother, Ruth, and me alone in the house.

I escaped the horror by being taken to our Uncle Ray and Aunt Adah Sims's home. Ruth, however, stayed in the house with Mother. I was told years later that Ruth was terrified—screaming at Mother to get out of the house.

As Sarah Massey's account of her and her sister's experiences attests, the violence that erupted during the 1946 strike took its toll on children.

Ruth thought that she and Mother were going to be killed. Saturday afternoon, after the police had once again driven away, Mother went to the front porch with a gun and fired it into the air, trying to scare the crowd, but the mob continued to advance on our home, throwing rocks, painting obscenities on the house, and trying to break into the house. Finally, early Saturday evening, April 13, the day before Palm Sunday, my mother and sister left the house and went to Uncle Ray and Aunt Adah's house.

The damage to our house was unbelievable. Dishes were broken, pictures were ripped off the walls, wallpaper stripped, clothes were stolen or shredded. Games, toys, dishes, pots, pans, household goods were all destroyed or taken. Furniture was broken and thrown into the yard. A three-inch hole was drilled into our piano, and the vandals tried unsuccessfully to cut the legs off the piano. A large steel beam was lifted and rammed through our front window. Nothing but wreckage remained inside the house, the result of incredibly thorough rage.

Because I was only five years old, I did not understand why people had destroyed our house. I did not know what a strike was, and I did not know what "crossing the picket line" meant. The word "scab" had been painted on the outside of our house, and when I asked what that word was, I was told it was a bad word that the bad people had painted on our house. No other explanation was given to me at the time.

Monday, the day after Palm Sunday, Mother, Ruth, and I went back to our house. Someone from the newspaper was there and took our picture, which was featured on the front page of the *Montana Standard* on Easter Sunday, April 21, 1946, four days before my sixth birthday.[83]

Sarah and her family moved to an apartment in Uptown Butte for several months while their house was being restored. Her family received donations of clothing and toys, including a tricycle for Sarah. Ruth went back to school, where she was the subject of name-calling and teasing. When the family returned to their restored home shortly before Christmas 1946, they received a surprise visit from men of the McQueen Athletic Club bearing gifts of toys, books, and clothing for Sarah and Ruth and household items for their parents.

Sixty-five years later, Sarah carried the memories of that traumatic time.

When I reflect on the damage done that weekend not only to our home but to the homes of other supervisors, it shocks and saddens me to realize that the young people and the men and women who participated in the rioting were being taught that violence and destruction was an acceptable way to deal with conflict. I also find it hard to understand how some people tend to oversimplify conflicting values, which then get reduced to "us" versus "them" and allows people to act violently toward others without ever really knowing who they are or what they stand for. Perhaps someday we will move beyond treating each other this way. I certainly hope so.[84]

While few Butte children were the targets of mob violence as experienced by Sarah and Ruth Massey, strikes were defining moments of childhood for many. Children experienced solidarity and support, deep uncertainty about their families' futures, and the painful divisions of "us" and "them." Adults still carry memories of childhood slights when they were teased at school for their hand-me-down clothes. Children "walked on eggshells" at home to avoid upsetting an "already upset household." Adult economic worries preoccupied children's thoughts as well. Children were often keenly aware of the fact the grocery bills were adding up, and power bills were not being paid. Some kids remembered strikes as times of "more drinking and no money." Some took on more responsibilities at home in order to try to keep things on an even keel. Some internalized the sense of shame their parents voiced about seeking welfare assistance. Some can still taste the free commodity cornmeal and powdered milk that supplemented their meals. Others recalled the tensions at home and their fathers' resentment as their mothers tried to find paid work or increase their work hours.

Families went without basic medical care. Children made do with old glasses and worn shoes. Christmas might mean a single present or presents for the younger siblings only. One woman remembered the 1959 strike as the year she got a box of crayons for Christmas.[85] Children did not ask for more. They witnessed the differences between their families and the families of schoolmates who were not affected by the strike. Some were amazed at the sheltered lives of some of their peers. "They just didn't have the same experiences that we did. They thought we were making it up."[86] Some recalled their peers as just plain cruel. In the end, children learned that mining was a "hard, hard" life that took its toll on everyone.[87]

Celebrating Community

While strikes brought notions of "us" and "them" into sharp relief, childhood memories are also shaped by the joy of celebration. Sometimes the Anaconda Company displayed its corporate benevolence through generous support of community spirit at holiday time. The Hill glowed at Christmas with lighted trees perched atop gallows frames, and Butte children enjoyed Company-sponsored parties at Halloween and Christmas. The Butte Miners' Union also fostered community spirit with the celebration of Miners' Union Day. June 13 marked the anniversary of the union's founding in 1878. While the date honored the lives and labors of mining men, it also celebrated the contributions of all of the city's working men and women. It was a citywide holiday. Thousands would gather for a grand parade, speeches, an afternoon of picnicking and competitive games at Columbia Gardens, and dancing into the night. John T. Shea recalled upwards of ten thousand miners, dressed in their best clothes, marching in the parade when he was a youngster in the 1920s. "I was never so proud in my life as to walk holdin' my father's hand. It was a great thing," John remembered.[88] Steve Sherick, who grew up in Butte in the 1930s, described Miners' Union Day as a "big deal."

They used to have a Miners' Union Day parade. It would start at the Miners' Union Hall, and they would walk all the way down, like the Fourth of July parade, and go all the way back. And the first one of those I was in, I must have been about four or five years old because I can remember my dad carrying me. A lot of guys carried their kids. He had his white cap on and his bib overalls, and we'd march back, get in the car, and go up to Columbia Gardens. At the Gardens, there were competitions. They had first-aid teams from every mine, and they had a lot of miners working then. And they had the mucking contest, and they had the drilling contests. And so that was a big day up there. [They had] sack races and ice cream [for the kids], and you didn't pay for nothing. The Miners' Union paid for that. It was great. It was really something.[89]

Jule McHugh remembered the events of the day.

We would go to the parade, although it wasn't more than a march, but they had the Elks and the Eagles drill teams and the miners' band. . . . After the parade, we went to the Gardens, where they had all the contests. We weren't interested, but we watched them anyhow. These were the drilling and shoveling contests. But we loved the first-aid contest. Each mine had a first-aid team, and the contests were held in the pavilion. Everybody would be cheering for their favorite mine to win.[90]

Vadis Stratton grew up with a more skeptical view of the celebration: "They used to fine the miners if they didn't march in the parade. And my dad didn't like walking in the parade, but they'd fine them if you didn't. And then they went up to the Gardens. But my mother mostly took me. Anything free. They'd give you ice cream. For the kids, you know."[91]

Celebrations extended beyond the reach of mines and mining. Sporting events were a core part of community celebration as were ethnic and religious holidays. Butte youngsters vividly recalled the twinkling lights of Uptown Butte at Christmastime and family trips through Meaderville to witness the Meaderville Fire Department's elaborate Christmas display. Children in Butte's Italian community joined their parents in door-to-door holiday visits on New Year's Day, sharing food and drink with their neighbors. Jewish families gathered at the Finlen Hotel each year for a Passover Seder dinner. As Mary Trbovich recalled, Serbian youngsters could hardly wait for Easter and Christmas to come. "Our parents would prepare for two weeks in advance for each holiday. How they ever did this without refrigeration I'll never know. Of course, in those days we didn't know what it was so did the best we could and survived.[92]

Following the Julian calendar, Serbian families celebrated Christmas on January 7 and New Year's on January 14. Starting at tender ages, Serbian girls joined their mothers in holiday food preparation at Holy Trinity Orthodox Church, preparing recipes handed down from grandmother to mother and daughter.

However, it is the "all-American" celebration of the Fourth of July that stood out in many childhood memories. As Mary Lou Kane Fitzpatrick described:

The elaborate life-sized Christmas displays created by the Meaderville Volunteer Fire Department delighted Butte children.

On the Fourth of July, the parade used to come out West
Broadway to Excel[sior] Avenue. My Grandma Driscoll's
house was in the 700 block on Broadway, so we would go
down and sit on the porch and watch the parade go by. It had
all kinds of floats and bands, clowns, the whole nine yards. . . .
In the afternoon, we'd set off firecrackers. Every Fourth of July
I had a new dress made out of something fancy like organdy.
[Then we] lit sparklers, and by the time the day was over, I had
a dress full of nothing but little teeny holes where the sparks
had caught the clothes on fire. There was no such thing as
jeans for girls back then. All the girls dressed like ladies.[93]

Catherine Hoy remembered the Fourth of July as the time when
"we really tore loose."

We had the big parade, you know, and . . . we got a new outfit.
Fourth of July and Easter and Christmas we always had new
clothes. And my mother and grandmother and these other
families, there was about, oh, five or six families, and they all
had between six and eight children. So, we'd all cook up these
big meals. Boiled the hams, legs of mutton. I don't mean lamb.
I mean old mutton. And then boiled the chickens, you know,
baked the bread, all that affair. Then put it in baskets, and we'd
go to the parade, and then after the Fourth of July parade we'd
all jump on these outdoor cars and go to the Gardens.[94]

Bessie Sherman remembered a particular Meaderville tradition:
"On the Fourth of July, my dad always got us a pine tree to put up in
the backyard. It was a custom then. We would sweep the yard extra
clean and enjoy the shade of the tree during the days of the celebration.
All the stores in Meaderville would have a tree in front of their buildings, too."[95]

The McHugh household had one particularly memorable Fourth of
July when Jule was a girl:

We always had fireworks. No big displays . . . but we always
had fun. One night we sure had our own fireworks. Johnny
brought home two roman candles. We had never seen one
before and didn't know what to do with them. So, Ma lit
one—in the house. Well, we were all running, and she was
all over the house screaming. I think it must have been the
longest roman candle ever made as the "shoots" kept coming
out and hitting us in the behind, and Johnny was trying to get

it away from her. But, finally, it fizzled out. You can be sure we set the other one off outside.[96]

Children of Meaderville took pride in the grand floats created each year for the Fourth of July parade by the Meaderville Volunteer Fire Department. These works of art took weeks to build. During the 1940s and 1950s, the fire department dominated the competition, taking top prize for best float year after year. The float themes invoked images and joys of childhood—the circus, the Playtime Unlimited Train, Cinderella, and Mother Goose—and each year some lucky children had the pleasure of riding on the float in the parade.

Children of Meaderville took pride in the grand floats the Meaderville Volunteer Fire Department created each year for the Fourth of July parade. These works of art took weeks to build and dominated the competition, taking top prize year after year. This one participated in 1956.

Children were both keen observers of and active participants in the social and cultural life of Butte. They acquired rich cultural knowledge as they moved in and beyond neighborhood boundaries and negotiated the complex relations of belonging and difference. As open-pit mining operations began to expand in the mid-1950s, significant spaces of attachment to neighborhood, ethnicity, and community belonging were lost forever.

Janie Payne's East Butte neighborhood was consumed by the Berkeley Pit. She described what it was like to be unable to return home: "It affects your roots in some ways. I cannot take my son to my old grade school and say, 'This is where I went to school. This is the neighborhood I grew up in' because it is not there. So to maintain our family history, it's all pictures. This is what the neighborhood looked like. This is where my uncle used to teach boxing. My great-uncle taught boxing to a lot of people in this community, and those places are now gone."[97]

CHAPTER THREE

———

Saving Children

Little waifs and homeless children will be taken in and cared for until homes can be found for them. . . . By combined effort such as comprehended in this scheme, it lies in our power to relieve hunger and distress, to lighten the burdens of the unfortunate, to soften the sorrows of the bereaved, to whisper words of encouragement and hope in the ears of the downfallen, to modify or disperse the gloom, sorrow, and despair that cloud so many human hearts, and invoke for them the dawn of sunlight and hope.

—William A. Clark's speech at the
1900 grand opening of the Paul Clark Home

Starting in the early twentieth century, Butte was a focal point of reform efforts directed at children and youth who were deemed dependent—lacking parental supervision and support—or delinquent—in trouble with the law. Adults concerned with the welfare of children sought to intervene in young lives, and their ideas and actions reflected an understanding of childhood as a time of both innocence and vulnerability to forces of vice and corruption. Reformers' actions were also colored at times by assumptions about gender and sexuality and by class-based attitudes regarding the needs and the worthiness of "other people's children," particularly the children of poor and working-class families. Over the decades, adult reformers and advocates, professionals and volunteers alike, directed their collective energies toward the care and control of children in order to protect them from harm, save them from the streets, and guide them on the right path to adulthood.

The accounts of efforts to improve children's lives in Butte reveal the powerful place of children and childhood in public policy and sentiment. Moreover, these accounts contribute to a more complicated

Built by copper baron William A. Clark and named in memory of his son, the Paul Clark Home opened its doors in 1900.

understanding of childhood that oral histories and individual memories do not tap.

Childhood and Charity in the Progressive Era

The Progressive Era was a time when reformers were especially concerned with the growing numbers of poor and working-class children of immigrants drawn to America's industrial cities. These reformers worried about the unhealthy conditions in which children lived, worked, and played and about the criminal potential of these youngsters if left unsupervised. Some reformers focused on charitable efforts to shelter and supervise children deprived of parental care and support due to death, desertion, or dereliction. Others advocated increased government intervention on children's behalf, including child labor laws, compulsory public education, programs for organized and supervised play, public health initiatives, and a youth-centered justice system. The children of Butte were the targets and beneficiaries of both of these types of efforts.[1]

The Associated Charities of Butte, a volunteer organization made up primarily of women from prominent and professional-class families, was launched in 1897 with the motto "Help the worthy poor help themselves."[2] In line with the thinking of the era, poverty was considered a moral failing, and dependent children were understood to be at risk for inheriting undesirable traits such as laziness from their parents.[3] In the organization's first biennial report, dated January 1, 1900, Associated Charities president Mrs. A. S. Christie was strident in purpose and clear in the organization's moral compass:

A "parasite" or in other words, a pauper, we must avoid creating.
. . . We must recognize that the most hopeful work that can be

done is in saving children from beggary and vice. They must be taught to feel the responsibility that their parents never felt; taught, if possible, the skills their parent never learned; given the character their parents never had. Proper care and environment would mean moral and social advancement to hundreds of our little products of the streets and alleys.[4]

The Associated Charities' initial charitable efforts were modest. The organization provided coal to needy families, distributed flower bouquets to the sick, and established a soup kitchen for Butte's poor with financial support from prominent business owners.[5] During 1898 and 1899, they also found adoptive homes for three children and made arrangements to send another twenty Butte children to institutions such as St. Joseph's Orphanage in Helena, which had been established by the Sisters of Charity of Leavenworth, a Catholic religious order, in 1893. The work took on new purpose, however, once one of Butte's major benefactors decided to build a local home to provide for needy and homeless children. William A. Clark, infamous Copper King, power broker, and, for a time, U.S. senator, had a soft spot in his heart for the children of Butte. Clark had lost his son Paul at age sixteen as a result of a sudden illness. In his son's memory, Clark funded the

Associated Charities of Butte, a volunteer organization made up primarily of women from prominent and professional-class families, operated the Paul Clark Home, which offered shelter to Butte children whose parents were unable to provide for them due to death, illness, dereliction, or poverty. This photograph shows the home's reading room.

construction of the Paul Clark Home, which offered shelter to Butte children whose parents were unable to provide for them due to death, illness, dereliction, or the grinding effects of poverty. He enlisted the Associated Charities of Butte to manage the facility. The Paul Clark Home opened its doors in 1900.[6]

During its first year of operation, two hundred fifty-three children were placed in the Paul Clark Home, and dozens more were cared for in the day nursery set up to serve the needs of working women. A weekly sewing school drew an average of fifty girls who were instructed in the skills the women of the Associated Charities saw as essential. "When we consider how much of the misery among the poorer classes is to be attributed to the lack of knowledge on the part of mothers to mend, darn, and sew, we cannot fail to appreciate the value of this important department," Christie wrote in the organization's 1904 annual report. The Paul Clark Home's young residents, referred to as "inmates," were scrubbed clean and dressed in uniforms made by older girls attending the sewing school. Their comportment was under the close scrutiny of Associated Charities matrons, who were always on the alert for signs of trouble that would lead their young charges on a wayward path.[7]

The women of the Associated Charities set about running the Paul Clark Home with zeal. They organized gala events to help fund their operations and planned benefits to support children's outings to

William A. Clark provided Butte children with free children's days at Columbia Gardens and transportation to and from the attraction on the specially named streetcar (below, circa 1905).

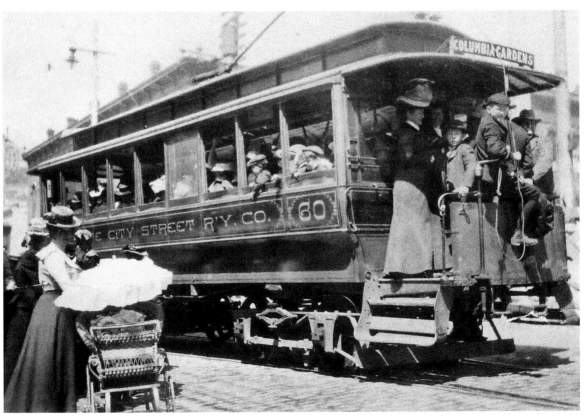

art exhibits and to Columbia Gardens. In 1901 W. A. Clark himself donated two hundred tickets for the children to attend an art exhibit and arranged for their participation in Children's Day at Columbia Gardens. The women organized amusements for the Fourth of July and dinners for Thanksgiving. At the Home's annual Christmas open house, the children, dressed in their best uniforms, played host to and provided the entertainment for Butte's social elite, and at a Christmas party complete with Santa Claus, they received gifts courtesy of the Clark family and local donors.[8] The children and their gift-receiving behavior were under the watchful eyes of the Associated Charities board members; those youngsters who eagerly made their way to Santa and his bag of toys were deemed unaccustomed to restraint and chastised for taking too literally the notion that "God helps those who help themselves."[9]

At times, the efforts of Associated Charities suggested that the organization had come to a deeper understanding of the realities of poverty that shaped the lives of so many Butte families. In the minutes of November 1901, it was noted that the group was "giving away used clothing to miserably clad children without shoes or stockings. Many children are unable to attend school because they have no food even." In a press release dated December 10, 1901, Associated Charities claimed that "Nobody need go hungry in the Greatest Mining Camp on Earth" and called for donations of clothing and food for the many mothers with children who were asking for help for the first time. By the time the 1904 annual report was written, the women were decrying the overwhelming nature of need in Butte. They had dished up over thirteen thousand meals from the soup kitchen and were serving an average of thirty-two children a month in the Home. The organization's minutes noted that "The past year has been one of unceasing activity for our organization. Two shut downs in the mines have entailed much suffering among the poor, and we have been at times unable to supply all the demands made upon us."[10]

However, the Associated Charities meeting minutes also illustrate the group's preoccupation with the worthiness of the children in their care. As board president Mrs. Christie declared in her 1902 annual address: "One of the first essentials to a wise and efficient ministry in behalf of the dependent poor is the sifting out of the unworthy. To feed and clothe unworthy people is not only an imposition upon the giver and an injustice to the worthy, dependent poor, but it encourages indolence and fosters pauperism and crime. It breeds imposters on the one hand and dries up the fountain of benevolence upon the other."[11]

In order to counter these tendencies in the Paul Clark Home's inmates, Christie put forth a modest proposal: the "establishment of a penny savings bank for the encouragement of thrift, the lack of which is one of the fruitful causes of dependence among the poorer classes.[12] The profit in many lines of business lies in the saving and using of small things while the dependent condition of many families is traceable to unwise expenditure and the lack of a disposition to save a small part of their earnings."[13] Mrs. A. H. Jones, board president in 1908, recommended that the children be charged a small fee for clothes they received from the sewing school or for garments donated by the Needlework Guild.[14] This practice, she asserted, would further instill in them a sense of economic value and the importance of savings and thrift.

The women of the Associated Charities, informed by their own class-based assumptions, made judgments about the parents of children in their care. Their views also influenced the ways in which they saw the children themselves as potentially lacking in responsibility, skills, and character and thus vulnerable to the vices of the street. Ironically, at times it was that very street wisdom the matrons deemed so dangerous that could be a child's saving grace. Consider the story of little Eddie Bennett. On August 15, 1902, the Paul Clark Home planned a picnic at Columbia Gardens for the young inmates. Eddie was among the excited group of children who boarded a special streetcar in Uptown Butte for the trip. Over the course of the day, the children picnicked beneath the trees, twirled on the merry-go-round, and visited the zoo.[15]

Unbeknownst to the matrons, Eddie had gotten separated from the group. No one missed him as the youngsters boarded the streetcar and headed home at the end of the day. As the sun began to set, Eddie began to walk, heading, he hoped, for the Paul Clark Home, located several miles from the Gardens. He descended to the outskirts of town and made his way through Uptown Butte, passing unnoticed through the throngs filling the streets, bars, and restaurants on a summer's evening.

Long past dark, Eddie was found trudging along West Park Street, mere blocks from the Paul Clark Home, and taken to the police station. Eddie, described as a "bright little fellow," was exhausted, but he "manfully held back tears" as he told the officers how he had gotten lost and, after thinking the matter over, had come to the conclusion that there was only one way to get home and that was to walk. Eddie Bennett was five years old. Little Eddie, it seems, was resourceful and streetwise, attributes worrisome in the eyes of the Paul Clark Home matrons yet integral to the resilience of children growing up in the harsh urban conditions of Butte's early days.[16]

Associated Charities was not the only philanthropic group to champion the cause of Butte children. A number of charitable organizations operating across the state also took an early and active interest in Butte children. By 1903, for example, St. Joseph's Orphanage in Helena housed 94 boys, 120 girls, and 32 infants in the "baby ward."

Given Butte's relative proximity to Helena and its strong Catholic contingent, St. Joseph's was a valuable resource for placing dependent children from the Mining City.[17]

The Sisters of Charity of Leavenworth were a force to be reckoned with when it came to saving unfortunate children from Butte. On one occasion, the nuns were asked to intervene on behalf of five Butte siblings, ages two-and-a-half to ten years, whose mother had died and whose father was reported to be a drunkard. A determined Sister Rose Vincent traveled from Helena to Butte in January 1903 to see to the children's welfare. Despite her familiarity with poverty and distress, the scene she encountered made an impression.

It was in the dead of winter, and yet the little boys were clothed only in ragged overalls and jackets and worn out shoes. They had no stockings, no underclothing, no shirts. The little girl had on a man's undershirt, a pair of ladies' stockings, ladies' shoes, and a skirt. They lived in two little rooms about eight feet long by six feet wide. In one of these rooms was a stove in which there were a few coals. Slinking over the stove, ragged, dirty, and unkempt, was the drunken father. There were no lights in the room nor facilities for procuring them. The only furniture consisted of a rough table and two boxes. The two beds were confused masses of rags. The children were eating when the sister found them. They had bread and hot water and that was all.[18]

The father at first resisted Sister Rose's efforts, but she persisted, assuring him his children would be well cared for at St. Joseph's. Reluctantly, he let them go. From the perspective of the orphanage staff, the children were "infinitely better off" as they "know want no longer and do not see their father." The account offered no indication of how the children made sense of their experience of having lost both their mother and their father in such a short time.[19]

Charitable institutions that focused exclusively on "wayward" girls were also coming into existence in Montana. The Florence Crittenton Home, located in Helena, began operation in the early 1900s. The home was dedicated to "retrieving wayward girls from a life of error" and carried out its mission by housing pregnant girls and young, single mothers and arranging placements for their infants. The home also served as a refuge for girls who were homeless and victims of abuse. In keeping with the thinking and practice of the times, pregnant girls were moved out of their home community until their babies were born, and they were encouraged to place the infants for adoption. Butte was one of six Montana communities that hosted a Florence Crittenton Circle, which provided support for the Helena-based facility, made referrals, and helped raise funds to cover costs of housing and maternity fees for residents. In addition, the Circle was a conduit for placing babies into adoptive homes.[21]

The House of the Good Shepherd, a Helena-based institution founded by the Sisters of the Convent of the Good Shepherd, also sought to intervene in the lives of girls deemed "wayward." The sisters began their ministry for troubled girls upon arrival in Helena in 1889. They soon outgrew their small quarters, and in 1909 they opened a new facility with room for 150 girls and twenty nuns, which also housed a school, a laundry facility where the girls were employed, and a gymnasium.[22] Butte officials concerned with the physical safety and moral character of young girls on the streets of Butte made regular referrals to the House, which was noted for strict discipline and rigorous work demands as antidotes to potential delinquency.

Child Welfare: From Charitable Cause to State Concern

In addition to the work of charitable organizations, the State of Montana took up the cause of dependent, neglected, and delinquent children as a matter of public concern. In 1893 the State responded to the need to house "orphan, foundling, and destitute children" by funding the construction of the Montana Children's Home in Twin Bridges. The home was to provide for the nurture, discipline, and schooling of dependent children. That same year, legislation was passed to establish the State Reform School for boys and girls ages eight to twenty-one "found guilty of any crime, vagrancy, mendicancy, or incorrigibility." The school was to provide its inmates with training in "morality, temperance, and frugality and instruction in the different trades and callings of the two sexes."[23]

In March 1903 the State Bureau of Child and Animal Protection was established and charged with investigation into reports of abuse and neglect of children and animals. Otto Schoenfeld, a strident advocate, became its first director. In his inaugural report to the legislature, Schoenfeld outlined the mission and responsibilities of the bureau: "The two classes of society under consideration, children and animals, differ only from other classes by reason of their helplessness, and for this reason it has been deemed necessary to pass special laws for their protection." Although Schoenfeld praised the work of Montana's charitable organizations, he firmly believed that the State had a responsibility to children. If parents failed in their duties, he argued, it was up to the State to step in so that children do not grow up to be "vagabonds and criminals, idle and vicious, inmates of jails, reform schools, penitentiaries, hospitals, and insane asylums."[24]

With a meager budget and little assistance, Schoenfeld valiantly sought to "prevent evil from growing" and dedicated himself to children, whom he often described as Montana's "most valuable asset." Schoenfeld featured cases from Butte in his biennial legislative reports to illustrate both the seriousness of child welfare concerns and the significance of his bureau's work. He argued the urgent need for a deputy humane officer specifically assigned to Butte to handle the city's high volume of child protection cases and was successful in securing funding for the position; P. J. Gilligan served as Butte's humane officer for a number of years, consistently earning high praise from the bureau.[25]

One of Schoenfeld's concerns was "rushing the can," a common practice in Butte in which parents sent their children to the corner saloon to purchase a bucket of cold beer and rush home with it. "The practice may not be looked upon by the public generally as a very grievous one, yet it is but the stepping stone to worse habits," Schoenfeld argued.

> Taught from infancy, almost, to entertain no hesitancy about
> entering saloons to get "a can of beer for papa or mamma,"
> the child grows believing the groggery a necessary part of the
> world's business. Long before he reaches his majority he himself becomes an habitual visitor and patron of the saloon, and
> it is but a few months later that we find him a prisoner before
> the police magistrate as a common drunk.[26]

Schoenfeld's hardest work was the investigation of infant deaths, and cases from Butte proved to be his most difficult. As early 1900s Silver Bow County coroners' registers reveal, the bodies of infants were occasionally found in mine shafts, their identities and the circumstances of death unknown. In December 1903 Schoenfeld was called in to investigate the death of an infant boy who had been strangled "by tying the sleeves of a woman's waist around his neck" and then wrapped in old clothes and thrown into a shaft at the Travonia Mine. Schoenfeld described the atrocity in his annual report and voiced his frustration at being unable to find and punish the "heartless criminal who perpetrated the act."[27]

At times, Schoenfeld sought legal action on behalf of children. He found a kindred spirit in Judge Michael Donlan of Butte, who oversaw a broad range of cases involving dependent, neglected, and delinquent children in the early 1900s. While the two showed little sympathy for parents who were "drunk and dissolute," they paid close attention to the needs and wishes of children and took swift action on their behalf whenever possible. For example, in 1906 Schoenfeld brought the case of the Barrett children before Judge Donlan. The children, ages seven, three, and four months, had been found "groveling in rags and filth" in "habitation not fit for hogs." Mrs. Barrett blamed her husband for never bringing home his wages from the mine, but a police officer testified to finding Mrs. Barrett herself too drunk to care for her children. Despite her protests, Mrs. Barrett was sent to the county poor farm and the children to the state orphans' home in Twin Bridges. When asked about the case pending against Mr. Barrett, Judge Donlan declared that if he had his way the man would get twenty years. Schoenfeld said the man should get the whipping post.[28]

Humane Officer P. J. Gilligan also found Judge Donlan to be a champion of children who listened with a sensitive ear. Donlan was moved to action by the tears of eight-year-old George Carlisle, whom Gilligan brought before the court in 1910. Young George's mother was dead and his father absent. The boy had come to Butte with an aunt and uncle as a toddler. George had recently been found crying on the street by a police officer. When the officer asked where he lived, George reported that he had no home. He had been taken in by another family for a time, but they had moved away and left him behind. Officer Gilligan brought George's aunt and uncle before the court, and Judge Donlan questioned them regarding the boy's care. The uncle claimed that he had offered to pay for George's care, but Donlan questioned his sincerity, noting that the child's clothing and shoes were in tatters. Young George, fearing the judge might make him return to his aunt and uncle, began to "weep bitterly" as he told Donlan that he was fearful of his aunt who had abused him in the past. Judge Donlan took George seriously and assured him that he would not be forced to go back. Officer Gilligan made arrangements for the boy until a family home could be secured for him.[29]

Judge Donlan was a strong advocate for the protection of children, but at the same time he was sensitive to the struggles of parents whose life circumstances challenged their abilities to care for their children. In a 1907 case, for example, Donlan took to heart Mrs. Annie Ward's touching situation and her desire to fight for the custody of her nine-year-old daughter Hazel, "a pretty little girl with bright red hair." According to the *Butte Miner*, Mrs. Ward was an "inmate of a resort in the red-light district of Dillon." She openly admitted to having taken up a "life of shame" and blamed her husband for her unfortunate circumstances. Mrs. Ward told the court that her husband had been severely injured in a mining accident, and as a result she and the child had been left penniless. Desperate, she had left the child in "good hands" as she took up work as a prostitute. She claimed that she found out only by accident that her child had been sent to the state orphans' home and adoption proceedings were under way. Donlan, apparently swayed by Mrs. Ward's claim that she was "not beyond redemption," issued a continuance so that she could have adequate legal representation in making her case for regaining custody of Hazel.[30]

Butte in many ways served as a proving ground for Montana's nascent system of child protection. The State Bureau of Child and Animal Protection's work as well as court cases in Butte in the early twentieth century served to highlight the importance of child welfare as a public issue rather than private concern. The child welfare cases also revealed both the complexity of children's lives and children's determined efforts to advocate for themselves, their interests, and their well-being.

Wayward Children

During the first decade of the new century, Butte's law enforcement and judicial leaders were also preoccupied with youngsters on the city streets and their potential to go astray, as evidenced by regular court appearances of children on charges of truancy, theft, arson, and general incorrigibility. Until 1899 there was no separate court system in the United States for children, but soon thereafter, following in the footsteps of youth advocates in Chicago, several states passed legislation creating special youth courts to deal with young offenders.[31] In 1907 the Montana legislature approved legislation to establish a juvenile justice system to ensure that "a delinquent child shall be treated not as a criminal but as misdirected and misguided, and needing aid, encouragement, help and assistance."[32]

The 1907 legislation prohibited the confinement of juveniles in a county jail with adult prisoners, and the Silver Bow County officials found themselves at a loss regarding what they should do with youthful offenders. The sheriff complained that his sole option might be to "handcuff them and tie them to posts in front of the courthouse or hobble them and turn them loose on the courthouse lawn." It was suggested at a county commissioners' meeting that the basement quarters under the county jail, formerly used for the detention of opium fiends, might be fitted up for juvenile offenders. Those quarters were deemed to be not very secure, however, and some expressed concern that the isolation would be very severe punishment for a solitary young offender confined there.[33]

Further efforts to create a separate juvenile court system in Montana came to fruition in 1911. In December 1910, shortly before the opening of the legislative session in which the issue would be addressed, Judge Alexander McGowan of Butte's police court made a public endorsement of the proposed new legislation as "the only way to save the Butte youths from the course they are now on." McGowan, however, did not rail against parental failures as the cause of delinquency. Instead, he addressed the toll that Butte's harsh environment took on its young people.

> The boys of Butte haven't had their chance in life. I remember
> where I was born and recall my boyhood days in California.
> The grass was green around my home and the trees were
> shady. Apple and other trees were all around and I had fun.
> But there is nothing of that sort for the boys of Butte. They
> have no place to play but in the streets and there is not even a
> place to go swimming. Why should anyone wonder if the boys
> of the city go wrong? I am greatly interested in the work for
> the juvenile court and should the movement be successful it
> would be a great benefit to Butte.[34]

In Butte, prior to the state's establishment of a youth court, delinquency cases were frequently referred to Judge Michael Donlan. Once the juvenile court was established, Judge Donlan became the leading figure in meting out discipline and justice to the Mining City's wayward children. Donlan blended paternalism with the power of law and concerned himself as much with the welfare of young people as with their particular acts of delinquency. His reprimands of parents who were negligent in their duties were often more forceful than those directed at children accused of delinquent acts.

In 1907 the cases heard by Judge Donlan included an appearance by a ragtag band of eight- to ten-year-olds accused of arson following a fire on Easter Sunday. On that day, John Ruffato and his friends Fred, Chelsea, and Willie Gogginoni had paid a visit to Columbia Gardens, which was closed for the season. With matches and contraband cigarettes in hand, the boys headed to the grandstand for shelter from the April winds. Beneath the grandstand, they spotted a fallen bird's nest. With the strike of a match, the nest—and the grandstand—went up in flames. The stunned youngsters fled.[35]

In their appearance before Judge Donlan, Fred, Chelsea, and John tearfully confessed to their crime, claiming the fire was accidental; they had "simply wanted to see what effect the heat had on the nest." Ten-year-old Willie, however, was adamant in his denial. With crossed arms and jutted jaw, Willie held his ground, telling the judge he had nothing to do with the fire as he had "sworn off" his cigarette habit two years ago. Given the boys' tender ages, the superintendent of Columbia Gardens did not want them to face a criminal charge of arson and possible placement at the State Reform School. Instead, the youngsters were released to their parents with a stern warning and reprimand by Judge Donlan.[36]

Both Judge Donlan and State Bureau of Child and Animal Protection director Otto Schoenfeld recognized that the distinction between dependent and delinquent children was often blurry, and they found common cause in their efforts to keep youngsters from going down the wrong path. Schoenfeld argued forcefully that State intervention in the lives of children was an important measure to prevent the development of "vicious and criminal elements." He offered high praise for Butte's Industrial School, established in 1903, for its successes in early intervention with wayward boys. The residential school could provide up to forty boys with basic schooling and manual training. Donlan made discerning use of the Industrial School in his efforts to curb the criminal inclinations of Butte's youthful offenders. He generally favored remand to the Butte Industrial School over the State Reform School in Miles City, which he saw as a potential training ground for a criminal element rather than deterrent.[37]

Juvenile court was largely a male space in Butte and elsewhere. Butte, however, was on the cutting edge of intervention with girls at risk of the perils of the street. In 1913 the city hired its first policewoman, Amanda Pfeiffer, who blended Christian ministry and law enforcement to rein in wayward girls.[38] On rare occasions, young girls appeared before the court with tales of life circumstances that posed challenges to their innocence. For example, in 1909 two "little girl waifs, May Lynch, 13, but small for her age, and Lillie Hawkins, reportedly 9 years old," appeared before Judge Donlan, accused of truancy and frequenting lodging houses.

Their mothers are dead and their fathers' whereabouts are unknown. Both girls are incorrigible truants and relatives could not take care of them. It was hard for the truant officer and humane officer to catch the elusive little waifs. The grandmother of May Lynch was aged and feeble and had lost all control. The girls had secured a few dollars from their home and had rented a room in a cheap lodging house on South Main. The landlady was warned that she could be liable for prosecution for harboring the girls. It was deemed very dangerous for little girls to go to such places and other lodging house keepers were given the same warning. It was also learned that the girls had spent part of the money they had surreptitiously secured at their homes to purchase candy, ribbons, and other articles that are dear to the childish heart.[39]

Upon hearing the case, Judge Donlan initially committed the girls to the House of the Good Shepherd in Helena. The next day, however, Donlan rescinded his decision and opted instead to send them to the St. Joseph's Orphanage, contending that they were of "too tender an age" to be sent to a reformatory.[40]

Youth court involvement with girls generally occurred in cases where their moral and sexual innocence was deemed at risk. Concerns about "promiscuity" were expressed exclusively in relation to girls. Girls were also likely to receive more severe consequences than were boys. For example, Judge Donlan's ire was aroused when young girls were found frequenting saloons and roadhouses. He was quick to issue commitments to the State Reform School or the House of the Good Shepherd and even quicker in his condemnation of roadhouse proprietors who contributed to the girls' moral corruption.[41]

Preoccupation with the morality and sexual innocence of girls featured prominently in the annual reports of the State Bureau of Child and Animal Protection as well. Otto Schoenfeld expressed concern for the vulnerability of young girls to "licentious brutes" and "lowlife villains" who might lead them on the downward path. In his 1906 report, Schoenfeld praised the House of the Good Shepherd and the Crittenton Home for "retrieving wayward girls from a life of error" and leading them "gently along the narrow path of right and virtue thus almost unconsciously imbibing qualities which make the true woman."[42]

J. M. Kennedy, Schoenfeld's successor as the director of the State Bureau of Child and Animal Protection, took aim at dance halls as a threat to the innocence of young girls: "The cheap public dance hall has become a public menace and nuisance. The public dance hall is the brazen big sister of the wine room; its baneful influence is even more far reaching and destructive. Montana needs a law that will prevent very young girls from attending public dances unaccompanied by their parent or guardians."[43]

At times, cases of juvenile delinquency were directly tied to Butte families' everyday struggles to survive. For many families, staying warm during Butte's long winters required stealing coal, and theft was a family activity. Sometimes children gathered coal that had fallen from the trains; other times they helped the process. Many old-time Butte residents described climbing onto the train cars and tossing coal to younger children waiting below. When the weather was cold, the mothers desperate, and the children young, company officials and local police might look the other way. But the practice was so commonplace that, from time to time, especially when young rascals were on their own and spring was in the air, businesses, police, and courts took action. For example, in early April 1913, the *Butte Miner* reported that "Three boys, ages 8, 9, and 13, are brought before Judge Donlan for stealing coal from South Butte Coal Co. They are charged with incorrigibility. 'A person would have to stand around with a shot gun on Saturdays to stop the kids from stealing coal' says coal company representative." Donlan warned the company against taking the law into its own hands. He sentenced the older boy to time in the Butte Industrial School until his mother could pay four dollars to replace a lock on the coal warehouse that the boys had broken. The younger two were sent home with their mothers after being given a warning by the judge.[44]

Issues of dependency and delinquency continued to be further defined, codified, and documented in ensuing years. Advocates called for increased State funding for child-serving institutions and legal changes that would allow for greater oversight of children and youth. Concern for wayward girls persisted, and in 1917 the women's clubs of Montana joined forces with the State Bureau of Child and Animal Protection to successfully lobby for the construction of a separate state reform school for delinquent girls. Judgments about the manners and morals of parents continued to play a central role in advocates' theories about "other people's children," although child welfare and youth court cases drew less media attention as concerns over privacy increased. And conditions in Butte continued to test the mettle of the city's humane officers. As humane officer Paul Ozanne wrote in his 1922 report: "Because of the complexity of Butte's population and its incongruous customs, habits, and temperament, the demands upon the Humane Officer are at once varied and trying and his activities and experiences are replete with acute conditions, some which beggar description."[45]

Organized Play

The organization and oversight of children's play was an important arena for reformers' advocacy and action since a child unsupervised on the streets was considered a delinquent in the making. As the professional field of child guidance developed in the first two decades of the twentieth century, experts argued that organized, supervised play was essential to children's moral, physical, and cognitive development. Some claimed that play was a deterrent to crime and others that team play was necessary to rein in individual energy and promote social skills. Groups such as the Playground Association of America advocated public funding of organized play and formal playgrounds throughout the country.[46]

The national playground movement, which promoted safe, supervised, and structured play spaces and activities, had a difficult time gaining traction in Butte. Despite early efforts of such Butte organizations as the Marian White Arts and Crafts Club, the city was slow to embrace and support public playgrounds. When experts visited Butte, they chided local officials for failing to provide Butte children with safe, adequate playgrounds and adult-supervised outlets for recreation.[47] In 1911, for example, Professor Henry Curtiss, a playground advocate from Massachusetts, addressed this concern in a lecture to the College Club of Butte on the importance of city playgrounds as a means of delinquency prevention.[48] Butte's lack of public playgrounds also raised concerns for U.S. Children's Bureau investigators during their assessment of the city in the 1920s.[49]

The connection between supervision and delinquency prevention captured the attention of Butte's chief probation officer David J. O'Connor. As a result of the tough economic times in Butte, the Industrial School closed at the end of the 1922 school year. In April 1923 O'Connor began to mobilize forces to reopen the school, arguing that it was much more effective for both deterrence and reform than was the state school for boys in Miles City. Like his predecessors Judge Donlan and Humane Officer Gilligan, O'Connor feared that time in the State Reform School could teach impressionable youth more about crime than correction.

> It is hardly right to send boys to Miles City for breaking
> windows and for trivial offenses, as the class they meet up
> with there is made up of anything but petty offenders. Boys
> sent to that institution usually have been convicted of some-
> thing more than petty crimes, and it stands to reason that
> association with the criminally inclined will often lead a

good boy astray, and when he comes out of Miles City he is worse than when he was sent there.

O'Connor argued that incorrigible youth should be dealt with close to home, where they could be "given a good education, proper training, and a chance to make good."[50]

O'Connor was successful in his mobilizing efforts to reopen the Butte Industrial School. He then set his sights on the prevention of juvenile crime and delinquency. O'Connor was a vocal advocate for organized athletic programs in Butte grammar schools as a means of countering incorrigibility, eliminating the "evil of idleness," and derailing delinquency. In 1926 O'Connor's efforts were praised in the *Butte Miner*:

> Rugged Butte youngsters, who under the old order might frequently turn their abundant energies toward activities which would brand them miscreants, now have capitulated to the lure of healthful American sport, Mr. O'Connor says. So enthused have Butte youngsters become with district and rural football, basketball, and hockey that they have little or no time for mischief which discomforts the city's grown-ups, damages property, and causes endless investigations and lecturing by juvenile authorities.[51]

O'Connor claimed that it had been several months since a Butte boy was sent to the State Reform School and that he received few calls now from citizens concerning the lawlessness of youth. He credited the YMCA, the Knights of Columbus, and the Butte Independent Football League for their work in organizing youth sports leagues, and he argued that these efforts had "shifted the scene of play in Butte from the streets to the playground, gymnasium, and rink."[52]

Child's play continued to worry Butte's business leaders. In 1930 the Butte Chamber of Commerce invited L. H. Weir, field secretary of the Playground and Recreation Association of America, to Butte to assess the situation of recreation for Butte children and to provide recommendations. Weir offered a critical summary, noting that the city owned only two parks, schools had inadequate play facilities, and other sites such as ball fields and skating rinks were privately owned. Weir was also troubled by the fact that many Butte playgrounds were simply old mine dumps.[53]

The recreation initiatives of the 1930s sponsored by the Works Progress Administration reiterated the message that a strong public recreation program was key to delinquency prevention. WPA programs promoted activities for young boys and girls, teens, adults, and families as a whole. They offered sports leagues, social clubs, dancing, music lessons, gymnastics, and boxing. In some Butte neighborhoods, they provided the spark for clean-up of gullies, hillsides, and empty lots for use as parks and play areas. As the city weathered the Great Depression, a few lasting changes occurred. Meanwhile, children continued to entertain themselves on slag heaps and in mine yards, taking in their neighborhoods and the industrial landscape about them as their own wondrous amusement park.[54]

The Depression Era and the Welfare of Children in Butte

Butte families were already struggling to get by when the nation's economy collapsed, ushering in the desperate years of the Great Depression. The community's widespread misery, especially the plight of poor Butte children, drew the attention of a group of women determined to do good. In October 1931 about fifty of "Butte's prominent young women" came together to form the Butte Junior Service League, "which will foster the interests of its members in the social, economic, educational, and civic conditions of this community and make efficient their volunteer services. They immediately began to form committees, plan meetings, and organize activities."[55]

The Junior Service League's first initiative involved a partnership with the East Side Neighborhood House, a community-based organization that developed programs and activities in partnership with neighborhood residents. According to a feature in the *Montana Standard* in November 1931, the partnership between the Junior Service League and the East Side Neighborhood House looked promising. The Neighborhood House had a solid reputation and knowledge of community need, and the young women had boundless enthusiasm and connections to Butte's wealthier residents. The article praised the members of the fledgling organization for their self-sacrificing work to "promote the welfare and increase the opportunities of little children, to lighten the burdens that press on the brow of the aged, and to contribute to the happiness of the unfortunate. . . . This new organization is composed of a membership that, were it so minded, might spend its time in pursuit of pleasure in the social whirl, but which elects to work with those who are endeavoring to make Butte a better place in which to live."[56]

In December 1931 the League organized a Christmas benefit for East Side tots at the Neighborhood House, complete with Santa Claus, treats, and toys. By February 1932 they had organized a daily program in cooperation with a local dairy to provide a glass of fresh milk and graham crackers for needy children of the East Side neighborhood. Sixty gallons of milk were distributed a day, serving upward of five hundred children. When the East Side Neighborhood House was forced to close its doors for a time in late 1932, the Junior Service League lent support to the efforts of the Silver Bow Emergency Relief Association, providing layettes for needy infants. The *Montana Standard* praised the efforts of the "young matrons and single girls, all from good homes" who "are not only contributing of their spare time, but give constantly, in ways that are never known, of their money."[57]

The work of the Junior Service League offers engaging insights into class relations in Butte. The League was continuing a tradition of charitable work focused on concern for "other people's children." Members were the daughters of Butte's social elite, whose mothers may well have given of their time to the Associated Charities a generation earlier. The Junior Service League was regularly featured on the pages of local newspapers throughout the 1930s. The League's cabarets, holiday balls, summer dances at Columbia Gardens, teas, and theme parties were events not to be missed by Butte society. The members of the social circle connected to the Junior Service League moved through the Depression years relatively unscathed, and the women likely saw no

In October 1931 about fifty of "Butte's prominent young women" formed the Butte Junior Service League to "foster the interests of its members in the social, economic, educational, and civic conditions of the community." Here, they dole out milk to children who have lined up, buckets in hand.

irony in wearing their furs as they ladled milk to youngsters lined up with buckets and mugs in hand. At the same time, League members' dedication to children was without compromise and continued to find renewed forms of expression over the years.

The Junior Service League was indefatigable in its organizational activities. In 1934 the group launched a fund-raising effort for the "Crippled Kiddies Drive." In 1936 the League's children's theater department began to organize and present puppet shows. The organization sponsored Christmas parties for children in Butte's three WPA nursery schools, providing the children with toys and candy. Puppet theater became a hallmark feature of the League's entertainment for the children. Little Billy Hardle, writing in November 1938, was surely impressed: "Dear Junior Service League, Our class saw the puppet show and we thought it was just fine. Everything was so little and pretty. This was the first puppet show I saw and I liked it better than a movie."[58]

Aid to Dependent Children

Despite their energetic dedication, however, the young women of the Junior Service League were only able to scratch the surface in terms of addressing the needs of Butte children in the depths of the Depression. Employment in the mines dropped by 84 percent between 1929 and 1933, and families turned first to charities and then to the State of Montana for relief. Butte and Silver Bow County had nearly six thousand residents on relief, and it was using a major share of the state's child welfare resources by 1931. Uncertainty and poverty permeated children's everyday lives.[59]

Through enabling legislation of the Federal Social Security Act in 1935, the State of Montana was able to provide more extensive child welfare services and economic assistance to poor families and dependent children. In March 1936 the director of the U.S. Children's Bureau approved the state's child welfare plan, which provided greater resources for investigation and placement of dependent and neglected children, guided by a philosophy that no child should be removed from his or her family for reasons of poverty alone.[60]

The Social Security Act also established enabling legislation for the Aid to Dependent Children (ADC) program, which Montana enacted through passage of the Public Welfare Act of 1937. Under the act, the powers and duties of the State Bureau of Child and Animal Protection were transferred to the newly created Montana State Department of Public Welfare. Through the ADC program, financial assistance could be provided to families with children under the age of sixteen who were deprived of parental support as a result of death, illness, absence, or incapacity. The federal government, the State of Montana, and individual counties shared equally in the payment of monthly support. Initially, the maximum monthly payment to a caregiver was eighteen dollars for the first dependent child and twelve dollars for additional children. By December 1937 Butte had 175 families participating, with 392 dependent children receiving an average of thirty dollars per month in ADC assistance. Throughout the later years of the Depression and well into the "recovery" period of the early 1940s, an average of 200 families and 425 children, a tip of the iceberg in terms of need, were receiving ADC. Interestingly, those numbers began to increase by the late 1940s, a signal that the postwar years were not years of economic recovery for all Butte families.[61]

Postwar Promise and the Well-Being of Children

The post–World War II years saw another burst of women's social and philanthropic organizing on behalf of Butte children. In 1944 a group of women founded Butte's Soroptimist Club, an affiliate of the international Soroptimist organization. The club was dedicated to the betterment of professional women, civic improvement, and the promotion of international peace, sisterhood, and good will. The small group had big plans for Butte. Their first major undertaking was the creation of a receiving home for dependent, neglected, abused, or abandoned children in Butte. Mary Phillips, one of the club's founding members, also served as the Silver Bow County child welfare agent. She was a tireless advocate for dependent and neglected children, and at every turn she called for a community facility to meet these children's needs.

The club's history and the realization of their collective dream to build a children's receiving home in Butte were featured in *Ladies Home Journal* in 1950. Writer Margaret Hickey captured the dynamic spirit and sense of possibility of this group of women who blended charity work and community development to create a home away from home for Butte's children. Hickey's article also reflects white middle-class assumptions about "other people's children" that informed child welfare work circa 1950. Hickey wrote:

> This is a story about a little boy who was so thin his arms
> were about the size of a broomstick, and so hungry that he
> scavenged in garbage cans like an alley cat. This is also a story
> about a two-year-old girl who had had so little to eat that she
> didn't have the strength to lift a spoon to her mouth when
> she got one. And the story of two children, shut in a car on
> a freezing night in January and forgotten by their parents.

And another child, about five, with dark, straight hair and big, black, Indian eyes, who was found playing in the street one midnight—and if she ever had a home, no one, not even she, knew about it.

It is also a story about a group of businesswomen who created a home for these lost and hungry children who had no place to go but jail when their parents abandoned or neglected them. The setting is Butte, Montana—but it could be anywhere. There are, unfortunately, sad-eyed and starving children in any city you wish to name. The welfare workers know it; the police know it; and when the city's civic-minded don't know it, it's because they hate the thought and won't face it.

... In May 1947, only three years after they'd organized, [the Soroptimists] found their house. A condition of the Child Welfare Department was that it must be near schools and churches. This was; in fact, it was in one of Butte's best residential neighborhoods. A demand of the club was that it should be big enough to hold at least twenty children. This could: its two-story brick walls held twelve rooms and two baths. Moreover, it was in pretty good condition, needing only fresh paper and paint—and the cost was only $5,500.[62]

Soroptimist Club members were relentless fund-raisers. They went door to door, badgered business owners, held white elephant sales, raffled a car, hosted a night of dog races, organized rummage sales, sponsored a concert and a tea, and held a charity ball. Within a year, they had raised enough money to buy the house outright. The doors of the Soroptimist Home for Children were opened on November 1, 1948, and within two weeks it had twenty-five residents. Children came to the home via the county child welfare office, and the county paid one dollar per day for each child's care. The home received its license from the State of Montana as a child-care facility in 1950 and earned the praise of state child welfare officials.[63]

According to Hickey, the children entrusted to the care of the home were impressed, too:

One youngster, sent back home when her parents were reunited, ran away and came back to the home. A child turned up ragged and disheveled at the police department and said he'd heard that they had all the ice cream they could eat at a home in Butte, and he wanted to live there. A baby, who, its departing mother said crossly, had never smiled in her life, began to gurgle and crow with happiness. The thin one grew

Butte's Soroptimist Club organized in 1944, near the end of World War II. Club members established a receiving home (left, circa 1950) for dependent, neglected, abused, or abandoned children.

fat. The starved one began to creep. Five bright-eyed kids who looked and acted like young tramps when they were first removed from their disreputable home and drunken parents by the courts police became honor students—and were taken by foster parents.[64]

The Soroptimist home became a key resource in Butte's child welfare system in the postwar years. It was often praised for providing a safe and welcoming sanctuary—and occasionally criticized for being sparsely appointed, inadequately staffed, and lacking professional direction. The home kept up its commitment to Butte children over the long haul even as changes in the field of child welfare in the 1960s resulted in greater use of foster homes and less reliance on receiving homes for younger children.[65]

Butte's Junior Service League also continued its efforts on behalf of Butte children in the postwar years. The League continued to entertain Butte youngsters with its puppet shows. Members organized and funded the "Play-Go-Round," a mobile playground that brought games, activities, and youth workers to city parks on a rotating basis. They sponsored pet shows that brought a fascinating menagerie of Butte youngsters and their furry and feathered friends to local parks and playgrounds. They also hosted well-child conferences and clinics, and in the 1950s they were instrumental in organizing campaigns for vaccination of low-income children against polio.

Junior Service League
pet shows were popular
with Butte kids.

In the postwar years, numbers of child welfare investigations
continued to rise as resources expanded and services grew more profes-
sionalized. Economic hardship contributed to the struggles of many
Butte families, as evidenced by the slow but steady growth in ADC
cases between 1945 and 1960. In oral history accounts of hard times in
Butte, residents spoke about their parents' resistance to "welfare" and the
shame they felt when necessity pushed them to seek public assistance.
By the 1959 strike, however, many mining families had exhausted the
generous support of family and neighbors and turned to public welfare
into order to feed their children.

––––––––

Inquiry into the efforts to care for and control "other people's children"
provides further insight into childhood in the Mining City. Hardships
in many forms were daily realities for many families, and children were
not protected from those burdens. Public and private entities, professional and volunteer alike, committed remarkable energy and resources
to making Butte safe for children—and to keeping residents safe from
children gone astray. The dedicated work of reformers and advocates
speaks to the significance of children in community life. Moreover,
advocates' sustained, organized efforts show how central children and
issues of childhood were to the development of policy and public institutions in Montana in the twentieth century. Their work also reveals
ways in which underlying assumptions regarding gender, class, sexuality,
and morality shaped both understandings of young people's needs and
capacities and approaches to intervention. Perhaps most fundamentally,
these efforts show that children, in Butte and beyond, were intimately
involved in and affected by the social, political, and economic world
surrounding them.

CHAPTER FOUR

Child's Play

Risk and Resilience

We used to sleigh ride. It wasn't sleigh riding. It was tobogganing. And these toboggans were homemade. You know, two sleds, and it would hold sixteen kids on that toboggan. We would pull that toboggan all the way up Anaconda Road for about two miles, and then we'd ride down, which took us about five minutes. It took us about two to three hours to get up there. That was really something.

—Catherine Hoy

BUTTE CHILDREN grew up in a rough-and-tumble world as they claimed slag heaps, mine yards, and city streets as their playgrounds. Stories of child's play in early Butte are rife with danger and derring-do, but as Butte youngsters played with and around the dangers of mining life, they forged their identities as hardy survivors in the process. Stories from the streets, school yards, and sports teams provide insights into children's collective strength and competitive spirit. These stories reveal both tough and tender moments as children established their turf, protected siblings, built alliances, and negotiated power. Memories of childhood escapades are marked with both pride and chagrin as adults recall their brash acts and shake their heads wondering how they survived. They are also marked by losses as mining life took its toll across generations.

Power in Numbers

Even as Butte's population peaked in 1917 and then began to decline, the number of children continued to rise, and children and miners vied for space on the Butte Hill. Memories of childhood are marked

Butte children grew up in a rough and tumble world as they claimed slag heaps, mine yards, and city streets as their playgrounds. Above, children play at the Gagnon Mine, circa 1900.

These six at right may be posing in their Sunday best (circa 1940), but their playground stretches out behind them.

by stories of groups of youngsters who organized themselves in their neighborhoods, created their own forms of play, and took responsibility for watching out for one another. As Catherine Hoy stated:

> There were, I'd say, fifty to sixty kids in [our] area. And they all went to St. Mary's School at this time. We had to cross the railroad tracks from our house to St. Mary's School. And, believe me, it was snow. They say ankle deep, but it was knee deep getting back and forth to that school. But it was nice,

and we got along real well. [There were] lots of fights and lots of quarrels. But they managed. There was one thing about the kids on Anaconda Road and the people in Dublin Gulch. They all stuck together. They had their fights and their quarrels, but they stuck together. If one was in trouble, you'd best know everybody was on the helping side of it. But the miners were really something else. You know, as I said, there'd be from two to three thousand miners going up and down that road every day. And you got lost in the shuffle if you happened to be on the road at the changing of shifts.[1]

John Onkalo grew up in Finntown, where the houses were "skin to skin" and the neighborhood teeming with children.

There was always a gang around to play with. As far as excitement, there was always something to do. Like this hillside here, this was our favorite playground, up on the side of the hill. We had what we called cabins. We'd just dig a hole, a hole in the ground high enough to stand up in, and we'd cover it over. We'd rustle scrap nails and pipe, anything we could find on the hillside, and then we'd go up to the dumps and pick up sheet tin and boards or anything we could find that we could use to cover it over with and put a layer of dirt on top of that. Then that would be our secret meeting place.[2]

As Packey Buckley, Patricia Canty, Kay Antonetti, and John Onkalo described, children occupied a wide swath of the social and physical space of Butte. They were intrepid explorers, continually staking claims to their turf and embarking on new adventures.

We played up on the side hill. We would make up a game, you know what I mean. They had a football field up there, and you would play—it was right up there above the first tracks, and we called it the "side hill"—and all of the guys would stand beneath the bridge. Twelve and fourteen guys would stand beneath the bridge just talking, just talking.[3]

When we weren't in school, we were outdoors playing. We played on the Cinders, the ball field down there. We used to go for long walks with our lunch tucked under our arms or bike rides. We went for lots of hikes in back of Big Butte, down to the Brown's Gulch area. And then, of course, all of the neighborhood kids were involved, too, so we had lots of friends that did all kinds of things with us. . . .

We played an awful lot of really wild games when we were kids. We used to go running through the neighborhood playing chase and "commandoes." . . . We had what they call rubber guns. You could put a clothespin on top of a gun-shaped thing and snap them. You'd make these long rubber bands out of inner tubes that could shoot about twenty feet. We also dug a lot of foxholes in our backyard, and I can remember one time at dinner my dad saying, "I'm going to make a rule. You can't dig foxholes any closer than five feet to the foundation of the house. Otherwise our house is going to fall down." We actually dug long, skinny foxholes. We played war with each other.

Other girls might have been out playing dolls or something like that, but I was always playing war and "commando" with my brothers. So, all around the neighborhood we could shimmy up between the garages, especially the two garages next to the family next door to us, and get up on the roof. And we used to walk around on that roof all the time, surveying the neighborhood. My dad would have killed us if he ever found out. But that was our lookout, and you'd look over the neighborhood—make sure none of the enemy was coming. We played stuff like that all of the time. . . . We kind of protected our neighborhood.[4]

Everyone in the neighborhood, all around, everyone knew everybody. And all us kids played together. There was a playground across the street from us. We played ball and kick-the-can, and we'd go around and ring neighbors' doorbells and then run, you know. We had a wonderful childhood. We had a big hill behind us that we'd sleigh ride down and skied a few times on funny little old-fashioned skis. Then Big Butte was just over Zarelda Street, just four blocks up. And we'd go up there and bring our lunch and play. And we'd play in the Gulch. We went all over. Nobody worried about their kids. We'd go play in the morning, come home at noon for lunch, then go again 'til dinner. And then we'd played outside again in the evenings. Everybody knew you, so you could never do anything bad.[5]

Weathering Winter

The mile-high city of Butte is precipitously perched on steep hillsides that descend abruptly to the flats of the Summit Valley floor. Just as miners made their way up and down the Butte Hill to the mines each day so did children come to know the steep streets, gullies, and gulches that shaped the contours of school, work, and play. Butte winters were long and harsh, and children weathered them with aplomb. On snowy days, eager children, with Flexible Flyers and homemade toboggans in tow, shared the Hill with weary miners trudging their way to and from their shifts. John Onkalo remembered:

> As far as the mining population, man, the hillsides used to be black with men when they were changing shifts. You'd see men walking up the Hill and other men walking down the Hill. I remember as a young boy we used to do a lot of our sleigh riding on the hillside up here behind the old Pennsylvania Mine. We'd go up what we called the "first tracks"— railroad tracks—and we'd coast on our sleds from there down to Broadway. A lot of times if there was fresh snow during the night, that snow would be soft, you know, not good for sleigh riding. But after the shift had gone that morning, why, man, it was packed. There was a hard-packed trail. We'd get up there, and we'd come scooting down that hard-packed snow, which, of course, made it tougher for the poor guys that had to come down that after the next shift again.[6]

Butte's topography provided children a ready-made ski hill in winter, with cross-streets and railroad tracks serving as only minor inconveniences. Bobsledding and tobogganing were favorite past-times, despite the potential for disaster. As Elinore Sterrett Shields Penrose recalled:

> Centerville had a very steep hill coming down, with a railroad track that crossed the street at right angles. One winter when I was old enough to ride the big sled—we had a great big Flexible Flyer—Dad told me that I could go up the hill in Centerville with Kenny and Cliff, who were my friends. We started out on a beautiful winter's night, sparkling snow, and we walked from our houses, from Zarelda and Alabama streets. We went up Alabama, and then we cut across the Gulch, and we went up Centerville Street and went way up beyond the railroad track even. I don't know why none of us thought about the train track. We just should have had better sense. Here we were coming down, and I think Kenneth was lying down and Cliff was on back. When they got on, I pushed and then hopped on, and off we went. It was a little bit icy and very cold, and suddenly I saw the track. We went over it, and we

jumped six feet. With the three of us on that sled, we landed hard and the runners were bent underneath it, and we were just sick. . . . Well, we turned it over, and the fellas pulled the runners back into place as best they could. And we got on and went on again, but more slowly and a little bit more scared.

Danette Harrington spent many a winter's day playing on Anaconda Road.

Half the time you couldn't get the car up the road. You had to leave your car and pack your groceries up. My father spent the best years of his life shoveling this road, which was about six hundred yards long. It was wonderful to sleigh ride. Dad would spend all day out shoveling and sanding. He would shovel it manually and sprinkle a box of sand. And then he would go in and have dinner, and we would go out with our little shovels, and we would be throwing the snow back so we could sleigh ride for the night.[7]

Sledding down Butte's steep streets was risky business. Reports of accidents and injuries from children's winter adventures were commonplace in both personal stories and the daily news. The *Butte Miner* described one such accident in December 1909:

Sled Crashes into Pole Injuring Two Little Maids
Coming at top speed and crashing into a telephone pole with a frail sled was the experience of Laurine Thurwell and Madeline McCroon of Centerville last Tuesday. Stunned and bleeding, they were picked up and carried home where physicians were sent for. It was discovered that Miss Thurwell had suffered a broken nose and severe bruises and her playmate Miss McCroon had her scalp laid open by its contact with the pole. Both girls are recovering rapidly and will be at play again soon.[8]

Butte's winters provided Butte children with a long skating season as well. The Holland Ice Rink was a second home for many Butte youngsters over the years until its closure in 1951. As an article in the *Montana Standard* reported: "Rosie DesJardins, now 90, recalls the many times she skated there. Rosie won skating medals in Butte and at competitions in Canada in 1932 and 1933. . . . On Friday nights at the rink, she remembers that the band closed with 'The Olde Gray Mare She Ain't What She Used To Be,' which was appropriate because, after everyone cleared off the rink, a horse stabled nearby would pull a scraper over the ice before crews flooded it for the next day."[9]

Elinore Sterrett Shields Penrose also enjoyed afternoons at the Holland Ice Rink as a young girl: "We'd go down there, and they had big, high fences so that when the sun came out it didn't spoil the ice. I loved to skate. But I was light, and I wasn't big, and every once in a while they'd get me in the crack-the-whip. One time the whip broke in the middle, and I was at the end. And you should have seen what happened. I went flying, and I hit my hip, and it scraped away the flesh clear down to the hip bone. I never showed it to my mother."[10]

For many Butte children, the free neighborhood rink was the draw. Kids would strap on hand-me-down skates and wobble their way from home to rink for a hockey game, racing practice, or a few rounds of crack-the-whip. John T. Shea grew up in Corktown during the Depression. A little ingenuity went a long way in winter as John and his friends crafted makeshift hockey equipment from the materials at hand.

> When I grew up, it was tough times, and you become acclimated to those times. We played hockey. "Shinny," we called it. Little Sego milk cans, we'd fill them full of water and freeze them. And then you would get a broom with everything cut off of the broom, you know, the bristles. And we'd play shinny with them. You put cardboard inside your overalls, in case you get hit in the shin. Oh, I got hit right above this eye. There is still a scar up there under that eyebrow. Boy, it hit me. Blood all over the place. I went up to the drugstore. They had a drugstore up there. He put something on a chunk of gauze, slapped it on. They weren't too worried about it. But then, I'll tell you one thing, kids took care of kids. The older guys made sure nobody picked on the younger guys. And as you got older, you know, you did the same way.[11]

Given the popularity of skating and the recognized need for recreation, ice rinks began to receive government support during the Depression years. In 1936 young people were hired through the National Youth Administration, a New Deal youth-employment program, to create and maintain skating rinks around the city. On December 6, 1936, the *Montana Standard* proudly announced that "22 rinks comprising 249,000 square feet of ice will be operated in the city this winter."[12] The largest was at Clark Park, where a new hockey rink was added.

Youngsters flocked to skating events and competitions over the years. They practiced on neighborhood rinks and converged on Clark

Butte's cold winters provided Butte children with a long skating season. They practiced on neighborhood rinks and converged on Clark Park (above, 1940s) to compete for their schools in citywide speed-skating contests.

Park to compete for their schools in citywide speed-skating contests. Each year, the Clark Park rink was the site of an ice carnival, which began in 1919, and various speed- and figure-skating competitions. Children cheered on the city's best as they defended their titles and moved on to state and regional competitions. In 1939 the honor of Ice King and Queen went to Babe O'Farrell and Patsy O'Connor, who went on to represent Butte at the Banff Winter Carnival. In 1952 Butte's state-of-the-art Civic Center opened. Among its special features was an indoor ice arena that hosted hockey leagues, visiting professional ice shows, and training space for local speed and figure skaters. For fifteen cents, Butte children could use the rink during public skating hours. While the smooth ice was a treat, it did not replace the pleasure and accessibility of the neighborhood rink.

And when the temperatures warmed and the ice melted, children took their competitive spirit outdoors with track meets in the spring and jacks, marbles, and hopscotch on street corners in summer. In the 1940s and 1950s, the sounds of the "Play-Go-Round" bus, sponsored by the Butte Junior Service League, signaled mobile neighborhood fun ranging from spirited volleyball matches to pet shows in which bunnies and mixed-breed mutts squared off with snakes and occasional bear cubs for "Best of Show." And in the fleeting dog days of summer, youngsters headed for Bell Creek to try their luck in a fishing derby. On July 4, 1953, Tommy Laird and Maureen Tinsley were the first-place finishers.

Tommy caught a one-pound, eleven-ounce rainbow—and Maureen an eight and seven-eighths-ounce rainbow.[13]

Mine Yards as Playgrounds

Year-round, Butte children honed their risking-taking skills in and around the workings of the mines, incorporating the gallows frames, slag heaps, settling ponds, and train tracks into their social worlds. In contrast to expert calls for safe, designated sites for child's play, Butte youngsters preferred the allure of the mine yard. They built forts from pilfered mine materials, organized potato roasts behind slag heaps, and dangled from ropes suspended from ore train trestles. Memories of play are intertwined with elaborate details of the mechanics of mining itself. Frank Carden grew up on Butte's East Side, where he developed a fascination for the grit and intrigue of the mine dumps and shafts.

> We used to drop rocks down the holes in the coverings of the old mine shafts and listen to them as they'd hit the wooden walls on the way down and finally splash in the water at the bottom of the shaft. No one knew how deep these shafts were or if the covering was rotten and would let one fall through. But no one ever fell in that I know of, and no mining company ever put new covers on or fenced these dangerous holes to keep the kids out. When you think of the immensity of these dumps and how close together they were, it makes you think the underground must have been pretty hollow with drifts, raises, tunnels, and shafts for all that dirt to come out of and

Year-round, Butte children honed their risk-taking skills in and around the workings of the mines, incorporating the gallows frames, slag heaps, settling ponds, and train tracks into their social worlds. This boy swings on a guy-wire.

what kind of dangerous chemicals the present environmental-
ists would have found in those dumps.[14]

Lucille Martinesso Sheehan was drawn to the copper tanks—
large tanks containing scrap iron used to precipitate copper from mine
water—as her playground in the 1920s.

Lucille Martinesso
Sheehan, circa 1926

> We always played in Meaderville. . . . We used to play in the
> copper tanks. We'd play with the copper water. [It was] just
> about three or four blocks from home. We'd have little milk
> cans, and we'd fill 'em with water, and we played in there. It
> was all around the copper tanks. They had these piles all over,
> you know, of their debris. And we'd play around there. They
> were like big troughs, and we'd go around there and play in
> the water. I'm ninety years old and still here, so it didn't do any
> damage to us.[15]

Copper ponds and tanks captured children's imaginations for
decades. Danette Harrington, who grew up in the 1940s, recalled:

> When we were kids, up above our house in the back, between
> Anaconda Road and the Bell Diamond Mine, were the copper
> ponds, and we used to go swimming there. My mother used
> to get so angry because my brother, the only thing left on his
> jeans were the brass little pieces of buttons, and the pants just
> got eaten alive, and the tennis shoes. Back then kids wore the
> black canvas tennis shoes, and the eyelets would rot out of
> them. They didn't last three weeks. Then we'd go over to the
> cement ponds that were on Anaconda Road. That's where the
> Company had its own cement company. And they went up
> and emptied their trucks out, and it was wonderful because
> it ran downhill. And when they flushed the trucks out, the
> cement that wasn't used eventually made a wonderful cement
> pond. So then we would go up after the shift closed down, and
> we would turn the hoses on and fill that with water, and that's
> where we swam.[16]

As Danette's childhood experiences reveal, girls and boys alike
tested their mettle with their mine yard adventures.

> We had a transformer that was huge. It was probably one
> hundred feet high or bigger. We used to spend all the time

in the world up there. We'd go and hang ropes on it. We'd go steal some rope from the mine yard and tie it to the thing and make a swing. You'd climb the first eight feet, and then you'd get on the level. The brave guys would go up to the next level and tie the rope on the second level. You would spend all day taking turns, throwing the rope from corner to corner. . . .

We used to give the gunmen [security guards for the mine yards] a run for their money. The gunmen at all of the mines had a little gunman shack. Every hour the gunman would punch his clock. They had a little clock that they wore on their hip on a heavy two-inch strap. It looked like a canteen. The gunman had certain rounds he had to go on and punch the clock to designate that. We used to play around the machinery or wherever. The minute he would leave, we would go in the gunman's shack. He had naked ladies, like out of *Playboy,* along the walls. We would tear them off because, oh, yuck, what did he want to look at those filthy women for? It became a wonderful game. The minute he left the shack we would go in and tear all the stuff down.[17]

When not playing on mine features, the gang might gather for a more traditional game such as marbles. Pictured circa 1920 in Finntown are (top, left to right) Mary Takala, Lempi Koski, Helen Amtilla, Vera Bendio, Minnie Trevithick, Hilea Takala, and (bottom) Jack and Walter (no last name listed), Emil Koski, John Button, Hjalmer Koski, unidentified, William Vincent [?], Charles Griffis, and John Takala.

Some adventures were a bit more tame yet rich in ingenuity and discovery. Tom Holter grew up in McQueen. His childhood forays to the mines led him to the discovery of other treasures.

When we were kids, we had the Main Range just east of McQueen. It wasn't a working mine. We'd go up there, get a bunch of wood, and come down and build a cabin, a skating-rink cabin. The Main Range had little tunnels, and we'd climb through the tunnels. We'd bring empty buckets, and we'd walk from McQueen up to Black Rock, and we'd bring home buckets full of wild raspberries. And our parents would make raspberry jelly or raspberry pie. My aunt Mamie and I would go up there and pick them wild raspberries. East of McQueen . . . there were a bunch of chokecherry bushes. We'd go up there and pick buckets full of chokecherries. By the time we got home, our teeth would be all black. People would make chokecherry wine, chokecherry jam.[18]

Linda Raiha's family relocated from the East Side to Company-built housing in McGlone Heights, at the base of Big Butte, when Linda was eleven. At first she found this foreign terrain daunting, but she and her siblings soon adapted.

We did a lot of climbing up the Big M. Mom would give us lunch, and we would climb the Big M and spend the whole afternoon up there, just inventing our games up there. There were caves and rock formations, and they would become our

Lucky children like this boy at the Parrot Smelter had bikes with which to get around in Butte and the nearby countryside.

The Meaderville girls softball team (left, circa 1920) included (front row, right to left) Margaret Pierce, Annie Moore, Dillis Pierce, Loretta Moore, Sally Pierce, (center row) Theresa Ferrando, Inga Johnson, Julia Morello, Hazel Pomroy, (back row) coaches Dominick Ruffato and Anton Bertoglio. The child in front is not identified.

houses. It was a lot of fun. You'd use your imagination a lot. We'd spend hours and hours up there. It took half a day to hike up there. It kept us out of Mom's hair. We had a lot of neighborhood kids at that time, and we organized all kinds of games.[19]

Linda was the only one of her siblings with a "store-bought" bicycle, which she shared. Her younger brothers, however, put their ingenuity to work to acquire their own bikes. They scavenged enough old parts to build themselves serviceable bicycles. Their universe expanded as they biked to Brown's Gulch to camp and Bell Creek to swim.

Children crafted their play to the contours of mining. Whistles from the mine yards sent them running home for lunch, and the 9:00 siren was the warning to head home for the night. And in between time, many children honed their athletic skills on makeshift playing fields built from the vestiges of mining. As John Sheehy, who grew up on Butte's north side, explained: "We didn't have ball fields really. . . . One of the things that happened was that the Company, with all those forges, had cinders that they had to get rid of. They had all kinds of places on the north side where they brought those cinders up by horse and wagon and deposited them on their property in the neighborhood. They'd become the basic platform for a ball field, especially the football field."[20]

Makeshift baseball was a favorite of Catherine Hoy.

We played baseball, and at one time it was called "tippy." We had a big, flat stick, you know, and I don't know what it is called now, but we used to call it a "tippy." A flat stick, it was shaped like an oar. And we had fights. Girls on one side, boys on the other, and we'd hit that stick back and forth. We had bases that we used to run back and forth like the baseball team. The girls could play ball as well as the boys. I don't think there was any difference in the girls and the boys in those days.[21]

By Danette Harrington's time, the game had changed a bit. A Dublin Gulch neighbor had a backyard pond that had fallen out of use. It was filled with empty beer cans. When bats and balls were scarce, Dublin Gulch kids would grab sticks and cans for a rousing game of beer-can baseball.

Children on Butte's East Side congregated on the upper and lower playgrounds at Grant School, which had been created by leveling two large lots that had formerly served as mine tailing dumps. As Edward Jursnich described, they were completely barren of grass, and their "only semblance to playgrounds was that they were located near a school and often crowded with children."[22] They served as the playing fields for endless variations on baseball in which the rules changed depending on the number of players.

Dozens of gallows frames, the above-ground structures for the hoists that carried miners deep beneath the ground, towered over the city. From a child's-eye view, the formidable frames were the ultimate monkey bars, and only the best and the bravest could scale them.

Kids would tie a rope on the Belmont gallows frame or the East Park Street Bridge, hang onto the rope, and swing off the ground. . . . The Belmont ore trestle was about seventy-five feet above the street level and built in such a wondrous manner that the kids could climb up the steel support towers without any trouble whatsoever. Most of us could not go any higher than fifteen or twenty feet before we got scared and had to come down to think things over. But there were those who could climb clear to the top and, wonder of wonders, without any trouble get right up to the top deck, where they would shout down to us groundlings so we would know they were brave enough to make the top deck.[23]

At times, children made it home safely by sheer luck, as Danette Harrington's experience attested.

Another night we decided to do something a bit more adventuresome. We went to the Kelley Mine. There were five of us, four girls and a boy. We went up in the crusher. We snuck in and went in the crusher and rode the conveyor belt to the top of the ore bins. We got caught, and everybody started to run. The ore bins at the Kelley are big. They must have been about six stories high. The rocks came out of the crushers and down those chutes and came out on the conveyor belt into those bins. They drove the trains up, and there was a platform where the ore cars would come over. They would open the chutes, and the rocks would come down and fill the ore cars. We had never been up there, and we thought it would be fun. I was no little girl. I was probably twelve or fourteen at the time. And we got caught, and they chased us. I came down those six stories on a rope. My hands were just all raw coming down the rope. And, well, you were out for yourself then. You couldn't depend on the other person, and you couldn't take care of anybody. We ran and ran. There were cop cars and gunmen. They chased us for almost four hours.

Danette and one of her companions, who sported a bleeding lip from the incident, took refuge in her friend's house, hiding under the bed until the coast was clear.[24]

Adventure by Train

With mining came the hauling of wood, coal, and ore and the perpetual rumble of freight trains. Children found plenty of adventure to be had along the tracks. John Sheehy's North Montana Street house was located directly above a tunnel for the Butte, Anaconda & Pacific Railway.

I spent a lot of time as a young kid at the sides of that tunnel—first of all, playing on that grade. We would take railroad spikes and pretend that they were trains or railroad cars. We'd dig trenches around and run the spikes on the rails, playing railroad. And another thing that I can remember us doing is going down and sitting on the side when the train passed. And if you sat at the head of the underpass and just stared straight ahead, pretty soon you were moving. It was an optical illusion. You were moving, and the train was standing still. I did that often. It was a wonderful sensation. I was always, always fascinated by those trains. They would pass by every two or three hours. They took ore out of the Hill, and they brought lumber back and coal back.

In one of those years, I had a neighbor named John Connors. He was a remarkable climber. He could climb anywhere.

His nickname was Dead Eye, Dead Eye Connor. Anyway, we were good pals, about the same age. We'd go over to the Stewart Mine where the woodyard was. The woodyard was on one side of Main Street, and the mine was on the other. And in that woodyard, the train came in on a high trestle. And then you came to a fence right below the end of that trestle. It would be maybe thirty feet high at the end of the trestle. So, we'd climb the fence and get over to where were called laggins. I guess the word is "lagging." And it's a piece of lumber. It would be about two inches thick and about twelve feet long and about six or eight inches wide. They used those for timber down in the mines. They must have been pine, I guess. And you could split them right down into the size that would fit in your kitchen range. We'd go there, Dead Eye and I, and get three or four of those things and go to the end of the trestle and throw them off. And we'd throw them so that they would land on the end, and they would not break. And then we'd go outside and pick them up and take them home and chop them up right away. And I think about that now. The top of that trestle was right about the same height as the sixth floor of the Hennessy Building [Anaconda Company headquarters]. And we were only about a quarter mile away. I'm sure those men looked down and saw the two kids out the window.[25]

Betty Henderson shared the love and adventure of trains. "Oh, I love trains. As kids we used to dam up the railroad tracks, and the engineer, he'd come, 'toot, toot, toot.' 'You damn kids, get them dams down.' Oh, we'd lay under the track and hold our breath as the train went over. We'd lay under the water trestle. We'd lay there and let the train go right over the top of us."[26]

Through their fascination with trains, Betty and her friends met a lot of travelers, whose company and conversation enhanced their adventures.

The bums would come off the trains, and they'd come down for food. . . . My mother and dad were better off for food than some people. We always had food. Dad said he never had food when he was a kid, and, by gosh, we were going to have food. . . . Mom and Dad didn't know about it until we were grown up, but we'd bring the bums back to the house. They'd say, "You got anything to eat?" and we'd grab some canned food for them.[27]

For some youngsters, the proximity of a train yard simply meant access to an easy, if illicit, form of transportation. When Danette Harrington's father was working at the Anselmo Mine, he would drive to work. Keeping with Catholic tradition, the Harringtons did not eat meat on Friday. On occasion, Danette and her brother would hitch a ride on the westbound train running through the mine yard adjacent to their house and hop off when the train slowed at the Excelsior Street intersection near the Anselmo Mine. They would borrow the car, drive to a place on the Flats that made great fish and chips, order takeout, return the car, and hop an eastbound train home, fish and chips in hand.

Play and Piracy

For many Butte youngsters, there was a fine line between play and piracy. Just as miners' stories are laced with accounts of smuggling Company supplies from the mines in their lunch-buckets, so do children's stories tell of theft from the mines and railroads as an accepted practice.[28] The gathering of coal, wood, and scrap metal as part of child's play often helped to supplement the family income or keep the stove going on a frigid winter night. Catherine Hoy described the necessity of what she termed "petty stealing":

> We used to steal coal. Get sacks of coal and put it on our sled
> and sleigh ride down the hill with the sacks of coal on it. You
> had to, with those big pot-bellied stoves, you know, try to keep
> warm, to keep warm, ten below zero, and every one of the
> kids would be just freezing to death. And we'd all congregate
> around that great big stove, trying to keep warm.[29]

Ann and John Onkalo lived, played, and scavenged by the St. Lawrence Mine as kids.

> [Ann] They used to dump lumber up by the St. Lawrence
> Mine down onto the dumps. Why, women and kids would go
> rushing up to bring home wood to burn. They'd dump it, but
> it was just waste wood. Boy, any mother that noticed it would
> whistle to her kids, and when you'd see somebody going, you'd
> all scramble for it. . . .
>
> [John] I used to enjoy that rustling wood. I used to go up on
> the Hill all the time and rustle wood off the dumps. That's
> when they used to dump everything outside. There was no

using it for fuel down in the mine, you know. Each scrap would come up with the waste, and they'd put it over the dump.

[Ann] We used to get sawdust down at the Belmont Mine. Fill gunnysacks with it. Five gunnysacks on a wagon. I remember another girl and I, we made the rounds of every butcher shop Uptown once, and nobody would buy it. Then we got back to the house that her parents were renting. The building, it had a row of outdoor toilets, . . . and the landlord bought fifty cents worth of sawdust from us.[30]

Sometimes children and adults conspired in appropriation of minor items from the mines for the common good of the neighborhood kids. As Danette Harrington described: "Mickey Kelly was a carpenter at the Kelley mine yard. He was great. He would build stilts for all of the kids. We would use them for awhile, then it would be time for a potato roast, so we'd take the stilts and burn them for the roast. About a week later, we'd be back at the mine yard to get more stilts, and Mickey would always build us some."[31]

As these stories suggest, children's play offered up-close experiences with mines and risk. Children honed their skills and bravado as they embraced Butte's industrial terrain as their playground.

Death and Loss

Stories of childhood also reveal that the consequences of play could be serious, and at times fatal. The detritus of mining could turn playgrounds into mine fields, robbing youngsters of life and limb. While memories of broken bones and bruised bodies are common place in adult recollections, newspaper accounts document the frequency of debilitating and fatal injuries resulting from children's play in and around the mines.

For example, nine-year-old Frank Shovlin, son of a local police officer,

had one eye probably totally destroyed and received other injuries shortly after noon yesterday through the accidental explosion of a percussion cap. The little boy was not far from his home and he and three other children had found the cap with a small end of fuse attached to it. The children lighted the fuse and then the Shovlin boy held the match under the cap. Immediately there was an explosion that cut the right eye of the boy badly and also lacerated his fingers. None of the other children were injured.[32]

In 1910 Percy Honeychurch, fifteen, and Frank Barry, thirteen, died of electrocution while they were swinging a piece of baling wire over the transmission line of the Rarus Mine. According to the newspaper report, they had cast the wire over the power line and then were swinging on the wire, apparently trying to break down the line. In the process, they sawed the insulation off the cable. Their bodies were badly burned. The news account first described the teenage victims as "little boys, ignorant of the danger," then noted that the boys had "flirted with death before." Numerous complaints had been made regarding the "mischievous pranks of this crowd of boys," and they had been brought to the attention of the sheriff's office.[33]

The mixing of child's play and danger is a recurrent theme in news reports. Curiously, the fact that explosive devices were often found about town in the path of children's play was not questioned, nor was mention made of Company accountability for the mine fields that extended well beyond the mine yards. Decade after decade, the injuries continued. In June 1916 thirteen-year-old Willie Ritchie lost a thumb and two fingers in an explosion "when a giant cap he was playing with near his home exploded. Neighbors attracted to the scene by the report of the explosion found the lad in great pain but his first words were, 'Don't tell mother.'"[34] In 1934 ten-year-olds Robert Olson and Clarence Lemier were hospitalized for injuries received when a dynamite cap they were playing with exploded: "They were playing near the Blue Bird gas station on the Anaconda Highway. First they found an ice pick near the Oro Fino Ice Company at the foot of Big Butte. Then they found the dynamite cap and started picking at the cap, which exploded."[35]

The city of Butte was rocked by tragedy on July 4, 1932, when six young men were killed in an explosion. The group, all from McQueen, had lifted some blasting caps from a mine yard and begun to set them off around town in the early morning of July 4. About 1:00 A.M., when they ran out of explosives, they returned to the mine yard to find more caps, and the pile exploded. All six were killed. Residents came together in mourning, and a joint funeral for the six was held at Holy Savior Parish. News reports of the tragedy refer to the victims as "boys," even though all were over age eighteen.[36]

However, the deaths of friends and schoolmates did not seem to serve as deterrents for other young adventurers drawn to the pleasures—and dangers—of risky play. Children died on train tracks and under streetcars. They lost life and limb from explosions and accidents. They bore witness to loss from early ages. And they joined in the curious fusion of grief and celebration at wakes and funerals in a community where premature death touched so many families. Childhood memories of wakes and funerals provide windows into children's understandings of death and loss and their efforts to assimilate profound events that adults failed to explain to them. It is notable that the same sense of wonder, curiosity, and emotional energy that children bring to play comes through in accounts of witnessing and making sense of the rituals around death. And play provided children with a way of coping in the moment.

Jule McHugh was born in Dublin Gulch in 1906. Her father died when she was eight. His body was brought to the family home for the wake and covered with sprays of flowers. Jule was one of ten children, and her father's wake was on Halloween. Caught in a powerful mix of emotions, Jule and her siblings invented their own way of coping:

> We had a circus. We soaped windows. Joe had a bogus ten-dollar bill on a string, and he would set it outside the door. Everyone that saw it would stop to pick it up, and Joe, around the corner, would pull the string. At one time, they were three or four deep trying to grab it. We stayed over at Mrs. Nugent's, a boardinghouse, and we never saw such an abundance of food—cookies in big boxes, cases of oranges—and did we have a party. We were trampolining on the bed in our black sateen bloomers, and someone came over from the wake and told us to pull down the shades. Best Halloween we ever had.[37]

As a child, Catherine Hoy was taken by the activities surrounding a funeral.

> There were a lot of heartaches, you know. Children got killed in the cars up on Anaconda Road, you know, fell between the cars and were killed. There was a lot of heartaches. But you hadn't seen anything until you went to an Irish wake up there. Didn't you ever go to an Irish wake? Well, then you missed something. They kept the bodies at home. You didn't take them to the undertakers like they do now. They prepared the bodies and fixed them at home. They had them in a big room, and all the mourners came up. And everybody in the neighborhood cooked something. They had a big ham, chicken, dessert, cakes, and so on. Then they'd have this wake, and all the neighbors would come in and say how sorry they were and so on and so forth. Then at midnight, you know, they'd have this big feast in there with all the liquor they wanted. There

was twenty, thirty saloons on that highway, so we weren't short by any means. But then they'd all eat and have a good old time up to the wake and enjoy it. And then the funerals were something else. [Undertaker] Fat Jack [would drive] the hearse on funeral day. And all the Irish drinking. . . . Of course, the kids weren't allowed, but lots of times the kids got in on it. We made it our business to attend.[38]

John Onkalo was four years old when he attended his first funeral.

I remember my fourth birthday. That was in 1916. A good friend of the folks died, and we went to the funeral. In those days, it was mostly horse-drawn vehicles. There were some automobiles but not very many. When you'd go to a funeral, why, you'd go and rent a horse and buggy in the summer or in the wintertime a horse and sleigh. That's the way you'd go to the funeral. Well, the Finns, a lot of them it seemed, after the funeral, they'd go charging around to one of the roadhouses after the funeral. I enjoyed that. They'd go to the roadhouse, and you'd get some pop to drink. I really got a kick out of that.[39]

John T. Shea revealed his Irish humor as he recounted memories of a funeral he attended as a child.

When I was a kid, we lived up on Missoula Avenue. When I was little, right across the street was Guinness Shea, and their daughter was my godmother. They were like grand-parents. Guinness died, and they had the wake at home. Right away, my mom started cooking, and she put the big wreath on the door. They had the three wooden chairs [to hold the casket], and then they put down the kneeler. The first night went well. They had more or less family. The second night they had the "keenies," the ladies who sit at either end of the casket and wail and cry. Then the third night it was more or less for everyone. Sometimes they'd say, "The wake was so good they postponed the funeral." Anyway, the ladies were in the front room saying the rosary, the "keenies" were wailing, and the guys were in the kitchen, drinking and smoking big cigars. Pretty soon, they run out of chairs. And O'Neil says to Murphy, "Well, himself is just laying there. Aren't there three chairs in the living room? [So they take the chairs support-ing the corpse.] Well, about that time doesn't himself Father

O'Brien arrive. Seeing the corpse standing in the corner, he says, "It's a sacrilege" and comes into the kitchen and says, "Can we have three chairs for the corpse?" And the fellas say, "Hip, hip hooray! Hip, hip hooray! Hip, hip hooray!"[40]

Helen Evankovich grew up in Finntown. Each week a neighbor woman would drive Helen and a group of children to Sunday school classes at the Finnish church. After Sunday school, the children were given Finnish language classes. One time, Helen recalled, the neighbor woman took Helen and her young friends along to a wake. "Well, us kids never could go to wakes. But we all ended up going to the wake with her, . . . and she made us each go up and kiss him. I remember that I didn't like it. . . . And if you didn't kiss him, you at least had to touch him and that was so he wouldn't come back, which I think was a pretty good thing."[41]

Kay Antonetti recalled the death and wake of her uncle when she was a little girl.

> That was when they waked them at home. They had him in the living room by the window. We kids would stay out and play, and they had a big porch in front. Everybody was there at the house, in the dining room and the kitchen and outside, eating and drinking. Then when it cleared out pretty much, my cousin Marian and I climbed up the little steps, and we felt him. I remember poking him with my finger. We tried to lift his hands, and they were hard as a rock. He'd always lie down after supper, and when he'd get up, there would always be quarters or nickels or dimes between the couch or on the floor, and he'd always say, "You can have it." I remember the two of us, Marian and me, looking at each other. I said, "No more nickels and dimes." And she said, "No."[42]

Tom Holter was an altar boy at Holy Savior Church, where he participated in many funeral services as a boy. The service itself offered the opportunity for some fun.

> From Holy Savior you could see when the funeral procession was coming, passing over the bridge towards East Butte. You could see the funeral from there, and when the funeral reached there, we started ringing the bell. And we'd jump up with the bell. We were able to go up with the bell. The bell was so strong and so forceful that it would lift us right up. We thought that was something. We'd jump right up on the rope,

Tom Holter, Meaderville, circa 1935

Kids hung out in self-organized groups, looking out for one another. These boys and girls appear to have stopped to admire a car while en route home from school, circa 1910.

and we'd go up and down with it. But we had to watch and see where the funeral was, coming over the overpass, and then we'd start ringin' the bell, so the bell would be ringin' when the funeral procession came in.[43]

Butte children transformed the machinations of mining into child's play, the mine yard terrain as familiar to many of them as to those who mined the copper. In turn, their playful spirits provided a buffer and source of resilience in the face of adversity and loss that touched many young lives.

The Gang's All Here

Butte children took pride in the camaraderie of their neighborhood gangs. Stories of neighborhood youth gangs and turf battles at times take on legendary proportions in Butte. William Burke's colorful account captures a bigger-than-life image of Butte's boyish brawlers and of the wink-and-nod acceptance of physical force as a form of play.

Butte had a great gang of kids in them days, too. They were tough, and their reputations had traveled far and wide over the country. You could write a book on their carryin' ons in Dublin Gulch and the East Side alone. It is the truth that

Father McGlynn used to ride with the grocery wagons when they were makin' their deliveries up Dublin Gulch. The kids respected the priest, and he was about the only one the little devils would listen to.

. . . They traveled in gangs and could throw a rock through a knothole at a hundred yards. It's a fact they had to build a separate correction school out on the Flat just to take care of them. They were as wild as the hills that surrounded them and fought like devils amongst themselves and with the other gangs. There were very few of them that didn't have scars all over their noggins from the belts from rocks they'd received.[44]

Reports of gangs and violence seem prone to exaggeration. John Onkalo offered a more tempered perspective. John grew up in Finntown, and when asked about trouble with the boys from Dublin Gulch, he replied:

I guess you might say that we were friendly enemies. I don't know. In fact, it got to be such a habit. When I was going to Washington Junior High, there was a kid there. We were good friends, but he was from the Gulch. Naturally, we were kind of opponents. We used to arrange to have rock fights after school. We'd go, "Okay, you be down there at the Moonlight dump." He says, "We'll come down." So I'd get a bunch of guys together, and we'd go up to the Moonlight dump, and pretty soon we'd see a whole bunch coming over from the Gulch, but they'd be uphill from us. Boy, then the rocks would start flying. But it was never really serious. There were a few scratches and knobs and stuff, bloody noses, maybe. Sometimes you'd get into a little hand-to-hand combat. But outside of that, why, it wasn't too bad.[45]

John T. Shea contended that trouble arose only if you strayed outside your turf: "The real trouble was between the kids from Centerville and Walkerville. There were lots of problems when those two groups got together. The Centerville kids went to the Dream Theater in Walkerville on Saturday afternoon. Once that show was over, you were expected to get back over that hill where you belonged. If you didn't, there'd be trouble brewing with the Walkerville gang and the local sheriff, Mike Peters."[46]

Catherine Hoy wanted the record to show that fighting was not solely the domain of boys in Butte.

You know, my grandkids ask me, "Grandma, who was the best fighter?" Of course, I had to tell them I was. Because I was. I was, really. I came out ahead all the time. . . . We [girls] loved [to fight]. We were in the battling just as well as the boys. We had sides, you know, one side and the other side. Well, then the fight would start with two, and by the end of the fight there was about fifteen or twenty kids all mingled and mixing it up. . . . Boys and girls mixing it up at the same time.[47]

In Linda Raiha's experience, fighting was just something you learned to do to protect younger siblings and stick together as a group.

My younger brother was always getting in fights, and my brothers and sister would come and get me. The neighbors always said, "You didn't fight one Raiha. You had to fight them all." We defended each other. There was that family unit there. We had to fend for ourselves a lot of the time, so we clung together. We were one unit.

I remember when we moved to Walkerville. They did not like outsiders. My brother, who liked to fight anyway, fought almost every day until he finally became one of them. I had to defend my brother. I spent all of my time defending him. He was terrible. He'd start fights, then he'd say, "My sister Linda is going to come and get you." He always got beat up because he had a big mouth and a little body. I got tired of it. Finally, there was one time when I was in junior high. This big, huge guy was sitting on our lawn waiting for me when I came home one day. He said, "Your brother says you're going to take care of me" because he had beat John up. He looked like a house. He looked like a grown man. I just looked at my brother and said, "I don't think I like you that well. . . . He's yours." That was the last time I ever had to fight.[48]

For the most part, talk of gangs in Butte is a reference to close-knit groups of neighborhood youth who played together, competed against one another, sometimes fought one another, and watched one anothers' backs. For example, Edward Jursnich described his "gang," the Ranga-tangs, as a group of East Side boys who developed strong and lasting friendships as they went to school and played sports together, organized wienie roasts and other outdoor adventures, and talked about girls.[49] However, when those growing up in Butte in the 1920s and early 1930s spoke of gangs, they told stories of the fabled Overall Gang. Catherine Hoy recalled them as a group of pranksters rather than thugs.

They were a rough-and-tumble bunch of kids, from age sixteen to about twenty, I guess. Mischievous. They'd steal tires when the car was running. Tires and hubcaps, stuff like that. Or take a horse and buggy and put the horse in backwards. Or unharness the horse, and when the driver got in, the horse walked off, and the wagon stood there. They weren't as bad as some of the kids' gangs nowadays. They got blamed for everything, but they stayed pretty much to their own community up on Anaconda Road, Dublin Gulch. . . . They'd go down in Finntown and all those places to fight.[50]

John Sheehy recalled a more serious side to the Overall Gang's activities and contended that these were not "boys" at all, but young men, out of work and in trouble.

Well, it was a group who lived in the north side, pretty much around our neighborhood. This was in the early period of Prohibition. These men were young, really. I would guess in their twenties. They couldn't have been too old because they died fairly young. What they would do is that they would drink whatever kind of alcohol they could get because Prohibition had closed down the saloons and so on. They had the bootleggers to get booze. And there was quite a crew of them. Once they got addicted to that alcohol, they quit working. Wherever they could pick up some money, they'd steal something, and they were just a problem around that neighborhood. There must have been about ten or fifteen around our area. What they drank, among other things, was rubbing alcohol and Sterno. And what they would do is take the Sterno and put it in a stocking, a silk stocking, and squeeze it, and the alcohol came out. And they drank it. They died young.

The Overall Gang disappeared in the early 1930s. They died, most of them. They had names like Gyp the Blood. I do recall that one of the Overall Gang was charged with stealing something downtown. His trial came up in Justice of the Peace Court. . . . This man was charged with [theft], and the rest of the gang came down and testified that he couldn't have been there, he wasn't there that night, and the man got off free. And the thing that was nuts about it was that they each got two dollars for being a witness, [and] they spent [it] that night.[51]

While talk of gangs takes on a mythic quality, a fundamental truth remains: Butte children had power in numbers and were a force to be

When John Shannon photographed his daughter, Marian Shannon (left), and her friend Patricia McCauley in the 1920s, he caught members of the infamous Overall Gang lurking below the water tank on the upper right of the photograph. The gang was made up of young men who roamed the streets and caused trouble in the Dublin Gulch and Finntown neighborhoods.

reckoned with. Adults put considerable effort into building youth organizations and offering entertainments to harness or quell young energy. Children were courted each week with free trolley rides to Columbia Gardens, and they were gathered by the thousands to take part in Arbor Day celebrations there. And, for a time, children were treated to free entry to the "pigpen" to enjoy Mines League baseball and football games at Clark Park.

On summer afternoons, the stadium at Clark Park would be packed to capacity with thousands on hand for the start of game. As Vince Dowling recalled: "I remember spending a lot of time in the 'pigpen' watching those Independent League games. Only a handful of kids had enough money in those days to go to the games, so the way to get in was to go to the 'pigpen' at the end of one side of Clark Park and watch the game for free behind this wired fence. The 'pigpen' was always filled with kids when the Independent League teams played at Clark Park."[52]

The 1923 League playoffs were a classic example. The Butte Electric Railway ran trolleys to shuttle fans to watch the Clarks, who had won eleven straight games in the Mines League. The Clarks were facing their rivals, the Anaconda Anodes. A record crowd surpassing ten thousand watched the Clarks defeat the Anodes 13 to 5 to win the series. Over eight hundred of those in attendance were children who had gotten free admission to the "pigpen."

By the following season, however, Butte youngsters were at risk of losing their "pigpen" privileges due to the actions of a few "hoodlums." According to May 1924 news reports, children had been caught using mirrors to reflect blinding lights in the eyes of ballplayers, and such "dangerous as well as uncalled for tactics is only one of the offenses that have justly stirred the powers that be to arms."[53] The final straw came with a case of auto theft. Butte youngsters had regularly earned pocket money at the games by watching cars to prevent vandalism. At

Butte children enjoyed power in numbers and were a force to be reckoned with. Adults put considerable effort into building youth organizations and offering entertainments to harness or quell young energy. Children were courted each week with free trolley rides to Columbia Gardens (above, circa 1905) for activities that would keep them out of trouble.

the May 16 ball game, one of the young watchmen made off with the car he was being paid twenty-five cents to watch. Benevolence gave way to ire and harsh warnings. Butte youngsters were publicly chastised: "Youngsters of Butte are on the verge of forfeiting their privilege of seeing all ball games at Clark Park free. . . . A few young hoodlums, showing more than anything a lack of training at home, have become so obstreperous at recent Mines League games that officials have declared an ultimatum, ordering the section closed to the youngsters for the rest of the season and possibly for all time if order is not voluntarily maintained."[54]

While Butte's youngsters may not have acquiesced gracefully to the expectations of adults, they must have managed to maintain a modicum of order in their own ranks as "pigpen" privileges continued. At the same time, they sought to push boundaries, reinvent rules, and claim their own spaces. As John T. Shea described, all it took was a little ingenuity: "Another way to get in free was to carry the headgear for some of the players. You walked right on the field with them and served as manager for the day."[55]

Butte children were also team players. Although the playing fields may have been leveled slag heaps and the equipment makeshift, many children pursued a passion for sports. Children both created their own informal neighborhood teams and took advantage of the formal, adult-organized sports activities available to them. Hodgepodge East Side baseball teams with shifting numbers of players practiced before, during, and after school, running around bases made of gunnysacks. Some went on to play for Grant School and on citywide leagues.[56] Grade schools sponsored baseball, basketball, football, and track teams in which students took part in neighborhood and citywide competition. From the 1930s, the Catholic Youth Organization (CYO) sponsored athletic and social programs for boys and girls in Butte's Catholic schools. CYO boxing was a favorite among the boys as they filled the Knights of Columbus gym to train and fight. Girls turned out for basketball. Pat Sullivan was a star hoopster, leading her St. Lawrence O'Toole team to victory in the CYO league in 1939 and to the state Class A championship in 1940.[57]

St. Lawrence O'Toole School was also home to a scrappy young football team in the mid-1940s. At that time, with men away at war or engaged in war-production work, adult coaches were scarce. Eighth-grade boys were called on to coach the newly formed fifth-grade football team. Jim Cortese, a member of the fifth-grade team, wrote:

Undaunted by the lack of gear or adult expertise, we practiced on the rocky soil near the Blaine School each day in

September and October. We did drills and a bit of training and ran, tackled, and kicked. We made a lot of noise, dispersed a lot of energy, went home and ate big dinners, and formed lasting friendships with our teammates. And frequently at the end of practice, the whole team climbed up on the rock wall, and each kid lit up a cigarette. In these ways, the St. Lawrence No-Name team prepared to take on the world. The following year, the team got sponsorship from the Men's Club, a coach, helmets, and uniforms. In 1948 they won the Class C championship.[58]

The East Side Neighborhood House provided youngsters with a hardwood court for basketball until it was converted into a church after World War II.[59] East Side youth then joined youngsters citywide for Saturday basketball leagues sponsored by the YMCA. Saturday trips to the "Y" could be challenging ventures for children who rarely left the confines of their neighborhoods. The YMCA offered free swimming lessons for children. Learning to swim often entailed a long walk or a bus ride and the potential for confrontation. As Edward Jursnich described: "My very first visit to the 'Y' left an indelible impression. At about six years old, I tagged along with my older brother Ray, reluctantly undressed in front of everyone, and entered the pool. It was different and scary. I did not know how to swim, so I climbed into the pool and stayed at the shallow end where I could stand on my tiptoes and keep my head above water level."[60]

Just as Edward was gaining some confidence, an older, bigger kid came into the shallow end and began "ducking" the little kids, holding them underwater until they were gasping for air and terrified. An older East Side boy came to the rescue, grabbing the bully by the neck and "giving him a taste of his own medicine."[61] Even though the YMCA and other organizations offered adult-supervised activities for youngsters, children also learned to count on the neighborhood gang and the protection of older youth to keep them safe.

Happy Halloween

At times grown-ups were simply willing to recognize the power and place of children and give them cause to have some fun. Halloween in Butte is a case in point. Of all the holidays, Halloween stood alone as a celebration by and for children. Butte children took their Halloween fun seriously. They were eager for treats and ingenious with tricks. John Onkalo described Halloween antics of his youth:

Mostly we made a lot of noise and were kind of mischievous. I can't remember the kids every really doing any real damage, outside of maybe making a mess. We'd dump garbage cans, then roll the cans around and maybe stack them up in the middle of the street. But there wasn't much traffic in those days. . . . You'd have an arc light at an intersection. Well, the rope from the arc light would be hooked up to the telephone pole on the corner on a ring, but it was way high up. You'd shimmy up enough to get hold of it, and then you'd pull it off the hook and release it. Of course, that would drop the light down, so it would be just hanging a few feet off the street, you know. Then the power company would have to come down. Somebody would report it, and then they'd have to pull it back up into place again and rehook that ring on the telephone pole. But as far as any real damage, I don't think there was much of that. We'd rattle doors and knock on windows and soap windows. And stuff like that was about the worst part, the soaping part.[62]

Principal Isabel Kelly seemed to embrace the philosophy "if you can't beat 'em, join 'em" in initiating Halloween parades at Grant School in 1924. The parade became an annual event with costumed youngsters from schools across the city marching in force.

The celebratory spirit of Halloween also came to life in an unexpected place: Charley Judd's New Deal Bar. Charley Judd and Esther Zannon were newlyweds in 1942 when they purchased the New Deal Bar on South Arizona Street from Esther's father, an Italian immigrant who had operated a drinking establishment at that location during Prohibition. Across Arizona Street from the bar was Silver Bow Homes, a New Deal housing initiative and one of the country's first public housing projects, which replaced the Cabbage Patch shantytown. Initially, Silver Bow Homes housed older people, especially widows. Women raising children on their own during World War II joined the mix, followed by young families after the war.

Charley and Esther turned the New Deal Bar into a community gathering place, selling "pick candy" for kids and welcoming their Silver Bow Home neighbors. During their first year in the neighborhood, the Judds hosted a Halloween party for the children at the housing project. The event was a success, and the community space at Silver Bow Homes could not hold the number of children in attendance. The next year, Charley and Esther moved the event to the New Deal Bar, and so a Butte tradition was born. For one day a year, the New Deal did not

Every year, Butte photographer C. Owen Smithers took photographs at the annual Halloween party at Charley and Esther Judd's New Deal Bar and made a poster showing the night's activities and participants.

serve alcohol, and children were special guests for a night of revelry and treats, where they could fill pillowcases with candy, popcorn, and toys.

The party became an annual event, open to all Butte children. The Judds raised four sons in the apartment above the New Deal and created an extended family of Butte children every Halloween. Charley initiated creative fund-raising efforts over the course of the year to purchase party supplies. Two spaces in every football pool were designated "Halloween," providing a chance for the party fund to win one hundred dollars. The party budget quickly surpassed two thousand dollars, as did the number of children in attendance each year. In 1952 two thousand children consumed one ton of candy, fifteen boxes of apples, four barrels of popcorn, and thirty pounds of cotton candy. For a few years, Charley added fireworks to the festivities, until an errant rocket targeted a group of young ghosts and goblins, and Charley had to fling himself in its path, sustaining a serious wound to the face in the process.[63]

Over the years, patrons gave up their favorite seats at the bar for the night and helped distribute candy. In 1950 the Butte stockyards donated a large stock tub so kids could bob for apples. The mayhem was such that the tub was first moved outdoors, then abandoned altogether. But

November 1 would roll around again, and New Deal patrons would start contributing to the following year's effort. Over the course of the year, Charley Judd and the New Deal Bar would also lend support to student scholarships, Little League baseball, CYO basketball, and the Sacred Heart football team. And once television came to Butte, the New Deal hosted children and adults to view weekly favorites such as *Chicago Wrestling*.[64]

Saturday Matinee

Uptown Butte was a cosmopolitan center with a host of department and specialty stores, restaurants, ice-cream parlors, dance halls, and theaters to attract young and old. Children were early and enthusiastic patrons of Butte's many show houses. And, by 1907, city officials were preoccupied with the influence of stage entertainment on the young people of Butte. For example, in October 1907 a city ordinance was passed that forbade showing performances judged to be "immoral." Alderman Jerry Mullins was vocal about his concern over recent productions at the Grande Theater: "I think it is a shame and disgrace for any playhouse to be permitted to be able to hang out any such sign as the one now in front of the Grande Theater.... I have noticed young girls standing opposite the theater reading the title of the week's bill, while their young minds were becoming to some extent polluted by the morbid thoughts aroused by the suggestive title, 'Why Girls Go Wrong.'"[65] Alderman A. B. Cohen concurred: "We must take steps to stop this evil, which has been the cause of great harm to the young people of Butte."[66]

But the power of the stage and silver screen outweighed the pomposity of city officials, and young people flocked to the theaters. For the modest price of admission, they could be transfixed and transported. Ads in the *Butte Miner* circa 1914 offer a taste of local theater fare. The Ansonia featured the three-reel motion-picture drama *The Billionaire*, along with a two-reel drama *The Toll*, a short comedy, and music by the Ansonia Orchestra. At the American Theater, audiences were treated to *Million Dollar Mystery*, while the Orpheum was presenting *The Voices of Angelo*, *The Mysterious Package*, and a performance by singer extraordinaire Alex Barthild. The Empress, not to be outdone, featured performances by the Jackson Family Cyclists, the Roland West Players, the motion picture *The Criminal*, and the melodious surprises of Bert Ralton and Lucille Latour. By 1915 Uptown Butte housed nine theaters featuring an array of vaudeville entertainment and motion pictures.[67]

The stage and screen made an impression from the start. Children attending a live performance of *Uncle Tom's Cabin* watched transfixed as Little Eva, played by a Butte girl, was hoisted on a cloud in a jerky ascent to heaven. Images of the Ku Klux Klan were seared in their memories after viewing *Birth of a Nation* at the Ansonia Theater. They remembered the smell of garlic that permeated the Elysium Theater, a favorite of Butte's Italian community. And the Liberty Theater had a reputation for easy entry; boys and girls could sneak in at the end of one movie and be set for the next show.[68]

Stories of Saturdays at the movies held a special place in memories of childhood. Butte children were eager and savvy consumers of movies and tucked away precious earnings for the price of admission. When money was short, children pooled their pennies to pay for one admission, and the intrepid ticket holder would then make his or her way to the alley exit where friends would be awaiting illicit entry. Kevin Shannon remembered: "It was great sneaking into the show. You were frowned on if you paid. So one guy would pay. We'd raise the dime between us. One would open the exit, and we'd go in."[69]

Boys were not the only ones who dodged the ticket booth to see a show. Dolores Barsanti would sneak into the Rialto Theater with her sister and girlfriend: "Dan Kailin [ran the theater]. He was a big man, and he used to catch us by the nape of the neck and throw us out. But then he got to liking me and my sister and girlfriend, and he used to let us sneak in."[70]

Entertainment in Butte theaters attracted old and young alike. In this case, "Caribou Bill's Famous Dog Team" drew a mixed audience of spectators to the Orpheum circa 1902.

John Sheehy recalled sneaking into the movies at times and other times paying with money from his newspaper sales. Once he had established his corner as a newsboy, he was lucky enough to have a regular customer who provided him with free movie tickets.

Movies were great for us as a kid. I liked the old cowboy movies, with a guy playing the piano. When I was selling papers, there was a guy who took a liking to me who played the piano at the Ansonia Theater. That was located right next to the Symon's Department Store, the next building over. That was one of the theaters. On that street, you had the Broadway and the Ansonia. The Rialto, it was a beautiful theater on Park and Main. But, anyway, when I was selling papers on Saturday nights, that man, when the theater closed down, would come over and give me five tickets for the theater for the next day. That was kind of a treasure. I could take some friends the next day, on Sunday, and see him playing.[71]

For Dorothy Martin, movies offered a great way to learn to read.

Going to the movies, that's where I learned to read. I could read before I went to first grade. That's probably why I got my first promotion. My Uncle Isador loved to go to the movies. Charlie Chaplin and all. He always liked to take me. I went a lot. He used to read the subtitles in the beginning, but then as we went more frequently, he got kind of tired, and it was annoying to the other people around. So just watching and hearing and seeing, I picked up the words. It's like flash cards. That's what they really were, flashing on the screen.[72]

John Wallace Cochran became an avid fan of Westerns at an early age: "Some of my spending money went for movies, and many were the Westerns featuring Harry Carey, Hoot Gibson, or Tom Mix that I sat through. Admission at the Ansonia on West Park Street was a dime, while at the Liberty on West Broadway it was only a nickel. Occasionally I delivered handbills for the Harrison Avenue Theater and received free tickets as pay."[73]

Frank Carden spent many a Saturday at the Lyric Theater on Butte's East Side.

The Lyric Theater was also known as the East Side Opera House. It operated for years, mostly as a "B"-run house— mostly cowboy Westerns and serial movies. The serials would run over a period of a couple of months, and each serial would be half an hour. The actors, during the thirty minutes, would get themselves out of one jam and end up getting themselves into another jam just at the end. You would have to come back next week to find out how they would extricate themselves from this dangerous and life-threatening situation, only to have to come back next week and so on and so on until the end of the serial.

These usually would be run in mid-week to bolster attendance, which was not as good as it was on weekends. They told us of the dangers of the "Yellow Peril," . . . which threatened our way of life, and the perils of Ruth Holland and Pearl White, two actresses who made a good living playing in these pictures.

On Saturdays and Sundays, you'd usually have what we later called a "cowboy opera," which consisted of Cowboy Pete Morris being shown riding his horse from east to west and then west to east to rescue the heroine. Pete never kissed or hugged the heroine but was often seen hugging and kissing his horse. He had a great following of kids at that time, and every time he kissed the horse, they would whistle and cheer him like the girls of a later period did to Frank Sinatra. However, none of them got to the point where they fainted like Sinatra's fans, but you could tell they practiced hard on the whistling bit. These movies were in black and white and were silent.[74]

Movies held their magic over time. John Mazzola and Kay Antonetti recalled Saturdays at the movies in the 1930s and 1940s. Kay remembered:

As a child, we'd go to movies. These two cousins who lived down the block were cowboys. They were, like, five and six years younger than I. I would take them every Saturday to the Park Theater for all the cowboy shows and Abbot and Costello. We'd get in for a can of soup that would go to the poor people or else pay something like a dime. All we would see were all the cowboy shows. And these little guys would be in their cowboy outfits. They had the holsters and the cowboy hats and everything.

Then when we got in high school, my friends and I would go to every military show, and we'd cry our eyes out. All the old shows with John Wayne and all. . . . And then I worked as an usher at the old American Theater when I was sixteen. And that was a ball. It was right on Park Street, so you saw everybody. I had a wonderful time.[75]

For John Mazzola, movies provided his first opportunities for dating.

We'd go up on Saturdays to the Park Theater for a nickel. They'd have two features, the Three Stooges, cartoons—they'd have some news, for a nickel. Then on weeknights you'd go to the Montana Theater or the Fox Theater. Pal Night, they called it. Two could go for fifteen cents. Big bag of popcorn was only a nickel. [Sometimes we'd take girls to the movies.] We'd try to get them into dark places. I liked being around the girls, but I didn't like my friends to know I liked being around them. So I'd get off in a dark corner. We never smooched or anything like that, but we'd watch the movie and laugh and have a friendship. But I'd have been mortified if somebody I knew saw me with a girl. And most of the time they had to pay their own way.[76]

Theaters offered both escape and connection as children joined their friends and heroes riding into the sunset. Closer to home, radio continued to captivate children throughout the 1950s, until its magic was eclipsed by the arrival of television. Linda Raiha remembered the importance of radio in her childhood.

I was a great lover of the radio. I used to listen to all those stories like the Lone Ranger and Dick Tracy. There used to be a thing on the radio about the temperature from the School of Mines. I used to wonder all of the time, "Where is the School of Mines?" And when we moved up to McGlone Heights, lo and behold, we passed the School of Mines. I was thrilled. I didn't have any idea it was in the same town. To me, that was like a different town, so far away.

I loved the Lone Ranger on the radio. The radio was so warm. I used to sit in the kitchen and wrap my arms around the radio and listen to the show. We had a wood stove. We never had regular heating on the East Side, so the radio was so nice and warm.[77]

Columbia Gardens: Every Child's Dream

While mine yards and movie halls provided the settings for many childhood memories, the most poignant place of child's play in Butte

Columbia Gardens—every child's dream—included acres of lawn, forested picnic grounds, a lake, a zoo, a playground, pavilions, a penny arcade, and a roller coaster. This panorama is dated 1914.

was Columbia Gardens. Columbia Gardens was a lush and lovely sixty-eight-acre park purchased by William A. Clark for use as a community playground. Tucked in the folds of the craggy mountain ridge east of Butte, Columbia Gardens was a world apart from the gritty, churning, haze-filled Mining City.

Columbia Gardens opened to the public on June 4, 1899. Its first pavilion was built in 1900, and Clark invested one hundred thousand dollars in its expansion and development in 1902. It contained acres of

Columbia Gardens gardeners planted twenty-five thousand pansies each year to give children the pleasure of picking a handful once a week on Children's Day, photographed here circa 1905.

grass, greenhouses, intricately designed flower gardens, and a lake, zoo, playground, pavilions, and penny arcade. Clark initiated Children's Day at Columbia Gardens in 1907, marking Thursdays as the day Butte children anticipated through the summer months.

Children and adults alike were captivated by the giant wooden roller coaster, the biplanes, and the carousel of hand-carved wooden horses. But beyond the amusement rides were the luxuriant grounds and gardens themselves. Acres of lawn and forested picnic grounds awaited eager children and their overworked parents. Massive greenhouses supplied the flower gardens. Twenty-five thousand pansies were planted each year simply to give children the pleasure of picking a handful once a week on Children's Day.

After Clark's death in 1928, Columbia Gardens was sold to the Anaconda Company, which kept it operating until Labor Day 1973. Much to the outrage and dismay of Butte residents, the Gardens were closed to make way for the mining of a new vein of copper. When the Gardens, including the beloved carousel, were destroyed by a suspicious fire in November 1973, it was almost too much for the hard-hit community to bear. For the better part of the century, Columbia Gardens had been both site and symbol of the joys of childhood.

Marie Butori offered her vivid memory of the Gardens, her words conveying the spirit of childhood.

> Columbia Gardens was beautiful. The ACM Company
> thought the miners needed [a place like that]. . . . If you got
> the chance to ride to the Columbia Gardens on the trolley car,
> you thought you really had it made. . . . You went to the Gardens
> free 'cause they paid for everything. . . . And when you
> got up there, they had a popcorn stand just as you come in the
> gate. Then they had that little fish place where the kids could
> fish and get little prizes. Then you go up farther, and they had
> ice cream there. And then when you got to the top, they had

airplanes. It was like a carnival, and they had airplanes that flew around and went up in the air. They had the [carousel], where everybody had their own favorite horse, and you'd fight for the horse when you went on. And when you left there, then they had a roller coaster. A lot of people didn't go on the roller coaster, but we always did. I thought it was great. It had about three big dips, and it went around twice.

They had these big pot stoves built into the ground. And every Thursday we all went out. . . . They were made like cement. . . . It was real old-fashioned, and everybody cooked on it. Everybody took their turn cooking. And they had one big pavilion, and it had all kinds of tables and benches, so you then could go in there and eat your lunch if you wanted to. But sometimes we just went and had a place by ourselves.

They had the cowboy swings, and they had a ring that you grab on to. It was just round and went around, and you'd hang on to it and swing around. And if somebody didn't like you, they'd push you into the pole. They had a beautiful garden there. On one side, they had a garden in the shape of a butterfly—big and all the different colors, you know, in there. On the other side, it was like an Irish harp. And they had a man who took care of it all the time. . . . It was really a beautiful place—and the Anaconda Company paid for all that.[78]

Elinore Sterrett Shields Penrose recalled Columbia Gardens as

the most beautiful place for a place like Butte that for a long time had been ruined by smoke. Nobody had lawns. Nobody had flowers because of the soot from the smelters. . . . Once a week in the summertime, they had open streetcars, no sides on them, big red ones, and you could get in. And all the kids would run for the streetcar, take our lunches, and go out to the Gardens. Then just about three o'clock they'd open up the pansy gardens, and they'd let us all go in and pick flowers. Of course, by the next week there were hundreds more. We were doing their work for them. The fellows would put them in their hats to take home to their families.[79]

For Lucille Sheehan, Columbia Gardens represented a precious place.

We'd have picnics when one of the kids had a birthday. We'd have everything ready, and we'd go out to the Gardens. And there'd be big tables. And they had everything there for you to play with. And you'd bring your food, and, oh, we had such a wonderful time. And holidays we'd go up there, too. But you'd have to go early enough to get a table and so that you could get around a stove there. They had those big stoves. Oh, it was a wonderful place, and for the kids, they had everything. They had the cowboy swings and other kinds of swings, and, of course, they had the roller coaster and the biplanes and the merry-go-round.

[We would take] the streetcar. There was no other way. And then on Thursday they had Children's Day, and you could go out and pick pansies. They had this huge spray of pansies, and they'd open the gate, and everybody'd go in, and they used to mess up the whole place. And then it was so pretty, they had, in one section of the gardens, the butterfly and the harp.

They had so much, and you could stay out there all day long. They had the dance hall, and they used to have all the dances out there. And the main dances that came to Butte were out there at the Gardens. They were name bands. Frankie Clark was out there. Jack Benny was out there. Bennie Goodman, Glenn Miller, even Lawrence Welk. They said it was the best dance floor in the Northwest.[80]

A special trolley (above, circa 1910) transported children to and from Columbia Gardens.

John Sheehy went every Thursday to Columbia Gardens as a youngster.

[We would go] on the streetcars. They provided the transportation on Thursdays for all of the kids, so you'd grab a streetcar on Thursdays about nine o'clock in the morning and go up there. Occasionally you'd bring lunch with you and eat lunch out there. Once my father took me to the Gardens when I was quite small. I'd guess I was four or five years old. We went up to the upper part of the gardens, and he found a grassy spot there where he laid down and fell asleep. And when he woke up, I was gone. I remember crying. Someone brought me down to the place where you got on to the streetcar. I remember crying there. And along came a neighbor boy. Well, he got me on the streetcar and got me home. Then my father came walking up the street. He was glad to see me, I'm sure.

Over the years, my mother loved to go up there. Any kind of a holiday in the summertime, we'd be out there. On Sundays, out cooking on that great big stove they had—beautiful, big stove. It had a big chimney in the middle and out on the sides a place to throw wood in, not just wood but logs. And you'd get that fire started, and on top of the stove was a piece of steel about [one inch] thick and longer than this table. There was plenty of room for lots of pots and pans on the stove. So, all those people who were out there picnicking on each side of that, it could take care of several hundred people that way. And nearby they did have a covered area with tables inside underneath. Usually by the time we'd get there, it would be occupied. But if it did happen to rain, you could go in there and get shelter. Besides, you went out there for the fresh air anyway. There were all kinds of tables outside, with benches and all that they provided. And down close to the arcade there, that was a place where you could sit on a bench and watch the people go by if you were a people watcher. And they had the rides, which I liked a lot. You could ride for a nickel on the carousel, and the airplane cost a dime, and I liked that. And I especially liked the roller coaster.[81]

For Nancy Klapan, Columbia Gardens "was just all by itself and a thing you can't even imagine unless you lived it."

Thursdays, every Thursday, during the summer was Children's Day, and all of us, all my friends, packed a sack lunch and waited at the bus stop. The city buses were free every Thursday for kids, and we would get on the bus. I lived down on the Flats, and we would take the bus up to the corner of Park and Main and get a transfer, all free, and then wait for the Columbia Gardens bus, and we would all go up to the Gardens for the entire day. The biplanes and merry-go-round were a nickel, and the roller coaster was a dime, but you didn't do that until you were a little older because it was really scary. You would spend the entire day at the Gardens. Not a care in the world, just eat your lunch, play on the playground for hours, on the cowboy swings and the merry-go-rounds up there, and then walk all the way home. It was magic. And every Thursday, every single Thursday, we did that. And as soon as Thursday was over, we couldn't wait until the next one. Then we would walk the boardwalk. They had all kinds of arcades at the boardwalk and an ice-cream store. All wood, all quite magic.[82]

The magic of Columbia Gardens lived on in memories of Butte childhood, but the start of open-pit mining operations in Butte portended its demise. As Dolores Kangas stated, "I am sure W. A. Clark turned over in his grave when he heard it was gone. He fixed that up for the families so that the miners when they got off work, they had a place to go besides home. People aren't happy about that even today. But that's what they do, and it's hard to fight big mining companies."[83] The loss of Columbia Gardens brought to a close a special chapter on childhood in Butte.

CHAPTER FIVE

School Days

*My father is a miner and very caranky man. He drinks quite a bit of licker
and likes to rush the can. His hair is red his eyes are blue. He wears a 44 vest
and is a darling dady and his name is Richard Best.*

—Blaine School student essay, circa 1927

CHILDHOOD and schooling go hand in hand, and schools are key
sites for understanding young people's social lives and relationships. Stories of childhood in Butte are replete with accounts of the joys
and miseries of school days, of children's keen impressions of teachers
and fellow students, and of the ways in which lessons children learned
were not necessarily those being taught. Broader social and political
issues also played out in classrooms and school halls. At school, children
learned about and negotiated class and ethnic relations, lived experiences of belonging and difference, and became active consumers and
producers of popular culture. Vignettes of school experiences across the
decades offer windows into shifts and continuities over time.

Starting School

Schools and schooling played central roles in Butte's social and cultural
life. As Butte's workforce grew so did the neighborhoods, numbers of
children, and commitment to education. Six public and three Catholic
elementary schools were built in the first five years of the twentieth
century. Elementary schools took on the character of their neighborhoods, and many became centers of social life for children and adults
alike. For example, Franklin School opened in Meaderville in 1903. The
three-story building housed both an elementary school and, until the

1940s, a nursery school. From the start, the school sought to respond to the needs of its working-class, ethnically complex neighborhoods of Meaderville and McQueen. The Grant School, built in 1898 at 526 East Galena Street, served Butte's ethnically diverse East Side. Carl Gegurich described Grant School as "a dividing line in East Butte. All the Swedes and English lived on one side of the school, and the Croatians and Slovenians were on the lower side of the neighborhood on Cherry and Plum streets."[1]

Grant School fourth grade, 1916. John Laitinen, who grew up in Finntown and started at Grant School in 1916, remembered his school as a mix of Finnish, Cornish, Croatian, Slovenian, Serbian, Mexican, and Chinese students.

In the early 1900s, schools were the gathering points bringing together immigrant children and first-generation U.S. citizens in a cacophony of culture. For many Butte children, English was a second language, often learned through struggle upon entry into grade school. Children of immigrants described their experiences of shifting back and forth between English and their native tongue over the course of the day. Ann Pentilla's parents emigrated from Croatia, and Croatian was her first language. Ann recalled starting first grade: "I didn't talk the American language. A lot of children couldn't. Everyone talked their own language."[2] Ann was on the verge of failing first grade when a patient teacher by the name of Stella McGovern came to her aid. Ann retained her fluency in Croatian and, as the eldest child in her family, became the English teacher for her younger siblings.

GRANT SCHOOL

The Grant School on Butte's East Side held a special place in many childhood memories. The school was built on a "parcel of slag dirt that was hauled up from the tailings of the underground mine tunnels."[3] In its early days, Grant School housed five hundred first-graders through eighth-graders. John Laitinen, who grew up in Finntown and attended the Grant School, remembered his school as a mix of Finnish, Cornish, Croatian, Slovenian, Serbian, Mexican, and Chinese. However, it seemed all of his teachers were of Irish descent—with a McCarthy, Barclay, Mulholland, Greenough, and Price among them and Isabel Kelly as the school's longtime principal. Miss Kelly was a firm believer in schools as spaces for celebration as well as education. She instituted Halloween events at Grant School in which children showed off their homemade costumes in an all-school parade, marching from the school grounds through the neighborhood. Youngsters at Grant also celebrated St. Patrick's Day, a holiday dear to Miss Kelly's Irish heart. In the 1930s, the school drew national media coverage for its St. Patrick's Day celebration. According to the story, "My Wild Irish Rose" was sung by a Chinese student because none of the handful of Irish students at Grant knew the words.[4]

The school retained the ethnically diverse character of the surrounding neighborhood over time. But, as a latter-day principal of the school recalled, "Fights were very few about race but lots about football." Although their playground space was modest at best, Grant School children prided themselves on their athletic skills. The Grant School Bulldogs won the Class C football championship in 1930 and took home top honors in the citywide track meet in 1937. Sports standouts such as Eso Naranche and Milt Popovich got their start on the Grant School football team. Naranche, a beloved and talented Butte High football player, enlisted in the U.S. Army at the start of World War II and was killed in combat in Tunisia in 1942. Popovich, another Butte High football hero, played professional football for the Chicago Cardinals.

The youngsters' competitive spirit went beyond sports. According to a former principal,

> We always had a contest going on—marbles, . . . jump rope, yo-yo, jacks, hopscotch—and prizes were hard to get. The contests were between rooms or school wide. A Grant kid was a competitor. For prizes we collected for corporate America: soup labels, bottle tops, gum wrappers, etc. But the ends never justified the means 'cuz the Grant kids would go to any length to get a Coke cap. Dump garbage cans—never pick them back up, search saloons, maybe visit a supermarket and remove soup labels, etc. It finally became expedient to get prizes from the PTA.[5]

Grant School students enjoyed music, the arts, and pageantry. First-graders got to play in the rhythm band and perform at PTA events and school pageants. Parents were actively involved in the festivities, crafting finely hand-stitched

Ring-around-the-rosy on the school playground, circa 1910

Each year from 1936 to 1954, graduating eighth-graders at Grant School embroidered their names on the auditorium stage curtains. As alumni, many took pride in returning to show off their handiwork to their own children. Pictured here is the eighth-grade class of 1949.

Perhaps one of the most memorable features of Grant School was the auditorium stage curtains. Each year, graduating eighth-graders got to embroider their names on the curtains. Boys took sewing classes in their eighth-grade year to develop basic proficiency in embroidery. Girls took a home economics course as well, and some of the better seamstresses would lend a hand to boys who were daunted by needles and thread. Near the end of the school year, students were brought to the auditorium in small groups to complete the delicate embroidery.[7] The curtains were then rehung for graduation ceremonies. It was a fitting ritual to close out the elementary-school

Grant School football champs, 1932. One of the school's principals recalled that "Fights were very few about race but lots about football."

costumes for their youngsters. Over the years, school leaders sought to recognize and celebrate the cultural traditions of Grant students, with varying degrees of success. For example, there was the time that the principal welcomed a parent's request to bring a piñata to school to teach children about a Mexican tradition of celebration and provide the children a lesson in sharing. The principal enthusiastically organized a school assembly. He recalled:

> The piñata is in place on the stage controlled by a rope on a pulley. After the first swing, I thought, if that bat flies out of his hand, someone is going to get brained. We moved the piñata up and down to the gleeful squeals of 150 to 200 students. Remember, we are on the stage and the students are seated by grade one through six. That means when that candy hits the stage those Grant kids starved for sweets are going to invade. I had a funny feeling in my stomach. Suddenly, it broke, and the invasion was on. The stage was covered with paper-wrapped caramel kisses. Why no one got crushed in that onslaught only my guardian angel knows. One kid told me afterward that his feet never touched the ground. The stage was about three feet high—just right to crush first-graders. But, once again, peace was restored at the Grant School. A principal went wearily home much wiser.[6]

careers of youngsters who had taken to the stage in countless programs and performances over the years. The practice was initiated in 1936 and continued until 1954, accumulating hundreds of names. School alumni took pride in returning to the school to find their names and show their handiwork to their own offspring. Grant School eventually fell victim to the mining operations that ravaged Butte's East Side. The school was torn down in 1975. The curtains now hang in Hell Roaring Gulch, a historic mining town reconstruction that is part of the World Museum of Mining.

Aili Goldberg lived in Finntown and attended Grant School. Like Ann, English was Aili's second language. She recalled that "Mother never spoke a word of English. For a fact, I didn't either when I started the first grade here. But it wasn't unusual because it seemed like all the rest of us were in the same boat. We were the first generation, and the language was spoken at home. We didn't speak English at home."[8]

Mary Gussino Mencarelli remembered the difficulties that she and so many children at Grant and Franklin schools faced as they struggled to learn English: "My brother Joe and I really struggled in school. All my mother and father spoke at home was Italian. Yet, when we went to the Franklin School, all our teachers allowed us to speak was English. When we came home at night to do our homework, we could not receive any help from our parents because they did not know the English language. Joe and I were always shuttling between Italian and English."[9]

Some Butte children served as interpreters for their parents, while others were discouraged from speaking anything but English. Some children with stronger English language skills helped peers who were struggling. At times, children could only bear witness to their schoolmates' struggles. John Mazzola attended Grant School. A poignant memory of school days and the challenges of learning English stayed with him.

> I want to tell you about the kids from all these different ethnic countries. They all spoke Finnish, Serb, Croat, Italian. They came to school, and I'll tell you the teachers had a tough time because they had to teach those kids to speak English. There was one little kid, wonderful little Serb kid. He was reading the paper and everything, and he said, "The soldiers are marching down the street, hammer, hammer." Teacher came over and hit him on the knuckles with a ruler. She said "Read that right." "The soldiers are coming down the street, hammer, hammer." It was "hurrah, hurrah." And he couldn't pronounce "hurrah." And that was "hammer."[10]

In addition to their diverse languages, schoolchildren also brought other aspects of their cultural traditions to school, including their home remedies for childhood illnesses. Butte's winters were notoriously long and cold, and school buildings were rambling and drafty structures. Children trudged to and from school, taking in the toxic residues from the mines and the smelters. Along with their books and pencils, children also carried a host of preventative medicines and remedies with them. Lucille Sheehan grew up in the Italian community of Meaderville. Her mother used a concoction made with camphor to rub on the chest for a cold. If there was an epidemic, she sent Lucille to school with a chain of garlic around her neck. Steve Sherick, who grew up in McQueen, captured the ambience of a school full of children fending off disease:

> They'd rub your chest with Mentholatum or Vicks or just plain lard, put a piece of red flannel on top of that, then thread some garlic cloves and either put them around your neck or pin it on that flannel, and then send you to school. When you think of a class full of kids all that way . . . we must have smelled terrible. Here is this mongrel bunch of kids dressed with all of these home remedies. . . . And when you got a cough, my mother would mix a potion for it. It was three parts brandy, one part honey, and two parts lemon juice. She would put it in a little bottle to take to school. She always said to shake it before you'd drink it. So you'd get a little cough, you'd shake it, take a sip, the cough settled down. We were in third or fourth grade. The teachers never said anything. They just conducted the class. And I wasn't the only one carrying the little bottle when I had a cold. We were all like that.[11]

Catholic Schooling

The strong early influence of Butte's Irish immigrant community fueled the proliferation of Catholic education in the early 1900s, but the city's rapid growth in the early 1900s meant that school construction could not keep pace with the rates of student enrollment.[12] The start of Sacred Heart School is a case in point. The school, established to serve Butte's East Side, held its first classes on September 8, 1901. As Sister Mary Angelina Buckley described:

> That morning 147 children marched to the "gymnasium" which the City Drug Company had donated to be used as a school until better accommodations could be provided, and there seated on camp-stools they listened to the principal, Sister Mary Cecilia, as she efficiently organized the classes. Apparently everybody was happy, for to the oft-repeated question of the pastor, the Reverend J. J. Callaghan, "Isn't this the finest school you ever saw, children?" the enthusiastic and unanimous reply was, "Yes, Father." . . . Six weeks after the opening of the school, the Pastor appeared one morning and announced that he had "a fine new building." Immediately a line of marchers formed and triumphantly proceeded to . . . a recently vacated meat market. . . .

Sacred Heart School fieldball champions, 1936. From left to right are (front row) Ann McEnaney, captain Mary Sutey, Mary Dika, (center row) Betty Garland, Ann J. Spencer, Helen Susak, Betty Jo Rogers, (top row) Catherine Murray, Marrion Stanaway, Rosemarie Susak, Phyllis Ruthledge, and coach Irene Pappas.

Sacred Heart basketball team, 1926–1927. From left to right are Joe Murray, unidentified, Neamer Murray, Tuma Kiely, unidentified, B. Stanaway, and (first name not listed) Riely.

In November the basement of the new church was completed and furnished so it could be used as a temporary church on Sunday and a school during the week. Two classes occupied the sacristies; a portion of the church was curtained off, and there the school found its third site in three months. . . . Enrollment grew rapidly to 800. In December 1904 when the superstructure of the church had been completed, the entire basement was used as a school.[13]

Catholic high school education had its start with St. Patrick's School, above circa 1905, the first parish-based school to expand its curriculum beyond elementary school. St. Patrick's graduated its first high school class in 1896.

Catholic high school education had its start with St. Patrick's School, the first parish-based school to expand its curriculum beyond elementary school. St. Patrick's graduated its first high school class in 1896. Sister Mary Xavier Davey taught virtually every subject, from German to advanced trigonometry.[14] In 1904 Sacred Heart School began to offer a commercial high school curriculum, and St. Lawrence School soon followed suit. In 1907 Bishop John P. Carroll proposed a "central" Catholic high school to bring graduates of the school's seven Catholic grade schools together under one roof for their further education. Central Catholic High School opened its doors as a coeducational institution in 1908 under the direction of the Sisters of Charity of Leavenworth.

Sister Syra, the first superior of the school, recalled that first day of school in 1908:

> We had 170 students on the first day of school. And 170 students were all we could accommodate. However, that afternoon 10 husky boys reported for class. We told them that we had not desks or other facilities for them. One of them, John

Ward, acting as spokesman, said, "Sister, we don't care if we have to sit on the floor, we're going to go to school here." That settled it. They didn't have to sit on the floor, but they did have to double up with other students.[15]

It was not long before the new high school was overcrowded with students, but the economy of the World War I era hampered plans for building a larger school. Bishop Carroll was an advocate of separate schooling for high school boys and girls. With the completion of a new building, the high schools became sex segregated. In 1924 Boys Central High School opened under the tutelage of the Irish Christian Brothers, and the old high school was destined to become Girls Central High School. The commencement exercises at Central High School in 1926 brought an end to coeducation in Butte's Catholic high schools for the next forty-five years.[16]

Catholic education was a dominant influence in Butte. By 1924 Butte had nine elementary schools and two high schools run by the Irish Christian Brothers, the Sisters of Charity of Leavenworth, and the Sisters of Charity of the Blessed Virgin Mary. Children and adults alike talked about education in Butte in terms of a "public versus Catholic" distinction. As Helen Nicholls described, "There was the usual rivalry between Catholic schools and public schools. It wasn't violent, it wasn't cruel, but it was there. We always considered our schools better than their schools and vice versa."[17] This divide represented an important

The ball flies in a Butte High School versus Bozeman High School football game played at Columbia Gardens in 1910.

axis of belonging and difference in Butte. Both within and beyond schools, the distinction between "public" and "Catholic" created a meaningful shorthand for locating oneself in a larger scheme of community and belonging.

Rivalries and competition played out along those lines, perhaps best exemplified by the annual cross-town football game between Butte High School and Central High School, each vying for the title of city champion. The two teams met for the first time in 1915, and the game became a much-anticipated annual match-up. Although Butte High School dominated the rivalry, with thirty-five victories to Central's three between 1915 and 1960, Central was a determined competitor, and, for the most part, good sportsmanship reigned. During one pregame parade, the Butte High marching band stopped in front of the Knights of Columbus Hall and played the Butte Central fight song since Central did not have its own band at the time.[18]

Progressive Education

The education of Butte children was a community priority, as evidenced by the numbers of schools and size of enrollments. Young children throughout the city had access to neighborhood-based elementary schools. Butte High School was touted as one of the largest and most thoroughly equipped secondary schools in the Northwest. Butte High School students of the early 1900s had a choice among four courses of study: English, scientific, classical, and commercial. In addition, students could take part in a broad range of extracurricular activities ranging from sports teams to academic, athletic, and social clubs. Boys and girls alike took part in glee clubs, band and orchestra, and a host of organizations for those interested in drama, foreign languages, speech and debate, chemistry, journalism, and puppetry. A few student organizations were sex segregated, such as the all-male Student Senate and the all-female Etiquette Club. Opportunities in sports were broadly egalitarian in the early 1900s. While basketball and football dominated boys' sports, girls had opportunities to take part in the Athleta Club,

GOOD SPORTSMANSHIP?

Camaraderie and good sportsmanship fell by the wayside in 1939 when the pregame festivities for the cross-town match turned riotous. Mun Doran was a freshman at Central High School at the time. He recalled trouble beginning to brew after the bonfire and pep rally at Cinders Field: "They formed a snake dance at the Cinders and moved from the ball field straight up Park Street to the Uptown business district. The snake dance went into the American Candy Shop and the American Theater. After that, all hell broke loose in the area."[19]

As Patrick Kearney described in *Butte's Big Game*, young people began throwing eggs and rampaging in the streets. The police and fire departments were called in, but the crowd took over the fire trucks, turned the hoses on the firemen, and overturned a police car. They looted and vandalized thirteen downtown businesses that night. Once the dust settled the next day, business leaders and school administrators issued a statement: there would be no more Butte High–Butte Central city championship games until Butte youth could be counted on to behave themselves.[20]

which encouraged athletic participation for all girls, the swim club, and girls' basketball. Over the years, the possibilities for both boys and girls expanded to include golf teams, ski clubs, tumbling, tennis, and more.[21]

The accomplishments of Butte's schools and schoolchildren were a source of pride for Robert Young, director of the Butte Board of Education: "There are no brighter or better behaved children to be found in the entire country east or west than attend the Butte public and private schools. This is chiefly owing to the high character of Butte's laboring classes, of their respect for law and order, and their desire to see their children become intelligent, self-reliant, and law abiding citizens."[22]

Butte also embraced the progressive education movement with the opening of the new Washington Junior High School building in September 1915. Junior high students attended classes in Butte's city jail for a time as they awaited the opening of their new school building. The new school, which welcomed five hundred seventh and eighth grade boys and girls that fall, was Montana's first "fully organized" junior high school. It set high hopes for the possibilities of public education in the Progressive Era. Supporters of the junior high school described it as a "social laboratory in which the student no longer 'prepares for life,' as the older conceptions of education expressed it, but who actually participates in real life activities under proper guidance in the class room and shop."[23]

The new philosophy emphasized development of the "intellect, character, and skills" youngsters needed to succeed in a "new era." According to Leo King, Washington Junior High principal, "We live in an era of industrial, material, and inventive progress. The schools of the past were almost totally organized for the white-handed professionals, with little or no heed given to the great masses of industrial workers who are doing the world's work."[24] In contrast, the junior high intended to prepare boys and girls with vocational training and "industrial intelligence" as well as "literary and scientific intelligence."[25]

The junior high curriculum offered students a choice between a general high school preparatory course and a vocational course geared for those more likely to go to work than to high school. The vocational program offered courses in bookkeeping, mechanical drawing, woodworking, metalworking, printing, clerical work, carpentry, cabinetmaking, patternmaking, domestic science, dressmaking, and millinery, with students tracked along gender lines into preparation for "men's" and "women's" work.[26] On the surface, it appeared that progressive educators had crafted a program well suited for the children of Butte's vibrant working class. However, a closer look at schooling in the early 1900s reveals tensions between the goals of educators and the needs of families.[27]

Compulsory Education, Truancy, and a Struggle over Values

The progressive education movement championed compulsory school attendance laws to ensure that "future citizens" were prepared for their adult responsibilities. Montana, in line with national trends, passed compulsory education legislation in 1903. Despite most parents' desires to see their children educated, attendance requirements were not embraced by all Butte residents. Some youth actively resisted schooling. Some parents resented State involvement in the sanctity of the family. Others struggled with meeting the demands of state law and the needs of their families, whose livelihood depended on the labor contributions of children. While parents might value the idea of education, practical realities made other demands. Many children were getting real-world experience and "industrial intelligence" through their contributions in family enterprises rather than in the classroom. At times, these conflicting values and competing demands played out in truancy cases brought before Butte's longtime youth court judge Michael Donlan.

In a February 1911 case, thirteen-year-old Mary Palia appeared in Judge Donlan's court charged with truancy. The *Butte Miner* reported:

> It was charged that the girl had only been in school for 25 out of the past 110 days and she had been roaming around the streets at all hours of the night. Mrs. Palia attributed her inability to control her daughter to the fact that several other youngsters in the neighborhood had been sick with chicken pox lately. It was also reported that she had been allowed to attend shows uptown. The girl tearfully promised to mend her ways and go to school regularly. She was allowed to go home with her mother on the promise that she would attend school and cease her night roaming.[28]

On the court's docket that same day, Eugene Moriarity, age ten, and his brother Graten Moriarity, age fourteen, were also charged with truancy. According to the *Butte Miner*:

> Officer Gilligan said the boys had not attended school since December 12. The mother admitted that she had kept the boys out of school to help her make a living for them and several other small children. Mrs. Moriarity said her husband had deserted her and she had a hard struggle to exist. The woman was admonished that the compulsory education law must be complied with even if it was necessary for her to get some help from the county.[29]

The rights of parents, responsibilities of youth, and role of the court as enforcer of compulsory public education played out dramatically in Judge Donlan's courtroom in April of 1911. *Butte Miner* headlines read "School Boy Must Not Peddle Milk."

> That the compulsory school law must be complied with regardless of business considerations was explained yesterday morning by Judge Donlan to Mrs. J. Berryman of North Walkerville. The judge was quite emphatic in this declaration when Mrs. Berryman decried it impossible for her 14-year-old son Eddie to go to school for the reason that the family revenues depended upon the proceeds from a dairy business and it was necessary for the boy to drive the wagon on the early morning route and attend to other work in connection with the business.
>
> Mrs. Berryman said her husband at present is a cripple with rheumatism and could not do the work himself. The judge declared that the boy must go to school regardless of all other considerations and that if he did not he would be committed to the industrial school where he would be compelled to attend to his books.
>
> "You will not send him to the industrial school," declared Mrs. Berryman in a defiant tone of voice.
>
> "Be careful what you say, madam," said Judge Donlan, the warning being given in a firm tone of voice. "The law must be complied with in regard to this boy as well as other boys of his age. You must make some other arrangement for the peddling of that milk and this boy is ordered committed to the industrial school as you seem to have a disposition to defy the court's admonition to send the boy to school."
>
> Truant Officer Fox said the boy had not been to school for a month, and his parents seemed to imagine there was no way to compel him to go as long as his services were needed in the milk selling business.[30]

In contrast to truancy cases, some Butte youngsters did their utmost to stay in school even when family support for education was lacking and work obligations were looming. For example, Ann Pentilla's father did not see the value in high school education for his daughters. After completion of eighth grade, they were expected to go to work. Ann, however, was determined to further her education. "I went to business college. I worked as a cashier from twelve to eight in the morning and went to night school. I took me two years just to finish my bookkeeping course."[31]

Butte Business College, Normal and English Department, circa 1900

Frances Ferrian Lenz attended Sacred Heart and St. Patrick's schools as a child, where she excelled as a student. "The nuns made us learn those multiplication tables backwards, frontwards, and upside down." Frances's father had died when Frances was a little girl, and resources were scarce for her family. Upon completing eighth grade, Frances was determined to continue her education. She borrowed fifty dollars from an aunt to pay tuition for Butte Business College. While attending school, Frances worked as a live-in "nurse girl,"

Father Joseph Gilmore presided while family and friends overlooked the Sacred Heart eighth-grade graduating class of 1926.

running errands and doing chores for a family in exchange for board, room, and five dollars a month, which went to repaying her aunt.[32]

The son of a baker, John Sconfienza juggled school and work from the time he was a young child.

> I wanted to go to high school and play football, but the folks, they couldn't see that. You were just foolish to play football, so I went to business college. In fact, in the seventh grade the teacher flunked me because I didn't go dressed up. I figured I wasn't any better than the others, and I went with my copper-toed shoes. In them days to save your shoes, the parents had to put the copper toes on them. I went with my copper toes and a new pair of overalls. I didn't go dressed up. She flunked me. There was three or four of us that was flunked for not dressing up. We wasn't going to be sissies. We was tough guys.[33]

School Lessons

Butte children learned powerful lessons about culture, class, belonging, and difference through their school experiences. Children took measure of their teachers, forged bonds with their classmates, and learned much more than reading, writing, and 'rithmatic in the process. Butte residents' recollections of their school days provide provocative insights into what was taught, what was learned, and how children made sense of schooling.

Many folks described the close ties that formed among their neighborhood gangs during their elementary school years. Lula Martinez grew up in a Mexican family on Butte's East Side, where "the kids would all fight together, then eat together, and go to [Grant] School together."[34] With eleven children in the Martinez family and four more boarders in the household, Lula's mother prepared bottomless pots of beans and soup and managed to feed the kids in the neighborhood as well. John Laitinen was part of the East Side neighborhood gang, and he took part in a few rock fights and fistfights with Dublin Gulchers. "We fought after school each day on the hill up to the mines. These fights seemed to unite all of the East Side kids regardless of nationality."[35]

Catherine Hoy attended St. Mary's School, which served the Irish neighborhoods of Dublin Gulch and Corktown. For Catherine, school was a part of her rough-and-tumble neighborhood experience.

> Kids in school, you know how they fight. Maybe one got a little better grade than the other, and one, he was a little

St. Mary's School, above, served the Irish neighborhoods of Dublin Gulch and Corktown. The first-grade class is pictured here circa 1910.

smarter than the next one. Well, then they went up to the alley and fought it out, to really see which one of them won. They were really some gangs of kids, and, like I said, I don't know of anything nicer, a nicer way of life, than we had up there. . . . And then on Sundays we all went to church, went to Mass. That was our big day. And we all dressed up in our best clothes, high shoes, and our long, white dresses. Curly hair and so forth. We always managed. That's the one thing we did do, was to keep up our religion. Most of us graduated from St. Mary's School, went on to Central High School, and graduated from there.[36]

Hoy recalled that the nuns at St. Mary's "ruled the roost," managing fifty to sixty kids in a classroom with one teacher and a school that was cold and drafty with a boiler that was unreliable. "At one time, they used coal—they used all kinds of coal—and then the Anaconda Company got generous, and they piped steam from the Stewart Mine into St. Mary's School. So that warmed it, but that didn't warm it [much]. You still sat with your overshoes and coats on during school hours."[37]

Father Michael Hannan and St. Mary's eighth-grade graduating class, circa 1925

John Sheehy attended St. Mary's School and Boys Central High School. Education was highly valued in John's family, and he, too, found a passion for learning.

My mother and father, they didn't have much beyond an eighth-grade education. But they had lots of literature. They learned in Ireland very well in what they called "hedge schools." They had to have schools away from the English.

I was very good at school. I had no problems with it at all. I had a good memory in those days. St. Mary's School was staffed by sisters, and I remember some of them. In high school, it was all brothers. And, boy, I tell you, they were teachers, and they were tough.

I went to Butte Central and became a pretty good tumbler. Well, there was this brother, Brother McMahon, an amazing man. He was a great teacher. . . . He taught us how to build pyramids. And he taught dramatics. I acted in some plays. We used boys for girls. It would be at commencement at the end of the year when [the plays would be performed]. The plays were always Irish. We did one that was a very sad story about a woman who lived on the seacoast of Ireland, and she had six sons. She had lost five sons and her husband, drowned in the sea, out fishing. And the last one was going out. And he drowned, and they were bringing him home. That play was so sad. The old Irish woman sang, "They're all gone now.". . . And there was a line in it, you'd have to read it to get the Irish language out of it, but she said, "In the big world, old people die before the young, but in this place the young do the dying."

The *Resurrection of Dinny O'Dowd* was the other side of the coin. It was a comedy. This woman is being courted. She's a widow. She thinks she's a widow, and she is being courted by somebody or other. And along comes her husband. . . . It was kind of funny. And there were other plays like that. Let's see, Brother McMahon would have been in Ireland at the time of that great Irish dramatic development, of the Irish theater, people like Yeats. He was the most remarkable teacher I ever saw, that man. And the other brothers all had their own abilities. They were wonderful teachers as far as I was concerned.

And I did play football. I stayed out of high school for a year so I could play football. Between my junior and senior years, I stayed out of school, just sat around home. [I stayed out] so I could grow. I was only about 120 pounds as a junior, and I got up to about 140 or so when I played football. I played my senior year at Butte Central. I went to the library every day, which was really kind of a great thing because I just kind of assimilated all of that. I was also reading all of the newspapers. About Joe Brown and the great Joe Louis coming along as a great boxer . . . . So, I did lot of reading. I read all kinds of newspapers. And the Butte labor paper in those days was how I kept up on economics from the perspective of the working man.[38]

Aili Goldberg attended Grant School as a child. She and her siblings were responsible for getting themselves up in the morning because her mother left in the early morning hours to work in a nearby boardinghouse. The children counted on the support of neighbors for help getting ready for school. "My oldest brother wasn't very old either, but he had to hear the alarm clock to get us up to go to school. And a neighbor lady combed my hair or braided it, and it was such a fuss and holler that my mother finally had it cut. . . . I didn't care. Anything was better than having it pulled so tight that your eyes were just squinting."[39]

John Sconfienza began first grade at Holy Savior School, where he learned an unforgettable lesson in the power of a teacher over a vulnerable six-year-old. He also learned about the strength of his own will to stand up for himself and resist adult authority.

> I went to Franklin School. . . . Well, I started at Holy Savior. What happened was I raised my hand. I had to go. The sister shook her head. I don't know what the reason was. Then coming out just before lunch, coming down the steps, I made a mess. . . . I didn't go back because I dirtied my pants. Then old Father Pirnat come down here. I was back in the baker shop there, taking a bath in the old washtub. We had no bathroom or anything. [I was] in the old washtub. He begged me to go back, and I said, "No, I'm not going, and that's it." I was in the first grade. Six years old. So I didn't go back. . . . But I was mad at the sister.[40]

John T. Shea grew up in Corktown and attended both Blaine and St. Mary's schools. From young John's perspective, tough boys were easily bettered by tougher nuns. His teachers were stern disciplinarians who did not shy away from physical punishment as a means of classroom control.

> The thing is you never went home and told them you got hit. I can remember one day Sister Leonard gave me a wallop. It was right before lunchtime, and I must have done something wrong. I went home, and my dad was working the graveyard [shift] at the Emma [Mine], and he was up already, and he said to me, "Were you fighting at lunch? What happened to your face?" I couldn't lie to him, "Sister Mary Leonard slapped me." And I got one on the other side to match it. The nuns were tough, and I had the toughest nun in the room, Sister Mary Leonard.[41]

In contrast, John Mazzola found his teachers to be empathetic to the challenges their students faced. John went to Grant School, a home away from home for many kids from Butte's East Side. His teachers saw children's potential and brought out the best in them.

> The teachers bordered on sainthood. I'll tell you they had the patience of a saint with the children. They spent extra time with them. We were poor. We knew we were poorly dressed.

I don't know if they realized that some of us were not well fed. Although in my family we never missed a meal in our life, some of those kids were worse off, lots worse off than ourselves. One girl, a Scandinavian girl, would come to school in a man's coat, long underwear, and miner's boots. She never had anything—real poverty. It'd be forty-five-, fifty-below-zero weather, [and] she'd walk to school. And she still maintained her dignity. She turned out to be a lady and a princess . . . in spite of her humble beginnings. . . . Most of these kids turned out to be pretty darned good. We had doctors, we had lawyers, we had an astronaut from the East Side. We had scholars, poets, artists—I myself am a sculptor. I've been an artist all my life. Some were quite famous. They overcame their humble beginnings. . . . One thing about the Grant School, it produced some of the best athletes in the state of Montana. We had football players, we had basketball players, we had track men. I myself was a track man when I was a kid.[42]

Lula Martinez came up against the limits of Butte's mythic melting pot as an elementary school student. For Lula, school was a place where she was labeled as "different," not by her classmates but by her teachers.

As children we didn't know there was a difference, so we got along fine. It was when you're already between the ages of ten and eleven and going to school when the teachers started to say, "Well, you gotta sit over there. All the Mexicans sit on that side." And in those days they did, and then we found out that there was difference. . . . When I grew up in Butte and was going to school, there was a lot of discrimination.[43]

Perdita Duncan recalled parallel experiences with discrimination as a black child growing up in Butte. She experienced the everyday workings of racism as a child, such as not being able to attend white churches or eat in certain restaurants. Perdita was the only black child in her grade-school class. "They couldn't discriminate against just one person. We all sat in alphabetical order. I was a 'D,' and the 'Ds' were pretty close to the front." At the same time, she remembered that some teachers would not call on her in class. Her parents prepared her and her siblings for the realities of racism and attempted to instill a strong sense of pride and identity. As Perdita remembered, "I learned very early that I was a colored girl growing up in a white community and that my name was Perdita Duncan. After that, nobody could crush me." Perdita described the racism in Butte as "subtly done. You were just kept out of certain places, and by the time I was coming along, there were still certain places I couldn't go, and I just never bothered."[44]

Kay Antonetti grew up in an Irish Catholic family in the ethnically mixed Big Butte neighborhood located in the northwest corner of Butte. She attended Immaculate Conception School and Girls Central High School. She loved her school. At the same time, she never forgot the harsh lessons offered by one of her teachers at the expense of her classmates.

> We made our First Communion in a little tiny chapel that was in the basement, before the big church was built [in 1938], and that was lovely. I had wonderful nuns except for the one in the sixth grade. She was terrible. My dad always used to say she must have been pushed into the convent. She didn't want to go, you know? Maybe she had a bad love affair that fell through, and she went into the convent. . . . I remember one day we had this one girl who later became a Maryknoll missionary, and she was kind of a tomboy. She came to school, and she had painted her fingernails, and the polish was all over. And Sister made her stand in front of the statue of the Blessed Mother all day with her hands out like this [shows her arms extended, palms down], saying that she was sorry that she did that. Sister told her that the Blessed Mother would never do that to herself. So the poor girl stood there all day like this, and then she'd start to put her hands down, and Sister would shout, "Put those hands up." And another day a boy . . . a really nice kid . . . I don't know what he did, but he was reciting something. He was up in front of the room. Sister had a book in her hand, and she took it, and she hit his head against the book, just back and forth. Well, the next morning we were standing, saying our prayers, and the door was closed. All of a sudden that door flew open, and here comes the mother and the son. I thought the mother was going to hit the nun.[45]

Linda Raiha had fond memories of her first-grade teacher who helped her through a hard year. Linda's mother was pregnant and had given birth to a baby girl who was stillborn. Her mother was in the hospital for a period of time, and her father was trying to work and manage the children at home. Linda missed a lot of school that year and was at risk of being held back. With her determined effort and her teacher's support, Linda was promoted to second grade. Linda came to love school. She had lots of friends and, as the eldest of eleven children, found school to be a place where she did not have to be responsible for taking care of her younger siblings.[46]

Robert Hole longed to be in school with his classmates. He was one of several Butte children who had been diagnosed with rheumatic fever in the late 1940s. Robert and nine other youngsters were hospitalized in a special ward at St. James Hospital. He spent three years in the hospital, from 1947 to 1950, confined to bed. Robert credits the "Heart Fund," the American Heart Association's rheumatic fever program launched in 1946, for providing the resources for care that his family otherwise could not afford. He recalled:

> I was all by myself. I can remember there was a divider with a curtain separating the beds. I can remember there was a girl next to me, and she finally died. There were ten of us, and I was the only one who lived. . . . None of those kids gave up. They all died because they couldn't cure them. . . . You know how the Heart Fund cured me? They took my blood out of me and gave me a blood transfusion. . . . That saved my life. And what also saved my life was penicillin. I was taking pills and shots of penicillin, one thousand units twice a day. . . . When I got the fever, I was going to Franklin School at the time. We had moved to Meaderville. Then when I come back out of the hospital—that was three years—it made me three years behind in school, so I was always two and a half years older than all my classmates. So at my eighth-grade graduation I was two years older than the other kids.[47]

Tom King attended grade school in Butte in the 1950s. At about age seven, he began to experience epileptic seizures, as many as thirty or forty a day. Tom liked school as a child and fondly remembered teachers who took him under their wing. "The McNelis sisters lived on Woolman Street, where I used to live. They were teachers. One of the sisters, Sarah, taught at the high school. And Mary taught elementary school. Mary would walk me to school. She would come down about two blocks and I would come up about two blocks, and we would meet and walk up together. She wanted to make sure that I didn't have a seizure going up to school. She really helped me a lot."[48]

Tom also recalled being ostracized at times because teachers or fellow students did not understand his illness. Tom was not allowed to take part in physical education classes, so he joined the drama club and played the trumpet in the junior high band. When he went to high school, however, Tom was denied entry into the Butte High School marching band due to his epilepsy.

For some children, the classroom provided entrée to a world apart from the rather bleak landscape of the Mining City. Karen Butler's best memory of school came from the fourth grade when she took part in the Bird Club.

> I still meet kids in town who recognize each other from the Bird Club. You know, Goldfinch Hannah and Bluebird Rudy.... The teacher [organized] it, and we just studied all these different kinds of birds. And we had a president and a treasurer and all those kinds of things. I don't think we ever went outside. It was all book learning. Outside was not all that great in Butte at that time 'cause there wasn't a lot of grass and trees.... I remembered as a child reading books about kids walking down the street and kicking the leaves, you know, or raking the leaves in the fall and jumping in them. It was just foreign to me. We had no leaves, so the Bird Club didn't go outside looking for birds.[49]

When former students reflected on the move from their neighborhood elementary schools to junior high or high school, many recalled the profound culture shock they experienced as they entered these more cosmopolitan spaces. Young people were pushed out of the comfort zones of their tight-knit neighborhoods that, for many, had constituted their "whole universe." Some, especially youngsters who spent their grade-school years in neighborhoods comprised largely of mining and other working-class families, described becoming conscious of class differences for the first time. They encountered fellow students who drove cars, sported new clothes, and ate lunches made with store-bought bread. Some gingerly branched out and built new friendships, and others held on tight to their neighborhood gangs as they negotiated this unfamiliar terrain.

Aili Goldberg described her entry into Butte High School:

> There was definitely a class distinction in high school. Because if you were from the East Side, you were from the East Side. That was different from somebody... from Snob Hill, over there on the West Side.... There were just different classes [in high school]. You weren't included in any of their social activities or anything. It would be a rare day that you would be invited to anything when they had social functions at home. But it seemed like we never cared to cross that line anyway. We were happy on our own.[50]

Girls Central High School students wore simple blue-serge uniforms, which, ostensibly, served to blur class distinctions marked by clothing. The girls, however, were aware of the nuances of class, noting how they could tell the difference by "the sweaters they wore and stuff like that." Many girls could afford only one uniform: "You would air them on the weekend. You can imagine what we must have smelled like with all that wool."[51] Helen Bush attended St. Patrick's School and Girls Central. She recalled that tuition was $5.00 a month or $7.50 for two children in the same family.

> We wore uniforms, and in the four years of going to Central
> I had a brand-new uniform [to start], and then when I was
> a senior, I got a new uniform, and then that passed on to my
> sister, so we ended up with three uniforms between the two
> of us for eight years of schooling. . . . It was a jumper, a navy
> blue jumper with a plain top and pleats. [The pleats were not]
> from the waist down; they were inserted maybe four inches
> apart, and they hung below the waist. You know, it was a flap
> around the front and the back and the pleats and then just a
> plain white, short-sleeved blouse. And we did have a couple
> of blouses each, but we really struggled to even get through
> Central. And it doesn't sound like very much money, but at
> the time it was.[52]

Teaching and Learning: Miss Marguerite MacDonald's Classroom

Memories of childhood from an adult point of view reveal powerful impressions of schools and schooling, but children's own writings about their families and social worlds provide poignant and prescient insights into their lives. Longtime Blaine School teacher and principal Marguerite MacDonald preserved some of the writings done by her students in the 1920s. Their words illuminate ways in which children observed and made sense of class distinctions, coped with poverty and inequality, and made social assessments and moral judgments.

For example, a 1925 essay about young Theodore's longing for long pants reveals his awareness of the markers of class as well as age differences. "I would like long pants to wear on Sunday. They look nice on the children who wear them. The children who wear them are not very poor. Their mothers and fathers have good jobs and make all kinds of money. I can not have long pants till I am older. There are very few people wearing long pants. One Sunday I watch the boys going down

Washington Junior High, Butte's first middle school, opened in September 1915. The boys in short pants in this circa 1920 graduating class call to mind young Theodore's essay expressing his longing to exchange his short pants for long ones.

with long pants on. Six went down with short pants on and 1 with long pants on," he wrote. While long pants might be indicators of "growing up," for Theodore they also marked a distinction between the "haves" and "have-nots."[53]

Mike Milji's response to Miss MacDonald's 1926 "letter to Santa" assignment offered more than an opportunity to practice spelling. The letter provides a window into his childhood world. His appeal to Santa Claus speaks to cautious hope in the wake of past disappointment and modest expectations for a hard-earned gift.

> I hope you will bring some thing to my house. I would like to get some books to read. Please do not bring me any toys or any skats because I do not know how to skat. I only want two or three books. Do not bring much things because you will not have any thing for the boys and girls. I have bean good to my mother and father. I bring coal and wood when my mother tells me to. I can not bring it in when I am gone out. My brother has to then. I hope you will remember me when I was to the flat. Then you came and gave me a string full of candy. You will come to my house this year because you did not last year.

Miss MacDonald took his request to heart, and it seems that she intervened on young Mike's behalf, perhaps encouraging a classmate to pass along her books to Mike. While appreciative, Mike was also confused by the gesture and the possible meanings behind it.

Dear Elisibeth,

I think you where very good to give me three books for Christmas. I like every one of them. Miss Macdonild was telling how good the book of North ward ho was.

I do think you was very kind to give me them. I was redding of Tresuier Island. I do think it is vary vary vary good. I was thinking why you sent them books to me. I let my brother read the books to. Will you please right me a letter telling me why you sent me the books you can give the letter to the princabil or sent it to my house. I thank you vary vary vary much.

Some items in MacDonald's collection of children's work capture the students' understanding of morality, practical ethics, and audience, as illustrated in responses to their teacher's 1926 assignment "What is the best (and worst) thing a child can do?" Peter Stokina wrote: "The Best thing a child can do is to sit in position and do what His teacher tells him to do. The very worst thing a child can do is clog the toilets."
According to Doris,

The best thing a child can do is to be polite when a person's speaking to them. If your reading a book when a teacher come in to talk to you you should close your book and listen. Why I think this is because what she says is important and she wants you to know it.

The very worst thing a child can do is to talk back at their mother or father or tell your mother to be still. Why I think this is because you only have one mother and father and should be good to them while their living.

Miss MacDonald also provided children with opportunities to comment on trends of the times. Her students were keen observers of 1920s popular culture. The Roaring Twenties brought the age of jazz, entertainment on the silver screen, and a newfound freedom of expression. Millions of movie fans across the country were captivated by Rudolph Valentino in *The Sheik* (1921). The dangerous and sensual image of the sheik was matched by a "new breed" of young woman, the flapper, who wore her hair bobbed and her skirts short, who listened to jazz and smoked cigarettes, and who took pleasure in flouting the gendered rules of social behavior.[54] High school girls in Butte were sporting bobs and Marcel waves. Butte High band teacher Madam McPherson would not permit any saxophone in her band, claiming the instrument was "too sexy." Butte elementary schoolchildren were swept up in the moment as well, finding themselves at once repelled by and attracted to these seductive images of young manhood and womanhood. Their judgments of sheiks and flappers suggest careful and detailed observation.

Rosie Jecevich wrote her essay on "My Idea of a Sheik":

My idea of a sheik is, the sheik wears silk shirts some wear sweaters. Some do not wear hats. They have side burners down to their cheeks. They wear balloon pants. They wear silk stocking low shoes and long pants. There stocking are rolled all the way down to there ankles. They have rings on their both hand and a wrist watch. They wear powder. They smoke "Old Gold cigarettes." They only smoke half of the cigarette and then throw it away. Some of them have there pants laced up in back. They wear the belts with there name on it. What I like to see is when a flapper and a sheik get together the flapper giggles. It sounds like she is squealing. When he is laughing he laughs in a low voice. It sounds like a laughing record. When a flapper and a sheik dance they twist around and the flapper's dress goes out flat. You can see her rolled stockings. The sheik's pants go out at the bottom it is a lot of fun to see them dance.

George Williams titled his paper "Flappers":

A flapper is a girl that goes around with her head up in the air. She wears lipstick an eighth of an inch thick on her lips. And rouge all over her cheeks. They wear their dresses short and you can see their fancy garters with tassels on. They pull their coats from one side to the other. When you see them dancing they wear flare bottom skirts and they go out like an umbrella. They wear those little kiss curls that comes out the side of their head. And when you speak to them they say "hellew." The one I saw was going like anything. And her heels went clip clip on the sidewalk.

Millicent Bennetts also wrote about flappers:

The flappers nowadays are very rude. They wear their dresses too short. They wear little bob curls. The flappers use powder and lipstick. The flappers carry compack. They keep their money in their stockings. The girls have high heels. The men are fancy too. The flappers talk so queer. They sometimes say, "he lo" for "hello." The underwear has pockets so they may put anything in it. I wouldn't mind being a flapper myself. The blumers are green, pink, red, peach, yellow, and purple. They are not old fashioned. They pull their coats in and it shows their shape. I think Miss Matthews is a flapper because she has her hair bobbed. She has it curled. Has very pretty dresses. They are short like the flappers. I think she will always be a flapper.[55]

Political Education

Schools were also sites where Butte youngsters learned broader lessons in politics and economics affecting the community, state, and nation. Examples drawn from across the decades reveal ways in which school settings were variably used to instill "American values," encourage cultural pride, and discourage deviant tendencies. They also illustrate how children and youth experienced and made sense of broader political, economic, and social forces and events shaping American lives.

The intense political climate at the time of the United States' entry into World War I offers a case in point. Popular support for entry into the war was weak in Butte, where a large immigrant workforce was wary of President Woodrow Wilson's desires for U.S. political and economic expansion. Critics and resisters of the war effort soon found themselves censored, and in 1917 the U.S. Espionage Act was passed, making it a crime to speak against the State. Following the national trend, the Montana Council of Defense and a host of local councils were organized in 1917. Their focus soon shifted to pro-war propaganda and the censorship and criminal prosecution of those who questioned the United States' involvement in the war, fostering strong anti-German sentiment and a climate of suspicion.[56]

Schoolchildren were directly affected. German language classes were banned, and in some parts of the state children were called upon to participate in the burning of textbooks that had references to German history and Teutonic civilization.[57] All Montana libraries were ordered to destroy such books as *Writing and Speaking German, German Songbook, A Summer in Germany,* and *First German Reader.*[58] Lesson plans around the country were being reconfigured by the Committee on Public Information propaganda. As Clemens Work described in *Darkest before Dawn* (2006), in Montana required eighth-grade history curriculum for 1918 included sections on "Why America Entered the

War," "The German Autocracy," and "The War Message and the Facts Behind It."[59]

In Butte, store manager Alma Swift had made the obligatory purchase of a liberty bond but refused to volunteer her time in the 1918 bond campaign, stating, "Nothing doing. Let the profiteers pay for that." In response to her refusal, her boss threatened to fire her and to have her sister, a Butte grade-school principal, investigated. Miss Swift backed down and subscribed for a fifty-dollar liberty bond but was still let go from her job.[60]

Writings of children and youth in Butte schools reveal both heightened attention to patriotism and response to the anti-German sentiment of the times. For example, the following piece, written by a Butte High School student, was published in the 1918 school yearbook, *The Mountaineer.*

The Sentiments of a Loyal American of German Birth

A—iss Autocracy
A pain it me gifs.
B—iss der Brute
Vot in Chermany lifs.
C—iss a Coffin
Dot's all he vill get.
D—iss Democracy
Der best vot iss yet.
E—shtands for Eitel,
Der son unde der heir.
F—iss die Frenchmen
Dey sent dem home leer
      (empty).
G—iss for gans (goos)
His gans ist gecooked.
H—iss for Hoch,
But no more he'll be hoched.
I—means Insane
Dot's der poy Eitel Fritz.
J—means die Junkers
Ach Donner und Blitz.
K—iss der Kaiser
Who says "Mee und Gott."
L—He's a Lugner
For talking such rot.
M—iss for Murder
In vich Jounkers shine.

N—dot Narr Wilhelm
Iss no friend of mine.
O—he's ein Ochs (ox)
He boasts qvite a lot.
P—iss for Potsdam
It's going to pot.
Q—iss no Qvestion
Dot Wilhem gets likt.
R—iss der Rock
He vil git ins Genick (neck).
S—iss die Strafe (punishment)
He's giving poor France.
T—iss for Taugenichts
      (worthless),
Ve'll schlagen his pants.
U—iss der U-boat
Mit no trace may dey sink.
V—shtands for Victory,
Hey vot you tink?
W—iss die worlt
Full mit blood and mit tears.
X—iss der double-cross,
Vich eferyone fears.
Y—iss our Young Men,
Dey go now to fight.
Z—iss die Zeit (time)
Ven Right Will Beat Might.[61]

At times, schools also served as powerful sites for education in cultural identity and politics. St. Mary's School provides an intriguing example. Attached to St. Mary's Parish, St. Mary's School opened its doors in 1904. The school encompassed the heart of Butte's Irish community. Father Michael Hannan came to the parish first in 1906. After a brief stint away from Butte, Hannan returned to lead the parish from 1912 until his death in 1928. As William Fischer described in his thesis on the parish, Hannan took a strong interest in parishioners, knew all of the children, and had a deep concern for the poor. He was known for his personal visits to the homes of the ill and bereaved. Hannan was also a militant champion of the cause of freedom in Ireland.[62]

Under Hannan's guidance, the children of St. Mary's Parish were young recruits into the cause of Irish independence. The school incorporated Irish history and Gaelic language classes into the curriculum. Schoolchildren were a receptive audience to plays addressing the struggle for Irish independence, such as *The Trial Scene and Vindication of Robert Emmett,* performed by parish members. Key players in the movement for a free Ireland were regular visitors to the church and school, and the scholarly life of St. Mary's pupils was intimately bound to the politics of Irish nationalism. In addition to donning their Sunday dress to welcome Irish independence leader Eamon de Valera in 1919, St. Mary's students sang a rousing version of "Irish Freedom" to honor the 1921 visit of Mary MacSwiney, sister of freedom fighter Terence MacSwiney, who died in 1920 as a result of a hunger strike.[63]

Butte schoolchildren learned powerful lessons in political economy during the Great Depression. Their stories of school days during hard times also speak to young people's resilience, determination, and uncertainty. Work was scarce, so more young people in Butte were staying in school.[64] Butte High School began to run two shifts a day in order to accommodate the increased number of students. Others sought opportunities in New Deal youth programs. Former district court judge Arnold Olsen graduated from Butte High School in 1934. He recalled:

Some classmates quit to join WPA and CCC projects, working on Harding Way, sewers, the football bowl east of Montana Tech, and sidewalk paving. Some boys went on the bum and lived in hobo camps. A few went to gold camps in California, which were about the only mines operating at the time. Those who stayed in school seemed to do better in the long run. Some were in such deep poverty that they never recovered. . . . Sewing rooms at the Arizona Street and Caledonia Street fire stations were another WPA project which provided many of the clothing and shoes worn by students.[65]

Shoes and clothing were precious items, requiring care. As Olsen's classmate Marge Rowling remembered, "I had one blouse, which I pressed every day."

The Butte High Class of 1934 kept traditions alive, though, complete with the prom in the spring. Girls wore second-hand dresses, boys wore hand-me-down suits, and "only the rich had corsages." They danced the night away, displaying their prowess for waltzes, foxtrots, and the chicken scratch, a variation of the Charleston, danced to the tune of the "Twelfth Street Rag."[66]

John Sheehy was in high school during the depths of the Depression.

> I graduated in 1936. What I remember was day to day things. I enjoyed school. I was happy there. And it was kind of an escape, too. . . . We were very clannish and very aware of the fact that we were not high mucky mucks. It is kind of hard to describe. We were in a very poor poverty situation, and that had to affect us. At that time, in 1936, nobody on the north side was going to go to college. That just was not in our future, unless you were going to be a priest. The only two people who did go to college, just before the war, were myself and Jack Walsh, who came to Carroll [College], a very smart boy. In my case, there had never been the thought in our house about going to college. I would probably head for the mines as all my neighbors did.
>
> My father did not want us to work in the mines. None of my brothers worked in the mines. What I want to get across here is that nobody on that north side ever had the thought of going to college. . . . But in 1936, just before my graduation from high school, well, I went out to the prom at Columbia Gardens. On the way back, our car was struck by a driver from the other side, and our car went around behind him somehow. I guess he hit the front wheel. We went down over a cliff to the streetcar tracks below. I was the only one hurt in the car. I slashed my wrist. . . . All through the summer months I was wrapped up in bandages and such. In September, right about a day before college opened, my father came in and said, "You've got to go to college." Just like that. And very quickly, the family got together.[67]

John attended college first at Montana State University in Missoula and then at the Montana School of Mines in Butte. He pursued a law degree, practiced as an attorney for many years, and went on to serve as a justice of the Montana Supreme Court. As he described, it was a twist of fate that turned what had previously been an unimagi-nable future into a reality.

With the United States' entry into World War II, schoolchildren in Butte and around the country were called to patriotic duty. Memories of the war years provide telling examples of the ways in which national politics become part of children's lives. Recitation of the Pledge of Allegiance became a daily practice in Butte schools. Schoolchildren were recruited into the buying and selling of U.S. savings stamps and bonds. Children took their responsibilities seriously as they joined in the collective effort. "On Stamp Day, Mabel Erickson, our third grade teacher, sold us stamps, which we licked and pasted into little blue booklets," Edward Jursnich wrote in his memoir of childhood on Butte's East Side. "The stamps were ten cents each, and when the booklet was filled, it was worth $17.80. It could be taken to the bank and exchanged for a bond, which, at maturity in ten years would be valued at $25.00."[68] Children also participated in community-wide scrap drives, and schools were designated collection sites for scrap iron, copper, steel, and rubber.

Older youth found themselves facing adult decisions regarding military service. John Mazzola enlisted at age seventeen.

> I was supposed to graduate in June of 1943, but in February of '43 I got patriotic. I thought, "Well, this war is going to be over. I want to help my brothers, and I want to help my country, too." So I joined. I went and enlisted. Anyway, it was a common thing for us. You'd be surprised how many of my schoolmates did the same thing. Get up in the middle of a class and just walk out and go to join the army or go in the navy. Some even came back and sat in the classroom and got their diplomas. I had enough credits, so they gave my sister my diploma.[69]

For a single year, 1945, the Butte High School yearbook changed its name to *The Salute*. Its dedication is a sobering reminder of the cost of war in lives of young people: "This is a Salute to those who have gone and to those who will go; to those who will return, and to those who will not. May God bless them wherever they may be."[70]

Political education took a different turn at Immaculate Conception School in the postwar era. As fears of Communism swept the nation, teachers and parents at the school mobilized around another presumed evil—comic books. Their concerted efforts were under way by the spring of 1944, when Sister Aurea gave a spirited talk to the parent-teacher organization on the dangerous nature of such subversive reading, and a group of seventh-grade Thespians performed a play on the evils of comic books. The subject remained a pressing concern one year later as Sister Mary Annuncio and Sister Aurea again addressed the parent-teacher meeting regarding the dangerous effects of comics upon young, impressionable minds. A resolution calling for greater vigilance about children's reading material was introduced and adopted by the group.[71]

In March 1948 a group of fifth-graders took to the stage with their lively original play about a righteous angel defeating the evil of comic books. That fall the PTA invited Sister Mary Corita of Chicago to offer her insights on the deplorable nature of the "wide circulation of inferior comic books."[72] By April 1949 the PTA had invited an agent of the FBI to speak on juvenile delinquency. While the minutes of the meeting are scanty, one might wonder if he, too, made the insidious connections among comics, crime, and Communism. Finally, in 1953 the PTA made the connection between comics and Communism explicit. As the PTA minutes described: "The menace of Communism was recognized by the Catholic Press long before it was acknowledged by the secular press. Since PTA mothers are banded together for good, we cannot be mediocre. . . . Mothers should take active part in discussion clubs and active resistance to indecent literature. Mothers are responsible for what their children read. We need good reading at all ages. We are what we read."[73]

The concerns voiced by the nuns and parents of Immaculate Conception resonated with growing adult fears across the nation regarding the "youth problem" in the postwar era.[74] Comics, introduced in the 1930s with the invention of the "superhero," had gained widespread popularity. Following World War II, comics took on a new dimension, with superheroes gaining novel atomic powers.[75] By the late 1940s and early 1950s, however, the growing popularity of crime and horror comics had stirred adult fears.

By 1948 anti–comic book anxieties were topics of school and church meetings around the country. They were further fueled by the work of psychiatrist Fredric Wertham, who, in a series of articles in popular magazines, argued that comic books were a stepping stone to delinquency, violence, and corrupt morals. Boycotts, censorship, and organized comic book burnings around the country followed. In 1954 three days of congressional hearings were held on the impacts of comics on impressionable young readers and the presumed links between comics and delinquency.[76] While there is no evidence that the Immaculate Conception PTA advocated burning of comic books, they were surely on the cutting edge of concern about the corrupting effects of comics.

Immaculate Conception School was not unique in its preoccupation with Communism and the future of its students. John McGinley attended St. Joseph School during the 1950s. As John recalled, Cold War concerns overshadowed creativity.

> Beyond cutting and pasting construction paper, coloring in a coloring book, church choir, and piano lessons for the gifted few, there was very little exposure to art in the Catholic education system of the 1950s Butte, Montana. *Sputnik* was circling the earth, and any child with an IQ in the triple digits (or even mid-range doubles) was being groomed to be a priest, nun, or possibly a great Catholic scientist who would go forth and meet the Red Menace face to face in the cold reaches of outer space.[77]

And the Band Played On

Music and musical education were central parts of the social and cultural worlds of children in Butte. John Mazzola developed an affinity for opera at his grandmother's side. Jule McHugh, Kay Antonetti, and John Sheehy recalled the fiddle tunes and dancing of Irish shindigs in their family homes. Kevin Shannon turned his fine-tuned ear for Irish music into a childhood musical career. And generations of Butte children developed their musical appreciation and talent alongside Gina Rubatto Zanchi, a remarkable musician and educator. Zanchi was born to Italian immigrant parents in 1915 and came with them to Butte when she was eighteen months old. She grew up in the Italian neighborhood of Meaderville, speaking both English and Italian. Her father worked in the mines and her mother in Lucina's boardinghouse, which became a second home to Gina.

Music was an important part of Zanchi's childhood. Both of her parents loved to sing, and the family owned a piano. Gina began to take piano lessons at age ten. Gina was a dedicated student, under the watchful tutelage of her mother and Mrs. Wolette. Gina performed publicly for the first time at age fourteen, playing in a trio with a saxophone player and accordionist at the Rochina Calvetti boardinghouse in Meaderville.[78] That was the start of a weekly dance gig for which the trio was paid.

When Gina finished grade school, she did not go on to high school in Butte. Instead she moved to Salt Lake City, Utah, to study accordion. Her family had taken a train trip to Salt Lake City and had met a master teacher who happened to live in the rooming house where the family had stayed.

Music played an important role in Butte family and school life. This 1913 cameo with banjo came from the family page of Jim Hanley's photograph album.

Gina pleaded with her parents to let her return and study with him. As Gina described, "He had such expression. . . . He played from the heart and soul. And you just had to learn that. He was just great. I can't tell you. You know how some people can project some feelings? That was the way he was. He'd play, and it was just beautiful, just beautiful." And so Gina's parents gave their teenage daughter permission to travel alone by train, live with the family who ran the boardinghouse, and study accordion from a master teacher. Gina stayed for nearly two years and described that as a magical time of nothing but music, music, music.[79]

At age seventeen, Gina returned to Butte and took over as the director for the St. Helena Parish choir. She performed in bands and was part of a local orchestra. Within a few years, she began her long career as an accordion teacher. A number of her students went on to play in bands, including the forty-member accordion band that Gina

The Butte High School Band won the coveted slot of Honor Band in the 1948 Tournament of Roses Parade in Pasadena, California. One year later, the band was photographed when leaving for Portland, Oregon, where it led the Rose Festival Parade.

directed. Steve Sherick, who grew up in McQueen and began performing at the Alaska Bar as a youngster, was one of Gina's top students.[80]

Henry Schiesser, longtime director of the Butte High School Band, was also a demanding and dearly beloved teacher. The band he directed was the pride and joy of Butte. It was, on the one hand, a great equalizer, bringing young people from Butte's diverse communities together in harmony. It was also an elite group that prided itself on top-notch talent and reputation. Henry Schiesser served as the music director for the Butte public schools from 1939 to 1957. He was born in Iowa and grew up in Chicago. He was a child prodigy on the violin. Orphaned at age twelve, Henry made a living playing violin in Chicago movie theaters and other musical venues while earning a degree in music education from Vandercook College. During the Depression, he took a job as a music teacher in Glasgow, Montana, where he met Jean, the woman who was to become his wife in 1938. Jean earned her musical degree from Willamette University, and the couple moved to Butte with their infant daughter Karen in 1939.[81]

The Schiessers became a musical institution in Butte, with Henry creating a marching band and symphony orchestra with a national reputation, Jean serving as artistic director and choreographer, and Karen marching up front, a diminutive majorette nearly from the time she could walk. In fact, when the Butte High School Band won the coveted slot of Honor Band in the 1948 Tournament of Roses Parade in Pasadena, California, young children were not allowed to march in the parade. The Schiessers had to get special permission from the parade officials to allow nine-year-old Karen to march. They sent proof that Karen had marched her first five-mile parade with the band at age four in Butte and was a veteran of many long parades. Karen was the youngest person to march the entire distance of the Pasadena Rose Parade—which she did while twirling two batons.[82]

The trip to the Rose Bowl parade was an unforgettable time for the 136 members of the band. The trip was funded in part through subscriptions by Butte residents. It was the first time a band outside California had been named the Honor Band. The Butte youngsters performed before a crowd of 1.5 million people along the parade route. On their return trip, the band performed before a crowd of twenty thousand in downtown Las Vegas. They marched fifteen blocks through streets "lined deep" with spectators, then played a twenty-minute concert in the heart of the city. The Las Vegas chief of police claimed, "I have never seen so many people up so early in this 24-hour city."[83] The band was greeted with a homecoming celebration complete with fireworks when it arrived in Butte on January 3, 1948.

Henry Schiesser was known as a strict disciplinarian, demanding nothing less than the best from band members. At the same time, letters sent from former band members to Schiesser reveal the close bond some students developed with him over the years. Particularly poignant are letters from young servicemen during World War II. For example, a handwritten letter to Henry, Jean, and Karen from a young serviceman named Ray reveals the sense of familial bond that some band members felt for the Schiessers. Connection to Butte, the band, and the Schiessers provided a lifeline to a time of youthful innocence for young people living the realities of war.

Thursday, March 1, 1945

. . . I spend most of my spare time now looking back at when I was in the band and orchestra. Those were the golden days. Not a care in the world and just living from one rehearsal to the next. Sure would like to be there now. I heard "Overture 1812" over the radio the other nite and it sure brought back fond memories. A yr. ago at this time I could have sat right down and played my old part right thru, but I'm afraid that's all past history too now. I spend some of my time each day tooting on an old battered up coronet that one of the boys had, and I can't even remember the easy parts anymore. Remember how easy it was for me to memorize a solo? Now I don't even remember any of them any more. I'll sure be in an awful hole when I get out of this navy. I know you won't be able to write me until it's all over with so I'll ask a few questions sort of pointed at a month from now.

How did the solos and the "double trio" come out? There is no doubt in my mind but what they did excellent. Is Willie playing as good as you thought he would be this time? I sure do miss playing over his lessons with him and also that march music you used to lend me. I know we could sure use some good stuff like that out here right now.

Bill was home not so long ago. Did you find out what kind of set up he is going to have? What I really want to know is this—is he going to be on a ship or a shore station? . . .

Guess that by this time I have competition with Karen going to school. Before I get to see her again, she'll have a list of boyfriends a yd. long. Anyway she's still first on my list. I'm sort of at a disadvantage way out here. No girls at all.

Have you heard from H.E. lately? He hasn't written to me for quite some time now. Next time you write to him tell him

I'm still alive and that I intend to see him again when I get to be a civilian again. . . .

Not too far off now is Bohunkus Day. Is the band going to parade as usual? After that comes track, the Prom, and then Graduation. Are you going to lose many of the good kids this time? . . .

Love Ray

P.S. If it's not too much trouble, would you send me a list of all the kids from the band & orch who are in the same boat as me. By that I mean serving Uncle Sam so as you can continue to have these wonderful concerts every year.[84]

Ray's longing speaks not only to the power of the band but also to the significance of schooling in young people's lives. As teachers sought to train, discipline, socialize, and inspire, students were claiming schools as their own spaces and creating their own ways and means of learning. On the one hand, children learned powerful lessons about their "place" both inside and outside the classroom. On the other, schools opened young people's worlds of possibility both within and beyond Butte.

CHAPTER SIX

——

Learning to Labor

Selling papers was good work. Every kid wanted to do it. And it made you aggressive, very aggressive. When you had a district, your area that you sold papers in, nobody could come into that area and sell a paper unless you weren't tough enough to stop it. He either bought the paper back off of you, or you fought 'em.

—Kevin Shannon

Butte children honed their entrepreneurial spirits from a tender age through their paid and unpaid labors and acquired lessons in responsibility, economics, and justice along the way. Women, men, and children alike pooled their labors, resources, and earnings to hold the body and soul of family and community together.

In reflecting on the place of labor in their childhood experience, men and women who grew up in Butte from the early 1900s through the post–World War II era described work as a key part of their lives. For some youngsters, opportunities for education were curtailed when they were called upon to work full-time after losing their fathers to mine-related illnesses or accident. As Jule McHugh described:

> All the Gulch kids went to work early, as our fathers died so young from the mines. It used to be said, "Many a Gulch kid raised his mother." My father was fifty-two when he died from silicosis, and Tom's father was killed in the Speculator fire. That's why Tom didn't go to high school. He had to quit and go to work. The family was only here for one year from Aspen when their father was killed, and Grandma was left with seven kids. She went to work, too.[1]

Butte children honed their entrepreneurial spirits from a tender age through paid and unpaid labor and acquired lessons in responsibility, economics, and justice along the way. Their work took place in the heart of Uptown Butte (above, circa 1934), in their neighborhoods, or in private homes.

Jule herself went to work as a teenager, sacrificing school for work. She got a job at the Blanchard Creamery wrapping butter.

It was way down on the south of Butte, and the Gulch was on the north. And I had to work from 8:00 to 5:00, so I ran all those blocks every morning. There were no coffee breaks, and when we got there, we went into a room and put on some kind of wooden clogs. And we stood all day in the brine from the butter vat. There were about eight of us on both sides of the table, and no one was allowed to speak. The boss would put up this big block of butter, and when he cut it into pounds, we had the wrappers ready. And then they were moved to the end of the table and packed in boxes. . . . I had to quit school to take the job, and a few days after school got out, we were laid off since we were extras on temporarily. There I was with no job and no school.[2]

Tony Canonica, who grew up on Butte's East Side, began working at age nine. He attended Sacred Heart School, served as an altar boy, and belonged to the choir, but he claimed his real education came from the Butte streets. At various times in his young career, Tony was a newspaper boy for the *Free Press, Eye Opener, Butte Daily Post,* and *Montana Standard.* He also worked for People's, Belway, Liberty, Ansonia, American, and Rialto theaters as ticket seller, usher, janitor, advertiser, and film carrier. He became an iconic figure in Uptown Butte as he carted heavy cans of film to theaters in his little red wagon.

Many children juggled the demands of work and school in order to contribute to their family income. Accounts of children's paid and unpaid work are inflected with both pride and resignation. These are not stories of victims forced to toil against their will or of Dickensonian maltreatment. Rather, they speak to the complex economic lives of children. Children were players in a family and community economy, both contributors and consumers. And for many working-class children, there were harsh lessons learned early in life about the value of hard work. Despite the grinding efforts of their fathers and mothers in mines, smelters, garages, stores, boardinghouses, hospitals, and restaurants, economic security often remained an elusive goal.

Historical Perspective

Child labor had become an issue of public concern by the turn of the twentieth century. At that time, nearly seven million children were engaged in some form of paid labor in the United States. Children worked in mines, mills, factories, agriculture, and on the streets.[3] Social reformers who were coming to view children as a special group in need of protection took up the cause of child labor. Labor unions also championed the cause, although not necessarily for the altruistic purpose of protecting children. From a union perspective, child labor could be exploited by industry to undercut wages and protections for adult workers. Thus, the cause of child labor reform also served as a means of protecting the rights and gains of adult union workers.

Montana took up the issue of child labor early on. Otto Schoenfeld, the first director of Montana's State Bureau of Child and Animal Protection, addressed the issue in his first biennial report to the state legislature in 1904. He noted that the law was very clear in prohibiting the employment of children under fourteen years of age and that no children under the age of sixteen could be employed in the mines. He addressed the importance of compulsory education, making the point that children deserved the right to an education and that parents had the obligation to protect them from work that would interfere with their schooling. Schoenfeld concluded: "It is not the object of the law to bring children up in idleness, and no one objects to teaching children at a very early age to be useful. Every person of good judgment will approve training children in habits of industry and usefulness, but child labor, as meaning work injurious to the bodies, minds, and souls of children, is a wholly different matter and one the people of this State will not tolerate."[4]

While reformers voiced concerns over the exploitation of children's labor, educators championed innovations in manual labor training to prepare youngsters for careers in the trades and domestic service. Both of these adult preoccupations seem somewhat disconnected from the on-the-ground realities of many young people in Butte. The homes, streets, and businesses of Butte provided many children with hands-on work experience well before they had reached their fourteenth birthdays. Children contributed to household work and family income starting at a young age. They sold newspapers and magazines, filled miners' lunch-buckets, and worked in stores, restaurants, and private homes.

Newsboys

Many a Butte boy earned his first dollars selling magazines and newspapers on the city's busy streets. Boys purchased the papers at two for a nickel and sold them for a nickel a piece. They established their street corner turf and defended it with their fists as necessary. Once established, the rights to the corner might be passed along to younger siblings as an older boy moved on to other employment. By 1903 newsboys hawking the *Anaconda Standard,* the *Butte Daily Post,* and the *Butte Miner* numbered in the hundreds.

That year, a curious combination of temperance advocates, businessmen, and union leaders joined forces to form the Butte Newsboys Club to provide organized recreation and supervision of these young entrepreneurs who "roamed the streets" of Butte. The weekly meetings of the club soon drew upward of one hundred participants to conduct formal business, hear guest speakers, and enjoy a variety of entertainment. On one memorable occasion, the boys were treated to an inspirational speech by "Noodles" Fagan, honorary national president of the newsboys club, at the Majestic Theater on Broadway Street.[5] The club was designed on the model of a miniature city, with boys elected to positions of mayor, city council members, and aldermen charged with oversight of the social and moral discipline of the members. The Carpenters' Union provided free use of its union hall as a meeting

This circa 1890 photograph of two young paper carriers came from Daniel W. Tilton, who ran a bookstore in Butte that also printed and sold newspapers.

space. Other community members donated apples and candy for snacks at meetings. Members of the Women's Christian Temperance Union were also on hand to intervene with boys deemed in need of "reclamation."[6] In addition to regular business meetings, the organizers arranged outings to Columbia Gardens and Gregson Hot Springs and annual banquets in their efforts to mold streetwise youngsters into "future citizens." They presented each member with a club badge to attach to the lapel of his coat and wear with pride. The club also sought to represent the boys in the business dealings with the newspapers.

However, the newsboys developed their own sense of political organization as well, adopting strategies of collective action from Butte's unions. For example, as Dale Martin described, Butte newsboys went on strike on January 5, 1914, when the *Butte Daily Post* changed the rates it charged boys for the papers. Carriers with regular routes did not join the strike, and they were subject to attack by the striking newsboys. "The striking newsboys cast about the business district, seizing the *Post* from sellers who were still working, from carriers, and even customers. . . . City police eventually acted to clear the areas around the newspaper office. Two truant officers had little effect on the rambunctious newsboys, many of whom stayed on the streets after curfew."[7] The next day, the *Post* refused to reduce its wholesale prices and halted street sales. In the afternoon, the boys marched through Uptown Butte with banners supplied by the IWW that read "An injury to one is an injury to all" and "Direct action gets the goods," among other slogans.[8]

The *Daily Post* would not negotiate. Local elders, who had played key roles in the organizing of the newsboys club, urged the boys to end the strike. Club officials claimed that members were not responsible for the sporadic acts of violence and that those acts were incited by IWW activists and carried out by youth who were not members. The boys soon voted to go back to work, but they called another strike in 1919, resulting in a one-day disruption of delivery.[9] The next day, soldiers garrisoned in Butte took over the delivery.

The Butte Newsboys Club remained active until 1931, when it was officially disbanded by Judge Frank Riley, who ruled that it had outlived its usefulness. According to Riley, the club had been established at a time when organized recreation for Butte children was sorely lacking. With organizations such as the YMCA to provide recreational outlets, Riley contended, the club was no longer needed.[10]

Many men who grew up in Butte had powerful memories of their work on the streets selling newspapers and magazines. Their efforts to establish their turf, their sense of place in the city's social and economic

A curious combination of temperance advocates, businessmen, and union leaders joined forces to organize the Butte Newsboys Club to provide recreation and supervision for the young entrepreneurs who "roamed the streets" of Butte at all hours. Above, members wear lapel pins issued by the club circa 1905.

life, and their dedication to long hours were formative childhood experiences. However, membership in the Butte Newsboys Club was not often part of their stories. Perhaps the club meant more to the adult organizers than to the boys themselves.

John Sheehy began his career in newspaper sales at age eight. His earnings went to help support his family. He recalled taking part in one of the fabled newsboys' strike.

> Whatever I did make, I turned everything over to my mother. Twenty-five or thirty cents. I sold the *Butte Daily Post* until I was about a sophomore in high school. I don't understand how [the strike] got started. There were all kinds of us. I remember that we all gathered in front of the *Butte Daily Post*. This was the alley side of the *Butte Daily Post.* And going down these stairways, the presses were down in the basement. And on the other side going down, it was Galena Street, Galena and Main Street. We all crowded around the front of that building, making all kinds of noise. We got two papers for five cents. And you sold them for a nickel, so you made two and a half cents. For a dime, we got four newspapers, so you got two for a nickel. And we struck for three for a nickel. And there were two hundred or so newsboys. [I was] not quite in high school but coming close to it. The police came down in what they called the "Black Mariahs." That's another name for the paddy wagon. Well, the Black Mariahs came down, which were actually just trucks with a section in the back with two seats on each side. They same down, and we all crowded around the Black Mariahs and said, "Take us all." And they gave up. The policemen left. They didn't take anybody because they couldn't figure out who to take.
>
> There was a Dr. Staples in Butte, who was a generation later than mine. Dr. Staples's father was the head security guard for the Anaconda Company. Dr. Staples once told someone in my family that his father had told him that I was leader of the newsboys. I really don't think that's quite accurate, but, anyway, that is what he was told. The older Staples kind of remembered me as being a radical, I think. He told his son that. But the newspaper strikes, there were probably two of them. We never did get three [papers] for a nickel.[11]

John Sheehy's work as a newsboy made him intimately familiar with mines, miners, and the street corners of Uptown Butte.

I had the Terminal Drug corner. It would be on the corner of Park Street and Dakota. The J.C. Penney Company was next door and across the street was the Terminal Drugstore. Across Dakota Street was Symon's store, and across from it was a bank. One of the banks was a Yegen Bank. . . . What I remember about it, neon signs had come out—it was the early days of neon signs—and on the top of that building they had a great big "6," which meant that they'd pay you 6 percent for your savings deposit. . . .

[I would sell the paper] in the afternoon. It was an afternoon paper. It came out at 4:00 or 4:30, something like that, right after school. [I would earn two bits or so] if I sold them all. Now, what made that possible—you've got to remember this—that all around the downtown area were places where the tenants were the men who worked in the mines, who were bachelors, where one room was enough for them. They lived in one room, went to a boardinghouse for a meal or one of the restaurants in town. That was your market for the newspapers because if they had a house, they would be on a regular newspaper route. There was a large number of bachelors, and they were the ones who'd buy those papers. And any time of the day or night Butte would be busy because those streetcars I mentioned brought them up to the mines before automobiles were so prevalent. So they ride up to the mine and come back. If they were on day shift, they'd come down into Butte. The day shift got off at 4:30, and they'd come pouring down from the Hill, hundreds of men. Every corner, all through Park Street and Broadway, had newsboys on them. We claimed those corners as our property. [You established your corner] with your fists. Once it was established, it was pretty much yours then. My brothers then worked that corner. [It got handed down.]

And the Sunday paper, there was an afternoon edition of that as well. There was an afternoon edition of the *Butte Miner*. The Sunday edition of that paper would come out on Saturday night. The first edition, which they called the "bull-dog edition," came out about 6:00 P.M. And we got those papers and stayed all night, until about 6:00 in the morning, out on the street selling those papers. And the reason we would do that is the day shift was getting off at 4:30. The night shift began at 6:00 and got off at 2:30 in the morning. And so, even at that morning hour, there would be another whole shift coming out of the Hill. Hundreds of men. So that would be the market for Saturday night and Sunday morning.

I do remember as a newsboy a special time was Christmastime. It was quite a joy to see. It was made joyous by the downtown merchants. They kept their stores open until nine o'clock at night from Thanksgiving to Christmas itself. They usually closed at 6:00. At that particular time, there were all kinds of people downtown shopping and so on. By that time, they had developed [phonographs], [and] people could listen to records. Music stores had loudspeakers outside their stores blasting out music. That's how I became a fan of Bing Crosby singing some of those Christmas songs. And there was a store not far from my corner, the Dreibelbis Music Company. It was about in the middle of this long block between Main Street and Dakota Street.[12]

John Mazzola started selling *Liberty Magazine* and the *Saturday Evening Post* when he was nine years old.

I would make one and one half cents on each magazine that I sold for a nickel. So, I sold fifty *Liberties* a week, and that was seventy-five cents. And I sold fifty *Saturday Evening Posts,* and that was another seventy-five cents. That was a dollar and a half. Big money. I'd bring that home to my mother. That wasn't my money. I'd bring that home. I never had to bring it home. I did it because I knew they needed it. I knew that, yes. I was proud to do that. My mother would hold out her apron, and I'd put the money in there. She managed to give me something, too, you know.

If my mother was alive today, she'd kill me. I used to go all through the red-light district and sell them to the prostitutes. I thought a prostitute was a telephone operator. I didn't know what they were. They were good about it. And once in while they'd give me an extra nickel even. I'd go all through there. I'd go to Chinatown. I'd go to the bars—the M&M, Walker's, all those places—and sell my magazines.[13]

Kevin Shannon began selling newspapers when he was eight years old.

You'd go down and you'd buy two papers for a nickel at the *Butte Daily Post.* . . .

The miners' night shift began at 6:00 P.M. and ended at 2:30 in the morning, when newsboys would sell papers to the hundreds of men pouring down off the Hill. The young man above is carrying his newspapers past the Park Theater in Uptown Butte in 1939.

Sometimes [you would] only buy two, and then you'd sell them and go back for more. You sold 'em for a nickel apiece, you made two and a half cents a paper. After [the miners' shift change] was [when] you sold the papers. I sold my papers at Hamilton and Broadway. [I had to fight for that spot.] I'd say that's what made us all aggressive. And you heard of Butte kids [being] tough. Well, to me that was one of the reasons. You had to physically fight him if you sold a paper in his district. . . . Naturally, the toughest kids had the best corner. Gus Carkulis had Park and Main. He was tough. He was tough. The Murphys had Dakota and Park. All the Murphys. It was up to the brothers to hold it. They had St. James Hospital in the morning. You had to be an independent [and establish your own corner]. [I sold papers] after school and then on Saturday night. The Sunday paper would come out early, and you'd go down and get them on Saturday night.[14]

Micah Downs's first job was also selling papers.

Most of my customers were in the Board of Trade and down to the Greek store on the corner across from Sundberg

The Board of Trade was part of Micah Downs's territory. "I'd sell one hundred papers a night," he recalled. "[I made] two and a half cents a paper."

Electric and sometimes as far down as Sewell Hardware. Some of my best customers worked in the mines. They'd buy three or four papers from me. I'd sell one hundred papers a night. [I made] two and a half cents a paper. I'd go down there and flip my earnings with that guy that ran that Greek grocery store—big, tall, lanky guy. He'd flip for a dollar. I got onto him, though, because he'd cheat. He'd take my whole night's earnings.[15]

Buckets, Boardinghouses, and Baby-Sitting

For many Butte girls, childhood chores were training grounds for service work. Older children often bore care-giving responsibilities for younger siblings. While their fathers toiled in and around the mines, their mothers, too, often sought to juggle paid work with family responsibilities. Girls learned quickly to turn domestic and care-giving skills into paid labor. Catherine Hoy recalled her early childhood training that prepared her for boardinghouse work:

I came from a family of six, and we each had our chores to do. My older sister had the two front rooms—we had six rooms— that consisted of a bedroom and a front room. My other sister had the kitchen, which was the hardest one of all, and I had the dining room area to do. And in that dining room we had a great big, long table. It was always set, and on the table we ate our meals. You know, we'd sit around that. At one time, we'd have from ten to twelve at that table. We always had a cousin or an uncle or an aunt or somebody living with us, you know. Just the old Irish tie. . . . That area was mine. I had to do that. And every Saturday, whether it needed it or not, we had to scrub the walls down. . . . And we didn't slipshod it. We used soap and water, Naptha soap and water. Walls and woodwork and that. And that table had to be scrupulously clean or else you didn't get your supper. It was just too bad. . . . We were assigned the chores, and that was it. You didn't hesitate about it. My mother . . . ruled the roost. . . . And when she said it was to be done, it was to be done.

The boys had to chop wood and the coal. You know how we'd get our coal sometimes? The coal cars would run back and forth on Anaconda Road. So, one kid would get in a coal car and throw out all of this coal. Then the rest of us would go along and pick it up and take it home. And the same with the mines. The mines would throw a lot of wood out, you know, that they'd bring up out of the mines. They'd give them ties and stuff like that. So, that was the boys' chores, to bring the wood home and saw it on Saturdays.[16]

Catherine soon went to work in one of Butte's many boarding-houses.

> I was what they called a bucket girl. And these bucket girls, you know, if the miners were nice to you, you gave them an extra cupcake or an extra piece of cake or an extra piece of fruit or something. But if they weren't, you know, I mean [if they were] smart alecks or something like that, they just got their usual sandwich. And this was all made with homemade bread. And the slices were about a half an inch thick. And you slapped the meat in there, and then you put another big slice on there. They really had to use their jaws to get around some of these sandwiches.[17]

Catherine's labors took her first to McManon's boardinghouse and later to Symon's Department Store.

> They'd feed from about two hundred men a day. See, they'd come in. The eight o'clock shift in the morning would be breakfast. And then there'd be lunch shift. And then there'd be the ones come off that shift at five o'clock, and they would come and get their supper. Then they'd go to their room-ing house. A lot of them roomed. There was a lot of rooming houses, too. I think they only paid about three dollars a week or month or something. There was quite a few boarding and rooming houses there on Granite Street: the Big Ship, the Broadway, all those places.
>   [Then] I worked at Symon's. I was a cash girl there, which paid fifty cents a day or three dollars a week, big money in those days. We'd take that money home to my mother, and she'd give us fifty cents to spend. . . . Well, the shows were on Park Street then. There was the Ansonia or the Crystal, a few of those. They were only a nickel to get into, so we'd go and look at the double features. We'd stay there half the day. Get a sack of popcorn or some candy or something like that. That was the height of our amusement.[18]

Aili Goldberg's father died when she was very small. Her mother worked in Finntown boardinghouses, and Aili, too, began working at

Thousands of miners needed lunches to eat during their shifts. Bucket girls, and sometimes boys, worked for businesses that sold them, washing the round lunch-buckets and filling them with pasties or sandwiches, dessert, and coffee or other beverage. These miners posed in the Clark Mine yard circa 1900. Their colleagues on the roof worked in the mine shop.

a tender age. She gained employment as a nanny and domestic worker for some of Butte's professional families. Aili recalled:

> Oh, yes, you took care of children and took care of cleaning and stuff. My first job was with Dr. McPherson. That was ten dollars a month, and you had Sunday and Thursday afternoon off. Dr. McPherson had three children. . . . You got up in the morning with them for breakfast time, and you worked until dinner was over. And if they went out in the evening, well,

then you were expected to stay with the children. . . . With Dr. McPherson, I lived in. But I worked for Dr. Staples's mother here, and then you didn't live in there. I worked for them, too, after school and during summertime. And that was better. That was three dollars a week. You went in the morning at nine o'clock, but I was through at five or shortly thereafter, which was better than most of them. And the kids had to pitch in with dinner and dishes and pick up the table. They were different. They insisted that the kids had to take turns drying dishes.[19]

Aili later joined the brigade of bucket girls.

Oh, buckets. Ohhh, buckets. Well, we'd have to know buckets. From early time, there was the old-fashioned—and I don't know if you've ever seen them—round bucket. And it has a little pie plate on top, a little dish. Different men wanted different sandwiches. And, of course, Friday was fish day, and it was a matter of remembering who didn't eat meat on Friday—it had to be cheese, or some wanted a jelly sandwich—who had milk and who had buttermilk and who had coffee, who had cream and no sugar, or sugar and cream. Oh, yes, we put up buckets. . . . The biggest job was washing the dirty things.[20]

Boardinghouse labor was not solely the domain of women and girls. Jim Hanley began his work life in a boardinghouse as well. One of Butte's largest boardinghouses was the Mullen House, which was run by Paddy and Nora Harrington, who had emigrated from County Cork, Ireland.

Paddy and Nora were my grandparents. It was a lot of work for them to run that place. As a kid, I had to help them by feeding and milking cows every day. The cows were kept behind the boardinghouse. During wintertime, I was required to haul coal and wood to the upper floors to help keep the place warm. There was just a ton of work that went into keeping up that place.[21]

As Bob Sherman recalled, there was work for "bucket boys" as well as girls.

Those boardinghouses were a real plus for kids trying to earn some money. I would leave the Franklin School during a break, go over to the boardinghouse, and pack a couple of lunch-buckets up to the mines for the workers. The buckets contained tea in the bottom with a meal and pie above it. After school, I went back up to the mines to retrieve the buckets. I got paid five cents for every bucket that I delivered, which was big money in those days.[22]

Packey Buckley got his early work experience in the boardinghouse his mother ran out of a two-story home on North Wyoming Street. His mother ruled with "Irish brogue and iron will," raising six children and providing room and board for seventeen miners for nearly fifty years.[23] But Packey resisted kitchen duty.

We used to call it the "graduation class.". . . You got the apple box, and you would stand at the goddamn sink. And you washed the miners' buckets, and they would have the ore on them. We used to call it the "graduation class." And I made up my mind that I wasn't going to "graduation class." I went to work in 1924 for Clinton [Drugstore] rather than do dishes. What did I do with the rest of my life? I wound up washing glasses.

Children often helped out in grocery and other retail stores. Ken Lutey told of starting at Lutey Brothers Marketeria (above) in 1914, when he was twelve years old, weighing dry goods and sweeping and cleaning at the end of the day.

Boys also helped with the Lutey Brothers deliveries, pictured at right circa 1915.

Clinton's Drugstore was right below Maloney's Bar. I was a freshman at Central, going on fourteen years old. I was thirteen. I worked there until 1928, and then I went to work at the Eclipse Grocery. I worked at the Eclipse after school. I would go to work at 3:00, and the store stayed open until late at night. If you had to stock the store, you would work 'til 7:00 and sometimes until 11:00. I would get out of school at 2:30 and run home and then go to 737 East Park and go to work.[24]

Even as the mining workforce contracted and boardinghouses were no longer a prominent feature of community life, children continued to contribute to the family economy. Linda Raiha grew up on the East Side in the post–World War II years. As the oldest child in a large family, she had responsibilities from an early age. Linda began baby-sitting for other families when she was in the third grade.

I had three families on the East Side that I used to babysit for. One of the families lived right alongside of Luigi's on East Park. He worked for the railroad, and she was a stay-at-home mom, and they had three kids. I babysat for them in the evenings from 7:00 to 10:00. I'd walk over, and then they'd walk me back. It was the same way with the other families. I would walk to their houses, and then they'd walk me back. I would work on school nights every once in a while and then on weekends.

I was already helping out with my sisters and brothers, so it just kind of lapped over into getting paid for it. I got paid about twenty-five cents an hour or whatever they could afford. They were just working families, too. It wasn't a lot, but to me it was huge. The money came home and was given to my mom. It never occurred to me that that might not be the way to do things. It was just what we did.[25]

That same year, Linda began selling Cloverleaf Salve door to door in Finntown. With her sales, she earned points that could be redeemed for prizes. Linda had her eyes on a Kodak Brownie, and she hustled with sales until she earned the camera. With her Brownie in hand, Linda became the Raiha family photographer. In high school, Linda began working as a live-in weekend babysitter for a couple who ran a bar with live music and had to keep late-night hours.

I would go on Friday night after school, and then my dad would pick me up or I would walk home on Sunday. I lived in, made meals, gave the kids baths, fixed their hair. I got them ready for Sunday school. Then the man and wife would get up, and I would go home. They had a little girl named Mary. I would have to sneak out because she wouldn't want me to leave. They used to have to take her upstairs so she couldn't see me leave.

Linda Raiha snapped this photograph of her brothers John and Marvin in Finntown when she was about nine years old. She used the Brownie camera she bought with money earned selling Cloverleaf Salve door to door.

. . . They used to live by my house on the East Side. That's how they found me. They lived by my parents. And then when we moved to McGlone Heights, it was inconvenient to bring me home at those late hours, so that is how I started staying there all weekend. I started that when I was fourteen, and I worked for them all through high school. We had a set amount that they paid me. I want to say it was fifteen dollars for the whole weekend. Somewhere like that. It would have been around 1957. That money went back into the family. We kids used to keep an allowance for ourselves. We paid our own way. We got our own annuals [school yearbooks], our own books, and stuff like that. If mom needed more money, she came and got it. We just gave her our earnings. She managed the household money.[26]

Linda's work responsibilities limited her social time. Throughout four years of high school, she was only able to attend one football game and one dance—on the same night—in her senior year.

A Family Affair

Many Butte families ran small businesses, and they counted on the labor of children to make a go of it. Some ran businesses in their homes, and others had family stores that provided employment opportunities to extended family and beyond. Many children juggled the dual demands of school and work from an early age. And some had the choice made for them. As Mabel Dean remembered:

> I was never allowed to go to high school, though, because the girls started smoking at the time, and my father said that you aren't going to learn that. So he started a little grocery store in the neighborhood, and I had to work there. It started first in our home. He took one of the rooms that we had that was supposed to be our front room and turned it into a little neighborhood grocery. We had that for a number of years, so I worked in there. But it was right in our home, you know.[27]

John Sconfienza began working in his family's Meaderville Bakery at age six.

> I had to work in the baker shop. My dad had the baker shop. Him and Savant, they had the baker shop, and then Savant quit and went to Walkerville. My dad bought his interest out, so him and my mother, they went ahead in the baker shop. As we kids got old enough to work there, we had to help out. There were no girls in the family. We had to rush home at noontime and help. My mother had two or three brothers there and a couple of cousins and all living in the same family. And I had to rush home and set the table and help her with dishes before I went back to school at lunchtime. Then after school, I had to rush home, help clean up in the baker shop.
>
> At ten years old, I started putting bread in the oven. My dad was slowing up. He didn't get a chance to finish the oven, and here was the bread already baked, and he had to pull it out with the old peel. My oldest brother, he didn't like to work in the shop. He done more work outside—on the wagon, the horse and wagon, delivering. I [worked] the inside. My dad got to slowing up, and at ten years old my mother said, "Let Johnny put the bread in the oven," which I liked. I went ahead and learned to put the bread in the oven. I had to get up on a box to reach them out of the oven. Before I knew it, I was on a peel there, putting eleven loaves in at a time. You start off with

five and get down to three, two, one. Start in the corner and then you work in the center. And in the center you get three or four lines, well, a full peel. Then you'd have to cut down as you're coming into the corner. Cut down from eleven to nine and seven, five, three, and then when you get in the right corner, you have a shorter run, less bread on the line in order to fill your oven right.

[The number of loaves baked] all depends how the business was. On Monday you start out with two sacks or maybe three sacks. Tuesday, you cut down. See, Monday, everybody would be out of bread, and you'd sell more bread. Then on the weekend, you'd make a little extra to carry you over for Sunday, Sunday being a holiday. You'd have to make a good deal more bread. It was all hand work. You made your own yeast. Kept you going all the time. You're never through in the baker shop. There's always work.

When I finished eighth grade, I went in and took up bookkeeping. I went to night school because in the day I had to work in the shop. When things quieted down in the shop, I went to day school. Then I took up shorthand and typing. I wasn't good in typing. But my shorthand, I could do shorthand all right. But the typing held me back. I had too many fingers. When they got busy, I had to work in the shop during the day, and I had to go to night school. As long as that didn't interfere with helping at home, all right, I kept a-going.

My dad first got the [delivery] truck in 1916. In fact, I was one of the youngest kids driving truck in the state, in 1916. I could just barely reach the pedals. I got in, and then my dad learned to drive the truck. It was harder for him, getting up in his age, learning shifting and that. I could shift, but my brother, 'cause he was the oldest, he wanted to go out on the truck. I had to work inside.[28]

Dorothy Martin's family ran Rosenstein's, a specialty market and ice-cream parlor in the heart of Uptown Butte. Dorothy had spent her early childhood years playing in the store and nearby neighborhood with her dog Tiny. She knew the store and clientele and made the transition from play to work readily.

The miners didn't come into our store too much. It was mostly business people. It was a lot like Gamer's Confectionery. We had in the back-room marble tables with the chairs. We even had a little one with chairs for the little ones. I grew up working in the store. When I was a little older, I could sell cigarettes, tobacco, anything, you know, over the counter. It was pretty easy. [We sold] tobacco, candy, fruit. Our front window was filled with beautiful fruit. It wasn't carried much in the grocery stores. In the wintertime, we imported. It was really fancy, like we would get grapes in great big barrels in sawdust shipped from California. And dates in big square blocks. And then at Christmastime, we made up dozens [of fruit baskets]. Just like people send out floral bouquets, they used to send out baskets of fruit. And I used to help my mother. We'd all work packing and decorating those baskets of fruit. [In the back of the store, we served] ice-cream sodas, and floats, root-beer floats, and the fancy dishes. They always had the fleur-de-lis glasses.

Lots of [high school kids and young people who were courting would come in]. And after parties and parades.... There were loads of parades, you know. There was the Miners' Union Day parade, there was the St. Patrick's Day parade, the Fourth of July parade. We couldn't handle the people almost. We employed several girls.[29]

Rosenstein's employed many Butte youngsters over the years. Shirley Trevena began working as a young girl, helping out in the care of her younger siblings and then caring for neighbor children. Her father ran a barbershop and later a sports shop, and Shirley worked for him, sweeping and cleaning the barbershop and counting worms in the sports shop. Her father helped her find a job at Rosenstein's, and Shirley gladly gave up worms for ice cream.

The Rosensteins were a Jewish family. And they had this ice-cream parlor up on Broadway. They had this really old building with ice-cream tables and chairs and big counters with candies and nuts. It was a great place to work. And they were great. Isador was the owner. And there was Ann. And there was Jake Rosenstein. And we had nicknames for every one of them, all of us girls.

It was a hangout for Boys Central, so I loved it. Anyway, Boys Central picked that as their place. They'd have ice-cream sodas and whatever and drive you crazy, but it was a neat place to work. [I worked there] after school and weekends for a couple of years. It was a fun job. And they had all kinds of knickknacks in that store, all kinds of Hummel statues and all kinds of glass cabinets. It was really a classy place, really nice.

It was all marble and glass and whatever. It was a wonderful old place. My first paycheck I got I bought my mother a set of dishes.[30]

John Mazzola worked alongside his mother as a young boy, an able assistant for her home-based enterprises.

Now, my mother was inventive. She used to make donuts. Now, the first Safeway store in Montana was right up the street here. And she had kind of a contract with them, or whatever you'd call it, and she supplied them with donuts in the morning. Before school I'd bring the donuts up. She made them by hand. The donuts were that skinny with a hole like that. And she used some kind of potato yeast or something. Her donuts got that big around. She sold the donuts for twenty-five cents a dozen. And she'd be up all night making donuts. And I'd be up in the morning before going to school, and I delivered all her donuts.[31]

Tom Holter began working at the McQueen Market at age ten. He went to work at his grandfather's store at age eleven, shortly after his father passed away.

When my dad was alive—I think I was ten years old— I worked at the McQueen Market. My cousin, his name was Tommy Fava. His boxing name was John Doe, he was a boxer. He and Tino Grosso, they opened a grocery store. It was a block away from Cesarini's Grocery. When I was ten, eleven years old, I worked for them. It was every day after school and all day on Saturdays for two dollars a week. Two dollars a week. And I used to have to stock shelves, pluck the turkeys and chickens, and scrub off the meat block. And sometimes, like during the holidays, I used to have to help them with the delivery orders. Two dollars a week.

Then I worked at my grandfather's grocery store on the weekends when I was in school. And I helped him in the summertime. It was my grandfather who came from Italy. It was my uncle that was running the store. He'd take me down there, and he'd give me a dollar. And then when I was fourteen—he delivered his orders in a little

Tom and Margaret Holter, grandchildren of Michael Ciabattari, play behind the Meaderville Grocery and Ciabattari family home in Meaderville, circa 1940s.

Advertisement in the Central High School yearbook, *The Centralite,* 1928

Plymouth coupe—and that's when I started to drive. He let me drive from one house to another, making deliveries.[32]

Kay Antonetti earned her first wages in her uncle's market as well.

My uncle had the butcher shop on Caledonia and Excel[sior], the Excelsior Market. I worked in the butcher shop on Saturdays, washing the meat pans. I hated it. Washing the meat pans and cleaning up and stuff. I was about eleven or twelve. I would get two dollars for a Saturday. And sometimes, like for Christmas or Easter, he would give me four dollars, and I was thrilled. I'd go at twelve; I'd bring him his lunch-bucket. And most of the time I'd sit in this little tiny back room. And they had mice sometimes. And the guys would throw water over on me. And I had one of my cousins, and I'd beg him to come with me, but he didn't like it. . . . Sometimes he'd come, and sometimes he wouldn't. But I did it, and it was fun. And they were nice to me.
Then I worked as an usher at the old American Theater. I was sixteen. And that was a ball. It was right on Park Street, so you saw everybody. I had a wonderful time. I worked after school so many nights a week. You'd get the last bus home. And then on Saturdays you'd open at twelve and work 'til it closed.[33]

Kitchen Crew

Butte's cosmopolitan flair featured a wide range of cafés, restaurants, and bars, where entrepreneurial youngsters were likely to find work. Lydia Micheletti came to Montana from Italy in 1922. Her family first settled in Elkhorn, outside of Butte. She learned to cook alongside her parents and began working in restaurants by age eleven. At age thirteen, Lydia began cooking for popular restaurateur Mike Solat in Meaderville, then moved on to other dining establishments throughout Meaderville. Lydia worked seven days a week for seven years without a day off. She recalled that the first time she had a day off was when she worked for Teddy Treparish, who ran the Rocky Mountain Café. She was amazed to see how beautiful the Mining City was, with its thousands of twinkling lights at night. So busy had she been in the kitchen that she had never had the chance to gaze at the night sky.[34]

Lydia earned respect from the kitchen crew and praise from diners, although some were not convinced that such a young girl could be the chef. Lydia recalled one time, during the big gambling days at the Rocky Mountain Café, when a man came into the kitchen with a roll of cash for the cook. According to Lydia, "I kept on saying I was the cook. But he didn't believe me. He asked the other girls in the kitchen, and they told him I was the cook, too, but he said I didn't look like a cook." He put all the money, except for a single dollar, back in his pocket and handed Lydia the dollar.[35]

Lydia went on to manage restaurants and later to open her own restaurant in Butte, which became a community institution. Many youngsters earned their wages bussing tables at Lydia's. Tom Holter was among them.

> When I was fifteen years old, I was bussing for Lydia at the old Lydia's [restaurant]. Lydia's, where it is now—she had another place just south of there. I was bussing for her when I was fourteen or fifteen years old, and my mother was washing dishes. I did that for a couple of years. And, oh, boy, when you'd get through there, you were tired. I would bus for Lydia's sisters, Connie, Constanza, and Rosella. They used to have the front part of Lydia's. And then the other waitresses had the back part of the room. They trusted me. When I'd clear the tables, I'd pick up their tips, and I'd put it in their spots. And they knew, well, I wouldn't dare cheat them. And they'd help me, and Lydia paid me. At eleven o'clock, Lydia fed everybody. She'd close the place, and you could have anything but steak. We had chicken, spaghetti, raviolis, and she'd feed you at eleven o'clock. And by eleven o'clock we were tired, tired and hungry. That was a busy place. Every night it was a busy place.[36]

In addition to his early-morning donut deliveries, John Mazzola found lots of ways to earn money, including working in his uncles' restaurant.

> When I was a kid, I cleaned sidewalks and chimneys, beat mattresses, rugs. I cleaned brick, anything that we could do to get a buck or two. When I was fourteen years old, my uncles

owned Walker's Café and Bar, that was like the M&M. I asked him for a job. My older brother was working there as a dishwasher. He said, "Tell Johnnie to come up and talk to me." He said, "You're kind of young, and you'll have to get a permit because you're underage—the child labor law. You get the permit, I'll hire you as a dishwasher." For two dollars and fifty cents a day. And you talk about work—hard, hard work. But I made up for all that hard work, you know, because the cooks, the chefs mostly, everything they cooked was in butter. And, boy, could they cook. They were wonderful cooks. So, there were Serbs, Croats, Italian cooks, Scandinavian cooks. And, boy, I'll tell you they were good.

Anyway, there were all these chefs, you know, and they like to drink. It's hot behind those stoves. So I'd go downstairs for the vegetables, and I'd bring them four or five bottles of beer. And when I got off work, boy, I'd have a t-bone steak and all the trimmings. That was pretty good. And I got two dollars and fifty cents a day. That was pretty good money. I brought that home to my mother.

I worked in the summers, too. And there again the prostitutes, they would come up to the restaurant at night when they got off work. I'd save a few little pork chop bones and stuff for them, and they'd give me a nickel or dime or twenty-five cents. So that was extra pocket money.[37]

The close proximity of Walker's Café to a local candy factory offered John another money-making opportunity.

The people upstairs above Walker's ran a candy factory, made caramel candies. And she said to my uncle, I remember, she said, "I wonder if Johnnie could get here in the morning before he goes to school and clean this place up for us, and we'd pay him a buck a day." I'd get there at six o'clock in the morning, and I'd clean the place up. And they'd take like darning needles—like this, two of them, one in each hand—and they'd poke a caramel like that. The tabletop was marble, and they'd take the caramel, and they'd stick it in the hot chocolate and put it on the table and stick it there like that and make a little swirl on top. And she said, "Try it." They were nice people. I started making caramels, but they never looked good, and she said, "Well, you can have all of your mistakes." So I'd go to school with a big bag of candy for my friends and one

for my mother. And I juggled all of that work and in the evening washing dishes. I juggled all that work and school. And
I was a good student. I got good grades, I was on the track
team, I was having fun, and I liked the girls, too. [I would
work at the restaurant] 'til 11:00. From 3:00 to 11:00. By the
time I got home, I was exhausted. But I was having fun.

You realize in those days you could get a hamburger for
five cents, a nice hamburger, better than you get at Wendy's
for a buck today. And a bottle of Green River pop for a nickel.
You'd get a whole pie for fifty cents. That money went a long
way. And my friends weren't working. I was lucky to have a
job. They weren't working, so I tried to finance them, too, you
know. And we'd go out, and we'd buy four pies, pineapple,
pumpkin, apple, cherry. We'd cut them into four pieces, and
we'd each have a slice of each pie. We'd each eat a whole pie.
I mean a fourteen-year-old could eat a whole pie. Wow.[38]

Helen Evankovich worked at the S & L Ice Cream Parlor after
school as a young girl. She grew up in Finntown and had absorbed the
language as a child. She recalled:

A lot of the Finn people came in, and I'd listen to them and
understand them. One time, this Finn kid came in and asked
his mom what she wanted [in Finnish], and she told him.
Well, I went and got it and came back. And he looked at me
and asked, "How'd you know that?" Everybody thought I was
Irish because I had dark hair, and they'd say, "I've never seen a
Finlander with dark hair."[39]

Val Webster was born into the world of boardinghouses and restaurant work. Her mother was working at the Mullen House when she
met Val's father. Her father died when Val was only six years old, and
her mother remarried a few years later. Val began work as a dishwasher
at the Silver Bow Café as a young girl.

The man that run the place knew me, and he knew I was a
young kid, but he kept me. When the union woman would
come around—Sarah Michaels was the business agent—he'd
duck and say I was the babysitter for his daughter, which I
was, too. He was very good to me. Through the rushes, I'd have
to stay and wash the dishes and wipe the silver, but they were
good to me. They were Greek. They were fabulous people to

work for. When I first went to work, I was making about five dollars a week.[40]

Val joined the Women's Protective Union at age sixteen. There she found an extended family of women workers under the fierce and dynamic leadership of Bridget Shea. Val herself went on to an illustrious career as business agent for the WPU.

Entrepreneurial Spirits

A striking feature of children's work in Butte is the entrepreneurial spirit kids brought to their money-making endeavors. Children fit work into the larger structure of their lives, getting up to make deliveries before school, delivering handbills for stores and theaters, running home on the lunch hour to pack lunch-buckets or iron shirts, and balancing school with live-in housekeeping and child-care employment. While many turned their wages over to their mothers, work also provided access to a little spending money to call their own. Many children, like John Wallace Cochrane, had sampled a variety of jobs before they reached their teen years.

> When I was a kid, I earned spending money by working at different jobs. For a time on Saturday mornings, I sold *Liberty* and *Saturday Evening Post* magazines house to house. Sometimes I gathered waste coal and ice at the Northern Pacific yards and resold it. I tried my hand at selling the *Butte Daily Post* newspaper on the street, even in the red-light district. Later I delivered newspapers house to house, the *Montana Standard* in the mornings and the *Butte Daily Post* in the evenings.
>
> The biggest event of my boyhood summers was the arrival of the circus. I remember rising at four in the morning to watch the three sections of the Ringling Brothers and Barnum & Bailey train wind its way down the grade along the mountain ridge east of Butte as it descended from the Continental Divide. Later in the morning, I would help the circus people set up their tents, working for a pass to see the show later under the big top.
>
> Some of my spending money went for movies, and many were the Westerns featuring Harry Carey, Hoot Gibson, or Tom Mix that I sat through. Admission at the Ansonia on West Park Street was a dime, while at the Liberty on West

Broadway, it was only a nickel. Occasionally, I delivered handbills for the Harrison Avenue theater and received free tickets as pay.[41]

Kevin Shannon turned his fine singing voice and keen ear for Irish tunes into a money-making endeavor as a young boy.

I used to sing. And I knew all the Irish songs. I capitalized on the Irish songs—the happy war songs and sad love songs. I knew all the songs, and I'd go into the bars, the old Irish bars, and sing those songs. And they'd see me coming, "Hey, kid, sing me a 'Come All Ye.'" You know what a "Come All Ye" is? Every Irish song starts with "Come All Ye." So they called them "Come All Ye's." And you'd sing 'em, and they'd pay you . . . maybe a quarter or more. I was maybe nine, ten years old. I have a terrific memory of all these old Irish songs. My dad collected records. He had some records you couldn't believe, of the rebel songs and John McCormick and all of those. I was raised around all the Irish—Irish from all counties. I knew what the Donegal people liked to hear, I knew what the Cork-onians liked to hear, I knew what the Clare people liked to hear, and I knew these places. If you were from Donegal, you went to Boyle's Bar. Oh, they loved dear old Donegal, yeah. I can remember exactly the first time I went into a bar and sang. It was in Con Bonner's bar, and Honey McDevitt was playing the "fuddle." He called it a "fuddle." He was playing "The Rising of the Moon," and I started right in singing it. I was makin' $4.00 a day through my singing and my route. It all went to my mother. I think she knew how I was makin' money, but she didn't say anything. She didn't want me in the joints. Then when I was fifteen, I went to work as a railroad man. I had been making $4.00 a day, and I went to work for $3.76.[42]

Young Frank Dornhofer had the job of getting ice for his family's icebox.

When I was maybe ten years old, everybody had iceboxes in them days. The Butte Ice Com-pany was at Lake Avoca, where the Country Club is now. The Butte Ice Company had a big business right at the end of the lake. Well, in

Advertisement in the Butte High School yearbook, *The Mountaineer,* 1912

the wintertime, they'd cut ice. They'd use a long scissor-saw and drill a hole in the ice, then saw the blocks up, and they'd come up big and high. Then they'd put them in a warehouse that was full of sawdust. You could keep the ice all summer if it was covered with sawdust. Sawdust is real good insulation, and the ice wouldn't melt. So, when we were kids, my brother and I had a little wagon. At seven, eight, nine in the morning, we'd go down to the ice company, and they'd be loading their truck with ice to be delivered. They used to chip the blocks, and there'd be chunks left, so they'd give us the chunks. We'd put them in the wagon and haul them home. And we'd have ice in the icebox.[43]

While hauling ice home did not earn Frank money, the trips to Lake Avoca provided inspiration for his boyhood money-making schemes.

There was a wooden spillway at Lake Avoca. The lake would go so high, and then the water would go over the spillway. There used to be shiners, little fish, and all the people that fished used to love them for baiting minnows. Well, we'd go down there with a gunnysack or a net and catch the minnows, then take them up to these sporting goods shops. There were three or four of them—Al Jackson's and the Bug House and two or three more. We'd sell them to the fishermen. People didn't have no money, so the only way kids could get money was to earn it themselves.

We used to go down to where the highway now comes up from Father Sheehan Park. There was a county dump right in there. We used to be on the lookout if somebody's dog would die or a horse would die and they'd take it down to the dump. Well, in two or three days it would be loaded with maggots. So we'd go down there with buckets and shovels and shovel all the rotten meat up and the maggots and take it home. We had quite a system. We had two or three nets or screens of differ-ent sizes. So we dumped the bucket of stuff on the top screen, and the maggots would wiggle down through the screen, and they'd hit the next one. And by the time they hit the third screen, it was just pure maggots. Then we'd take the maggots and put them in cornmeal and leave them in cornmeal for a day or so. And all the odor and everything—cleaned them right up. At the time, cigarette and pipe tobacco used to come in what we called tobacco cans. We'd put one hundred maggots in a can with cornmeal, and we'd take them and sell them at the same places that we sold the fish. We used to get ten cents a can, and they'd sell 'em for two bits.[44]

Frank and his brother were adept at mixing work and play. "We used to spend half the summer down there at Bell Creek. You'd build a dam three or four feet high, then dig a ditch so the water would run around it, and you'd have a swimming hole, three or four feet deep." In May and June, they would head to a marshy area south of town after a rainstorm. "Mushrooms would grow. We'd go down and pick them and take them to a café on Main Street and sell them. We'd fill a big bucket and get a dollar for it. That night the café would have a steak and mushroom special. That's how we made money."[45]

According to Edward Jursnich, many Butte youngsters earned cash working as shoeshine boys. Shoeshine kits were favorite projects for youngsters in manual-training class. Boys would build a hollow pine box with a hinged door and a raised piece of wood on top where customers would rest their feet. They filled the boxes with basic supplies, then headed for busy street corners in search of customers—ten cents a shine.[46]

The Depression Era and the Labors of Children

Many Butte children growing up in the Depression Era knew poverty. It became harder and harder for their fathers and mothers to provide for them. And, at a time when their earnings were all the more needed for family survival, young people found it harder and harder to contribute. It was not until 1933 that the Federal Emergency Relief Act and the Civil Works Administration began to offer jobs to needy workers in Butte. Most relief efforts were directed toward adult men, and men with dependents were able to get more hours of work than single men. Single men with no dependents could work enough hours to earn up to $32.40 per month. Married men without children could earn up to $35.50 per month. A man with two dependents could earn up to $46.00 per month, and maximum earning for men with a large number of dependents was $62.00 per month.[47] Women were able to secure some employment through the WPA sewing rooms. And one special program of FERA offered an eight-week vocational summer camp for girls and young women ages sixteen to thirty-five. While many young people took advantage of the sports and recreation programs sponsored by the WPA, more vivid memories remained of hard times and efforts to contribute to the family's economic survival.

As John Sconfienza recalled:

I kept working in the baker shop until the Depression. The bakers at that time, they were the first hit. Nobody was working, and the government was doling out the flour, everybody baking their own bread. The baker shop, we were small, and we were the first hit. Then when Roosevelt got in, everybody was on the dole—you couldn't blame them. And, in fact, people were getting the flour. I was bootlegging flour. People couldn't bake bread or didn't know how, so, all right, I'd take your twenty-five-pound bag or two, take it home, the folks would bake it, and give them bread. They done the work, and we traded and bartered.[48]

John Wallace Cochrane helped his father and neighbors haul wood from the national forests near Butte.

The wood was burned during the winters in the stoves and furnaces of the Cochrane, Johnson, and Moore families. Two of the favorite places to go were the Roosevelt Drive south of Butte and Sawmill Canyon west of Anaconda. My father had bought a secondhand Dodge truck (with an upside-down gear shift), and it was the job of either Mr. Johnson or Mr. Moore to drive the truck, for Dad never learned to drive. Sometimes the cutting crew spent several nights in a row in the forests—felling trees and sawing them into truck-body lengths—while the truck driver, whoever he was, made several trips back and forth. Even after the wood had been stacked in the family yards, the work was not over, for it was then necessary to saw the five-foot lengths into short pieces that could be more easily handled. The national forest issued permits to people to cut and remove this timber if the people would confine their cutting to "bug-kills," trees which had been attacked by pine beetles and whose needles were turning from green to brown.[49]

John Sheehy worked as a newsboy until he was a sophomore in high school, then got a paper route. However, he recalled, "That was right in the middle of the Depression. Boy, that was a tough time to be in the business of selling papers. Nobody had any money."[50]

Alex Koprivica began working as a young child during the Depression: "I remember as a kid taking my little red wagon with my brother George to the business district. We collected as many cardboard boxes as we could for resale at two cents a box to merchants in the fish market. It was one of the few ways to make money in those days. The wooden boxes we found were taken home to use as firewood. It was not an easy time for anyone."[51]

Joe Roberts was nine years old at the start of the Depression. During the 1920s, he recalled that his father had bought him "only the finest" toys, including a ditchdigger and a little bus that he could ride on. His family was able to weather the economic downturn due to his father's work as a plumber and pipe fitter. Still, he recalled the hard work and entrepreneurial effort it took to get by.

> [When] we came home from school, we worked, we chopped wood. We used to steal wood, steal coal. We used to go to the warehouses in those days. All the fresh food came in on bunker cars, and they would empty the cars. And then we would climb in, and we would steal the ice and we'd lift the pallets on the floors of the cars and pick up all of the vegetables that had fallen out of the boxes. And we would sell the ice and we would sell the vegetables, and we'd sometimes make as much as a dollar.[52]

At age fourteen, Joe saw an opportunity to earn money as a result of the federal work projects in Butte. He sold all of his childhood toys and put the money toward the purchase of a car. "I bought a Model T, and we made a truck out of it. And, of course, the people up where we lived on Wyoming Street, they had to find a way to get to the tannery on South Montana Street, the site of the WPA sewing room, so we used to haul them for fifty cents a week. Five days a week we would take them out and bring them back. Fifty cents apiece. Of course, gasoline in those days was six cents a gallon. It was a different life."[53]

Amidst the struggles of those years, there was an occasional triumph as well. Montana's first drive-in restaurant, Matt's Drive-in, opened in Butte in 1930. Mae Waddell became a regular customer as a girl. She and a girlfriend would walk from town to visit the cemetery on South Montana Street. Her friend's mother would give the girls a nickel so that they could stop and have a grape drink at Matt's Drive-in on the way home. The grape drink was a special recipe that the owner created from his father's wine recipe. As a teen, Mae got a job as a "curb girl" at Matt's. And the drive-in was where she met her husband. Mae and her husband later purchased the drive-in, ran it together, and employed their family members. The restaurant was home for their infant daughter Robin, who greeted customers first from her buggy and then from her walker. Once she could lift a tray, Robin was waiting on cars. When one customer suggested that she send her mommy out, Robin made it clear that she was the one to take his order.[54]

These accounts of childhood labor provide insights into the complex economic lives of children. Children, especially working-class children, developed a critical understanding of work and wages from a young age. Their stories also suggest that miners struggled to earn a "family wage," wherein the income of a single wage earner supported a family. In many cases, the money children earned made the difference between getting by or going without. Much of children's labor was also tied to a broader network of family and neighborhood businesses, and their contributions helped to sustain those businesses and strengthen family ties. Children took pride in their economic contribution as they honed their business acumen, awareness of family circumstances, and understanding of the lines between the haves and the have-nots. Their stories broaden our appreciation for the many forms of labor needed to sustain the "Richest Hill on Earth."

CHAPTER SEVEN

Memories of a McQueen Childhood

STEVE SHERICK grew up in the McQueen Addition. His recollections take us to the heart of Butte childhood in the post–Great Depression Era.[1] They provide a child's-eye view of mining life and community culture. And they paint a vibrant picture of the energy and curiosity children bring to their everyday worlds of school, work, and play.

Steve's story of childhood is inseparable from that of his father's boyhood story of immigration and arrival in Butte.

I was born in Butte at the Murray Hospital, January 22, 1935. My dad was a miner, and my mother was a housewife. By today's standards, it was a mixed marriage because my dad was a Croatian and my mother was Slovenian. It's a story in itself how they got together. The name was Americanized. It was originally "Seric," and then it became "Sherich" and "Sherick," and here's where we are. Anyway, my dad had been married before, and he was working in the woods as a logger in Oregon and Idaho. His wife died, and his baby died. The baby died at a month old, and his wife died from pneumonia about a month after that. So he was in a state of mourning, and he headed for the Fort Peck Dam, which was being built at the time, about 1933. My mother had been married before to a man who was a miner, and he died from silicosis as a young man. Now, his name was Sherick also. They were not related, and they came from different villages. My dad knew about those people because his mother used to say, "Never marry anybody from that village. It's too close." So, anyway, as he was traveling through, he stopped to see my mother and give her his condolences. Then he went to Wolf Point and worked on the dam.

Well, prior to my father stopping at the house, my mother and my grandmother, who were very superstitious, had gone to a fortune-teller. The fortune-teller said she would need a twenty-dollar gold piece before she could tell my mother the whole story of what she saw. So they went home and my grandma had a twenty-dollar gold piece. They brought the twenty-dollar gold piece to the fortune-teller. The fortune-teller takes off her silk bandana, lays it on a table, and takes the twenty-dollar gold piece. She puts it in the bandana, ties it up, and puts it in her bosom. And then she tells the fortune. When she got done with the fortune, she takes this silk bandana out, unties it, and the twenty-dollar gold piece is gone. All that's in it is dust.

So, being superstitious, my mother and grandmother thought, "Man, that's a hell of a message there." Well, what story did the fortune-teller tell my mother? This lady told my mother, "You've had a tough life. You've got two kids and your husband just died, but things are going to work out." And my mother had a lot of bills; they had just built a new house. The fortune-teller told her, "Things will work out because a man is going to come to your house, he is going to carry a suitcase, he is going to stay, and you are going to have one more son." Anyway, my dad shows up, carrying one suitcase. I still have the suitcase. And here I am.

I was born in 1935. When I was born, my brother was living at home, and he was twenty years older than me. He was in love, and he got married and left the house. I had a sister who was two years older than him, and she had left also. She was married and working as a nurse at the Murray Hospital. And they were named Sherick, which was kind of a crazy thing. So, anyway, that's how we grew up. We had this twenty-year span. I grew up in a different generation than my brother and sister, who were really my half-brother and half-sister. But I had the basic values that they had, being that their father was an immigrant and my dad was an immigrant.

My dad came to this country when he was fifteen years old. When the kids became fifteen, they would head for America. My dad said he didn't come to America because it was so good in America. They'd come to America because it was so bad in Croatia, back home. Well, two of his brothers had already gone to America. He's fifteen years old, and his

Steve Sherick grew up in the McQueen Addition on Butte's east side. In this 1930s view, McQueen is in the foreground, Meaderville in the center, and mines on the Hill in the background.

mother gets his ticket for him. He caught the boat in Bremen, Germany. I'd ask him, "How the heck did you get to Bremen, Germany?" And he'd say, "I walked." Sometimes you'd get in a cart, and somebody would give you a ride. And if you look on the map, that is a long ways. Bremen is on the North Sea. That's where he caught this boat. He gets up there, and he couldn't speak the language. But, he said, any dummy could say "Bremen," and people would point him in the direction, and he'd keep going.

He gets to the ocean and gets on the boat. He said they treated him like a piece of livestock. They put a tag on his collar, and he is on the ship. It took him, I don't know, it must have been a hell of a long time to come across the ocean. Then he had a train ticket to Chicago. But he has no concept of what these distances are. He was heading for Las Vegas. So, he gets on the train, and he had one crown with him. A crown was about fifty cents. So, he bought a pie from a vendor on the street and got on the train and headed for Las Vegas. He is going to meet his brother in Las Vegas, except he doesn't know where Las Vegas is. Well, he gets to Chicago, and the conductor points to get out. That is all he has a ticket for. He doesn't really know where he is except that it's Chicago. He still has no idea where Las Vegas is.

He gets off the train, and he is walking down the street, and he's lost and wondering, "What the heck am I into?" And comin' down the street toward him is a young guy who was about a year older than him. The guy looks at him and says, "Stevo, what are you doin' here?" Well, it was a kid that grew up in his same village. He said, "Well, I've got to go find my brother. He's in Las Vegas." So, the kid said, "I don't know where that is. Come on home. My father knows where those places are." They go and see the father, and the father says, "Las Vegas, that's farther than you have come so far. And you have to have a train ticket." Well, he didn't have a ticket, so the father says, "I'll get you a job laying track for the trolleys in Chicago." The father was working for the trolley company in Chicago. He said, "You save your money, and when you get enough money, you'll get a ticket and go to Las Vegas."

So, my father stayed with these people and got a job laying track. Now, he's got two brothers working in Nevada, he thinks. But the last word was "meet in Las Vegas." So, he saves his money, buys the ticket, catches the train, and away he goes. He said when he crossed the Mississippi River, it was like the end of the world. There were no lights at night. There were no houses in the daytime. We have a word called *polje,* which is like a desert, and he said that was all that was there—nothing. He said the only time the train would stop was to get water. It took him four days to go from Chicago to Las Vegas. And as the train is pulling in, the conductor yells, "Las Vegas, Las Vegas." The train stops, and he's the only one who got off.

At that time, there was the depot, the hotel with a bar, and that was it. My father said the only person he saw at the depot when he got off was the guy with the shade on, like they used to wear, the telegrapher. He said, "All I could hear was tick, tick, tick, tick, tick, tick." The guy stopped, came out, and pointed to my father. He had a bucket of water with one of those big ladles in it in case my father wanted a drink. My father went back outside, and he sat there wondering, "Now where in the hell am I?" There's nothing here, and his brothers aren't here. He didn't have any more money. He said all that was there were bumbleweeds—he called the tumbleweeds "bumbleweeds"—and the wind was blowing. So, he was sitting on the bench outside the depot, and all of a sudden he could hear Croatian singing—guys singing. He said, "I thought I was goin' crazy." And he looked, and here comes a team and a wagon with some guys in it. They were singin' to beat hell. And they had a jug of wine. They drive up, and it's one of his brothers. So, they hugged and had a drink and drove to the shade and cooled down. And his brother said, "Now we've got to go back" because he had taken this whole crew. The companies had these ethnic crews. They had a Croatian crew and a Serb crew and an Italian crew and an Irish crew. That's the way the companies would do it. They were building railroad. They were making cuts through Nevada and that part of the country. That crew was working at Ely, Nevada. Now, that's a long ways from Las Vegas. My father's brother had borrowed the team and wagon, and he told the foreman, "I've got to pick up my brother. He's in Las Vegas."

I don't know how long it took them to get down there with the team and all these guys, the whole crew. They said, "We're going to pick up Stephen." They had a big party that night. Then my uncle said, "We've got to go back. These horses and wagon aren't ours. And they are holding our jobs for us, so we've got to get back. And when we get back, you can't work with us. I've got another job for you with another crew until you learn how to work these kinds of jobs." They were paid by contract. They got my father a job as a water boy with a Mexican crew. So my father's second language became Spanish. I don't know how long he worked with the Mexican crew, but he could speak pretty good Spanish. When he worked in the mines, he could talk to those guys.

When my dad got to Butte, he and my mother decided to get married. And all this happened within a month. They get married, and he needs to get a job, and work was really hard to find in Butte at that time. But there was a fellow that came from a village that was close to the village my father was from who was Serb. Now, the Croatians and the Serbs are not in a love fest. But this guy who was Serb grew up in a part of Croatia. There are a lot of ethnics involved in all this stuff. It's not just a Croatian. It's a certain kind of Croatian. Anyway, they both came from an area called Lika, which made them like blood brothers. So, they found each other in Butte, and my dad said, "Geez, I just got married, and I have to get a job." The guy said, "Okay, I'll talk to the boss tomorrow, and we'll have a job for you." He came to the house and said to my dad, "You're going to work tomorrow. You and I are going to be partners." Now, that was unbelievable. Here are these two guys—a Croatian and a Serb. Some people would think they didn't have anything to do with each other. But they had this commonality in that they grew up in this neighborhood. A neighborhood was what it really was, only it was a geographic neighborhood.

My dad's partner and his family lived about three houses from us. He and my dad worked together as partners for a long time. They had an outstanding relationship. They'd come up to the house, and they'd drink. We always had a lot to drink at our house. And they'd drink wine and grappo and argue about politics that were a hundred years old, but they would never fight. They worked at the Mountain Con Mine, which was up the Hill, and they had to walk down to catch the bus on Park Street. If there was a problem, the two of them would stand back to back. They were both big guys, and there was no problem between the two of them. It was a beautiful relationship.

My dad was a miner, a contract miner. There were different kinds of miners, even contract miners. There was a drift miner—they are the ones that dig the tunnels. Then there was the stope miner—they are the ones that went up and broke the rock and cut it down. There was the raze miners that made the holes between the drifts. But my dad was a drift miner. And the reason they were contract miners is because they made a little more money. They got paid for how much rock they broke, how much pipe they laid, and how much track they put down.

As Steve described, McQueen was defined both by its geographic boundaries and its cultural character. It formed the contours of his childhood experience.

Well, McQueen . . . there was no end going north. The old highway used to make a big swing around McQueen and go up on top of the hill. To the west, Meaderville and McQueen were separated by a creek that ran through there. The creek didn't have a name as far as I know. On one side of the creek was Franklin School and the other side was Holy Savior

School. Holy Savior was in McQueen, and Franklin was in Meaderville. The playgrounds for the two schools were between them. And then on the south the separation was another creek that separated McQueen from East Butte. All of the streets in McQueen were named for trees.

When we grew up in McQueen, it a diverse ethnic community. We had Croatians, Slovenians, Serbs, Swedes, Finns, English, and Irish. So it wasn't a solid block of ethnics. And within that there were two churches. You had a Catholic church and a Methodist church. The Methodist church was known as the Protestant church. People belonged to one or the other. In McQueen we had two bars. One of the bars was

These underground miners, identified as Schmooke and Larson, are "setting up a drifter" to drill holes to fill with dynamite and blast the rock loose. They may have been working as stope miners, "the ones that went up and broke the rock and cut it down," according to Steve Sherick, or as drift miners—"the ones that dig the tunnels" (also called drifts).

run by a guy named Baldy. And the other was run by a fellow named Nick. So, one was run by an Irishman, and a Serb was running the other one. They were kind of the center points of communications. They organized some of the athletics. Athletics was always a big thing in Butte. Nick had a bowling alley. There was a baseball team based out of the bar called Baldy's, and that became the McQueen Club.

In McQueen we had the two grocery stores and two bars as well as a candy store that sold candy and ice cream. We called that the Tipperary, and it was run by people by the name of Pencrazzi. They sold penny candy and ice cream for a nickel. In Meaderville they sold all the same kind of stuff. Meaderville had a lot more bars because they had the main drag down there. They had two or three grocery stores. They had a place right below the Franklin School that sold penny candy—we called it "pick candy," one cent a piece—and ice cream.

We had a barbershop in McQueen, and there were two barbershops in Meaderville. At the barbershop in McQueen, we had a barber who had cataracts, he couldn't see very well. When he held the hand clippers—he didn't have electric clippers—he had to tip his head back, and he'd hold his eye open with the other hand and clip your hair. You could watch him in the mirror in your barber chair. Geez, he'd pull off as much as he was cutting.

Well, when you were old enough to get out of this sphere of influence and get to Meaderville, they had two barbers down there. They were both Italian. On Saturdays Texaco and somebody else had opera on the radio in the morning and afternoon. One barber's name was Fontana, the other guy was Orzo. And those old radios at the time had the copper wire up for an antenna. They'd turn the radio on in front of Fontana's. Fontana's was on the sunny side of the street, and he had benches. They were probably made at the Leonard Mine because he was not too far from there. These old guys would sit out there and listen to those operas. And in the back of the barbershop, they would play bocce, which is an Italian game with a small ball. I don't know how to play the game, but it was kind of a cross between bowling and marbles, I think. . . . And they would play that opera, and as kids, if we made noise, we'd catch hell. They tell you, "Be quiet, go on home" because they wanted to listen to the opera. And they'd play some of those songs that they all knew, and all those miners would be out there singin'. Now, that is some memory I've got of those guys—I can still see it. I was probably about eight or ten years old then.

Butte children grew up with expectations to be "good Americans" even as they were surrounded by the sights, sounds, and smells that marked the richness of Butte's cultural diversity. In spite of his parents' best efforts, Steve was absorbing Croatian language and culture along with his American experience. His McQueen neighborhood became the bedrock for a lifelong appreciation of language and culture.

It was kind of a crazy thing. Our folks had the mentality that they wanted all of us kids to be American, so they didn't speak the language to us unless it was a big secret. They'd tell you how to behave in Croatian, but they wouldn't have a big conversation because you were supposed to be American. As a result, we grew up with this crazy language. My dad spoke very broken English. My mother spoke perfect English. She had gone to the eighth grade. She could speak Slovenian, and she could speak Croatian. And she was a big lady. A lot of people thought she was Croatian because she could speak the language.

I have an accent. People comment about my accent. But the way we grew up it was kind of neat because you had all these people who are trying to speak English. And English was really bastardized. You had a Swede trying to speak English, and it was kind of a singing voice. I used to love to hear those guys who were Swedish talk. And the Finlanders had a different kind of accent. They didn't have a lilt. You could sense the difference. The Italians had a different accent. Slavs a different accent. So, that's what we grew up with. My grandmother would make a list to go to the grocery store. Bread would be "brd"; butter was "bdr."

The smells were just unbelievable. [If you were at a friend's house who was Italian,] it smelled different, and it tasted different, but it all tasted good. There were some outstanding cooks. My mother would make bread, these nice big loaves. She'd make a half dozen loaves every time she made it. And she didn't want you to cut those loaves while they were still hot. She took them out of the pan and put them on the racks in the kitchen, and, gee, they smelled good. I came home from school one day, and there they were. They smelled so good, and the Devil made me do it, and I cut into a loaf. God, it was good. It was still warm, and I put butter on it and ate that. And it was so good I thought I better have another piece. I ended up eating the whole damn loaf. I thought she would never miss one loaf out of that bunch that was there. See, that piece of gold on that tooth? I swallowed the gold—it went down with the bread. So I had to tell her I ate the bread, and the tooth was gone. It was probably a good thing I swallowed that piece of gold. She didn't thump me too hard. I had to go to the doctor, and he said, "What the hell, it looks like you'll get to eat some more bread because you've got to pan for the gold."

In the early fall, my dad would buy a pig. That pig was kept in a little fenced area that wasn't much bigger than that piano. But he could lay down and eat, and it was clean. There was no odor or anything. And other neighbors did the same thing. Then when those pigs were about the right size to eat, that became a ceremony, killing those pigs. So, tonight we're going to do our pig, so my mother would make a lot to eat, and my dad would have a lot of wine and stuff. Guys would all come over, and they had a big vat, and they'd boil water

Butte families often raised much of their food in backyard gardens. (top) Youngsters posed circa 1910 at 20 O'Neill Street in the Centerville neighborhood with a dog and goat in a yard where turkeys, chickens, and geese also lived. (bottom) This family at 145 East La Platte owned a turkey and a goat.

so they could shave the hair off of the pig. They'd cut the pig's throat, and they'd save the blood because they were going to make blood sausage. There wasn't a damn thing they didn't use. If my mother knew how to make toothbrushes from the bristles, we would have done that, too.

The next day, they'd go to the house next door and then to somebody else's, and so it would probably take a couple of weeks to kill the neighborhood's pigs. We all had smokehouses. They looked like little outhouses out in the backyard. My dad had barrels that he would put his brine in, and he would pickle his hams and bacons and the side pork. And the shoulders, he'd grind that up and make sausage, *klobase,* out of that. Then that would be smoked. It would take quite a while to cure the bacons and the ham.

Also in the fall it was wine time. My dad would make four hundred gallons of wine a year. The grapes would come in on boxcars from California. The Meaderville Mercantile handled the grapes. The first grapes that would come would be the zinfandel, the red grapes. It takes twenty-two boxes for fifty gallons of wine. Anyway, my dad would get the grapes, and we'd make crushed grapes. It takes about two weeks for the grapes to go through their initial fermentation. And then you drain it, rack that off, and squeeze off the mash. You either throw the mash away or give it to somebody with a still to make grappo. But then that wine that's racked off, you put that in different barrels, and you leave it for a year.

The whole process took place down in the basement. Where they made the wine had a dirt floor. It didn't have concrete because my dad said the concrete would screw up the wine. So, a couple of weeks later the white grapes would come, the muscatel. And we'd go through the whole process again. First of all, we had a thing that looked like a meat grinder, and we'd just throw the boxes of grapes in there and crush those grapes. And then when you're racking that wine off in two weeks, it's put through a press, and you squeeze those grapes and get all the juice out of them, and you come out with these little squares, and we'd throw that on the garden. We had a garden. In Butte you could grow outstanding vegetable gardens. You could grow potatoes, cabbages, turnips, carrots. It had to be cold weather stuff. We'd grow potatoes and cabbages and make sauerkraut.

Once in a while, Dad knew somebody who wanted to make grappo, and he'd give the mash to them to make grappo.

That wine they were making was a big thing. But making that grappo, that was the brandy they made after making the wine. First of all, a lot of people had stills. Then there was a law that passed that you could make two hundred gallons of wine for every male in the house. It didn't matter if you were one day old. My dad could make four hundred gallons. He had to get a permit every year to make the wine, and it had to be posted conspicuously down in the basement where we were making the wine. Well, the treasury people, they were called T-men when I grew up. They'd just randomly select houses in McQueen—they did it all over—they'd randomly select houses where they had a permit. And they'd check to see if your permit was on the wall and make sure you weren't making any more wine than your permit allowed. Now, my dad had a still. One day the word was out—T-men are in East Butte—but they're going to every door. So, the next day, the T-men were still coming, and they were working the south end of McQueen, and they were going to all houses.

Now, you could tell who was using a still. Did you ever smell whiskey or brandy being made? Did you ever smell a haystack when it was too hot? That's what it smelled like. Well, in McQueen, Meaderville, and East Butte, you could tell who was cooking the brandy. They'd take tires and chop them into pieces and throw them in the stove—they always had a woodstove—and burn that so it would go up the vent the same way, and, you know, a tire don't smell too good. But I know that cannot overpower the odor of brandy cooking. Guys like me could walk by and see who's got the black smoke and say, "They have a still going." And as soon as you took a deep breath, you knew what was cooking.

Here these T-men were coming on some kind of a mission. They were checking people for how much wine they had, and they were checking for component parts of the stills. Well, my dad, instead of hiding the still, didn't think they'd ever make it up that far. But, by God, here they come. So my mother runs down the basement, and there was a little sledgehammer down there. And she pounded the hell out of that [still]—it was kind of an inverted funnel over the top and then the coils—probably the hardest part to make. And she pounded the hell out of it. She broke the wrong part. Anyway, the T-men came to the house, checked it out, and said, "You got the parts for that still?" My mother told them, "No." "What do you use that tub for?" "My laundry." A lot of women did use the copper tubs for laundry. Well, my dad never did use the still after that because it was broken, and he'd have to find a craftsman to make those parts. But he could find somebody who had a still, and they'd make the grappo.

. . . I never liked wine. When I was a little kid, I must have been about six or seven years old, it made me sick. When they were racking that wine off, it was a real pretty red and it's sweet. It tastes like strawberries. And so, as they're racking that off, my dad and his friends are there. My dad had a cup, and he filled that cup and gave it to me. Dad and his friends were drinking the good stuff—the real wine. Well, I can remember this just like it happened today. My mother come down those steps and sees me with this cup of wine and says, "Don't be giving him that. He'll be sicker than hell from that. He'll be drunk." My dad says, "No, that's just the first run." Well, I did drink a lot of it, and I did get sick. I mean I got sick. And as a little kid when you are throwing up, it's coming through your nose and mouth and eyes and ears and every place else. That damn smell of wine, it gets to me today.

My dad, when he came home from work, he'd drink about a quart of wine before supper. When he came home from the mine, my mother always had a bottle of wine for him, and he would drink that waiting for her to put supper on the table. Then he'd be done drinking unless somebody came over that night. And in the summertime he'd drink beer instead of wine, and I'd go after the beer for him. They sold beer in buckets. You had a little bucket, the kind that Hansen Packing had for their lard cans. My mother would know what time he'd be coming home, and she'd say, "Go get the beer." And I'd take my quarter and run up to the bar and set it up on the bar. The bartender would fill the bucket up with beer and take my quarter, and I'd go back home. I'd get home about the time my dad was coming home. I was pretty small at the time. I had to reach up pretty high to get that bucket up on the bar. I delivered a lot of beer.

As Steve described, Butte children got their social bearings within the safety of their close-knit neighborhoods, which often took on the character of an extended family. Over time, their spheres of social life expanded beyond the neighborhood, providing both challenges and opportunities.

Butte's close-knit neighborhoods often took on the character of an extended family. Steve Sherick posed with fellow McQueen "relatives" at a youth picnic held by the St. Philip and Jacob Society at Nine Mile Reservoir about 1945. They are (row one, left to right) Bobby Pajnich, Joey Petrin, Leonard Gorsh, Bill Malesich, Lavenia Petrin, Donna Lubick, Beba Antonovich (holding an unidentified boy's head toward the camera), Grace Marie Odonovich, Butch Williams, Robert Kovacich (in cowboy hat), Joseph Gorsh (holding rope), Evelyn Kovicich, Joe Kovacich (holding watermelon); (center row) Eleanor Crnich holding Vincent Crnich, three unidentified boys, Betty Lou Balkovetz, Jo Ann Carsh, Liz Culum, Millie Oreskovich, an Antonovich boy, Danny Pajnich, Steve Sherick, Vince Crnich; (back row) two unidentified boys, Donny Orlich, an Antonovich boy, George Antonovich, and Beans Pajnich.

When you started out, you had a range of a block, maybe, but you had both sides of the streets. And on the corner was an empty lot, so we could play ball down there, baseball, softball, whatever. And we played the normal games of kick-the-can and hopscotch and that sort of stuff. When you got a little older, you got to go to the next street. Well, when I grew up on that block, there were hardly any boys. Across the street, there was a girl, and then that family left. And I'll be damned if another family didn't move in who had a girl. Two doors down was a girl, the next one down was a girl. And across the street from them was a girl. So my range was pretty limited to the bossy females when I started out. But once I moved out a block, the world changed; there were some males.

That was another thing growing up in McQueen—you grew up on this island, and you got to go a block, and then you got to go two blocks. I was, I don't know how old, ten, twelve years old, and my neighbor gave me a bicycle. Well, now you've got some range. You could travel. McQueen was built on a hill, and Meaderville was down at the bottom. You could fly down there on your bike, dink around, and ride on the old hills that were built on the mine waste.

Then we had that dump between McQueen and East Butte. That was there forever. During World War II, they'd have these scrap drives. As kids, we'd go pick up all the iron we could. And sometimes, in McQueen and Meaderville especially, there were houses that were vacated. So we'd go in and magpie all the stoves and pieces of stuff, and then we'd go down to the dump and haul it all down. It was great as a little kid. You'd get all dirty.

As little kids in McQueen, it was no big deal to take a gun and go hunting. A friend of mine and I used to go hunt jackrabbits, or at least shoot at the jackrabbits. We'd do things like that on the weekends as little kids. You know, Butte was pretty barren as I was growing up. There wasn't much vegetation. North of Butte was where the railroad track and the highway went around north of McQueen. When you went up past there, there was a nice draw that was green. A beautiful green. It had some quaking aspen in there growing. We called it "Pretty Place." The kids in McQueen, we called it "Pretty Place." And you never desecrated the place. It was unbelievable how beautiful it was up there. There was a little spring, and the water was running. "Pretty Place," that was above Yankee Doodle Gulch. We'd just walk and walk and walk.

There was a guy who lived up north of us, and he had a little pig farm. He had a few sheep and horses, and everything ran loose. The animals would come down between Franklin and Holy Savior School, where there was a dump. They'd come down there, eating what little bit there was to eat. And then they'd turn around and go back. There always were a couple of nice-looking colts, and I always liked animals. So, I said to myself, "I think I'm going to catch a horse." Well, down by the dump, they had two telephone poles. So I went to the dump, and I collected a lot of wire. I made a corral out of the wire between these poles. I made some jacks and hung up these wires and dropped some clothes and made some big wings out of these wires that I could run these horses in and catch these horses. And I thought what I could do was just narrow it down. I had the perfect plan, and I could have myself one of those colts. Then somebody blew the whistle on me being down there building a corral. It was a lot of work, [but I never got a colt].

There was a guy above him who raised goats. The man and his wife had claimed the mountain up there and had all these goats. My dad liked lamb and goat, so I went up there. Anyway, I don't know how I caught a kid, but I caught one. I thought, "Wow, my dad's going to be happy." So, I packed this goat home. And I must have been about ten years old then. I wasn't very old. This goat, to me, was a lot of weight. I'd throw him over my neck for a while and hold him in my arms. And I walked all the way home with that goat. I got a piece of rope out of the shed and put it around his neck, and he was jumping around out there. Then my mother says, "Where'd you get that goat?" "I got him up on the mountain. Daddy is gonna like that goat." "Did you steal that goat?" "No, I didn't steal him. I took him. He was just standing there." Well, my mother had a hell of a temper. She got all unglued that I stole this goat, and she said, "You've got to take that goat back."

And this is uphill, a couple of miles up there to that place. And you don't lead the goat. You can't keep him on a rope; you've got to carry him uphill. And Mother is hollering the whole time. So, I've got this damn goat, and I'm back out on the street, and she's following me, yelling at me all the way— threatening to beat the hell out of me if I don't get that goat out of there. "Go see that goat herder and tell him you stole his goat and you're bringing it back." She followed me halfway up there hollering at me, so I took the goat back.

Children knew the intimate details of their neighborhoods, from the rumble of the mine workings beneath their feet to the cinder-lot ball parks, train trestles, and slag heaps. Butte, however, was a wild patchwork of ethnic neighborhoods. As Steve described, once outside the safety of home turf, youthful bravado was tempered with uncertainty.

None of us knew anything about the other kids that were in the other schools. Now, we knew about the Harrison School because we went to Harrison with boys from Franklin and

Holy Savior schools on Friday afternoons for manual training. The girls came to Franklin School from Harrison and Holy Savior for home ec. We started that in the seventh grade.

Now, we're in the eighth grade, and sports were not nearly as organized then as they are today. For some reason, we were a lot smarter kids, and we knew how to organize a baseball game. We didn't need anybody telling us what size of rocks to throw and not throw. You did what you had to do. But in the eighth grade, they had a program at the YMCA. Well, we're all going to go on Saturday, and we're going to the YMCA, and we're going to play duck pins. I didn't have a clue what a duck pin was. A duck pin is a bowling pin, only it's much smaller, and it has a rubber band around it. You set the duck pins on the same spots you do a bowling pin. But you don't bowl with a bowling ball, you bowl with a duck pin ball, which is about six or eight inches in diameter with no holes in it. The game is played the same as bowling. We used to play up at the YMCA. And we'd be in teams. The teachers had us all organized before we got up there—who is going to be on what teams.

We're going into strange territory. We caught the bus and got off the bus in front of the Rialto Theater, which was on the corner of Park and Main. Now we have to walk to that YMCA over there, tell somebody who we are, and sign in. Well, there's a lot of strange-looking guys running around town on Saturday morning. You think about it, they were as scared of the world as we were. So, we get to the YMCA, but we knew some of those guys from these Croatian parties. These guys from Parrot Flats and the East Side and Floral Boulevard. Our fathers and their fathers belonged to the same lodges, so you went to the same churches and you went to the same funerals and you went to the same weddings. So, all of a sudden there is this bond of some kind because we knew each other a little bit. We didn't really know them, but I was a lot more comfortable with Yelenich than I was with O'Shea. The trip to the YMCA was a big, scary adventure. That was a big experience for the kids from McQueen to go up to the YMCA.

Many Butte children cultivated their entrepreneurial talents from an early age. Music played a key part in the cultural life of Butte residents, and some youngsters, like Steve, turned their musical talents into money-making opportunities.

I wanted to learn how to play the accordion. In 1943 my dad bought an accordion. I took lessons from a gal in Meaderville. She studied in Naples, and she was a hell of a good musician. Gina Zanchi was her name. I took lessons for about twelve or fourteen years. At that time, there seemed to be a streak of kids taking accordion lessons. I would guess that in McQueen there were maybe a dozen of us, all about the same age. Well, four of us hung together. One of us lived out at St. Ann's, but he still took lessons from Gina. The four of us started playing together. We probably had been taking lessons for a year, and we played together all through high school. When we went to college, those of us that were together played in college.

So that gave us a really different perspective. We had some different aspects for looking at that culture. You know, it was working class in McQueen. They partied hard, and they worked hard. The church at Holy Savior was probably the center focus of all activities, even though they did have activities in those bars. But they weren't bluenoses in Holy Savior Church. When they threw a party, there'd be a lot to drink down there and a lot to dance. So we played for a lot of the dances. As we got older, we played all over town. It gave you a different realm of reality.

I was eight years old when I started to play the accordion. When school was on, I got to practice an hour a day and then four hours a day in the summertime, which gets you pretty good at it. [I started playing] around town when I was probably ten or eleven years old. When I was twelve years old, I was playing in Finntown at the Alaska Bar. I played from 9:00 P.M. to 2:00 A.M. The Alaska Bar was kind of a tough joint. And it belonged to a guy named Antonoli, and his sister lived across the street from us. Antonoli would come down to visit his sister, and my mother would have the doors open while I was in there practicing. He called her and wanted to know if I could go work in his bar. And he paid—I don't know what it was— maybe twenty-five dollars a night. It was a lot of money, so my dad would take me up there at 9:00, and I'd go get in the corner and start playing. And at 1:30 or so my dad would come up to the bar and sit there, and at 2:00 I was done.

I'd have a kitty out there, and I'd get a lot of tips. I played up there a lot of weekends. When I was twelve, I had an uncle who lived in San Francisco, and he came up to visit. And he was a general agent for the Union Pacific Railroad. So, it's Saturday night, and he and his wife are going out with some

This youth musical ensemble gathered in the early 1950s: (front row, left to right) Pene Osello, Jim Troglio, Tom Holter, Guido Bugni, Vic Romano, Anthony Barango, Martin Favero; (second row) Bob Pajnich, Virginia Rosellini, Hazel Palagi, Mary Bianchi, Ann Bersanti; (third row) Jack Russell, Elsie Madlena, Dolores Conta, Tom Ciabattari, Minnie Petroni, Marie Lazzari, Marie Bersanti, Emily Fontana, Audrey Silva, Bernardine Silva; (top row) Steve Sherick, Jim Konen, Danny Pajnich, Danny Konen.

people. I'm getting dressed, and he wanted to know where I'm going. I said, "I'm going to work." "Where are you working?" "I'm playing at the bar up there." He thought I was kidding. So, the party they were going to was at the Finlen Hotel, and they came down to Finntown later, and here I am in there playing. He got so damn mad he could hardly wait to get home to ball my mother out for letting me play in the bar. He said, "Did you ever go up and see that bar? Christ, they're in there fighting and pushing and shoving each other." It never bothered me, you know. They were good to the kids. I can remember my uncle saying, "Twelve years old. You shouldn't be playing in no damn bar." I played in that bar a lot of times, and I played in a lot of bars.

Another friend of mine, Matt Mattich, also lived in McQueen. I don't know how, but we got a job setting traps for the trapshooters. I must have been twelve or thirteen. You'd set all these clay pigeons. They didn't have automatic pigeon setters. So one guy would have to be in the hole setting these clay pigeons, and the other guy would be sitting back here, and when somebody said "pull," you'd pull this lever, and it would kick these clay birds out, and they'd shoot at them.

That was on weekends, Saturdays and Sundays. And it paid good. That was out at the Five Mile. My dad had a car that was used on weekends. He didn't drive to work; he'd catch the bus. So, I get that job out there, but I don't have a car, and I had to get out there. I had to swear on a stack of Bibles I wouldn't speed, I wouldn't go any place else. Matt and I could make some big money if we can go out there. So Dad gave me the okay to drive the car so that Matt and I could go out there and set trap.

I also worked setting pins. Nick's Bar in McQueen had a bowling alley—one lane—and so on Sundays guys and gals would like to go up and have a beer, and they liked to bowl. They needed somebody to set pins for them. I only lived across the street from the bar, and somebody would see me down the street, and they'd whistle and holler, "Hey, you want to set pins?" So you'd go up there, and, of course, it was all by hand because there was no rack to set the pins. And you'd set up the pins and get paid twenty-five cents a game or whatever. And sometimes some change would come down the alley as a tip. And then there was the Winter Garden, I set pins there, too. You could go there on a Friday or Saturday night and work for as long as you wanted to set. They had a rack so you could throw the pins in, and once you set it, then you could jump over to the other one. You could do pretty good. You could do that every Friday night.

Steve was introduced to the value of union labor at age twelve.

I went to work for a tire shop in Butte changing tires. I was about twelve years old. It was a tire shop on Montana Street, and they paid me seventy-five cents a day. And it was four of us changing tires, and it was a busy place. Then one day here comes these three guys, and they're suited up. They come over and talk to the four of us, and they said to me, "How old are you, kid?" "Twelve." "You do everything they do?" "Hell, yes." "You do it as good as them?" "Yeah." I was pretty good sized, you know. They talked to these other guys, asked them what do they do. They went in the office with Old Man Barry. Next thing, they are comin' out of the office with Old Man Barry.

They said, "Hey, kid, Mr. Barry wants to tell you something." He was kind of kicking at the ground, and he said, "You're going to get a pay raise starting yesterday. You're getting a dollar and a half a day." Well, he doubled my wages—it was union wages. Three Butte teamsters had come down there, and they said to me, "Hey, kid, how do you get home?" Well, there was a guy I was riding with, Mel. They said, "Have him stop by the union hall up there, and we'll get you signed up, and we'll take care of you." Well, that wasn't hard. We stopped that night, and all was said and done. I think I did have to give them two dollars. So, I had those kinds of experiences, and as a kid growing up, you heard a lot of those kinds of things.

Some of Steve's most memorable work experiences occurred in the lively restaurants of Meaderville.

In Meaderville they had all these restaurants, the Rocky Mountain, the Savoy, the Top Hat, and all of that. They had regulars that they hired, the girls. And the gals wore little

Some of Steve Sherick's most memorable work experiences occurred in the lively restaurants of Meaderville. Among them was the Top Hat (left).

short skirts with a lot of petticoats underneath. When they bent over, the skirt would flip up. That was before panty hose, and they wore these tall socks with the garters. And so that was really a big deal. If they were having a big night, the floor managers would come out in the back and us kids played back there. They'd say, "You, you, and you." And they'd hire you. They might want three of you, and they'd say, "Go in and wash your hands." They'd give you a little coat, a little white coat, and you'd be a bus boy. I think they paid a buck a night to go in there and clean off the tables. But these young gals in their little outfits, when they bent over the skirts would tip up, and there was always some guy in there who'd had a couple of belts and would give one a pat on the rear end, you know. And when she'd come back out, she'd really be insulted, and she'd say, "Give the guy in the grey suit the spaghetti." And you'd walk out there and—boom—you'd dump the spaghetti on him. Then you got your towel, your white towel, and you start wiping spaghetti off a grey suit or a brown suit or any-thing else. There'd be so much commotion out there. There'd be people jumping up and down. Teddy Treparish's brother—his name was Gino—Gino spoke very little English. He was hard to understand even when he wasn't excited. He was the guy that would come out and pick out all of the people they needed. He was kind of the floor boss. He'd go crazy out there trying to clean this poor bastard off.

So, you'd trip and spill the spaghetti, and then you made it worse trying to wipe it off. And when you were going out the door, the waitress would give you a wink and give you a buck. So, what the hell, you made two bucks, and you got out of there. So any time I am at a restaurant and see some plate

Croatians were spread out in Butte's neighborhoods, but they came together for holidays and other celebrations. Pictured here is the St. Philip and Jacob Society (named for the St. Philip and Jacob Church in Novi
Vinodolski, a city from which many of Butte's Croatians immigrated) posing in front of the Holy Savior School
(left) and Church (right) in McQueen circa 1928, the year the church was dedicated. The photograph may have
been taken on May 1, a feast day.

fall, I always wonder if that was real or not. I was about twelve
or fourteen, in there you know—old enough to stay out late
at night. Not too late, though. My mother was a pretty good
watchman, so you'd have to be home at ten o'clock on a school
night. And weekends we'd play, and we had our jobs.

For many Butte children, religious and ethnic celebrations combined
to create formative parts of family and community life.

In McQueen we had a Catholic church. It had a Croatian
priest. Meaderville had a church with an Italian priest. In fact,
Meaderville's old church, St. Helena's, is up at the mining
museum now. It had a charter that all the Italians in the area
had to belong to that church. It didn't make any difference
whether you were in Brown's Gulch or up Elk Park. If you
were Italian, you went to St. Helena's. Holy Savior was just
for the neighborhoods of McQueen and East Butte. I went to
Franklin School, the public school, but I went to Holy Savior
Church for catechism. One time the nun sent my friend and
me to go do something in the sacristy. Well, my friend finds
this box of hosts in there; they came in something like a cigar
box. He says, "Did you ever eat these?" We had to try 'em, and
they were not too bad. My friend says, "You gotta eat more
than one to get any flavor out of 'em," so we ate that whole
box of hosts. Well, now what do we do? We just threw the

MESOPUST

Mesopust was a celebration of the Serbian-Croatian community. *Mesopust* comes from the Croatian word for "meat fat." According to the February 15, 1931, *Butte Miner,* Mesopust was an old Slavic celebration that resulted from a calamity three hundred years ago in a little Slavic village. The Slavs adopted the ceremony in gratitude that their sufferings were no worse than they were.

A carnivalesque event, Mesopust took place in the days before the start of Lent and was a time to cast off old fears and grudges, settle debts, and be renewed. For the occasion, community members created the Mesopust, a straw-filled figure, to personify the evil committed during the previous year. The trial of the Mesopust was held on the Tuesday night before Ash Wednesday. Each year, a prosecutor would be chosen, and the Mesopust was always found "guilty as charged" and then "executed"—carried in effigy, beheaded, and burned—on Ash Wednesday. All evil of the previous year was thereby reduced to ashes. Mesopust festivities also included a door-to-door collection for butter, eggs, and money used for the festivities.

Mesopust was celebrated in Butte from about 1915 to 1955. By 1932 over 2,500 people participated, involving the entire community. A highlight of the Butte Mesopust was a big dance at the Rose Garden Dance Hall.[2]

Butte's Serbian-Croatian community celebrated Mesopust before the start of Lent. In this 1914 image, the dummy that personifies evil in the community perches below the eaves of the saloon. Each year, the effigy was tried, convicted, found guilty, and burned on the Tuesday night before Ash Wednesday. The Croatian words written on the photo translate to "Men's Mesopust Organization."

empty box in the garbage, hoping maybe Sister will think it didn't show up. Anyway, Sister found out the hosts were gone. She was a really nice gal, and she just scolded us a little bit. Then along comes this other nun, I'll never forget her; her name was Sister Prudentia. I'm sure she was a golden gloves champ someplace in the world, and she beat the heck out of the both of us.

The Croatians were kind of spread out in Butte. You had the ones in McQueen, the ones in East Butte, the ones on the East Side there, and the ones out on Floral Boulevard. But they had a central location that was in East Butte. They owned a building which was called the Narodni Dom, which was the "People's Place." There was a big sign out there that said the "Narodni Dom." They would hold tons of dances, and they had a big stage and plays and that sort of stuff, and they had a big back bar in there. It was nicknamed the Bubniga, which means "Hit 'em." That was because they'd go down and have a party, and as time went on, depending on how much they had to drink, somebody would holler "Bubniga," and then the fight was on.

Oh, there were a lot of Croatian activities there. . . . And there was a place down on Floral Boulevard because there were so many Croatians down there on South Montana, down by Hansen Packing. There was a place down there that was a meeting place for the Croatians also. Mesopust was a Croatian Lenten celebration. That was really neat. Butte would have a big event. People would come from all over for that. And we'd have a trial. This was before Lent, like the Mardi Gras, with lots to eat and drink. Everybody would go, but certain people were designated to be the actors. There was the judge, the jury, the accuser, and the dummy, who was the accused. They had this big trial. The dummy represented all of the ill will and sins of the past year. So, they would hold up signs, you know— sickness, theft, all kinds of stuff—so whoever was the attorney opposing this thing, he'd be giving a hell of a speech on every one of those issues. And some of the other people would be saying that this dummy had really done all of these bad things. They would sentence him to death. Now, they did it two ways. One, they'd chop his head off, and they'd do that with a big sword. And they'd haul the parts off, and they'd put them on a pile of debris and have a big bonfire. Or two, they'd just cart him out and put him on the fire. They would always burn him at the end. The purpose was a cleansing of the past and starting anew. Tomorrow starts anew. . . . It would take place right out in front of the Narodni Dom. Sometimes they did it out at the Floral Boulevard, either place. They'd light the fire right out in the middle of the street.

They had a parade, and we got to go in the parade. They'd have a big drum, and somebody would be pounding the drum, and they be marching around. They'd march through the building a couple of times and around the outside and down the block, and then all the kids would be hollering, too. And then you'd have this big trial. After the trial, there'd be this big fire and more parade marching around. Things will be okay now. All the kids participated in Mesopust.

Easter was also a big deal to the Croatians. First of all, you planted grain in a dish, just wheat, just set it in the dish and sprinkled it with water and had a candle in the middle, and the wheat would sprout. By the time Lent was over, it would be about twelve to fourteen inches tall. Then you would dye the eggs. With this egg dying, they cooked a lot of different foods. And before Easter, Easter Saturday, they would have a blessing of the food. I'm talking about people coming with their baskets, bringing them to the church. My mother made *povatica,* and my dad made *klobasa.* And they had *nadif,* and they had green onions and *flansi,* and they had the eggs, and they had big baskets. It was not like it was a little thing. And the church, it would smell so good in there. And this would be done, oh, about six o'clock, I think, late afternoon or early evening. Saturday used to be kind of a fast day before Easter. You had Good Friday and that Saturday. All of this stuff could be eaten after—you had midnight Mass on Easter, so you could eat it any time after church. If you didn't make it to midnight Mass, you'd eat it in the morning.

In the morning, you'd take some eggs and put them in your pocket. And you'd wait for your neighbors to come, and then you cracked eggs. You'd bestow a blessing on everything and have a drink. And you'd hold an egg and crack it. Well, one of those eggs cracked, and if yours cracked, your neighbor got the egg. And if his cracked, you got the egg. You'd wish him well and have a drink and go to the next house. That was a big deal to crack the eggs. . . .

We had a series of holy days here at Christmas as well. The twenty-fifth is Christmas, and the twenty-sixth is St. Stephen's Day, and he is the patron saint of Croatians. So if your name is Steve or Stephen, you got to have a drink, or you gave a drink. You got to have a lot of company on St. Stephen's Day. My dad was a Stephen, and I was a Steve. So there would be a lot to eat on those days. But there was always a lot to eat during the holidays.

Then after St. Stephen's Day, the twenty-seventh is St. John's Day. Then all the Ivans, Johns, and Yonkos, they all have their day. So it would be more reason to eat and drink a lot. Then the next day is Holy Innocence—that's when Herod was going to kill all the kids, or did kill some. That was another day for another party. But every day was something, and you'd go to church. That little church we had, it had a big bell tower, and the bells would ring, and people would go to church and then have something to eat and drink during the holidays. And there was New Year's, it was a holiday. It was also a church holiday. They used to celebrate the circumcision then, but they don't do that anymore. Then on January sixth, that was little Christmas, and that was nearly as big a day as Christmas.

[The Serbian Orthodox celebrated Christmas the next day.] This was their Christmas Eve. Because of the Three Kings, the Epiphany was on the sixth, and their Christmas Eve was on the sixth; it was another reason for a big party. Then on the seventh was their Christmas, so you'd start all over again. Because the eighth was St. Stephen's Day.

Another eagerly anticipated Butte tradition was Bohunkus Day, a carnivalesque affair held each spring. As Steve described it, Bohunkus Day was an ethnic day: "It started out as a spoof. 'Bohunk' was a derogatory terms for all of the Slavs. The Slavs did—they kicked it off. It became a hell of a deal. It was a big deal—people in costumes, clown costumes. And they had a big parade Uptown. Everyone would get into the hype the week before, [asking] 'What are you going to dress as? What are you going to do?'"

In 1951, however, the event took a sour turn.

Well, George Haney was the principal of Butte High. He had an assembly for all the seniors. But, see, there were about four hundred to five hundred seniors. . . . So, George gives the big "thou shall nots" this day. And he said, "There won't be any pipes." Well, I was about a freshman then, and I thought he was talking about smoking pipes. But he was talking about beating each other with a piece of pipe. Well, there'd be no pipes, no alcohol, no anything else. He went over the rules

BOHUNKUS DAY

ohunkus Day was launched by Butte High School students in 1910 as their first senior "skip day" in what was to become a forty-year-plus tradition. Xenophobia was running high in Butte in the wake of a wave of immigration from the Balkan region, and the term "Bohunk" was the hostile epithet used to label these newcomers.

On Bohunkus Day, students collectively "broke the rules" by skipping class and frolicking through the city streets and businesses. The raucous event was marked by elaborate and outlandish costumes, street dancing, and comic theater. As described in a feature story in the *Butte Miner* in 1920: "Bohunkus Day, according to high school traditions, originated years ago when students endeavored to emulate the attire characteristic of the 'bohunk,' a member of a wandering class of vagrants without visible means of support."[3]

Butte High School students launched Bohunkus Day, a carnivalesque affair named in spoof after "Bohunk"—a derogatory name for Slavs—in 1910.

about ten times. The same rules, everybody agrees, no response from the kids, and we all leave.

Well, the parade was on Wednesday, and the band was going to play. I played in the band. . . . And here's all these kids in costume, and there's no organization to it, and they're all spread out. And there's some booze out there. When I grew up, beer wasn't the big thing. You had a beer, but a bottle of whiskey—there was a lot more status to that. Well, they had the parade, . . . and by the time I got back up Park Street with the band, hell, they were going through [Uptown] again, everybody in costume. They were starting to get a little goofy. They had some hammers and pipes, and they were banging the cars, banging the windows. They took out Symon's windows—Burr's—they had the big plate-glass window. They knocked those out of there. They were just like guillotines falling. Breaking those windows started the trouble Uptown, and then it turned into a hell of a fight in Uptown. The next

Over the years, part of the play included both mimicking and mocking cultural traditions, dressing not only in wild but also in gender-crossing attire, and performing political satire. For one day each spring, seniors would "forsake dignity to honor Bohunkus, Saint of Tramps."[4] In addition to a motley collection of tramps, Bohunkus Day 1930 also boasted roller-skating hula dancers, Norse Vikings, and Yankee doughboys. Bohunkus Day 1935 was another madcap affair, with its vaudeville-style show "Laugh of Nations." The "Laugh of Nations" ended its "musical and terpachorial discussion of world problems with a grand finale in which the school song and 1935 class song [were performed]."[5]

Year after year, the ribald celebration continued. Even a blizzard did not dampen the spirit of Bohunkus Day in 1951 as "the weirdly daubed and grotesquely garbed class members snake danced through the streets of Butte then gathered for their performance of the 'Bungling Brothers' Circus.'"[6] However, 1951 was the last year Bohunkus Day was celebrated.[7]

On Bohunkus Day students collectively skipped class, dressed up, and frolicked through the streets. The costume of this 1927 participant required thirteen decks of cards.

day, we had another meeting in the auditorium, and that was the end of Bohunkus Day.

———

McQueen created the social and physical stage of Steve's childhood, where the worlds of work, school, and played melded. In 1955 the Anaconda Company launched large-scale open-pit copper mining in Butte. Over the next two decades, the Berkeley Pit would consume McQueen, Meaderville, and the East Side. Steve and his neighbors can no longer stand on ground that was once their home and community. It is through stories and storytelling that memory and history are kept alive.

CHAPTER EIGHT

Childhood Matters

I think for the people raised in my generation, we were growing up in the '40s and '50s, and the people in that time had a different feeling about Butte than, say, the children in the '60s, '70s, and '80s. It's quite a bit different. The town was different. Schools were a lot different. Communities were much closer to one another. You knew your neighbor.

—Helen Nicholls

IN FEBRUARY 1960 the strike that had begun in August 1959 came to an end after 181 days. Some families had made the hard decision to leave Butte in search of opportunities elsewhere. Others faced the struggle of trying to catch up on overdue bills and regain their footing. The 1960 census showed Butte's population at forty-six thousand, a loss of eight thousand people since 1940. The promise of mining lay in the expanding open pit, which was consuming the close-knit ethnic neighborhoods that had built and defined the Mining City for the first half of the twentieth century. Parents worked doggedly to provide a better life and greater opportunities for their children than they had enjoyed. For many young people coming of age in Butte post-1960, those opportunities lay beyond the industry and community their parents and grandparents had worked so hard to build.

———

In closing, I want to return to questions posed at the start of the book: How might an exploration of childhood in Butte provide insights about the ways in which meanings of childhood and experiences of children were shaped by mining life? In turn, how might stories told from a child's-eye view provide new insights into Butte's history?

Butte children lived and negotiated the everyday complexities of working-class culture, ethnic relations, and neighborhood ties and ten-

Close-knit neighborhoods shaped the geography of childhood in Butte. Left, an unidentified boy, girl, and doll pose in a backyard, circa 1925.

sions. They learned early on the demands of hard work and the tolls of hard-rock mining. Hardly a family or a neighborhood block went unscathed by the death or injury of one of its members. Children forged their own identities as workers from an early age, deftly blending entrepreneurial spirit with a playful sense of adventure.

Many children were infused from birth with a fine-tuned sense of ethnic identity and history. They took pride in their intrepid forbearers who bid goodbye to family, community, and country and set out in search of a better life. And they grew up viewing their worlds through a prism of ethnicity. Butte children mapped their worlds spatially and culturally, identifying boundaries of belonging and difference by stores, streets, and schools. They both challenged and reproduced those boundaries as they sought adventure, employment, and friendships.

Children's accounts provide windows into the geography of childhood. They offer unique perspectives on mining life as witnessed from a child's-eye view. Their stories offer powerful and poignant insights into children's experiences of trauma and their resilience. Finally, they offer rich data on the capacities of children and youth and their contributions to family and community well-being.

Geography of Childhood

Accounts of childhood reveal the deep and complex ways in which the rhythms and structures of mining became part of the everyday worlds of children. For children of the Hill, the landscape of mining structured a fundamental geography of childhood.[1] Children, like their parents, moved to the metronome of mining, with the roar of the fans, bells, and whistles of the mine yards and the rumble of the trains creating

Childhood ties often forged lifelong bonds. The Meaderville girls pictured here always went on outings together, from left: (back row) Margaret Grosso, Amelia Grosso, Stella Lazzari Favero, and Violet Michelotti Botton; (front) Mary Michelotti and Mary Martinesso Ciabattari.

the rhythms of everyday life. Children who grew up in neighborhoods adjacent to the mines developed an intimate connection to and practical knowledge of the industrial workings of mining. Their homes and yards abutted slag heaps, train tracks, and gallows frames. Photos of Butte neighborhoods near the mines reveal the fusion of home and mine in children's community geography. While mine yards were tantalizing and risky places, they were also extensions of the physical space of home.

Childhood stories portray a strong sense of identification with the physical and social space of neighborhoods and boundaries. Children's accounts offer vivid descriptions of the ethnic composition of home neighborhoods, the social and material amenities therein, and the borderlands separating neighborhoods. Children were part of rich social networks, and they created strong social ties within their neighborhoods and developed understandings of common ground and difference in relationship to place. Neighborhoods were important places for building a sense of group loyalty and collective identity. Older children watched out for younger, and differences were set aside when the moment called for sticking up for one another.

The stories of children growing up in neighborhoods predominated by mines and mining suggest that their experiences were qualitatively different from those of children growing up on the Flats or the West Side, which were often characterized as areas where the business and professional classes and "Big Shots" lived. While the landscape of mining broadly defined Butte, children whose everyday lives were removed from close proximity to the mines did not share the same sense of intimacy with mining. Theirs was a more protected space. At the same time, children from more well-to-do families with access to cars and experiences with travel enjoyed a more cosmopolitan childhood. When youngsters came together in the common space of high school, children of mining families were clearly conscious of the markers of difference. No longer were they "all in the same boat" as in the close and insular space of their neighborhoods.

Stories of Butte childhood also speak to a rich cultural geography of children's lives. Children acquired knowledge of ethnic identity, belonging, and difference not only in their families but also in their neighborhoods. While mining created common rhythms of life, the social, cultural, emotional, and sensory connections nurtured in neighborhoods gave children a strong sense of place and belonging as well as a sense of boundaries that marked the limits of familiar terrain. Within those boundaries, children enjoyed considerable freedom of movement. Neighborhoods often served as extended families, where children benefited from the support of multiple caregivers and suffered under the surveillance of multiple disciplinarians.

Sometimes children counted on neighbors to help them get ready for school. Sometimes neighbors counted on children for childcare and domestic service so that they could juggle the demands of work and child rearing. Many children grew up among multiple households, incorporating boardinghouses, work places, neighborhood homes, street corners, churches, and the homes and stores of extended family into their everyday social geography. Their accounts of childhood help us to appreciate a broader sense of "home" in the everyday lives of children, especially working-class children, in Butte and beyond. Children developed both independence and relationships from an early age as they negotiated the streets of their neighborhoods and ventured outside

Swinging in Butte, circa 1950s. Gallows frames made a familiar backdrop to Butte playgrounds.

those boundaries. In contrast to the perspectives of child advocates concerned with children's well-being, working-class children described Butte streets not as dangerous places but as the connective tissue of their networks of family, work, school, and play.

The dynamic social geography of children's lives is also revealed in their stories about working. These stories speak not only to their ingenuity and entrepreneurship but also to the diverse intergenerational relationships that children forged. Through their work as bucket girls, boardinghouse workers, bus boys, newsboys, waitresses, and cooks, children mingled with adults of differing ages and classes. Aili Goldberg and Catherine Hoy became well acquainted with miners in the boardinghouses and restaurants where they worked. They knew miners' tastes and stories. John Sheehy knew the routes, shifts, and residences of miners who passed by his corner and bought a paper. He developed personal relationships with significant adults beyond his family who took an interest in him and helped shape his aspirations. John Mazzola got well acquainted with cooks, business owners, and prostitutes in his work as a bus boy, delivery boy, and newsboy. They shared common bonds based on the value and dignity of hard work. These children defied the notion that "modern" childhood was defined by peer relations and the narrow age-group socialization structured through schools. In contrast, they cultivated and maintained meaningful relationships across generations. They were active partners in these relationships, not passive recipients of adult attention.

Children learned early to stake claims to their neighborhood and defend their turf, at times with their fists. Their stories reveal that boys and girls alike enjoyed the freedom and autonomy to develop a social life of their own, on the streets and slag heaps and outside the watch and reach of parental authority. Both boys and girls also assumed responsibility for overseeing and defending younger siblings in their home neighborhoods and beyond. A certain pride in toughness comes through in the stories of girls as well as boys. Childhood on this hardscrabble terrain was characterized more by spunk, curiosity, and hardiness than by sentimentality, innocence, and dependence.

Child's-Eye View

As the stories of childhood suggest, children are astute observers of their social worlds, taking in the music, stories, conflicts, and celebrations around them and acquiring cultural knowledge at every turn. From their perches on the porches of boardinghouses, in kitchen cubbyholes, and on city street corners, they bore witness to a mining way of life and its human toll. Young people grew wise to adult ways from early

Skiers at Woodville, 1930. During Butte's long winters, young people took to the great outdoors. Some were fortunate enough to have skis and real toboggans.

on. They actively engaged with family, community, and culture. They absorbed the languages, habits, practices, and tastes of their families and neighbors just as they took in the toxic residues of the mines.

Children were not insulated from adult lives; rather they were actively trying to make sense of adult ways in order to better understand their own place in the world. John Sheehy and his brother Ed learned about loss, grief, and the depth of family ties to Ireland as they watched the neighborhood women gather at the family table to tell stories of "the Old Country" and read "letters edged in black." Kevin Shannon observed the nuances and diversity of history and place among Irish immigrants as he learned and performed the "Come All Ye's." Vadis Stratton learned basic lessons in cultural difference as she watched in wonder while her neighbors slaughtered a pig. Steve Sherick learned the power of ritual in community life as he took part in annual Meso-pust celebrations. They grew up steeped in appreciation of cultural knowledge and history.

Children of mining families were acutely aware of the financial uncertainty that came with mining. Many people described turning their childhood earnings over to their mothers. Some made a point of noting that they were not asked to do so but that they were simply aware of the need. Children had a clear, if unspoken, understanding of both family hardship and family pride. They contributed as they could even as they honored an informal "code of silence" about their contributions to the family economy.

This knowledge speaks to the complicated relationship between prevailing attitudes about childhood and the reality of many children's lives. The necessity of children's labor runs contrary to ideas about "modern childhood" as protected and labor free. It also challenges assumptions that adult male breadwinners are expected to be solely responsible for earning wages that will support a family and can earn enough to do so. Instead, many children witnessed the difficulties in making ends meet, despite their parents' hard work, and did what they could to contribute.

Children's observations of adults in their world reveal a well-honed sense of justice and fairness.[2] From their positions in school desks, children kept discerning eyes on teachers. As adults they still remembered the small kindnesses and large inspirations of particular teachers. In contrast, vivid accounts of abuses of power and demeaning treatment made indelible memories, whether one suffered as victim or witness.

Children were also keen observers of politics and culture, critically digesting messages about what it meant to be American, patriotic, different, "worthy," or risqué. Schools essays reflect children's attunement to popular culture and sensitivity to social distinctions. Youth-directed performances, such as those associated with Bohunkus Day, illustrate young people's awareness of and response to the broader political context of their lives.

In their working lives, children built ties with good customers and helped problem ones get their comeuppance. They clearly recalled who treated them fairly and who took advantage. They observed the social worlds of adults and learned from tender years how to navigate in those worlds. In their homes and churches, they observed and questioned the judgments made by adults around them regarding who counted as "us" and who counted as "them." Children also demanded

Bunnies made an appearance on Bohunkus Day in 1945.

to be heard, and they demonstrated on many occasions and in many settings that their views and experiences mattered. They made claims on behalf of their rights, interests, and well-being, showing that young people are quite capable of speaking for themselves, if adults are willing to listen.

Butte children witnessed the fractures of community life during strikes, and, at times, experienced those divisions in very direct and painful ways. They were implicated as both victims and perpetrators in the conflicts of the "adult" world around them. Children's descriptions of "walking on eggshells," "keeping an even keel," and "not upsetting things at home" speak to their acute sensitivity to the uncertainties and tensions that built up as labor contracts were under negotiation and the possibility of a strike loomed. Children experienced that tension, and the violence that sometimes accompanied it, firsthand. Butte labor politics became part of many children's everyday psychology.[3]

Children also witnessed and expressed confusion at the raw divisions of "us" and "them" that erupted in conjunction with strikes. From a child's-eye view, the man "behind the fence" offering a small treat was a "nice man," just as the neighbor needing help with a grocery purchase was a "nice lady." Children were thrust unwillingly at times into the either/or world of adults bound to labor-management struggles. Such binary thinking on the part of adults did not always make sense to children, and, for some, forged powerful and painful memories. Through those experiences, some came to question inequities of mining life and the rules by which powerful corporations and powerful unions play. Others resisted the ways in which adult notions of "us" and "them" were constructed and enforced.

Some still cringe when they hear the word "scab," and others embrace the meaning and power of the word. Some still remember the hardships in which doing without for months, then trying to get out of debt and catch up on bills defined and constrained family life throughout their childhood. Some still find it hard to make sense of the violence they witnessed as homes in their neighborhood were vandalized during strikes. And some, like Sarah Massey, still carry vivid memories of the terror and helplessness of being attacked in their own homes by members of their own community. Their experiences of conflict and hardship belie assumptions of childhood as a sheltered, protected, and "innocent" space.

Trauma of Childhood

Accounts of violence, suffering, and loss reverberate throughout this history of Butte childhood. Mining was dangerous work that exacted a heavy human toll on its workforce. Few mining families were left unscathed by the violence of the mines. Fear and uncertainty became unnamed and ever-present companions in mining families. As some narrators have described, the harsh and dangerous conditions of labor were often washed down with whiskey and beer at the end of the shift. Butte has been characterized as a hard-working, hard-drinking town. Bars and drinking played a central role in community social life for children as well as adults. Friday night was a time for many kids to wrangle quarters and Cokes from miners flush with payday cash. For some, it was a time to gently cajole Dad from the revelry and help him home. In some families, drinking may have dulled the violence of the mines even as it fueled violence at home. And yet domestic violence is a widespread social issue and certainly not unique to Butte. So what might be particular to Butte, and what might be the implications for the lives of children?

Many children in Butte grew up amidst the fears, uncertainty, and bravado wrought by the dangerous nature of the work. They knew the sirens signaling injury and death. Risk and danger were implicit, unspoken parts of everyday life. Children's play spaces were also fraught with risk. Moreover, children were privy to the tensions, anger, and fear that resonated through homes and neighborhoods as labor contracts were being negotiated and the possibilities of strikes and layoffs loomed. And they lived the painful and at times violent divisions of "us" and "them" when strikes divided the community. In this sense, many children bore witness to and embodied repeated experiences of trauma and fear over time. They carried the freight of risk, danger, and violence in many forms on their slender shoulders.

Perhaps the concept of intergenerational trauma is helpful here.[4] Intergenerational trauma has been defined as the cumulative emotional and psychological suffering over the life course and across generations that emanates from trauma experiences affecting groups over time. It considers how the hurts and injuries leveled upon one generation may have ripple effects into the next. Since experiences of trauma are ongoing and interconnected, group members may also suffer the consequences of unresolved grief and loss. The burdens can take a physical, psychological, and social toll over time as experiences of trauma are internalized and passed on. Alcoholism and interpersonal violence, as ways of expressing and coping with trauma and distress, can become structured into community life over time.

Consider the intergenerational nature of trauma and loss in the Butte context and the implications for children's lives. Children in mining families grew up with the truism that miners are lucky to live past forty. The potential for premature and violent death or debilitating injuries of fathers were facts of life. Sons might then follow in their father's footsteps into work in the mines, assuming the same risks. Mothers and daughters would ply their skills in service work, perhaps setting emotional healing aside in order to address the immediate needs of economic survival.

Not only did individual families live with the fears, dangers, and losses of mining, so did the community as a whole. Mining families of Butte experienced an intergenerational history of mining disasters, from explosions claiming dozens of lives to those of historic proportion such as the Granite Mountain fire. They also experienced an intergenerational history of economic hardship and insecurity, wrought by shutdowns, strikes, and layoffs, that made it difficult to "get ahead" in spite of their best efforts. Such trauma, loss, and uncertainty become embedded in community memory and identity and shape the backdrop of life for children and adults alike.

Families living with the danger and violence of the mines as a way of life learned to cope. The lore of Butte and the stories passed down celebrate the bravado of miners and mining, masking fears with humor and hyperbole. Likewise, stories of childhood feature hard-working, hard-playing children, socialized early to value toughness and tenacity over softness and sentimentality as attributes essential to making it in a mining way of life. Perhaps it is not surprising that alcoholism and interpersonal violence surface as problematic ways of expressing and coping with the inherent stress and trauma of mining life.

I do not want to overindulge a psychological interpretation here. Rather, I suggest that attention to intergenerational trauma may broaden our understanding of community struggle, of the forms of violence children witnessed and experienced, and of the ways that children as well as adults sought to cope with the tensions, conflicts, and dangers of mining life. With an understanding of the power of intergenerational trauma, one can better appreciate the profundity of loss many Butte people experienced as their beloved neighborhoods were consumed by open-pit mining. As the Berkeley Pit expanded, the very spaces of childhood were lost forever.

Risk and Resilience

The stories told here provide insights into the ways children made sense of struggles. They also illuminate the remarkable resilience of children, that is, their capacity to not only survive but thrive in the face of adversity. Some youngsters lived like boarders in their families' boardinghouses. They got themselves off to school, arrived in time for meals, and slept in backrooms and basements. Others took on familial responsibilities that both denied their childhood innocence and demonstrated their capacities as they cared for ill parents and younger siblings. Many moved fluidly between work and play, honing their social and entrepreneurial skills in the process.

Many childhood stories of play recounted here are also stories of resilience. They describe creativity, collective effort, tackling a challenge, overcoming fears, facing adversity, picking oneself up when things go awry, learning from experience, honing skills, and earning bragging rights. Children prided themselves on know-how and ingenuity. They took risks, outwitted adults, and staked claims to off-limits spaces of "adult" worlds. They took in the hard, harsh world of mining and made it their world.

Likewise, childhood stories of labor also underscore their resilience. Children took pride in their capacities and responsibilities as workers and caregivers. They were recognized and respected by adults for their skills and contributions. Many children were important contributors to their families' economic well-being. Their stories reveal their depth and breadth of knowledge about their worlds of work and the important social ties they built through their labors. This combination of practical wisdom and social relations constitutes another wellspring of resilience in the lives of Butte youngsters.

Children's stories also reveal a powerful connection to cultural heritage and history as another aspect of resilience. Accounts of growing up in Butte from the 1900s through the 1950s are rich in details of ethnic identity. Children knew their histories and took pride in the struggles and successes of the generations that came before them. The immigration stories of their parents and grandparents as young people became part of their stories of resilience and hope.

Revisioning Butte

Finally, what do these many stories of childhood teach us about Butte? Perhaps most fundamentally, these stories illuminate the meaning and purpose of mining life in Butte. So much of the historical literature about Butte has focused on the audacity of Copper Kings, the power of industrial capitalism, the grit and determination of hard-rock miners, and the epic struggles of union labor. Attention to women and gender has expanded and enriched understanding of Butte's history in addressing the social and labor force contributions of women and the constructions and complexities of gendered identities and relations. It is through a focus on children, however, that we come to appreciate how and why people called Butte home and engaged in the risky business of mining generation after generation.

People came to Butte in search of a better life for themselves. Many immigrated as young people themselves, assuming the risks, autonomy, and responsibilities of adulthood that belied their years. They stayed and struggled in order to build a better life for their children. They lived with the hardships and dangers of mining life so that their children might have a life beyond mining.

Tremendous collective energy went into the raising of children. From Butte's earliest days as a mining camp, schooling for children was a concern. While parents may have shied away from sentimentality, they demonstrated love and commitment to their children through their daily labors. Neighbors helped neighbors and created extended families from homes to boardinghouses to mine yards in their collective endeavors of child rearing.

Those who sought to intervene in the lives of "other people's children" did so with a commitment to their betterment. Their values and views, informed by particular class-based assumptions about proper childhood and parenting, at times clashed with those of the children and families they sought to "save" and support. At times their judgments of parents and children were harsh and their assumptions about character and capacity shortsighted. However, their vision was one of a better life for all Butte children. The Copper Kings themselves recognized the power and place of children in the city's political, social, and economic life.

Andrea Ciabattari and Tono Grosso, 1954. A child's-eye view offers fresh perspectives on Butte's rich history.

Children were, in fact, a powerful force to be reckoned with. Business people, teachers, police officers, judges, religious leaders, political groups, social organizations, and neighbors joined parents in the herculean work of child rearing. When children are taken into account, the social history of Butte gains new rhythms and hues. Community life was not only modulated by shift work in the mines and the possibility of strikes, it also moved to the pace of school days and, in summer, to the weekly rush of Children's Day at Columbia Gardens. Miners changing shifts competed with children for space on the Hill. Lunch-buckets were filled each day thanks to the work of children. A miner's daily connection to the world beyond Butte came through an exchange on the street with a youngster hawking newspapers. Neighborhood groceries and Uptown theaters counted on the labor and consumer power of kids. In short, children mattered.

A focus on childhood also illuminates the significance of Butte and its children to the development of child- and youth-focused public policies and institutions in Montana. Butte was the state's focal point of immigration, industrialization, and urbanization and,

Unidentified children, circa 1950s, with Kelley Mine headframe behind them. Children who grew up in neighborhoods adjacent to the mines developed an intimate connection to and practical knowledge of the industrial workings of mining.

as such, captured the attention of early-twentieth-century reformers. Tremendous economic investment, social capital, and political will was mobilized to ensure the welfare of children and keep them on the "right path" to adulthood. Reformers and advocates kept pace with the latest progressive practices and used Butte as the proving ground for both the need for and the possibility of positive intervention. It could be argued that response to conditions affecting children and youth in Butte defined the direction for child-focused policy and practice in Montana.

In sum, while accounts of children and experiences of childhood have largely been relegated to the margins of Butte's story, children themselves have been central to Butte's history. They were, quite simply, Butte's reason to be. Copper was merely the means to support them.

Notes

Introduction: The Meaning and Making of Childhood in Butte, Montana

1. Finn, *Tracing the Veins*; Finn and Crain, *Motherlode*.

2. Nybell, Shook, and Finn, *Childhood, Youth and Social Work in Transformation*; James and James, *Constructing Childhood*; James and Prout, *Constructing and Reconstructing Childhood*.

3. See, for example, Glasscock, *War of the Copper Kings*; and Calvert, *Gibraltar*.

4. Finn, *Tracing the Veins*; Finn, "A Penny for Your Thoughts"; Finn and Crain, *Motherlode*.

5. Coles, *The Political Life of Children*; Scheper-Hughes and Sargent, *Small Wars*; Stephens, *Children and the Politics of Culture*.

6. For example, Murphy, *Mining Cultures*, pp. 27–28, 129, 146–47, draws attention to children through the lens of women's efforts for family and community well-being. Peavy and Smith, *Frontier Children*, pp. 56, 100, 110, address the place of children in the West and make specific reference to the dangers facing children in mining camps such as Butte.

7. Ariès, *Centuries of Childhood*; Fass, *Children of a New World*; James and James, *Constructing Childhood*; Zelizer, *Pricing the Priceless Child*; Qvortrup, *Studies in Modern Childhood*; Sealander, *The Failed Century of the Child*.

8. James and James, *Constructing Childhood*; James and Prout, *Constructing and Reconstructing Childhood*.

9. Sealander, "The History of Childhood Policy," 176–77.

10. West, *Growing Up with the Country*; West, "Families in the West"; West, "Child's Play."

11. Peavy and Smith, *Frontier Children*.

12. Davin, *Growing Up Poor*.

13. Taksa, "Family, Childhood, and Identities"; Faue, "Retooling the Class Factory."

14. Nybell, Shook, and Finn, *Childhood, Youth and Social Work in Transformation*.

15. For a more detailed overview of this history of children, youth, and "trouble," see Finn, "Making Trouble," 37–66; Holloran, *Boston's Wayward Children*; Lindsey, *The Welfare of Children*; and Mintz, *Huck's Raft*, 154–84. For classic firsthand accounts, see Brace, *The Best Method of Disposing of Pauper and Vagrant Children*; and Brace, *The Dangerous Classes of New York*.

16. Finn, "Making Trouble," 39–40; Holloran, *Boston's Wayward Children*, 13–23; Lindsey, *The Welfare of Children*, 11–43.

17. Holloran, *Boston's Wayward Children*; Brace, *The Dangerous Classes of New York*, 91–92, 225, 231–32.

18. MacLeod, *The Age of the Child*, 30.

19. For further discussion, see MacLeod, *The Age of the Child*, 75, 101; and Cavallo, *Muscles and Morals*, 1–4.

20. Lindsey, *The Welfare of Children*; Mintz, *Huck's Raft*, 156–57; MacLeod, *The Age of the Child*, 26–30.

21. MacLeod, *The Age of the Child*, 26–31.

22. Sutton, *Stubborn Children*, 121; Trattner, *From Poor Law to Welfare State*, 118.

23. Roberts, *Juvenile Justice Sourcebook*, 163–82; Sealander, *The Failed Century of the Child*, 21.

24. Cavallo, *Muscles and Morals*, 1–13; MacLeod, *The Age of the Child*, 65–66.

25. Day, *A New History of Social Welfare*, 192.

26. Ibid., 239.

27. Ibid.; Gorn, *Mother Jones*, 137–38.

28. MacLeod, *The Age of the Child*, 76. See MacLeod, pp. 76–80, for a discussion of racial, ethnic, and geographic diversity in children's school attendance.

29. Hawes, *Children between the Wars*, 11, 21, 27, 126.

30. Finn, "Making Trouble," 47–48; Hall, *Adolescence,* xiii; Mintz, *Huck's Raft,* 189–90.

31. Day, *A New History of Social Welfare,* 238; Hawes, *Children between the Wars,* 51; Sealander, *The Failed Century of the Child*; Mintz, *Huck's Raft,* 180; Yarrow, *History of U.S. Children's Policy,* 3.

32. Hawes, *Children between the Wars,* 13–32; Jacobson, *Raising Consumers,* 1–15.

33. Hawes, *Children between the Wars,* 28.

34. Freedman, *Children of the Great Depression,* 19.

35. Hawes, *Children between the Wars,* 122–23; Freedman, *Children of the Great Depression,* 84; Mintz, *Huck's Raft,* 247.

36. Mintz, *Huck's Raft,* 252–57.

37. Flesch, *Why Johnny Can't Read.* The book stemmed from a widely read article by the same title that Flesch published in *Life* in 1955.

38. Yarrow, *History of U.S. Children's Policy,* 12.

39. "The Polio Crusade" Website; Yarrow, *History of U.S. Children's Policy,* 11.

40. Ibid.

41. Finn, "Making Trouble," 52–55; Cloward and Ohlin, *Delinquency and Opportunity.*

42. Sheehy, "A Seven-Year Old Looks at Butte in 1925," BSBPA.

Chapter One: Children of the Hill

Epigraph. Richard K. O'Malley, *Mile High, Mile Deep,* 42.

1. Glasscock, *War of the Copper Kings,* 57–60; Writers Project of Montana, *Copper Camp,* 296–97; Murphy, *Mining Cultures,* 3; Carroll and Mackel, *Revised Ordinances, City of Butte, 1914.*

2. See Glasscock, *War of the Copper Kings,* pp. 62–73, for introduction to the political and economic intrigues surrounding the emergence of the copper industry; and Calvert, *Gibraltar,* pp. 15–28, on Butte's early labor history.

3. Smil, *Creating the Twentieth Century,* 33–90.

4. Murphy, "Women on the Line," 7–8; Murphy, "Women's Work in a Man's World," 18–25; Murphy, *Mining Cultures,* 9–10.

5. Writers Project of Montana, *Copper Camp,* 18.

6. Calvert, *Gibraltar,* 4.

7. Emmons, *The Butte Irish,* 13.

8. Calkins, *Looking Back from the Hill*; Murphy, *Mining Cultures,* 4–10.

9. O'Malley, *Mile High, Mile Deep,* 2.

10. Emmons, *The Butte Irish,* 95.

11. *Butte City Directory,* 1900, 49–51.

12. According to Butte-Silver Bow Public Archives archivist Ellen Crain, the Cristoforo Colombo Society, whose membership was limited to men of full Italian descent, is one of the longest established fraternal organizations still in existence in Montana. It currently has eighteen members.

13. Filpula, *Meaderville Revisited*; Murphy, *Mining Cultures,* 148.

14. Kearney, *Butte Voices,* 208.

15. See "Ethnic Groups—Jewish," BSBPA.

16. *Butte City Directory,* 1900, 60–70.

17. Lee, *The Growth and Decline of Chinese Communities,* 105–7, 110–23.

18. Stewart, *1001 Things Everyone Should Know about African American History,* 127; Davenport, "The Pearl Club," 143.

19. Calvert, *Gibraltar,* 5. Glasscock, *War of the Copper Kings,* p. 73, notes that Butte's population doubled between 1876 and 1881, between 1881 and 1886, and again between 1886 and 1888.

20. Maney Ross and Finn, "Sisterhood Is Powerful," 34–40.

21. MacLeod, *The Age of the Child,* 40.

22. Pentilla interview.

23. Silver Bow County Coroner's Record, 1902, 156.

24. Pentilla interview.

25. "Triplets Born in Butte," *Butte Miner,* Feb. 17, 1903, in Astle, "One Hundred Years of Butte Stories," BSBPA.

26. MacLeod, *The Age of the Child,* 41–42.

27. Silver Bow County Board of Health, "Report of Investigation of Sanitary Conditions in Mines . . . in Silver Bow County," 1912, BSBPA.

28. Young, *The Public School System of Butte, Montana,* 17.

29. "Washington Junior High School," BSBPA.

30. Young, *The Public School System of Butte, Montana,* 27.

31. *Butte City Directory,* 1908.

32. Young, *The Public School System of Butte, Montana,* 43.

33. Ibid., 46.

34. According to Joseph Hawes, *Children between the Wars,* p. 45, one of the first junior high schools in the country was established in 1914 in Sommerville, Massachusetts, which points to the cutting-edge nature of Butte's school system.

35. Ostberg, "Sketches of Old Butte," 75, BSBPA.

36. Kearney, *Butte Voices,* 165.

37. Writers Project of Montana, *Copper Camp,* 237.

38. Ibid., 161. See Jacobson, *Raising Consumers,* for in-depth discussion of children as consumers in the early twentieth century.

39. For the history of Columbia Gardens, see Boyer, "Butte's Columbia Gardens"; Thompson, "Goodbye to the Gardens," BSBPA; and Kearney, *Butte's Pride.*

40. Andrea McCormick, "Union Day Taps Old Butte Spirit," *Montana Standard,* June 8, 1980, 25.

41. *Butte City Directory,* 1900, 19.

42. Murphy, *Mining Cultures,* 10.

43. Writers Project of Montana, *Copper Camp,* 303.

44. Toole, *Twentieth-century Montana,* 113, 116.

45. For detailed discussion of this era, see Toole, *Twentieth-century Montana,* 112–22, 127–35; and Calvert, *Gibraltar.*

46. Cunningham, "Annual Report, Associated Charities," Jan. 7, 1904, BSBPA.

47. O'Malley, *Mile High, Mile Deep,* 156.

48. Staudohar, "Dr. Caroline McGill," 86–87.

49. "Five Killed at Leonard Mine," *Butte Miner,* Apr. 24, 1913, 1.

50. Ibid.

51. Buckley interview.

52. Emmons, *The Butte Irish,* 71.

53. Brandjord, *State of Montana Department of Public Welfare Report . . . 1938,* 19.

54. Silver Bow County Poor Fund Investigation Records, 1909–1910, BSBPA.

55. Activities of the newsboys were regularly reported in the *Butte Miner.* A feature story on the newsboys, "Things That Are Being Done for the Newsboys of Butte," appeared in the *Anaconda Standard,* May 3, 1903, pp. 2, 7. See also Martin, "School for Struggle," 9–11; and Astle, "One Hundred Years of Butte Stories," BSBPA.

56. "Special Train on Arbor Day," ibid., Apr. 29, 1906, 6; "Another Arbor Day is Wanted in Butte," ibid., Apr. 4, 1907, 5; "Next Saturday Will Be Children's Day at the Gardens," ibid., May 22, 1907, 5.

57. "National Chief Scout and Founder of Movement in Montana Meet Here," *Anaconda Standard,* Feb. 11, 1920, in "Boys Scouts," BSBPA.

58. Astle, "One Hundred Years of Butte Stories," BSBPA.

59. "Girl Scouts," BSBPA; "Camp Fire Drive Nears Objective," *Butte Miner,* May 19, 1927, 4.

60. Notices of language and dancing classes appear in the *Butte Miner* by 1913. On Junior Auxiliary of the Temple, see "Jewish People of Old Butte," in "Ethnic Groups—Jewish," BSBPA.

61. "Children Free at Seton Indian Games," *Butte Miner,* July 26, 1914, 6. Chautauquas were a national popular education movement of the early twentieth century that spread widely through rural areas bringing diverse entertainers, musicians, and lecturers to broad-based community audiences.

62. "Schoolchildren Will be Shown How to Avoid Peril by Means of Motion Picture," *Butte Miner,* Mar. 15, 1913, 5.

63. "Open Air Story Hour at Gardens," *Butte Miner,* July 23, 1914, 7.

64. "Meaderville Young Men's Club is Growing Fast," *Butte Miner,* Apr. 4, 1913, 6; "School Dancing is before Board," *Butte Miner,* May 24, 1916, 6.

65. "Many Beautiful Babies are Seen at Second Annual Baby Show Here," *Butte Miner,* Sept. 22, 1915, 9.

66. In the wake of World War I, national attention was brought to the plight of children's health. Many of the young men drafted into the military were found unfit to serve due to malnutrition and poor health. Federal food programs and programs focusing on child health and nutrition began to develop in response.

67. Zinn, *A People's History of the United States,* 359–76.

68. Ibid., 362.

69. For a more detailed discussion of this time period, including the growing anti-German sentiment, see Gutfeld, *Montana's Agony;* Calvert, *Gibraltar;* Punke, *Fire and Brimstone;* and Work, *Darkest before Dawn.*

70. Toole, *Twentieth-century Montana,* 138; Calvert, *Gibraltar,* 113.

71. Sheehan, "Nun Rethinks Our Education," 55.

72. The total number of deaths in the Granite Mountain fire varies in published accounts. The most accurate accounting of the death toll, based on research by James Harrington, appears to be 168. See Harrington, "Mine Fatalities 1888–1996," BSBPA.

73. Punke, *Fire and Brimstone,* 110–11.

74. "Nipper" is a term for laborers who fetch tools for underground miners.

75. Quoted in Punke, *Fire and Brimstone,* 187.

76. McCormick, "Woman Inherits Mine's Heroic Legacy," *Montana Standard,* Nov. 5, 1978, 22.

77. Ibid.

78. Punke, *Fire and Brimstone,* 226.

79. Murphy, *Mining Cultures,* 27–28.

80. Punke, *Fire and Brimstone,* 236. Councils of Defense were being established across the country at the time.

81. See the Montana Sedition Project Website; and Work, *Darkest before Dawn.*

82. Punke, *Fire and Brimstone,* 225; Work, *Darkest before Dawn.*

83. Punke, *Fire and Brimstone,* 238–40; Toole, *Twentieth-century Montana,* 186. See also Calvert, *Gibraltar,* and Work, *Darkest before Dawn,* for detailed analyses of this political moment.

84. Astle, *Only in Butte,* 104.

85. Calkins, *Looking Back from the Hill,* 13.

86. Kaiyala memoir, BSBPA.

87. "Father and Daughter Die of Spanish Influenza," *Butte Miner,* Nov. 5, 1918, 5; Astle, *Only in Butte,* 104. Staudohaur, "Dr. Caroline McGill," p. 92, states that Butte lost one thousand people to the disease.

88. "Good Home for Every Orphan," *Butte Miner,* Dec. 24, 1918, 5.

89. McHugh, "The Gulch and I," BSBPA.

90. Duncan interview.

91. "Citizens' School Opens Monday," *Butte Miner,* Jan. 20, 1919, 6.

92. Goldberg interview.

93. The Catholic Church around the country encouraged parents to send their children to parochial schools in order to preserve cultural, religious, and ethnic identity and to resist the vigorous Americanization campaigns of the public schools. See Hawes, *Children between the Wars,* 39.

94. Hannan diary, BSBPA; Fischer, "Faith, Hope, and Ethnicity," BSBPA.

95. Jursnich, *Butte's East Side,* 99.

96. "Human Fly Visits Butte," *Anaconda Standard,* Aug. 29, 1920, 5.

97. Mintz, *Huck's Raft,* 216–17.

98. Montana Writers Project, *Copper Camp,* 308.

99. "Underfed Children of Butte to be Cared for by Women," *Butte Miner,* Apr. 1, 1921, 1.

100. "Salvation Army Day Nursery of Butte Starts Functioning," *Butte Miner,* Mar. 6, 1921, 5.

101. "Wants to Open Industrial School," *Butte Miner,* Apr. 13, 1923, 5.

102. See Murphy, *Mining Cultures,* pp. 145–48, for a discussion of the founding of the East Side Neighborhood House and the role of the Women's Auxiliary of the American Institute of Mining, Metallurgical, and Petroleum Engineers in its support and operations.

103. "Eastside Neighborhood House Wins Hearts of Kiddies," *Butte Miner,* Mar. 6, 1921, 6.

104. "Twenty-Two Thousand Gather at Columbia Gardens," *Butte Miner,* July 25, 1920, 1. Miners' Union Day was not celebrated and was replaced by Company-sponsored Miners' Field Day for several years as internal conflicts and corporate and state intervention weakened organized labor.

105. "9,500 Schoolchildren Return to the Classrooms on Monday, Sept. 11," *Butte Miner,* Sept. 10, 1922, 24; "Enrollment at High School is Greater Than Last Year," ibid., Sept. 27, 1922, 9.

106. "Boy Scouts Count in Life of Butte," *Butte Miner,* Mar. 14, 1923, 6.

107. Finn, "Seeing the Forest through the Trees," 215–17.

108. Higgins, *Horrors of Vaccination Exposed.*

109. "Schools Reopen Wednesday Morning," *Butte Miner,* Jan. 1, 1924, 6.

110. "Vaccine Case Now on Trial before Court," *Butte Miner,* Jan. 10, 1924, 1.

111. Murphy, *Mining Cultures,* 169–99.

112. Ibid., 176.

113. Ibid., 177.

114. "Butte and Central Meet in Annual Football Clash at Clark's Park Today," *Butte Miner,* Nov. 2, 1929, 1.

115. Hawes, *Children between the Wars,* 104.

116. Freedman, *Children of the Great Depression,* 14.

117. Ibid., 15.

118. Ibid., 41–43.

119. Murphy, *Mining Cultures,* 202–4; Hathaway, *Sixteenth Biennial Report of the Bureau of Child Protection.*

120. "Young Women of Butte Organize Junior League," *Butte Daily Post,* Oct. 31, 1931, 1.

121. "Junior Service League Planning Renewed Drive against Suffering in Mining City during Winter," *Montana Standard,* Dec. 4, 1932, 1.

122. Freedman, *Children of the Great Depression,* 13.

123. Hawes, *Children between the Wars,* 122.

124. Freedman, *Children of the Great Depression,* 17; Cohen, *Dear Mrs. Roosevelt,* 52.

125. Brandjord, *State of Montana Department of Public Welfare Report . . . 1938,* 21.

126. "Copper States Have Big Relief Rolls," *Eye Opener,* Oct. 13, 1935, 4. The article reports that Butte was second only to Phoenix, Arizona, in its percentage of residents receiving relief.

127. Renne, *A Preliminary Report of the Butte Economic Survey,* 34.

128. Ibid.

129. Ibid.

130. Shea interview.

131. Stratton interview.

132. Roberts interview.

133. Evankovich interview.

134. Martinez interview. See also Hawes, *Children between the Wars,* 118–19.

135. Freedman, *Children of the Great Depression,* 84–88.

136. "Strike Pickets at Leonard Accused," *Butte Daily Post,* June 27, 1934, 1; "Dynamite Sticks with Burning Fuses Hurled over Gate at Leonard," ibid., July 24, 1934, 1.

137. "New Style Serenades in Butte Strike Terror to Women and Children," *Montana Standard,* June 12, 1934, 1.

138. Finn, *Tracing the Veins,* 39.

139. "Strike Conference Reaches Agreement," *Montana Standard,* Sept. 14, 1934, 1.

140. "Of Interest to Us All That Still Eat," *Eye Opener,* May 18, 1935, 1.

141. Brandjord, *State of Montana Department of Public Welfare Report . . . 1938,* 49.

142. Renne, *Preliminary Report of the Butte Economic Survey,* 8.

143. Jursnich, *Butte's East Side,* 212.

144. Murphy, *Mining Cultures,* 212–16.

145. Prodgers, *Butte-Anaconda Almanac,* 2.

146. Mazzola interview.

147. Renne, *Preliminary Report of the Butte Economic Survey,* 1939, 3.

148. Ibid.

149. "$4,399,347 in Federal Sums Spent in City," *Montana Standard,* Mar. 23, 1941, 1.

150. Filpula, *Meaderville Revisited.*

151. Mary Murphy in *Mining Cultures* notes that investment in public recreation declined significantly with the end of WPA funding in the early 1940s. However, Butte children and adults continued to find and create their own entertainment through organized sports leagues, sandlot ball games, and community celebrations.

152. Trevena interview.

153. Mintz, *Huck's Raft,* 257.

154. "Honoring Montana's World War II Veterans" (Internet).

155. *Copper Commando* published names of all employees who served in World War II. See "Western Montanans Celebrated War's End," *Montana Standard,* Aug. 14, 1994, C4.

156. Ibid.

157. "A Message from Rear Admiral C. H. Woodward," *Copper Commando,* Sept. 5, 1942, 2.

158. "The Cry for Copper," *Copper Commando,* Oct. 7, 1942, 11; "A Message from Robert Patterson, Undersecretary of War," Nov. 6, 1942, ibid., 2; "Copper is Medicine: A Statement Prepared Expressly for *Copper Commando* by Major General J. C. Magee, Surgeon General of the Army," ibid., Jan. 29,

1943, 2. The *Copper Commando* was published from 1942 to 1945. Each issue featured statistics about the demand for copper as an essential wartime metal.

159. Finn, *Tracing the Veins,* 43.

160. Mazzola interview.

161. Mintz, *Huck's Raft,* 258.

162. Wilson, "War Bonds Drives" (Internet).

163. Jursnich, *Butte's East Side,* 64–65.

164. Trevena interview; Antonetti interview.

165. Crain and McCormick, "Butte's Cadet Nurses," 123–28, 136.

166. *Copper Commando,* Nov. 1944, 7.

167. Aug. 14, 1945, marks the day Japan announced it would surrender unconditionally. The official date is Sept. 2, 1945, marking Japan's signing of the official surrender. May 8, 1945, marks Victory in Europe Day, the date when the Allied forces accepted the unconditional surrender of the armed forces of Nazi Germany.

168. "Western Montanans Celebrated War's End," *Montana Standard,* Aug. 14, 1995, C1–2.

169. Antonetti interview.

170. "Western Montanans Celebrated War's End," *Montana Standard,* Aug. 14, 1995, C1–2.

171. "Mobs Wreck Dozen Homes," *Montana Standard,* Apr. 15, 1946, 1.

172. "Orgy Uncontrolled in Wild Night of Terror, Lawlessness," *Montana Standard,* Apr. 15, 1946, 1.

173. "Butte Quiet after Lawlessness," *Montana Standard,* Apr. 16, 1946, 1; "Butte is Calm for Third Straight Night," ibid., Apr. 18, 1946, 1; "No Action Taken on Butte's Lawless Gangs," ibid., Apr. 20, 1946, 1.

174. "Grim Wreckage Remains after Systematic Vandalism, Looting," *Montana Standard,* Apr. 16, 1946, 1.

175. Holter interview.

176. Anonymous interview.

177. Henry Schiesser "biographical summary," BSBPA.

178. Astle, *Only in Butte,* 174.

179. "Company Towns," 100–101.

180. "Report on Schools Building Program: Butte School District No. 1, 2–3," BSBPA.

181. Ibid.

182. Ibid.

183. Finn, *Tracing the Veins,* 55–57.

184. Harrington interview.

185. Stefanic interview.

186. "Mine-Mill! Anaconda! Your Neighbors Speak!" *Butte Daily Post,* Dec. 15, 1959, 1.

187. "Forces Joined to Help Needy," *Montana Standard*, Jan. 26, 1960, 1.
188. "County Says Relief Purse Empty," ibid., 1.
189. "2,400 Butte Families Receive Emergency Food and Clothing," ibid., Feb. 2, 1960, 1.
190. Ibid.
191. Ibid.
192. "Butte Aid to Needy Program Coordinated," ibid., Feb. 4, 1960, 1.
193. "Public is Requested to Continue Donations to Needy," ibid., Feb. 10, 1960.
194. "Peace Pact," *Montana Standard*, Feb. 12, 1960, 6; "County Says Relief Purse Empty," ibid., Jan. 27, 1960, 1; "Committee Appeals to Public as Food for Needy Runs Low," ibid., Jan. 29, 1960, 1; "Contributions of Food to City Pile Up," ibid., Jan. 30, 1960, 1; "More Surplus Food Arrives," ibid., Feb. 3, 1960, 1; "Tasty Meals of Surplus Food," ibid., Feb. 4, 1960, 5; "City Will Continue to Give Food and Clothing to Needy," ibid., Feb. 6, 1960, 1; "Public is Requested to Continue Donations to Needy," ibid., Feb. 10, 1960, 1.
195. "Ratification Ends Copper Strike—Workers Are Returning to Jobs," *Montana Standard*, Feb. 16, 1960, 1.
196. Ibid.
197. Kearny, *Butte Voices*, 186.
198. "Anaconda Company Announces Plans for Expansion," *Montana Standard*, Jan. 1, 1962, 1B.
199. Filpula, *Meaderville Revisited*, i.
200. Kangas interview.
201. Finn, *Tracing the Veins*, 191.
202. Brinkel personal communication.

Chapter Two: Mining Childhood

Epigraph. Anonymous interview, 1992.
1. Sheehy interview.
2. Penrose oral history.
3. Ibid.
4. Finn, *Tracing the Veins*, 150.
5. Mercier, "We Are All *Familia*," 270.
6. Carden, "A Walk from 228 Gaylord Street," BSBPA.
7. Anonymous interview (pseudonym).
8. Finn, *Tracing the Veins*, 188. Names used with permission.
9. O'Malley, *Mile High, Mile Deep*, 6.
10. Sheehy interview.
11. Anonymous interview.
12. Klapan interview.
13. Sherman interview.
14. Ibid.
15. Kearney, *Butte Voices*, 211.
16. Burke, "Sixty Years in Butte," BSBPA.
17. Sherman interview.
18. Butori interview.
19. Ciabattari, "Meaderville," 99–100; "Little Italy," *Montana Standard*, Sept. 3, 2006.
20. Penrose oral history.
21. Butori interview.
22. Kearney, *Butte Voices*, 196.
23. Sheehan interview.
24. Filpula, *Meaderville Revisited*, 41.
25. Sheehan interview.
26. Holter interview.
27. Ibid.
28. Ibid.
29. Pentilla interview.
30. Ibid.
31. Stratton interview.
32. Kearney, *Butte Voices*, 189.
33. Ibid.
34. Mercier, "We Are All *Familia*," 270.
35. Mazzola interview.
36. Ibid.
37. Ibid.
38. Ibid.
39. Ibid.
40. Ibid.
41. Wayrenen, "Growing Up in Finntown," BSBPA.
42. Ibid.
43. Ibid.
44. Onkalo interview.
45. Goldberg interview.
46. Ibid.
47. Thelma (Karki) Point Hjelvik, letter to the editor, *Montana Standard*, June 28, 1998, C3.
48. Fischer, "Faith, Hope, and Ethnicity," 27–30, BSBPA.
49. Kearney, *Butte Voices*, 181.
50. Ibid.
51. Hoy interview.
52. Sheehy interview.
53. McHugh, "The Gulch and I," 18, BSBPA.
54. Harrington interview.
55. Buckley interview.
56. Tarrant interview.
57. Brinig, *Singermann*, 34, 37.
58. Martin interview.
59. Henderson interview.
60. Mazzola interview.
61. Stratton interview.
62. Pentilla interview.
63. Practice referred to in oral history accounts.

64. Kaiyala memoir, BSBPA.
65. Ugrin personal communication.
66. Ibid.
67. Goldberg interview.
68. Sheehy interview.
69. "Boy Cries As He Describes Death of Step-Father," *Butte Miner,* Mar. 30, 1923, 7.
70. Ibid.
71. Ibid.
72. Hoy interview.
73. Ibid.
74. Ibid.
75. Antonetti interview.
76. Shea interview.
77. Betty Matesich quote, *Butte, America* DVD.
78. Butori interview.
79. Butler interview.
80. Anonymous interview.
81. McGregor interview.
82. Holter interview.
83. Massey, "My Memories of the Miners' Strike," BSBPA.
84. Ibid.
85. Anonymous interview.
86. This quote captures the sentiments of many people interviewed.
87. Ibid.
88. Shea interview.
89. Sherick interview.
90. McHugh, "The Gulch and I," 19, BSBPA.
91. Stratton interview.
92. Simonich, "Yugoslavian Community," 201; Paula J. McGarvey, "Food for the Soul," *Montana Standard,* Feb. 21, 2009.
93. Fitzpatrick interview.
94. Hoy interview.
95. Sherman interview.
96. McHugh, "The Gulch and I," 20, BSBPA.
97. Payne interview.

Chapter Three: Saving Children

Epigraph. "The Paul Clark Home—Formal Opening Last Night Was a Brilliant Social Event," Nov. 16, 1900, BSBPA.

1. See Abramovitz, "Social Work and Social Reform"; Ehrenreich, *Altruistic Imagination*; and Gordon, *Heroes of Their Own Lives,* for more detailed discussion of the ideologies informing activities of charity organizations of the late nineteenth and early twentieth century. Day, *A New History of Social Welfare,* describes the Progressive Era as a time of reform aimed at promoting government intervention to protect the well-being of citizens and to demand corporate accountability.
2. The founders came together and adopted the motto in late 1897. Philanthropic efforts got under way in 1898.
3. For a more detailed discussion of the Charity Organization Society movement and its underlying philosophy drawn from Social Darwinism, see Day, *A New History of Social Welfare,* 206–20.
4. Christie, "First Biennial Report, Associated Charities," BSBPA.
5. Ibid. The report also notes that Marcus Daly, Clark's archrival, donated 200 tons of coal to the Associated Charities to be distributed to needy families.
6. Ibid.
7. Cunningham, "Annual Report, Associated Charities," BSBPA.
8. Christie, "Second Biennial Report, Associated Charities," BSBPA.
9. "Happy Boys and Girls," BSBPA.
10. Cunningham, "Annual Report, Associated Charities," BSBPA.
11. Christie, "Second Biennial Report, Associated Charities," BSBPA.
12. The language of "dependence" in discussions of charity and public welfare has a long history predating Elizabethan Poor Laws and has been subject to much debate. In general, the term refers to those who depend upon others—whether that be family, charity, or the state—to have basic needs met. For an insightful discussion, see Fraser and Gordon, "A Genealogy of Dependency."
13. Christie, "Second Biennial Report, Associated Charities," BSBPA.
14. Jones, "Third Biennial Report, Associated Charities," BSBPA.
15. The story recounted in this and the following paragraphs comes from "Children Enjoy Outing," BSBPA.
16. The home was improved in 1908 and enlarged in 1920. It served children in need of care under various auspices until 1970.
17. "St. Joseph's Orphanage," *Helena Daily Record,* Oct. 5, 1903. Some parishes organized relief societies that tended to the needy in their congregation, especially widows with children.
18. Ibid.
19. Ibid.
20. "Beautiful Baby Boy for New Year's Gift," *Butte Miner,* Dec. 31, 1910, 7.
21. The Florence Crittenton Home was part of a national Christian service movement initiated

in the early 1880s by New York businessman Charles Crittenton. The history of the movement is described in Baumler, "Making of a Good Woman." Baumler notes that a Florence Crittenton Home was established in Butte in the late 1890s but was only in operation for one year. Reason for the closure is not clear but may be due to the Crittenton policy of not placing girls in their own communities.

22. "Helena as She Was" Website.
23. *Laws, Resolutions . . . 1893*, 190, 187–88.
24. Schoenfeld, *First Report*, 4–6. Throughout the country, organized efforts for the protection of children were initially under the auspices of the Humane Society. Laws for the prevention of cruelty to animals preceded laws for the protection of children and became the basis for such protection.
25. Schoenfeld, *Second Biennial Report*.
26. Schoenfeld, *First Report*, 18–19.
27. Ibid., 20; Silver Bow County Coroner's Register, 1900–1905. See Scee, "The Story to Be Told of the End of the Line," BSBPA, for an intriguing look at the high rates of suicide and widespread sense of hopelessness in Butte resulting from harsh economic, work, and living conditions in the early 1900s. Cases of infanticide at this time could also be considered in this context.
28. "Unfit to Care for Her Tots," *Butte Miner*, Apr. 8, 1906, 6.
29. "Small Boy Weeps in District Court," ibid., May 8, 1910, 5.
30. "Is Bad but Loves Child," ibid., June 18, 1907, 6. Donlan, apparently swayed by Mrs. Ward's claim that she was "not beyond redemption," issued a continuance so that she could have adequate legal representation in making her case for regaining custody of Hazel.
31. See Sutton, *Stubborn Children*, for a detailed account of the emergence of the juvenile justice system in the United States.
32. Malone, Roeder, and Lang, *Montana*, 257. See also Tascher and Withee, "A Chronology of Corrections: Montana," 438.
33. "No Place for the Youthful Offenders," *Butte Miner*, Apr. 4, 1907, 5.
34. "McGowan Endorses Law for Juveniles," *Anaconda Standard*, Dec. 24, 1910, 13.
35. "Boys Set Fire to Grandstand," *Butte Miner*, Apr. 12, 1907, 5.
36. Ibid.
37. Schoenfeld, *First Report*, 12.
38. Astle, *Only in Butte*, 56–57.
39. "Little Girl Waifs," *Butte Miner*, Oct. 8, 1909, 5.
40. Ibid.
41. See, for example, "Girls Danced in Roadhouses until 1 A.M.," *Butte Miner*, June 10, 1916, 5.
42. Schoenfeld, *Second Biennial Report*, 15.
43. Kennedy, *Fourth Biennial Report of the Bureau of Child and Animal Protection*, 7.
44. Boys Charged with Stealing Are Freed," *Butte Miner*, Apr. 5, 1913, 6.
45. Ozanne, "Report of the Butte District Deputy," in *Twelfth Annual Report of the Bureau of Child and Animal Protection*.
46. MacLeod, *Modern Childhood in the Progressive Era*; Cavallo, *Muscles and Morals*. The Playground Association of America was founded in 1906, with the height of the movement between 1906 and 1917.
47. Murphy, *Mining Cultures*, 141.
48. "To Speak on Playgrounds," *Butte Miner*, Jan. 6, 1911, 5.
49. Murphy, *Mining Cultures*, 157.
50. "Wants to Open the Industrial School," *Butte Miner*, Apr. 13, 1923, 5.
51. "Butte's Athletics for Kids Eliminating Incorrigibility," ibid., Jan. 24, 1926, 10.
52. Ibid.
53. Murphy, *Mining Cultures*, 157–58.
54. Ibid., 157, 210–13.
55. "New Welfare Organization Formed with Novel Ideas," *Montana Standard*, Nov. 17, 1931, 1–2.
56. Ibid.
57. "Junior Service League Planning Renewed Drive against Suffering in Mining City during Winter," *Montana Standard*, Dec. 4, 1932, 4.
58. Letter in Junior Service League scrapbook, BSBPA.
59. Murphy, *Mining Cultures*, 202–4; Hathaway, *Sixteenth Biennial Report of the Bureau of Child Protection*.
60. Brandjord, *State of Montana Department of Public Welfare Report . . . 1938*, 19. See also summary reporting, by county, of Aid to Dependent Children payments in *Statistical Report—Montana Department of Public Welfare*, 1939–1945.
61. This paragraph draws from Finn and Crain, *Motherlode*, 17–18.
62. Hickey, "Homeless Children in Butte, Montana," 23–24, 227–29.
63. Ibid., 227.
64. Ibid.
65. "No Place for Youthful Offenders," *Butte Miner*, Apr. 4, 1907, 5. In 1975, the facility changed its name to the Soroptimist Attention Home, with

a focus on diverting juveniles from jail. This chronic concern had plagued youth advocates since 1907, when the exasperated county sheriff had threatened to handcuff errant youth to the posts in front of the courthouse or hobble them and turn them loose on the courthouse lawn.

Chapter Four: Child's Play

Epigraph. Hoy interview.

1. Ibid.
2. Onkalo interview.
3. Buckley interview.
4. Canty interview.
5. Antonetti interview.
6. Onkalo interview.
7. Harrington interview.
8. "Sled Crashes into Pole Injuring Two Maids," *Butte Miner,* Dec. 17, 1909, 5.
9. "Memories: The Holland Rink," BSBPA.
10. Penrose oral history.
11. Shea interview.
12. "249,000 Square Feet of Ice Prepared for Skaters," *Montana Standard,* Dec. 6, 1936, 1.
13. "Fishing Derby Winners Listed," *Montana Standard,* July 5, 1953, 5.
14. Carden, "A Walk from 228 Gaylord Street," BSBPA.
15. Sheehan interview.
16. Harrington interview; Finn, *Tracing the Veins,* 185–86.
17. Harrington interview.
18. Holter interview.
19. Raiha interview.
20. Sheehy interview.
21. Hoy interview.
22. Jursnich, *Butte's East Side,* 119.
23. Carden, "A Walk from 228 Gaylord Street," BSBPA.
24. Harrington interview.
25. Sheehy interview.
26. Henderson interview.
27. Ibid.
28. According to local stories, many Butte homes are plumbed with pipes "the length of a lunch bucket."
29. Hoy interview.
30. Onkalo interview.
31. Harrington interview.
32. "Child Loses Eye through Explosion," *Butte Miner,* Apr. 15, 1908, 4.
33. "Little Boys, Ignorant of Danger, Unwittingly Electrocute Themselves," *Butte Miner,* Apr. 27, 1910, 1.
34. "Boy and Giant Cap a Bad Combination," *Butte Miner,* June 9, 1916, 5.
35. "Dynamite Cap Puts Two Ten Year Old Butte Boys in Hospital," *Butte Miner,* Mar. 11, 1934, 1.
36. "Holiday Blast Kills Six," *Montana Standard,* July 5, 1932, 1–2.
37. McHugh, "The Gulch and I," 6, BSBPA.
38. Hoy interview.
39. Onkalo interview.
40. Shea interview.
41. Evankovich interview.
42. Antonetti interview.
43. Holter interview.
44. Burke, "Sixty Years in Butte," BSBPA.
45. Onkalo interview.
46. Shea interview.
47. Hoy interview.
48. Raiha interview.
49. Jursnich, *Butte's East Side,* 271–73.
50. Hoy interview.
51. Sheehy interview.
52. Kearney, *Butte Voices,* 334.
53. "Kids May Lose Free Pen at Clark Park," *Butte Miner,* May 16, 1924, 11.
54. Ibid.
55. Kearney, *Butte Voices,* 334.
56. Jursnich, *Butte's East Side,* 121–23.
57. "Believe It or Not, Kids, Grandma Was a Star Hoopster," *Montana Standard,* June 28, 1998, C3.
58. John Cortese, "St. Lawrence No-Names Willing to Take On the World," *Montana Standard,* June 28, 1998, C8.
59. Jursnich, *Butte's East Side,* 94. The Neighborhood House was closed for a period of time during the Depression
60. Jursnich, *Butte's East Side,* 100.
61. Ibid.
62. Onkalo interview.
63. Judd, "Judd and Zannon Family History Project," BSBPA.
64. Ibid.; George Everett, "Butte Halloween Party Steeped in Tradition, *Great Falls Tribune,* Oct. 27, 2000, 15.
65. "Council Passes Ordinance Prohibiting Immoral Plays," *Butte Miner,* Oct. 3, 1907, 1.
66. Ibid.
67. Theater bills advertised in the *Butte Miner,* ca. 1914; *Butte City Directory,* 1915.
68. Stories recounted in various oral histories. See also "Theaters in Butte," BSBPA.
69. Shannon interview.
70. Barsanti interview.
71. Sheehy interview.
72. Martin interview.

73. Tretheway, "The John Wallace Cochrane Family," BSBPA.
74. Carden, "A Walk from 228 Gaylord Street," BSBPA.
75. Antonetti interview.
76. Mazzola interview.
77. Raiha interview.
78. Butori interview.
79. Penrose oral history.
80. Sheehan interview.
81. Sheehy interview.
82. Klapan interview.
83. Kangas interview.

Chapter Five: School Days

Epigraph. Blaine School student essay, ca. 1927.
1. Kearney, *Butte Voices*, 187.
2. Pentilla interview.
3. Jursnich, *Butte's East Side*, 60–61.
4. *Montana Standard*, July 21, 1975, news clipping.
5. Grant School principal to Badovinac, BSBPA.
6. Ibid.
7. Jursnich, *Butte's East Side*, 83–87.
8. Goldberg interview.
9. Kearney, *Butte Voices*, 211.
10. Mazzola interview.
11. Sherick interview.
12. Emmons, *The Butte Irish.*
13. "Sacred Heart School," BSBPA.
14. Sheehan, "Nun Rethinks Education," 53.
15. "New Girls Central High School Opens for Some Classes This Week," *Montana Standard*, Apr. 22, 1951, 1.
16. Sheehan, "Nun Rethinks Our Education," 53–56; "Butte Central—One Hundred Years," *Montana Standard*, July 4, 1992, supplement.
17. Nicholls interview.
18. The Knights of Columbus is a Catholic organization. See Kearney, *Butte's Big Game*, for more on the football rivalry. The teams did not play one another in 1917–1918 or in 1940–1942. According to Kearney, pp. 97–100, the game was cancelled in 1940 as a result of street dancing that turned riotous in 1939. Three games ended in ties.
19. Kearney, *Butte's Big Game*, 97.
20. Ibid.
21. This is not an exhaustive list of school-based activities. Butte High School yearbooks provide ample evidence of the variety of activities available to both boys and girls.
22. Young, *The Public School System of Butte, Montana*, 64.
23. *Washington Junior High Ingot*, BSBPA, quote from 1915 principal Leo H. King.
24. Ibid.
25. Ibid.
26. Ibid.
27. Young, *The Public School System of Butte, Montana*, 43.
28. "Girl Accused of Being a Truant," *Butte Miner*, Feb. 19, 1911, 5.
29. Ibid.
30. "School Boy Must Not Peddle Milk," *Butte Miner*, Apr. 2, 1911, 6.
31. Pentilla interview.
32. Betty Ann Raymond, "Frances Lenz Sees No Reason for Recognition," *Montana Standard*, Apr. 24, 1977, 19.
33. Sconfienza interview.
34. Martinez interview.
35. John Laitinen to Nick Badovinac, Dec. 13, 1989, BSBPA.
36. Hoy interview.
37. Ibid.
38. Sheehy interview.
39. Goldberg interview.
40. Sconfienza interview.
41. Shea interview.
42. Mazzola interview.
43. Mercier, "We Are All *Familia*," 271.
44. Duncan interview.
45. Antonetti interview.
46. Raiha interview.
47. Hole interview.
48. King interview. King noted that Henry Schiesser was no longer band director at the time he attended high school in Butte.
49. Butler interview.
50. Goldberg interview.
51. Anonymous interview.
52. Bush interview.
53. Blaine School student essays, BSBPA.
54. For more on this era in Butte, see Murphy, *Mining Cultures*, 71–105.
55. All selections in the section are found in Blaine School student essays, BSBPA.
56. Zinn, *A People's History of the United States*, 359–376; Punke, *Fire and Brimstone*, 213–25.
57. Punke, *Fire and Brimstone*, 239–40.
58. Toole, *Twentieth-century Montana*, 186–87.
59. Work, *Darkest before Dawn*, 87. See also National Security League, "A Suggestive Outline for Teachers," BSBPA.
60. Work, *Darkest before Dawn*, 141.
61. Heiman, "The Sentiments of a Loyal American of German Birth," 26, BSBPA.

62. Fischer, "Faith, Hope, and Ethnicity," BSBPA.
63. Ibid. See also Hannan Diary, BSBPA.
64. This was not the case in all parts of the country. As Freedman addresses in *Children of the Great Depression*, p. 31, in some parts of the country, schools were closing due to inability to pay teachers, and youngsters were leaving school in search of any sort of work.
65. "Reunion: Classmates of 50 Years Ago Find Time Brings Them Closer," *Montana Standard*, Aug. 12, 1984, 19.
66. Ibid.
67. Sheehy interview.
68. Jursnich, *Butte's East Side*, 64–65.
69. Mazzola interview.
70. Dedication to *Butte High School Salute, 1945*, BSBPA.
71. PTA minutes, Mar. 1, Nov. 8, 1944, Mar. 14, 1945, BSBPA.
72. Ibid., Mar. 10, Oct. 12, 1948, Jan. 12, Apr. 12, 1949.
73. Ibid., Feb. 11, 1953.
74. Adams, *The Trouble with Normal*.
75. Szasz, "Atomic Comics."
76. Nyberg, *Seal of Approval*; U.S. Senate Committee on the Judiciary, *Juvenile Delinquency (Comic Books) Hearings before the Subcommittee to Investigate Juvenile Delinquency in the U.S.*
77. McGinley, "The Nevada Street Art School," 200, BSBPA.
78. Filipula, *Meaderville Revisited*, 139; Zanchi interview.
79. Zanchi interview.
80. Ibid.; Sherick interview.
81. Henry Schiesser "biographical summary," BSBPA.
82. Ibid.
83. "Butte to Accord Its Band Warm Welcome," *Montana Standard*, Jan. 4, 1948.
84. Henry and Jean Schiesser Collection, folder 15, BSBPA, excerpts from handwritten letter. Note that Karen would have been six years old and starting first grade that year.

Chapter Six: Learning to Labor

Epigraph. Shannon interview.
1. McHugh, "The Gulch and I," 12, BSBPA.
2. Ibid.
3. Day, *A New History of Social Welfare*, 238; MacLeod, *The Age of the Child*, 106–17.
4. Schoenfeld, *First Report of the Bureau of Child and Animal Protection*, 18.
5. Ostberg, "Sketches of Old Butte," 69, BSBPA.
6. "Things Are Being Done for Butte Newsboys," *Anaconda Standard*, May 3, 1903, pt. 2, 7.
7. Martin, "School for Struggle," 9–11.
8. Ibid.
9. "Old Butte Newsboys Club Dissolved after Years of Service to Youth of City," *Montana Standard*, Apr. 12, 1931, 1.
10. Ibid. The judgment was requested in a suit filed by six of the eleven original trustees. The club's assets of several thousand dollars and title to lots that had been purchased to build a facility for the club were turned over to two of the trustees.
11. Sheehy interview.
12. Ibid.
13. Mazzola interview.
14. Shannon interview.
15. Downs interview.
16. Hoy interview.
17. Ibid.
18. Ibid.
19. Goldberg interview.
20. Ibid.
21. Hanley interview.
22. Sherman interview.
23. Andrea McCormick, "Buckley Boardinghouse: Butte's Little Ireland," *Montana Standard*, Mar. 16, 1980, 18.
24. Buckley interview.
25. Raiha interview.
26. Ibid.
27. Dean interview.
28. Sconfienza interview.
29. Martin interview.
30. Trevena interview.
31. Mazzola interview.
32. Holter interview.
33. Antonetti interview.
34. *Montana Standard*, July 27, 1976, 5; McCormick, "A Taste for Butte," 57–60.
35. McCormick, "A Taste for Butte," 58.
36. Holter interview.
37. Mazzola interview.
38. Ibid.
39. Evankovich interview.
40. Webster interview.
41. Tretheway, "The John Wallace Cochrane Family," BSBPA.
42. Shannon interview.
43. Dornhofer interview.
44. Ibid.
45. Ibid.
46. Jursnich, *Butte's East Side*, 117–18.

47. "All Needy Workers in Butte Will Have Jobs under FERA," *Montana Standard,* Apr. 1, 1934.
48. Sconfienza interview.
49. Tretheway, "The John Wallace Cochrane Family."
50. Sheehy interview.
51. Kearney, *Butte Voices,* 20.
52. Roberts interview.
53. Ibid.
54. Andrea McCormick, "Drive-in Serves Up Morsels of Yesterday," *Montana Standard,* July 27, 1980, 17.

Chapter Seven: Memories of a McQueen Childhood

1. This chapter is based on an interview with Steve Sherick.
2. "Butte Jugo-Slavs to Hold Mesopust," *Montana Standard,* Feb. 15, 1931, 1–2; McGrath, *Butte Heritage Cookbook,* 199–200. See also John Astle, "Mesopust," *Butte Weekly,* Feb. 7, 2001.
3. "Pupils Decide to Wear Beards—'Rubber Tire' Specs and Mustaches to Be Featured at 'Bohunkus' Day at High School April 16," *Butte Miner,* Mar. 25, 1920, 6. See also "Bohunkus Day," BSBPA.
4. "Butte High Schools Seniors Forsake Dignity to Honor Bohunkus, Saint of Tramps," *Montana Standard,* May 10, 1930, 1.
5. "Subjects of King Bohunkus," ibid., Apr. 27, 1935, 1.
6. "Snowfall Doesn't Dampen Spirit of Bohunkus Day," ibid., Apr. 21, 1951, 1.
7. "Bohunkus Day Merriment," ibid., Feb. 27, 1994, 12.

Chapter Eight: Childhood Matters

Epigraph. Nicholls interview.
1. I borrow the term "geography of childhood" from Jeffrey Shook, who has addressed "childhood by geography" in relation to the differential treatment of children in the justice system based on the particular state and judicial district in which they reside. See Shook, "Childhood by Geography."
2. See O'Kane, "Marginalized Children as Social Actors," for a discussion of children's sense of justice.
3. I draw this notion from Coles, *The Political Life of Children.* Coles describes how a nation's politics become part of children's everyday psychology.
4. There is a rich literature on the concepts of intergenerational and historical trauma, both in studies of family systems and in studies of social groups who have experienced histories of oppression. The concept of historical trauma has been used as a frame for understanding experiences of trauma, loss, and grief in Native American communities and among Holocaust survivors. See, for example, Weaver, "Indigenous People and the Social Work Profession"; Abrams, "Intergenerational Trauma"; and Brave Heart, "The Impact of Historical Trauma."

Bibliography

Abbreviations used in this bibliography include Butte-Silver Bow Public Archives (BSBPA); Drawer (DR); File Folder (FF); Manuscript (MS); Montana Historical Society, Helena (MHS); Oral History (OH); Oral History Collection (OHC); Oral History Project (OHP); Typescript (TS); University of Montana, Missoula (UM); and Vertical Files (VF).

Books and Articles

Abramovitz, Mimi. "Social Work and Social Reform: An Arena of Struggle." *Social Work* 43 (1998): 512–26.

Abrams, Madeleine S. "Intergenerational Trauma: Recent Contributions from the Literature of Family Systems Approaches to Treatment." *American Journal of Psychotherapy* 53 (1999): 225–31.

Adams, Mary Louise. *The Trouble with Normal: Postwar Youth and the Making of Heterosexuality.* Toronto: University of Toronto Press, 1997.

Ariès, Philipe. *Centuries of Childhood.* Translated by Robert Baldick. London: Jonathan Cape, 1962.

Astle, John. *Only in Butte: Stories off the Hill.* Butte, Mont.: Holt Publishing, 2004.

Baumler, Ellen. "The Making of a Good Woman: Montana and the National Florence Crittenton Mission." *Montana The Magazine of Western History* 53 (Winter 2002): 50–63.

Boyer, Lynne. "Butte's Columbia Gardens." *Montana Historian* 8 (1978): 2–7.

Brace, Charles Loring. *The Best Method of Disposing of Pauper and Vagrant Children.* New York: Wynkoop and Hollenbeck, 1859.

———. *The Dangerous Classes of New York and My Twenty Years among Them.* New York: Wynkoop and Hollenbeck, 1872.

Brave Heart, Maria Yellow Horse. "The Impact of Historical Trauma: The Example of the Native Community." In *Trauma Transformed: An Empowerment Response.* Edited by Marian Bussy and Judith Bula Wise. New York: Columbia University Press, 2007.

Bremner, Robert, ed. *Children and Youth in America: A Documentary History.* 3 vols. Cambridge, Mass.: Harvard University Press, 1970.

Brinig, Myron. *Singermann.* New York: Farrar & Rinehart, 1939.

Butte City Directory. Helena, Mont.: R. L. Polk, 1900–1940.

Calkins, Ray, comp. *Looking Back from the Hill: Recollections of Butte People.* Butte, Mont.: Butte Historical Society, 1982.

Calvert, Jerry. *The Gibraltar: Socialism and Labor in Butte, Montana, 1885–1920.* Helena, Mont.: Montana Historical Society Press, 1988.

Cavallo, Dominick. *Muscles and Morals: Organized Playgrounds and Urban Reform, 1880–1920.* Philadelphia: University of Pennsylvania Press, 1981.

Ciabattari, Andrea. "Meaderville." In *Butte Heritage Cookbook.* Edited by Jean McGrath. Butte, Mont.: Butte-Silver Bow Bicentennial Commission, 1976.

Cloward, Richard, and Lloyd Ohlin. *Delinquency and Opportunity: A Theory of Delinquent Gangs.* New York: Free Press, 1966.

Cohen, Robert, ed. *Dear Mrs. Roosevelt: Letters from Children of the Great Depression.* Chapel Hill: University of North Carolina Press, 2002.

Coles, Robert. *The Political Life of Children.* Boston: Atlantic Monthly Press, 1986.

"Company Towns." *Time,* Apr. 1, 1956, 100–101.

Crain, Ellen, and Andrea McCormick. "Butte's Cadet Nurses: Commitment to Country, Community, and Caregiving." In *Motherlode: Legacies of Women's Lives and Labors in Butte, Montana.* Edited by Janet L. Finn and Ellen Crain. Livingston, Mont.: Clark City Press, 2005.

Davenport, Loralee. "The Pearl Club: Black Women and Community Building in the

Mining City." In *Motherlode: Legacies of Women's Lives and Labors in Butte, Montana*. Edited by Janet L. Finn and Ellen Crain. Livingston, Mont.: Clark City Press, 2005.

Davies, Allen. *Spearheads for Reform: The Social Settlements and the Progressive Movement, 1890–1914*. New York: Columbia University Press, 1967.

Davin, Anna. *Growing Up Poor: Home, School, and Street in London, 1870–1914*. London: Rivers Oram Press, 1996.

Day, Phyllis. *A New History of Social Welfare*. 4th ed. Boston: Allyn and Bacon, 2003.

Ehrenreich, John. *The Altruistic Imagination: A History of Social Work and Social Policy in the United States*. Ithaca, N.Y.: Cornell University Press, 1985.

Emmons, David. *The Butte Irish: Class and Ethnicity in an American Mining Town, 1875–1925*. Urbana: University of Illinois Press, 1989.

Fass, Paula. *Children of a New World: Society, Culture and Globalization*. New York: New York University Press, 2007.

Faue, Elizabeth. "Retooling the Class Factory: United States Labour History after Marx, Montgomery, and Postmodernism." *Labour History* 82 (2002): 109–19.

Filpula, Joan M. *Meaderville Revisited*. Privately printed, 2008.

Finn, Janet L. "A Penny for Your Thoughts: Stories of Women, Copper, and Community." *Frontiers: A Journal of Women Studies* 19 (1998): 231–49.

————. "Making Trouble: Representations of Children, Social Work, and Pathology." In *Childhood, Youth and Social Work in Transformation: Implications for Policy and Practice*. Edited by Lynn M. Nybell, Jeffrey J. Shook, and Janet L. Finn. New York: Columbia University Press, 2009.

————. "Seeing the Forest through the Trees: The Green Legacy of Alma Higgins." In *Motherlode: Legacies of Women's Lives and Labors in Butte, Montana*. Edited by Janet L. Finn and Ellen Crain. Livingston, Mont.: Clark City Press, 2005.

————. *Tracing the Veins: Of Copper, Culture, and Community from Butte to Chuquicamata*. Berkeley: University of California Press, 1998.

Finn, Janet L., and Ellen Crain, eds. *Motherlode: Legacies of Women's Lives and Labors in Butte, Montana*. Livingston, Mont.: Clark City Press, 2005.

Flesch, Rudolph. *Why Johnny Can't Read*. New York: Harper and Row, 1955.

Fraser, Nancy, and Linda Gordon. "A Genealogy of Dependency: Tracing a Keyword of the U.S. Welfare State." *Signs* 19 (Winter 1994): 309–36.

Freedman, Russell. *Children of the Great Depression*. New York: Clarion, 2005.

Glasscock, C. B. *The War of the Copper Kings*. New York: Grosset and Dunlap, 1935.

Gordon, Linda. *Heroes of Their Own Lives: The Politics and History of Family Violence*. New York: Viking, 1988.

Gorn, Elliott. *Mother Jones: The Most Dangerous Woman in America*. New York: Hill & Wang, 2001.

Gutfeld, Arnon. *Montana's Agony: Years of War and Hysteria, 1917–1921*. Gainesville: University of South Florida Press, 1979.

Hall, G. Stanley. *Adolescence, Its Psychology and Its Relation to Physiology, Anthropology, Sociology, Sex, Crime, Religion, and Education*. Vol. 1. New York: Appleton, 1904.

Hawes, Joseph. *Children between the Wars: American Childhood, 1920–1940*. New York: Twayne, 1997.

Hickey, Margaret, ed. "Homeless Children in Butte, Montana." *Ladies Home Journal*, Sept. 1950, 23–24, 227–29.

Higgins, Chas. M. *Horrors of Vaccination Exposed and Illustrated*. Brooklyn, N.Y.: Chas. M. Higgins, 1920.

Holloran, Peter. *Boston's Wayward Children: Social Services for Homeless Children, 1830–1930*. Boston: Northeastern University Press, 1989.

Jacobson, Lisa. *Raising Consumers: Children and the American Mass Market in the Early Twentieth Century*. New York: Columbia University Press, 2004.

James, Allison, and Adrian. L. James. *Constructing Childhood: Theory, Policy, and Social Practice*. New York: Palgrave Macmillan, 2004.

James, Allison, and Alan Prout, eds. *Constructing and Reconstructing Childhood: Contemporary Issues in the Sociological Study of Childhood*. 2nd ed. London: Falmer Press, 1997.

Jursnich, Edward. *Butte's East Side: Gone but Not Forgotten*. Denver: Outskirts Press, 2009.

Kearney, Patrick. *Butte Voices: Mining, Neighborhoods, People*. Butte, Mont.: Skyhigh Communications, 1998.

————. *Butte's Big Game: Butte Central vs. Butte High*. Butte, Mont.: Skyhigh Communications, 1989.

————. *Butte's Pride: The Columbia Gardens*. Butte, Mont.: Skyhigh Communications, 1994.

Lee, Rose Hum. *The Growth and Decline of Chinese Communities in the Rocky Mountain Region*. New York: Arno Press, 1978.

Lindsey, Duncan. *The Welfare of Children.* 2nd ed. New York: Oxford University Press, 2004.

Long, Priscilla. *Mother Jones: Woman Organizer and Her Relations with Miners' Wives, Working Women, and the Suffrage Movement.* Boston: South End Press, 1976.

MacLeod, David. *The Age of the Child: Children in America, 1890–1920.* New York: Twayne, 1998.

Malone, Michael, Richard B. Roeder, and William L. Lang. *Montana: A History of Two Centuries.* Rev. ed. Seattle: University of Washington Press, 1991.

Maney Ross, Marilyn, and Janet L. Finn. "Sisterhood Is Powerful: The Labors of the Butte Women's Protective Union." In *Motherlode: Legacies of Women's Lives and Labors in Butte, Montana.* Livingston, Mont.: Clark City Press, 2005.

Martin, Dale. "School for Struggle: The Butte Newsboys Strikes of 1914 and 1919." *Speculator* 2 (Summer 1985): 9–11.

McCormick, Andrea. "A Taste for Butte: Lydia Micheletti." In *Motherlode: Legacies of Women's Lives and Labors in Butte, Montana.* Edited by Janet L Finn and Ellen Crain. Livingston, Mont.: Clark City Press, 2005.

McGinley, John. "Nevada Street Art School." In *Motherlode: Legacies of Women's Lives and Labors in Butte, Montana.* Edited by Janet L. Finn and Ellen Crain. Livingston, Mont.: Clark City Press, 2005.

McGrath, Jean, ed. *Butte Heritage Cookbook.* Butte, Mont.: Butte-Silver Bow Bicentennial Commission, 1976.

Mercier, Laurie. "We Are All *Familia:* The Work and Activism of Lula Martinez." In *Motherlode: Legacies of Women's Lives and Labors in Butte, Montana.* Edited by Janet L. Finn and Ellen Crain. Livingston, Mont.: Clark City Press, 2005.

Mintz, Steven. *Huck's Raft: A History of American Childhood.* Cambridge, Mass.: Belknap Press, 2004.

Murphy, Mary. *Mining Cultures: Men, Women, and Leisure in Butte, 1914–41.* Urbana: University of Illinois Press, 1997.

————. "Women's Work in a Man's World," *Speculator* 1 (Winter 1984): 18–25.

Nasaw, David. *Children of the City at Work and at Play.* Garden City, N.Y.: Anchor Press/ Doubleday, 1985.

Nybell, Lynn M., Jeffrey J. Shook, and Janet L. Finn, eds. *Childhood, Youth and Social Work in Transformation: Implications for Policy and Practice.* New York: Columbia University Press, 2009.

Nyberg, Ami Kiste. *Seal of Approval: The History of the Comics Code.* Jackson: University Press of Mississippi, 1998.

O'Kane, Claire. "Marginalized Children as Social Actors for Social Justice in South Asia." *British Journal of Social Work* 32 (2004): 697–710.

O'Malley, Richard K. *Mile High, Mile Deep.* Privately printed, 1986.

Peavy, Linda, and Ursula Smith. *Frontier Children.* Norman, Okla.: University of Oklahoma Press, 1999.

Prodgers, Jeanette. *Butte-Anaconda Almanac: A Day by Day History of Montana's Two Greatest Mining and Smelting Towns.* Butte, Mont.: Butte Historical Society, 1991.

Punke, Michael. *Fire and Brimstone: The North Butte Mining Disaster of 1917.* New York: Hyperion, 2006.

Qvortrup, Jens, ed. *Studies in Modern Childhood: Society, Agency, Culture.* New York: Palgrave Macmillan, 2005.

Renne, R. R. *A Preliminary Report of the Butte Economic Survey.* Butte, Mont.: Works Progress Administration, 1939.

Roberts, Albert R., ed. *Juvenile Justice Sourcebook: Past, Present, and Future.* New York: Oxford University Press, 2004.

Scheper-Hughes, Nancy, and Carol Sargent, eds. *Small Wars: The Cultural Politics of Childhood.* Berkeley: University of California Press, 1998.

Sealander, Judith. *The Failed Century of the Child: Governing America's Young in the Twentieth Century.* New York: Cambridge University Press, 2003.

————. "The History of Childhood Policy: A Philippic's Wish List." *Journal of Policy History* 16 (2004): 176–87.

Sheehan, S. "Nun Rethinks Our Education." In *Motherlode: Legacy of Women's Lives and Labors in Butte, Montana.* Edited by Janet L. Finn and Ellen Crain. Livingston, Mont.: Clark City Press, 2005. Reprinted from *Butte (Mont.) Montana Standard,* Aug. 24, 1975.

Shook, Jeffrey J. "Childhood by Geography: Toward a Framework of Rights, Responsibilities, and Entitlements." In *Childhood, Youth and Social Work in Transformation.* Edited by Lynn M. Nybell, Jeffrey J. Shook, and Janet L. Finn. New York: Columbia University Press, 2009.

Simonich, Ann. "Yugoslavian Community." In *Butte Heritage Cookbook.* Edited by Jean McGrath. Butte, Mont.: Butte-Silver Bow Bicentennial Commission, 1976.

Smil, Vaclav. *Creating the Twentieth Century:*

Technical Innovations of 1867–1914 and Their Lasting Impact. New York: Oxford University Press, 2005.

Staudohar, Connie. "Dr. Caroline McGill, Mining City Doctor." In *Motherlode: Legacies of Women's Lives and Labors in Butte, Montana.* Edited by Janet L. Finn and Ellen Crain. Livingston, Mont.: Clark City Press, 2005.

Stephens, Sharon, ed. *Children and the Politics of Culture.* Princeton, N.J.: Princeton University Press, 1995.

Stewart, Jeffrey C. *1001 Things Everyone Should Know about African American History.* New York: Doubleday, 1996.

Sutton, John. *Stubborn Children.* Berkeley: University of California Press, 1988.

Szasz, Ferenc M. "Atomic Comics: The Comic Book Industry Confronts the Nuclear Age." In *Atomic Culture: How We Learned to Stop Worrying and Love the Bomb.* Edited by Scott C. Zeman and Michael A. Amundson. Boulder: University Press of Colorado, 2004.

Taksa, Lucy. "Family, Childhood, and Identities: Working-Class History from a Personalized Perspective." *Labour History* 82 (May 2002): 127–34.

Tascher, Harold, and Clara Withee. "A Chronology of Corrections: Montana." *Crime and Delinquency* 3 (October, 1957): 438–39.

Toole, K. Ross. *Twentieth-century Montana: A State of Extremes.* Norman: University of Oklahoma Press, 1972.

Towne, Charles W. *A Short History of Butte, Containing a Few Statistics Pleasantly Told.* Butte, Mont.: Chamber of Commerce, 1925.

Trattner, Walter. *From Poor Law to Welfare State: A History of Social Welfare in America.* 4th ed. New York: Free Press, 1989.

Weaver, Hillary. "Indigenous People and the Social Work Profession: Defining Culturally Competent Practice." *Social Work* 44 (1999): 217–25.

West, Elliott. "Child's Play: Tradition and Adaptation on the Frontier." *Montana The Magazine of Western History* 38 (Winter 1988): 2–15.

_____. "Families in the West." *Organization of American Historians Magazine of History* 9 (Fall 1994): 18–21.

_____. *Growing Up with the Country: Childhood on the Far Western Frontier.* Albuquerque: University of New Mexico Press, 1989.

Work, Clemens. *Darkest before Dawn: Sedition and Free Speech in the American West.* Albuquerque: University of New Mexico Press, 2005.

Writers Project of Montana. *Copper Camp: Stories of the World's Greatest Mining Town, Butte, Montana.* Helena, Mont.: Riverbend Publishing, 2002. First published 1943 by Montana State Department of Agriculture, Labor, and Industry.

Yarrow, Andrew. *History of U.S. Children's Policy 1900 to Present.* Washington, D.C.: First Focus Publication, 2009.

Young, Robert. *The Public School System of Butte, Montana: Historical, Descriptive, and Illustrative.* Butte, Mont.: Board of Education, 1904.

Zelizer, Viviana. *Pricing the Priceless Child: The Changing Social Value of Children.* New York: Basic Books, 1985.

Zinn, Howard. *A People's History of the United States, 1492 to Present.* 2nd ed. New York: Harper Collins, 1999.

Film

Butte, America. DVD. Directed by Pamela Roberts. Bozeman, Mont.: Rattlesnake Productions, 2009.

Government Documents and Reports

Brandjord, I. M. *State of Montana Department of Public Welfare Report to the Honorable Roy E. Ayers, Governor, for the One-Year Period Beginning Mar. 2, 1937 and Terminating Mar. 1, 1938.* Helena, Mont.: State of Montana Department of Public Welfare, 1938.

Carroll, William E., and Alex Mackel. *Revised Ordinances, City of Butte, 1914.* Butte, Mont.: McKee Printing, 1914.

Cooney, Frank H. *Message of Governor to the Twenty-Third Legislative Assembly in Extraordinary Session of the State of Montana, 1933.* Copy in FF 12, Box 15, Montana Governors Records, 1889–1962, MC 35, MHS.

Hathaway, Maggie Smith. *Sixteenth Biennial Report of the Bureau of Child Protection Biennial Report, 1931–32.* Helena, Mont.: State of Montana, 1932.

Kennedy, J. M. *Fourth Biennial Report of the Bureau of Child and Animal Protection, State of Montana, 1909–1910.* Helena, Mont.: Independent Publishing Company, 1911.

Laws, Resolutions and Memorials of the State of Montana Passed at the Third Regular Session of the Legislative Assembly, 1893. Butte City, Mont.: Inter Mountain Publishing Company, 1893.

Statistical Report—Montana Department of Public Welfare. Vols. 2–8. Helena, Mont.: Montana Department of Public Welfare, 1939–1945.

Ozanne, Paul. "Report of the Butte District Deputy." In *Twelfth Annual Report of the Bureau* of *Child and Animal Protection, 1922–1924.* Helena, Mont.: State of Montana, 1924.

Schoenfeld, Otto. *First Report of the Bureau of Child and Animal Protection.* Helena, Mont.: Independent Publishing Company, 1904.

————. *Second Biennial Report of the Bureau of Child and Animal Protection, 1905–1906.* Helena, Mont.: Independent Publishing Company, 1906.

U.S. Congress. Senate. Senate Committee on the Judiciary. *Juvenile Delinquency (Comic Books) Hearings before the Subcommittee to Investigate Juvenile Delinquency in the U.S.* 83rd Cong., 2nd sess., Apr. 21, 22, June 4, 1954.

Internet Sources

"Helena as She Was: A Cooperative History Resource, http://www.helenahistory.org/good_shepherd.htm.

"Honoring Montana's World War II Veterans," *Capitolwords,* 58, June 12, 2012, e1034. http://capitolwords.org/date/2012/06/08/E1034-4_honoring-montanas-world-war-ii-veterans/.

Montana Sedition Project, University of Montana School of Journalism, http://www.seditionproject.net/.

"The Polio Crusade: Introduction." *American Experience,* 2009. http://www.pbs.org/wgbh/americanexperience/features/introduction/polio-introduction/.

Wilson, Linda D. "War Bonds Drives." *Encyclopedia of Oklahoma History and Culture.* Oklahoma Historical Society, 2007. http://digital.library.okstate.edu/encyclopedia/entries/W/WA020.html.

Interviews and Correspondence

Anonymous. Interviews by author, 1992.

Antonetti, Kay. Interview by author. Helena, Mont., July 29, 2009.

Barsanti, Dolores Silver. Interview by Rickey Cliff. Butte, Mont., Apr. 15, 2005. Transcript. OH 008, BSBPA.

Brinkel, Dolores. Personal communication. July 16, 2012.

Buckley, Patrick Michael "Packey." Interview by Joan Porter. Butte, Mont., Apr. 25, 2001. Transcript. OH 025, BSBPA.

Bush, Helen. Interview by Ellen Crain. Butte, Mont., n.d. Transcript. OH 026, BSBPA.

Butler, Karen. Interview by Martha Jessup. Butte, Mont., Mar. 9, 2002. Transcript. OH 028, BSBPA.

Butori, Marie. Interview by Katrina O'Brien. Butte, Mont., n.d. Transcript. OH 029, BSBPA.

Canty, Patricia. Interview by Maria Canty. Butte, Mont., Nov. 27, 2001. Transcript. OH 039, BSBPA.

Dean, Mabel. Interview by Stephen Wilson. Butte, Mont., Apr. 9, 2001.Transcript. OHC: Harrington Class: Dean, Mabel, BSBPA.

Dornhofer, Frank. Interview by Jacqueline Rautio. Butte, Mont., Nov. 28, 1999. Transcript. OHC: Harrington Class: Dornhofer, Frank, BSBPA.

Downs, Micah. Interview by author. Butte, Mont., May 20, 2009.

Duncan, Perdita. Interview by Mary Murphy. Butte, Mont., Mar. 18, 1980. Transcript. OHC: OHP: Perdita, Duncan, BSBPA.

Evankovich, Helen. Interview by author. Butte, Mont., May 27, 2009.

Fitzpatrick, Mary Lou Kane. Interview by Mary James. Butte, Mont., Feb. 9, 2001. Transcript. OHC: Harrington Class: Fitzpatrick, Mary Lou Kane, BSBPA.

Goldberg, Aili. Interview by Mary Murphy. Butte, Mont., Feb. 29, 1980. Transcript. OHC: OHP: Goldberg, Aili, BSBPA.

Harrington, Danette. Interview by author. Butte, Mont., June 10, 1993, and Sept. 6, 2011.

Henderson, Betty A. Interview by author. Butte, Mont., June 3, 2009.

Hole, Robert. Interview by author. Butte, Mont., July 10, 2009.

Holter, Thomas. Interview by author. Butte, Mont., July 1, 2009.

Hoy, Catherine. Interview by Ray Calkins. Butte, Mont., May 11, 1979. Transcript. OHC: R. Calkins & C. Smithson: Hoy Catherine, BSBPA.

Kangas, Dolores. Interview by author. Butte, Mont., July 23, 2009.

King, Thomas. Interview by author. Butte, Mont., July 30, 2009.

Klapan, Nancy. Interview by Seth Hertin. Butte, Mont., Apr. 15, 2005. Transcript. OHC: Harrington Class: Klapan, Nancy, BSBPA.

Martin, Dorothy. Interview by Mary Murphy. Butte, Mont., May 23, 1988. Transcript. OHC: OHP: Martin, Dorothy, BSBPA.

Martinez, Lula. Interview by Teresa Jordan. Butte, Mont., Apr. 2, 1986. OHC: Teresa Jordan: Martinez, Lula, BSBPA.

Mazzola, John. Interview by author. Butte, Mont., July 2, 2009.

McGregor, Helen. Interview by Mary Murphy. Butte, Mont., June 12, 2003. Transcript. OHC: OHP: McGregor, Helen, BSBPA.

Nicholls, Helen. Interview by Teresa Jordan. Butte, Mont., Apr. 23, 1985. Transcript. OHC: Teresa Jordan: Nicholls, Helen, BSBPA.

Onkalo, John. Interview by Ray Calkins. Butte, Mont., Feb. 5, 1981. Transcript. OHC: Ray F. Calkins: Onkalo, John, BSBPA.

Payne, Janie. Interview by James Hadley. Butte, Mont., Nov. 29, 2005. Transcript. OHC: Harrington Class: Payne, Janie, BSBPA.

Penrose, Elinore Sterrett Shields. Oral history recorded by Lynn Penrose. Butte, Mont., Sept. 3, 1984. MS. "Vertical Files—Biography: Penrose, Elinore Sterrett Shields." VF 0674, BSBPA.

Pentilla, Ann Skoll. Interview by Ray Calkins and Caroline Smithson. Butte, Mont., Apr. 27, 1979. Transcript. OHC: R. Calkins & C. Smithson: Pentilla, Ann Skoll, BSBPA.

Raiha, Linda. Interview by author. Butte, Mont., June 10, 1993, and Sept. 6, 2011.

Roberts, Joe. Interview by Julie Kerns. Butte, Mont., Oct. 19, 1994. Transcript. OHC: Harrington Class: Roberts, Joe, BSBPA.

Sconfienza, John. Interview by Ray Calkins. Butte, Mont., June 27, 1979. Transcript. OHC: Ray F. Calkins: Sconfienza, John, BSBPA.

Shannon, Kevin. Interview by author. Butte, Mont., Apr. 7, 2009.

Shea, John T. Interview by Corey Warner. Butte, Mont., Apr. 19, 2005. Transcript. OHC: Harrington Class: Shea, John T., BSBPA.

Sheehan, Lucille Martinesso. Interview by author. Butte, Mont., June 24, 2009.

Sheehy, John "Skeff." Interview by author. Helena, Mont., Nov. 17, 2009.

Sherick, Steve. Interview by author. Missoula, Mont., June 2, 2009.

Sherman, Bessie. Interview by Steve Sherman. Butte, Mont., n.d. Transcript. OHC: Harrington Class: Sherman, Bessie, BSBPA.

Stefanic, Bonnie. Interview by author. Butte, Mont., July 15, 1991 and Jan. 15, 2012.

Stratton, Vadis. Interview by author. Butte, Mont., June 4, 2009.

Tarrant, Colleen. Interview by Adam Lawrence. Butte, Mont., Apr. 15, 2002. Transcript. OHC: Harrington Class: Tarrant, Colleen, BSBPA.

Trevena, Shirley. Interview by author. Butte, Mont., May 26, 2009.

Ugrin, Laurie. Personal communication, Nov. 15, 2011.

Webster, Valentine. Interview by Mary Murphy. Butte, Mont., Feb. 24, 1980. "Vertical Files—Biography: Webster, Valentine." VF 0818, BSBPA.

Wendell, Herbert. Interview by Ray Calkins. July 1979. Transcript. OHC: Ray F. Calkins: Wendell, Herbert, BSBPA.

Zanchi, Louise "Gina." Interview by author. Butte, Mont., June 25, 2009.

Newspapers

Anaconda (Mont.) Standard
Butte (Mont.) Anode
Butte (Mont.) Copper Commando
Butte (Mont.) Daily Intermountain
Butte (Mont.) Daily Post
Butte (Mont.) Eye Opener
Butte (Mont.) Miner
Butte (Mont.) Montana Standard
Great Falls (Mont.) Tribune
Helena (Mont.) Daily Record

Unpublished Material

Astle, John. "One Hundred Years of Butte Stories." Manuscript Collection 350, BSBPA.

Blaine School student essays. Ca. 1927. Marguerite McDonald Collection, SM 007, BSBPA.

"Bohunkus Day." VF 1050, BSBPA.

"Boys Scouts." VF 1716, BSBPA.

Burke, William A. "Sixty Years in Butte as an Old Timer Tells It." "Vertical Files—Biography: Calamity Jane." VF 0246, BSBPA.

Butte High School Salute, 1945. Butte High School: YB 001, BSBPA.

Carden, Frank. "A Walk from 228 Gaylord Street to Park and Main Streets and Beyond in Butte, Montana in the 1920's and 1930's." Ca. 1987. TS. FF 14, Butte East Side Collection, PC 096, BSBPA.

"Children Enjoy Outing." TS. FF 5, Box 1, Paul Clark Home Collection, OC 39, BSBPA.

Christie, Mrs. A. S. "First Biennial Report, Associated Charities." Jan. 1, 1900. "Associated Charities," VF 1713, BSBPA.

———. "Second Biennial Report, Associated Charities." Jan. 2, 1902. "Associated Charities," VF 1713, BSBPA.

Cunningham, Mrs. M. L. "Annual Report, Associated Charities." Jan. 7, 1904. "Associated Charities," VF 1713, BSBPA.

"Ethnic Groups—Jewish." VF 1096, BSBPA.

Fischer, William. "Faith, Hope, and Ethnicity: St. Mary's Parish in Butte." Master's thesis, Montana State University, Bozeman, 1997.

"Girl Scouts." VF 1729, BSBPA.

Grant School closure clippings. FF 3, Butte East Side Collection, PC 096, BSBPA.

Grant School principal to Nick Badovinac. Letter. Ca. 1989. FF 8, Butte East Side Collection, PC 096, BSBPA.

Hannan, Father Michael. Diary. FF 1, Father Michael Hannan Collection, SM 059, BSBPA.

"Happy Boys and Girls." Dec. 19, 1900. TS. FF 5, Box 1, Paul Clark Home Collection, OC 39, BSBPA.

Harrington, James D. "Mine Fatalities 1888–1996." TS. 2012.093, BSBPA.

Heiman, Donald H. "The Sentiments of a Loyal American of German Birth." *Mountaineer*. 1918. YB 001, BSBPA

"History of Butte Grade Schools." VF 1899, BSBPA.

Jones, Mrs. A. H. "Third Biennial Report, Associated Charities." Jan. 8, 1903. "Associated Charities." VF 1713, BSBPA.

Judd, Stephen P. "The Judd and Zannon Family History Project." TS. "Vertical Files—Biography: Judd, Stephen." VF 0472, BSBPA.

Junior Service League. Organization scrapbooks. Box 18, Paul Clark Home Collection, OC 39, BSBPA.

Kaiyala, Waldemar. Memoir. FF 2, Box 1, Kaiyala Family Documents, LH 021, BSBPA.

Laitinen, John to Nick Badovinac. Letter. Dec. 13, 1989. FF 13, East Side Collection, PC 096, BSBPA.

Massey, Sarah. "My Memories of the Miners' Strike and the Destruction Done to Our House at 2213 Oak Street, Friday April 12 through Sunday April 14, 1946." June 2011. Academic Work M009.001, BSBPA.

McHugh, Jule. "The Gulch and I." N.d. MS. "Neighborhoods: Dublin Gulch-St. Mary's." VF1610, BSBPA.

"Memories: The Holland Rink." N.d. "Places & Parks in Butte: Holland Rink." VF 1793, BSBPA.

Montana Standard, July 21, 1975, news clipping. FF 3, Butte East Side Collection, PC 096, BSBPA.

Murphy, Mary. "Women on the Line: Prostitution in Butte, Montana, 1878–1917." Master's thesis, University of North Carolina, Chapel Hill, 1983.

National Security League. "A Suggestive Outline for Teachers." *Teachers' Patriotic Leaflets.* Vol. 1. Box 74, World War I Pamphlet Collection, Mansfield Library, UM.

Ostberg, Jacob H. "Sketches of Old Butte." 1972. TS. 978.668 OSTBE 1972, BSBPA.

Paul Clark Home. Carbon copy of press release. "Paul Clark Home," VF 1762, BSBPA.

———. Carbon copy of article, "The Paul Clark Home—Formal Opening Last Night Was a Brilliant Social Event." Nov. 16, 1900. "Paul Clark Home." VF 1762, BSBPA.

PTA Minutes, 1940–1960. Box 1. Immaculate Conception Church, OC 008, BSBPA.

"Report on Schools Building Program: Butte School District No. 1, Butte, Montana." "Schools: Statistics & Census, 1956." VF 1924, BSBPA.

"The Sacred Heart School." TS. FF 14, Butte East Side Collection, PC 096, BSBPA.

Scee, Trudy I. "The Story to Be Told of the End of the Line: Suicide in a Western American City, Butte, Montana, 1907–1914." Master's thesis, UM, 1988.

Schiesser, Henry. Biographical summary, 1906–1969. Henry and Jean Schiesser Collection, MC 082, BSBPA.

———. Letter. FF 15, Henry and Jean Schiesser Collection, MC 082, BSBPA.

Sheehy, John "Skeff." "A Seven-Year Old Looks at Butte in 1925." MS. "Historical Overviews: Sheehy, "A Seven Year Old Looks at Butte in 1925." VF 0751, BSBPA.

"Silver Bow County, State of Montana, School District No. 1 Census," Sept. 1910. School Census Record, GR.SOS.SB.001, BSBPA.

Silver Bow County Board of Health. "Report of Investigation of Sanitary Conditions in Mines and of the Conditions under which Miners Live in Silver Bow County." Dec. 1908 to Apr. 1912. TS. Silver Bow County (Mont.) Sanitary Conditions Report, 1908–1912, SC 89, MHS.

Silver Bow County Coroner's Register, 1902. Coroner's Register, GR.COR.SB.001, BSBPA.

Silver Bow County Poor Farm Records, 1922, 1926. County Poor Records, SM 109, BSBPA.

Silver Bow County Poor Fund Investigation Records, 1909–1910. County Poor Farm Records SM 109, BSBPA.

"Theaters in Butte." VF 0255, BSBPA.

Thompson, Judith. "Goodbye to the Gardens." Senior seminar paper, UM, 1987. Academic Works: AW T004, BSBPA.

Tretheway, William D. "The John Wallace Cochrane Family, Butte, Montana, Early Twentieth Century." Mar. 28, 1983. "Vertical Files—Biography: Cochrane, John." VF 0279, BSBPA.

Washington Junior High Ingot. Vol. 1, No. 1. 1916. "Washington Junior High." VF 1927, BSBPA.

Wayrenen, Ray. "Memories of Growing Up in Finntown." TS. FF 8, East Side Collection, PC 96, BSBPA.

Photograph Credits

Abbreviations

BSBPA—Butte-Silver Bow Public Archives
LC—Library of Congress
MHS—Montana Historical Society Photograph Archives, Helena
WMM—World Museum of Mining, Butte

frontispiece: Arthur Rothstein, photographer, LC-USF33-003115-M3
2–3: LC-USZ62-133271
4: BSBPA
7: BSBPA, PH 213
11: Courtesy Danette Harrington
16: N. A. Forsyth, photographer, MHS, ST 001.100
18: Courtesy Andrea Ciabattari McCormick
19: (top) Courtesy Andrea Ciabattari McCormick; (bottom) MHS, Lot 25 B1/1.02
22: MHS, Lot 8 B1/4.02
25: WMM, 34
26: N. A. Forsyth, photographer, MHS, ST 001.106
29: MHS, PAc 98-57.59
32: WMM, 163
38–39: BSBPA, PC 066
42–43: Al's Photo Shop, photographer, MHS, PAc 80-88 F8.3
52: Russell Lee, photographer, Library of Congress, photo courtesy BSBPA
54: Robert I. Nesmith, photographer, MHS, Lot 19 A1199
56: BSBPA, PC 096 F11
57: Arthur Rothstein, photographer, LC-USF33-003098
63: Walter Hinick, photographer, Montana Standard, Butte
65: MHS, ST 001.107
69: N. A. Forsyth, photographer, MHS, ST 001 108
70: MHS, PAc 98-57 68
72, 75, 77: Courtesy Andrea Ciabattari McCormick
80: BSBPA
83: Arthur Rothstein, photographer, LC-USF33-003097-M3
88: Middleton, photographer, The Maroon Annual (Butte, Mont., 1927), 58
90: Courtesy Danette Harrington
91: Courtesy Andrea Ciabattari McCormick
104: BSBPA, PC 096 F11

108: WMM
110: Courtesy Andrea Ciabattari McCormick
112, 113: Samuel Hamilton, photographer, from Harry C. Freeman, A Brief History of Butte, Montana the World's Greatest Mining Camp (Chicago, Ill., 1900), 55, 57
114: Carl Engelbach, photographer, MHS, 946-068
129: C. Owen Smithers, photographer, C. Owen Smithers Collection
133: BSBPA, PH 058 F8
134: C. Owen Smithers, photographer, C. Owen Smithers Collection
136: (top) MHS, PAc 98-57 79; (center) BSBPA, PC 096 B1 F4
142, 143: BSBPA
144: Courtesy Andrea Ciabattari McCormick
145: BSBPA, LH 021 B1 F9
146: Samuel Hamilton, photographer, from Harry C. Freeman, A Brief History of Butte, Montana the World's Greatest Mining Camp (Chicago, Ill., 1900), 84
147: Meaderville Volunteer Fire Department, Our Golden Anniversary Year, Fifty Years of Community Service, 1910–1960 (Butte, Mont., 1960), 16
156: Courtesy Andrea Ciabattari McCormick
157: BSBPA, PH 018 480
161: Courtesy Kevin Shannon
162: N. A. Forsyth, MHS, ST 001 126
166: C. Owen Smithers, photographer, C. Owen Smithers Collection
168: N. A. Forsyth, MHS, ST 001 070
172–73: (top) Todd Photographic, photographer, LC, PAN US GEOG Montana 16; (bottom) N. A. Forsyth, MHS, ST 001 120
175: WMM, 306
179: Avoca Studio, photographer, BSBPA, LH 021 B1 F13
180: BSBPA, PC 096 B1 F4
181: (top) BSBPA, PH 177; (center) BSBPA PC 096 East Side 2002.039
184: (top) Zubick, photographer,

MHS, PAc 96-8 10; (center) BSBPA, PC 096 F3
185: N. A. Forsyth, MHS
186: MHS, PAc 98-56 A1 15a
191: (top) MHS, 946-090; (bottom) BSBPA, PH 018 432
193: BSBPA
194: BSBPA, PH 018 261A
202: BSBPA, LH 021 B1 F18
212: BSBPA
217: C. Owen Smithers, photographer, C. Owen Smithers Collection
220: MHS, Lot 5 B3 09 05
221: BSBPA
225: Arthur Rothstein, photographer, LC-USF33-003128-M3
226: Arthur Rothstein, photographer, LC-USF33-003128-M4
229: BSBPA
231: Montana Standard, Butte
232: Ken Lutey, "Lutey Brothers Marketeria: America's First Self-Service Grocers," Montana The Magazine of Western History, 27 (Spring 1978), 54
233: Courtesy Linda Raiha
237: Courtesy Tom Holter
238: The Centralite (Butte, Mont., 1928), 106
243: The Mountaineer (Butte, Mont., 1912), 6
251: Al Hooper Collection
255: Robert I. Nesmith, photographer, MHS, Lot 19 B60
258: (top) MHS, Lot 8 B1 F5.01; (bottom) MHS, Lot 8 B1 4 09
262: Courtesy Steve Sherick
267: Courtesy Tom Holter
269: MHS, PAc 79-37
270–71: BSBPA
272: Neihter, photographer, BSBPA
276: BSBPA, PH 061 B1 Cyr Coll.
277: BSBPA, PH 061 B1 Cyr Coll.
279: BSBPA, 510.87 PH 001.1983.007.072
280: Courtesy Andrea Ciabattari McCormick
281: C. Owen Smithers, photographer, C. Owen Smithers Collection
283: Courtesy Andrea Ciabattari McCormick
284: BSBPA, PH 261
289: Courtesy Andrea Ciabattari McCormick
290: BSBPA, 510.074 PH 018.322

Index

Page numbers in italics indicate photographs.

Accents, variety found in Butte, 257

Accordion lessons and ensembles, 266, *267*

Adams, Mary H., 28

Adams School, 23

Adolescence, introduction of concept, 10

Adulthood, boundaries with childhood, 7

Aid societies, introduction of, 8–9

Aid to Dependent Children: during 1959 strike, 61; increases between 1945 and 1960, 134; introduction of, 49; significance of, 130–31

Alaska Bar, 266–67

Alcoholism and family life, 94–98; intergenerational trauma of, 287; role of bars in community and social life, 286; "rushing the can," 119

American Theater, 218

Ames, Dave, x

Amos 'n Andy radio program, 43

Amtilla, Helen, *145*

Anaconda Anodes baseball team, 162

Anaconda Road: dealing with class distinctions, 99; neighborhood camaraderie, 137; Overall Gang, 159–60; winter activities, 140

Anaconda Standard newspaper, 219

Ancient Order of Hibernians, 18

Ansonia Theater: admission price, 242; jobs for children, 218; matinees at, 167, 169, 228–29

Antonetti, Kay: acknowledgement, ix; childhood play, 137–38; dealing with class distinctions, 100; movie matinees, 170–71; music and music education, 211; nuns at Immaculate Conception School, 198; uncle's death and wake, 156; VJ Day, 55; wartime rationing, 52–53; work in family business, 238

Antonovich, Beba, George, and boys, *262*

Arbor Day, 32, 161

Armistice Day 1918, 37

Aro Café, 72

Associated Charities, 27, 112–16

Astle, John: acknowledgement, ix; Spanish flu epidemic, 36

Asylums and orphanages: nineteenth-century building boom, 8; reforming and improving, 111–18. *See also* Homes and orphanages

Baby-sitting, as childhood chore, 229–30, 232–33

Bait, gathering and selling, 244

Baldy's bar, 256

Balkovetz, Betty Lou, *262*

Ballfields, 137, 147

Barango, Anthony, *267*

Barbershops, 256

Barracks, militia, 84

Barrett family and children, 120

Barry, Frank, 153

Bars: effect on family life, 95; New Deal Bar, 1; role in community and social life, 286; "rushing the can," 119

Barsanti, Dolores, 168

Bartel, Andrew, 28

Baseball: Anaconda Anodes baseball team, 162; Clarks baseball team, 161–62; "tippy" baseball, 147–48

Basketball, Sacred Heart team 1926–1927, *184*

Beer buckets, 261

Bell Creek, 25, 142, 147, 245

Belmont House, 85

Belmont Senior Center staff, x

Belway Theater, 218

Bendio, Vera, *145*

Bennett, Eddie, 116

Bennetts, Henry, 35

Bennetts, Millicent, 204–5

Berkeley Pit: beginnings of, 1–2, 58; and childhood geography, 287; expansion of, 62–63, 110; and Holy Savior School, *63*

Bersanti, Ann and Marie, *267*

Bertoglio, Anton, *147*

Best, Richard, 178

Bianchi, Mary, *267*

Bicycles: building and acquiring, 147; usefulness of, *146*, 263

Big M, 146–47

Big Ship boardinghouse, The, 228

Bird Club, 200

"Black Mariahs," 222

Black Rock, 146

Blaine School, 23, 72, 163, 178, 201–5

Blanchard Creamery, 217

Block caving, 58

B'Nai Israel temple, 18

Board of Trade café, 226, *226*
Boardinghouses: children's meals at, 85–86; in Finntown, 82–84, 85, 86, 91–92; Lucina's boardinghouse, 211; lunch-buckets from, 69, 228, 230; McManon's boardinghouse, 228; Mullen House, 230; residents in 1900, *80*
Bohunkus Day, 215, 275–77, *276, 277, 284*
Botton, Violet Michelotti, *91, 280*
Boulevard area, South Montana Street, 77–78
Bowling: duck pins bowling, 265; work setting pins, 268
Boxing, 24
Boy Scouts: *Butte Miner* article praising, 41; expansion of, 10; introduction of, 32
Boyles Bar, 243
Boys Central High School, Irish step dancers, *88*
Bozeman High School, football game, *186*
Brinig, Myron, 92–93
Broadway Bar, 83–84
Broadway boardinghouse, 82, 228
Broadway Rink, 49
Broadway Theater, 25, 43, 169
Brown, Hi and Bruce, 49
Brown, Jerry, *72*
Brown's Gulch, 147
"Bubniga" bar, 273
Buckley, Mary Angelina, 183
Buckley, Michael Patrick "Packey": childhood play, 137–38; children's work and jobs, 231–32; Irish boardinghouses, 90–91
Bugni, Guido, *267*
Burke, William A., 73, 157–58
Butler, Karen, 200
Butori, Marie: April 1946 strike, 101; Columbia Gardens, 173–74; Meaderville, 73
Butte: 1930s view, *251;* coming of age during World War II, 50–55; demands upon humane officers, 125; education and early schools, 23–24; family life at turn of twentieth century, 20–22; first mayor,

92; population booms, 292n19; postwar period, 55–58; Progressive Era and children, 31–33; recreational opportunities in early twentieth century, 24–26; in Roaring Twenties, 40–42, 203–4; settlement and early history, 15–20; topography of, 138–39; women's and children's histories, 288–90; work life in early twentieth century, 26–31; World War I and aftermath, 33–40
Butte, Anaconda & Pacific Railroad, 66, 149
Butte Business College, 191, *191*
Butte Central High School, 194; football rivalry with Butte High School, 43–44, 187, 301n18
Butte Daily Post newspaper: ads during 1959 strike, 60–61; among Butte dailies, 218; newsboy strike against, 220–21; newsboys selling, 219, 242
Butte economic survey of 1939, 50
Butte High School: 1918 *Mountaineer* yearbook, 206; 1945 yearbook, *The Salute,* 209; and Bohunkus Day, 276–77; class distinctions among students, 200; Class of 1934 traditions, 208; first graduation, 23; football game against Bozeman High School, *186;* football rivalry with Butte Central, 43–44, 187, 301n18; marching band, *57, 57*–58, 212, *212,* 213; opening of new building in 1938, 49; student's German poem, 206; two shifts, 207
Butte Housewives' League, 36
Butte Ice Company advertisement, *243*
Butte Independent Football League, 127
Butte Industrial School, 23, 41, 123, 126–27
Butte Irish, The (Emmons), 30
Butte Junior Service League, 44, 128, 129, *129,* 130, 133
Butte Mine Band, *26*

Butte Miner newspaper: baby boy adoption advertisement, 118; Bohunkus Day, 276; child custody case for prostitute, 121, 298–99n30; community efforts to organize play for children, 127; domestic violence, 97–98; East Side Neighborhood House, 41; first triplets born in Butte, 22; juveniles sentenced for stealing coal, 125; Kid Wiley, the Human Fly, 39–40; Leonard Mine accident, 28; Mesopust celebrations, 272; newsboys selling, 219; school truancy cases, 189, 190; sledding accident, 140; Sunday "Children's Page," 41
Butte Miners' Union, 106–7
Butte Newsboys Club, 32, 219–20, *221,* 293n55, 302n10
Butte Public Library, 33
Butte-Silver Bow Public Archives, ix, 4
Butte skyline, 1914, *3*
Butte Women's Council, 33, 40, 293n66
Butte Women's Protective Union, 20
Button, John, *145*
"Buzzies," 66
Byrne Roller Rink, 24

Cabbage Patch neighborhood, 165
Cadet Nurses Corps, 53
Cafés, children's work in, 238–42
Calkins, Ray, ix
Callaghan, J. J., 183
Camp Fire Girls, introduction of, 32
Canonica, Tony, 218
Canty, Patricia, 137–38
Carden, Frank: mine yards and play, 143–44; mining landscape, 68; movie matinees, 169–70
Caringi, Jim, x
Carkulis, Gus, 226
Carlisle, George, 120
Carroll, John P., 185, *186*
Carsh, Jo Ann, *262*
Catholic Youth Organization (CYO), 163

Centerville: children's memories of, 72–73; garden and livestock 1910, 258; sledding in, 139–40; youthful gangs, 158

Central High School: 1924 division of, 186; 1908 opening, 23, 185–86; class distinctions among students, 201; dramatics class, 194–95; establishment of, 23; rivalry with Butte High School, 43–44, 187, 301n18

Central House (boardinghouse), 82

Cesarini's Grocery, 237

Chautauquas, at Columbia Gardens, 33, 293n61

Child care: Salvation Army nursery in 1921, 41; wartime demand for, 11; WPA nursery schools, 49

Child labor: historical perspective, 218–19; movements opposing, 9. *See also* Labor force: children's contributions to

Child psychology, introduction of, 9–10

Childhood: geography of, 279–82; historical perspectives, 7–12; jobs in, 26–27; potential trauma of, 285–87; risk and resilience, 287–88; theoretical perspectives, 6–7

Children: after World War II, 55–58, 131–34; boy on bicycle at Parrot Smelter, *146*; boy swinging on guy-wire, *143*; child-rearing practices at turn of twentieth century, 20–22; contributions during World War II, 52–53, *53*, 209, 263; contributions to labor force, 216–48; in early Butte photos, *4, 7, 22, 136, 157, 211, 258, 279*; in ethnic neighborhoods, 71–93; familiarity with mining industry, 64–71; and financial uncertainty, 283–84; influence in community, 160–64; and intergenerational relationships, 282; keen observations of, 282–85; and Kelly Mine 1950, *290*; and

labor unrest, 56–57; letters to Eleanor Roosevelt, 45; meals at boardinghouses, 85–86; organizing play for, 126–28; receiving homes for, 111–18; reform efforts on behalf of, 111–34; risk and resilience of, 287–88; in Roaring Twenties, 40–42, 203–4; and Rocky Mountain Garden Club, 41–42; state efforts to care for neglected children, 118–21; surrounded by mining landscape, *65*; and trauma of childhood, 285–87; and widowed mothers, 29–31

Children's Aid Societies, 8

Chile, copper mining in, 59

Christie, A. S., Mrs., 112–13, 114

Christmas celebrations: among Serbian and Croatian immigrants, 277; and Anaconda Company, 106; letter to Santa, 202–3; in Serbian Orthodox community, 108; Uptown businesses, 224

Church, J., 88

Ciabattari, Andrea: in 1954, *289*; First Holy Communion, *72*; in Meaderville, 1955, *77*

Ciabattari, Bart and Michael families, *19*

Ciabattari, Mary Martinesso, *91*, 280

Ciabattari, Tom, *267*

Ciabattari and Son Meaderville Grocery, *18, 74, 76*

Cinders ballfield, 137

Circus, Ringling Brothers and Barnum & Bailey, 242

Citizen Schools, 38

Civic Center skating rinks, 142

Civil Works Administration, 245

Civilian Conservation Corps (CCC), 207

Clarence boardinghouse, 82–83, 85

Clark, William A.: Children's Day at Columbia Gardens, *114*, 115; circa 1915, *32*; and Columbia Gardens, 25–26; efforts on behalf of children, 32; founding of Paul Clark Home, 113–14; remarks on

grand opening of Paul Clark Home, 111

Clark Mine yard, circa 1900, *229*

Clark Park: ice skating rink, 141–42, *142*; Mines' League baseball and football, 161–63

Clarks baseball team, 161–62

Class distinctions: at Butte High School, 200; and childhood experience, 8; and geography of childhood, 280; at Girls Central High School, 201; learning and dealing with, 98–106

Clinton Drugstore, 231, 232

Cochrane, John Wallace: children's work and jobs, 242; movie matinees, 169; wood gathering, 246

Cohen, A. B., 167

Cold War politics and education, 11–12, 209–11

College Club of Butte, 126

Columbia Gardens: Chautauquas, 33; Children's Day, 32, *114*, 161, 173; establishment of, 25–26; football game, *186*; importance to families and children, 171–77; juvenile arson case, 122–23; Miners' Field Day 1922, 41; panorama circa 1914, *172–73*; pansies circa 1905, *172*; photo circa 1900, *25*; photo circa 1905, *162*; trolley car circa 1910, *175*

Comic books, campaign against, 209–10

"Condo Vic," 83–84

Connors, John, 149–50

Conta, Dolores, *267*

Contract miners, 254

Cooney, Frank H., 45

Copper Commando newspaper: industry articles during World War II, 51, 295n158; Platter Chatter column, 54; special issue on McQueen Addition, 54–55

Copper tanks, 144

Corktown: Irish immigrant community in, 87; St. Mary's Church, 38; St. Mary's School, *193*

Cornish immigration and community: in Centerville, 72; Cornish Order of the Sons of St. George, 19; Cornish pasties, 74; first wave of immigration, 17; at Grant School, 179, 180

Cortese, Jim, 163–64

Cough syrup, onion, 94

Councils of Defense, 36, 205, 294n80

"Cousin Carl and his KGIR Happy Hour Kids Program," 42–43

Crain, Ellen, ix

Cristoforo Colombo Society, 18, 292n12

Crnich, Eleanor, Vince, and Vincent, 262

Croatian immigration and community: arrival in America, 250–54; Christmas celebrations, 277; Easter celebrations, 275–76; Mesopust festivities, 272, 272, 273–74, 283; St. Philip and Jacob Society, 270–71, 271; wine making, 259–61

Crystal Theater, 228–29

Cultural life at turn of twentieth century, 25

Culum, Liz, 262

Curtiss, Henry, 126

Darkest Before Dawn (Work), 205–6

Davey, Mary Xavier, 185

Davin, Anna, 7

Dean, Mabel, 234

Death and loss, dealing with, 152–57

DesJardins, Rosie, 140–141

De Valera, Eamon, welcoming, 38–39, 39, 207

Dika, Mary, 184

Disasters, children's awareness of, 70–71, 285–87

Discrimination: against Chinese and African-Americans, 20; against Germans, 36, 205–6; against Mexicans and African-Americans, 197–98

Domestic violence, 94–98; effect on families, 106;

intergenerational trauma of, 286–87; role of bars in community and social life, 286

Donlan, Michael, Judge: attention to needs of children, 120–21, 298–99n30; establishment of juvenile court, 122–23; juveniles in adult courts, 31; juveniles sentenced for stealing coal, 125; sentencing of girls, 124; truancy cases, 189, 190

Dornhofer, Frank, 243–44

Dowling, Vince: "pigpen" at Clark Park, 161; St. Stephen's Day, 87

Downs, Micah: acknowledgement, ix; work selling newspapers, 226

Dream Theater, 158

Dreibelbis Music Company, 224

Drift miners, 254, 255

Dublin Gulch: among other Irish neighborhoods, 87; children's work and jobs, 216–17; circa 1910, 16; dealing with class distinctions, 99; destruction of, 62–63; establishment of, 17; neighborhood camaraderie, 137; Overall Gang, 159–60; political and cultural roots, 38; St. Mary's School, 193; youthful gangs, 158

Duck pins bowling, 265

Duggan, Manus and Madge, 34–35, 294n74

Duncan, John, 20, 37–38

Duncan, Perdita, 37–38, 197–98

Duran, Mun, 187

Earthquake, Yellowstone Park, 1959, 59

East Butte: Croatian community in, 265; destruction of, 62–63; East Side Athletic Club, 32; East Side Opera House, 169–70; ethnic diversity of, 79, 179; Grant School class 1916, 179; Holy Savior Church, 271; Rangatangs gang, 159

East Side Neighborhood House, 79; basketball court, 164; closing of, 44; partnership

with Junior Service League, 128; recreational opportunities offered, 41; significance in East Butte, 79

Easter lilies and 1916 Easter Rebellion, 87

Eateries, in private homes, 76

Eclipse Grocery, 232

Economic survey of 1939, 50

Education: Butte Board of Education, 188; Catholic schools, 183–87; and Cold War politics, 11–12; compulsory education, 9, 189–92, 218–19; early Butte schools, 23–24; English as a second language, 179, 182; importance to families, 289; kindergartens and preschools, 11; Montana's first junior high school, 24, 293n34; music, 211–15; new Butte High School opening in 1938, 49; political education, 205–11; progressive quality of, 187–89, 293n34, 301n21; pursuing secondary education, 190–92; school uniforms and class distinctions, 201; starting school, 178–79, 182–83; student life, 192–201. See also individual schools

Emerson School, 23

Emmons, David: acknowledgement, x; The Butte Irish, 30

Entrepreneurship of children, 242–45; and geography of childhood, 282; and music, 265–67

Epidemics: polio epidemic of 1952, 12; Spanish influenza epidemic of 1918, 36–37, 294n87

Erickson, Mabel, 209

Ethnic neighborhoods: accents heard, 257; attachment to, 71–93; boundaries of, 72, 76–77, 80; Croatian community, 265; destruction of, 62–63, 110; diversity of McQueen Addition, 255, 257; diversity within, 82; Grant School class 1916, 179; growth of, 17–19; memories of, 71–77; as source

of ethnic identity, 280–81, 288;
sports teams and games, 24
Evankovich, Helen:
acknowledgement, ix;
childhood in Great
Depression, 47; children's
work and jobs, 241; traditional
wake, 156
Excelsior Market, yearbook
advertisement for, *238*
Eye Opener newspaper, 45, 218

Fagan, "Noodles," 219
Family businesses and children's
employment, 234–38
Family life: challenges to, 94–98;
childhood trauma, 285–87;
and financial uncertainty,
283–84; intergenerational
relationships, 282; resilience
of children, 287–88; at turn of
twentieth century, 20–22
Faue, Elizabeth, 7
Fava, Tommy, 237
Favero, Stella, *91*, 280
Federal Emergency Relief Act of
1933, 45, 245
Federal Social Security Act of
1935, 49, 130
Ferrando, Theresa, *147*
Fevero, Martin, *267*
Filpula, Joan, 62
Finnish immigration and
community, 82–87; Finnish
accent, 257; Finnish Hall,
18, 86–87; Finnish language
classes, 156; use of Finnish
language, 241
Finntown, 82–87; Alaska
Bar, 266–67; a game of
marbles, *145*; Hazel Block
boardinghouse, 91–92; and
Neversweat Mine, 1939, *83*;
youthful gangs, 158
Fire and Brimstone (Punke), 34,
35
First Communion, St. Helena's
Church, *72*
Fischer, William, 207
Fish bait, gathering and selling,
244
Fitzharris, Maurice, 35
Fitzpatrick, Mary Lou Kane,
108–9

"Flappers," in Roaring Twenties,
203–5
Flaxseed poultices, 94
Flesch, Rudolph, 11
Floral Boulevard, 265, 273, 274
Florence Crittenton Home,
117–18, 298n20
Fontana, Columbine "Bina," 75
Fontana, Emily, *267*
Fontana barbershop, 256
Football: Butte High School
vs. Central High School, 187;
game between Butte and
Bozeman High Schools, *186*;
Grant School Bulldogs, 180,
181
Forbes, David, x
Forges and blacksmiths, 66
Fourth of July, 115; 1932 explosion
and tragedy, 153; and fishing
derby, 142; parade and
celebrations, 50, 107, 108–10,
236
Franklin School, 23, 61, 182, 254–
55; 1903 opening, 178–79; and
surrounding neighborhoods,
264–65
Fraternal organizations, 18–19
Free Press, 218
Frontier childhoods, 6–7

Gaelic language instruction, 87,
207
Gagnon Mine, *136*
Gallows frames: play around, 148;
and playground swings, *281*
Games and sports: chase and
"commandoes," 138; duck
pins bowling, 265; in early
twentieth century, 24; Grant
School Bulldogs, 180, *181*;
high school football, 43–44,
186, 187, 301n18; ice hockey,
141; makeshift baseball,
147–48; in McQueen Addition
neighborhood, 262–63;
Meaderville Girls Softball
team, *147*; neighborhood
camaraderie, 135–37, 138, 163;
organized play for children,
126–28; ring-around-the-
rosy 1910, *180*; Sacred Heart
School athletes, *184*; skating,
140–42, *142*; skiing, *283*;

spring and summer, 142;
swimming lessons at YMCA,
164; tobogganing, 135; winter
games and sports, 135, 138–43;
youth sports leagues, 127
Gangs, of neighborhood
youth, 157–64; influence
of, 160–61; Overall Gang,
159–60; youthful gangs and
camaraderie, 157–59
Gannon, James, 72
Gardens: home-grown
vegetables, 258, 259; Rocky
Mountain Garden Club, 41–42
Garfield School, 23
Garland, Betty, *184*
Garlic, traditional uses of, 94
German: immigration and
community, 18, 36, 205–6
Ghenie, Kerrie, x
Gibson, Nancy, x
Gilligan, P. J.: appointment as
first humane officer, 31, 119;
Spanish flu epidemic of 1918,
37; truancy cases, 189
Gilmore, Joseph, *191*
Girl Scouts, 10, 32
Girl's Central High School, 186,
198, 201
Glynn, Joan and children, *54*
Gogginoni, Fred, Chelsea, and
Willie, 123
Goldberg, Aili: children's work
and jobs, 229–30, 282; Citizen
School, 38; class distinctions,
200; domestic violence, 97;
English as a second language,
179, 182; Finntown, 84–87;
grade school mornings,
195; growing up in Finnish
boardinghouse, 91
Gorsh, Joseph, *262*
Gorsh, Leonard, *262*
Grace, R., 88
Grand Opera House, 25
Grande Theater, 167
Granite Mountain Mine fire, 34,
287, 294n72
Grant School: accomplished
graduates, 197; children's
memories of, 47, 49, 82;
destroyed in 1975, 63;
eighth grade class 1949,
181; empathetic teachers,

196–97; establishment of, 179; fourth grade class 1916, *179*; Halloween parades, 165, 180; learning English, 182; makeshift playing fields, 148; ring-around-the-rosy 1910, *180*; significance in East Butte, 79, 180–81; St. Patrick's Day, 180; and sports, 163

Grappo, 82, 259–60, 261

Great Depression: children's jobs during, 245–48; distraction provided by movies and radio, 47–48; improving child welfare during, 128–30; lessons in political economy during, 207–8, 301n64; New Deal public policies, 10–11; onset and response to, 43–50, 295n126; toll on children, 10

Greater Butte Project, 58

Greeley School, nursery at, 49

Griffis, Charles, *145*

Groo, A., 88

Grosso, Margaret and Amelia, *91*, 280

Grosso, Martin "Tino," *72*, 237, *289*

Guidi Brothers grocery and meat market, 74 Gunmen and gunmen shacks, 145

Hall, Stanley, 10

Halloween: celebrations and traditions, 164–67; at Grant School, 180

Hanley, Jim, 211, 230

Hannan, Michael, 38–39, *194*, 207

Hardle, Billy, 130

Harrington, Danette: acknowledgement, ix; in Dublin Gulch 1950, 90, *90*; makeshift baseball, 148; mine yards and play, 144–45; miners' lunch-buckets, 69–70; 1959 earthquake, 59–60; petty thefts of wood, 152; play in mine yards, 148, 149; train rides in town, 151; winter 1948, *11*; winter games and sports, 140

Harrington, Jim, ix

Harrington, Paddy and Nora, 230

Harrison Avenue Theater, 169, 242–43

Harrison School, 23, 264–65

Hawes, Joseph, 10

Hawkins, Lillie, 123–24

Hazel Block boardinghouse, 91–92

Health: home remedies and practices, 93–94, 182–83; lack of basic medical care, 106; mining and mortality, 27–31; of mothers and children in early Butte, 20–22; rheumatic fever cases, 199; State efforts to care for neglected children, 118–21. *See also* Maternal and child health; Public policy and child welfare

Hebrew Benevolent Society, 18–19

Henderson, Betty: acknowledgement, ix; home health remedies, 94; train adventures, 150–51

Hickey, Margaret, 131–33

Higgins, Alma, 41–42

Higgins, C. M., 42

Historical perspective on childhood, 7–12

Hitchcock, Bill, 55

Hjelvik, Thelma Karki Point, 87

Hockey. *See* Ice hockey

Hole, Robert: acknowledgement, ix; rheumatic fever, 199

Holland Ice Rink, 24, 140–41

Holland Roller Rink, 24

Holter, Tom: in accordion ensemble, *267*; acknowledgment, ix; bell ringing at Holy Savior Church, 156–57; children's work and jobs, 239; circa 1935, *156*; ethnic markets, 76–77; labor unrest, 56; with Margaret Holter in 1940s, *237*; mine yards and play, 146; work in family business, 237–38

Holy Savior Church, 254–55, 271, *271*; bell ringing, 156–57; children's memories of, 82; funerals for victims of July 4, 1932 explosion, 153; opening as Jesuit mission in 1902, 23; significance in McQueen Addition, 75, 266

Holy Savior School, 271, *271*; and Berkeley Pit, *63*; start of, 23; and surrounding neighborhood, 264–65

Holy Trinity Orthodox Church, 108

Home eateries, 76

Home health remedies, 93–94

Homes and orphanages: Florence Crittenton Home, 117–18; nineteenth-century building boom, 8; reforming and improving, 111–18; Soroptomist Home for Children, 131–33, *133*. *See also* Asylums and orphanages; House of the Good Shepherd; Montana Children's Home; Paul Clark Home; St. Joseph's Orphanage

Honeychurch, Percy, 153

Hoover, Herbert, 43

Hopscotch, games of, 142

Horgan, Danny, *72*

Horrors of Vaccination Exposed and Illustrated (Higgins), 42

"Hot boxes," 66

House of the Good Shepherd, 118, 124

Hoy, Catherine: children's work and jobs, 227–29, 282; dealing with class distinctions, 99; Fourth of July celebrations, 109; funerals in childhood, 154–55; grandmother's Irish stories, 87–88; makeshift baseball, 147–48; neighborhood camaraderie, 136–37; Overall Gang, 159–60; petty thefts of coal, 151; tobogganing, 135; youthful gangs, 158–59, 192–93

Huie Puck, physician and surgeon, 19

Human Fly, The, 39–40

Humanities Montana, x

Hunger: during 1921–1922 work stoppage, 40; during 1959 strike, 60–61; effect on families, 106; food for strangers, 150; during Great Depression, 44; responses to malnutrition, 293n66; and work stoppages, 27

Hungry Hill, 38, 87
Hunting, 263

Ice carnival, 142
Ice for iceboxes, gathering,
    243–44, 247
Ice hockey, 141
Immaculate Conception School,
    198, 209–10
Immigration: arrival in America,
    250–54; Citizen Schools,
    38; Finnish immigration,
    82–87; German immigration
    and community, 205–6;
    importance of stories, 288;
    Irish immigration and
    community, 87–92; Jewish
    immigration and community,
    92–93, 108; love of music and
    opera, 81; Montana Sedition
    Act, 36; origins of Bohunkus
    Day, 275; succeeding waves
    of, 17–19. See also Cornish
    immigration and community;
    Serbian immigration and
    community; Slovenian
    immigration and community
Infant illness and mortality:
    infant bodies in mine shafts,
    21, 119, 298n26; measures
    to address, 33; at turn of
    twentieth century, 20–22
Influenza epidemic of 1918, 36–37
International Workers of the
    World (IWW): and 1914
    strike by newsboys, 221; at
    Finnish Hall, 86–87
Interviews, as source material, 5
Irish Christian Brothers, 186
Irish immigration and
    community, 87–92; attendance
    at Sunday Mass, 193; Boys
    Central High School Irish
    step dancers, 88; The Butte
    Irish (Emmons), 30; Catholic
    education, 183, 294n93;
    dramatics class at Central
    High School, 194–95; Gaelic
    language instruction, 87, 207;
    political and cultural roots
    of, 38; St. Mary's Parish and
    School, 207; St. Patrick's Day
    at Grant School, 180; support
    for Irish independence, 34,

38–39, 207; traditional Irish
    songs, 243
Isa Matti sauna, 83
Isakson, John, 97–98

Jackhammers, 66
Jacks, games of, 142
Jacobs, Henry, 92
J.C. Penney Company, 223
Jecevich, Rosie, 204
Jefferson School, 23, 47
Jewish immigration and
    community, 92–93, 108
Johnson, Carrie, x
Johnson, Inga, 147
Johnson, Tubie, 24
Jones, A. H., Mrs., 116
Jones, Mary Ann, 72
Jones, Mary Harris "Mother," 9
Judd, Charley, 1, 165
Junior Service League. See Butte
    Junior Service League
Jursnich, Edward: makeshift
    playing fields, 148; Rangatangs
    gang, 159; saving stamps and
    bonds during World War II,
    209; scrap metal drives during
    World War II, 52; shoeshine
    work, 245; swimming lessons
    at YMCA, 164
Juvenile courts and justice:
    dependent vs. delinquent
    children, 123, 126–27; girls and
    juvenile delinquency, 123–25;
    introduction of, 9; preventing
    and addressing delinquency,
    121–25; rising concern for
    juvenile delinquency, 9, 11

Kailin, Dan, 168
Kaiyala, Waldemar: bars and
    family life, 95; Spanish
    influenza epidemic, 37
Kangas, Dolores:
    acknowledgement, ix;
    expansion of Berkeley Pit, 62
Kelley, Con: dining at home
    eateries, 76; Greater Butte
    Project, 58
Kelley Mine, 148, 152, 290
Kelly, Florence, 9
Kelly, Isabel, 165, 180
Kelly, Mickey, 152
Kelly, Spider, 24

Kennedy, J. M., 124–25
Kersting, Aubrey, ix
KGIR radio, and children's
    programming, 43
Kiely, Tuma, 184
Kindergartens and preschools,
    public funding for, 11
King, Buddy, 24
King, Leo, 188
King, Tom: acknowledgement,
    ix; epilepsy and helpful
    teachers, 199; and interview
    with, 301n48
Kingston House, 82
Klapan, Nancy: boundaries of
    ethnic neighborhoods, 72;
    Columbia Gardens, 176–77
Knights of Columbus, 127, 301n18
Konen, Danny and Jim, 267
Kontola, Victor, 83–84
Koprivica, Alex and George,
    246–47
Koski, Emil, Hjalmer, and
    Lempi, 145
Kovacich, Joe and Robert, 262
Kovicich, Evelyn, 262
Kumpula, Anna, 98
Kumpula, Nick, death of, 97–98

Labor force: children's
    contributions to, 216–48,
    265–71, 282, 283–84
Labor history: and children's
    experience, 7, 56–57; "rustling
    card" system, 34; work life in
    early twentieth century, 26–31
Labor movement: and children's
    everyday psychology, 285;
    early development of, 17; Eye
    Opener newspaper, 45; labor
    newspaper, 195; laws regarding
    children, 218–19; and newsboys
    club, 220–21; union movement
    and children, 268–69; unrest
    during Great Depression,
    48–49; Women's Protective
    Union (WPU), 242
Ladies Home Journal, article
    on Soroptomist Home for
    Children, 131–33
Laird, Tommy, 142–43
Laitinen, John: East Side
    neighborhood, 192; Grant
    School, 179, 180

Lake Avoca, 243–44
Lally, T., 88
Larson (miner), *255*
Lazzari, Marie, *267*
Lemier, Clarence, 152–53
Lenz, Frances Ferrian, 191–92
Leonard Mine: 1913 accident, 28;
    photo, *29*
"Letters edged in black," 89
Liberty Magazine, children's
    work selling, 224, 242
Liberty Theater: admission
    price, 169, 242; jobs for
    children, 218
Little, Frank, 35
Lincoln School, 23
Livestock: forays into Butte,
    263–64; raising and slaughter
    of, 78–79, 258–59
Lone Ranger, The, 47
Lubick, Donna, *262*
Lucina's boardinghouse, 211
Lunch-buckets: children's
    memories of, 69–70; children's
    work preparing, 228, 230, 231;
    miners with, *70*
Lutey, Ken, 231
Lutey Brothers Marketeria, *231*,
    232
Lydia's Restaurant, 239
Lynch, May, 123–24
Lyric Theater, 169–70

MacDonald, Marguerite, 201–5
MacSwiney, Mary and Terence,
    207
Madlena, Elsie, *267*
Madlena, Peter and Clem, 76
Maki, Alex, 82
Maki, Bernice Favilla, *75*
Maki's Grocery Store, 82
Malesich, Bill, *262*
Maloney's Bar, 232
Marbles, games of, 142, *145*
Marching band, Butte High
    School, *57*, 57–58, 212, *212*, 213
Marian White Arts and Crafts
    Club, 126
Martial law declaration 1917, 34
Martin, Dale, 220
Martin, Dorothy: and Butte's
    Jewish community, 93; movie
    matinees, 169; work in family
    business, 235–36

Martinesso, Lucille, *75*
Martinez, Lula: childhood in
    Great Depression, 47; East
    Butte, 79; experiencing
    discrimination, 197; Grant
    School, 192; mining landscape,
    68
Massey, Sarah, 103–5, 285
Maternal and child health:
    receiving homes for children,
    111–18; responses to malnutri-
    tion, 293n66; State efforts to
    care for neglected children,
    118–21; at turn of twentieth
    century, 20–22
Matesich, Betty, 100–101
Mattich, Matt, 267–68
Matt's Drive-in, 247
Matule, Hank and Marcella,
    102
Mazzola, Columbine "Bina," *75*
Mazzola, John:
    acknowledgement, ix;
    benefit of intergenerational
    relationships, 282; candy
    factory, 240–41; East Butte,
    79–81; enlistment during
    World War II, 209; family
    business, 237, 239–40; home
    health remedies, 94; movie
    matinees, 171; music and
    music education, 211; selling
    magazines, 224; teachers at
    Grant School, 196–97; World
    War II, 51–52; WPA track and
    field activities, 49
McCarthy, W., 88
McCauley, Patricia, *161*
McCormick, Andrea, ix–x, *72*
McCormick, Michael, 26
McDevitt, Honey, 243
McEnaney, Ann, *184*
McGinley, John, 210–11
McGlynn, Father, 158
McGovern, Stella, 179
McGowan, Alexander, 122
McGowan, W., 88
McGregor, Helen, 102
McHugh, Jule Harrington:
    children's work and jobs, 216–
    17; Dublin Gulch, 89–90; end
    of World War I, 37; father's
    Halloween wake, 154; Fourth
    of July celebrations, 109–10;

Miners' Union Day, 107; music
    and music education, 211
McKinley School, 23
McMahon, Brother, 194, 195
McManon's boardinghouse, 228
McNelis, Sarah, 199
McPherson, Dr., 229–30
McPherson, Madam, 204
McQueen Addition
    neighborhood: 1930s view, *251*;
    businesses in, 256; destruction
    of, 62–63; establishment of, 18;
    ethnic and cultural mix, 77;
    Franklin School, 178–79; Holy
    Savior School and Berkeley
    Pit, *63*; July 4, 1932 explosion
    and tragedy, 153; "Memories
    of a McQueen Childhood,"
    13–14, 249–77; Nick's Bar and
    bowling alley, 268; "Pretty
    Place" grove, 263; raspberries
    and chokecherries, 146; special
    issue of *Copper Commando*
    newspaper, 54–55
McQueen Club, 256
Meaderville: businesses in,
    256; children's memories of,
    73–77; Christmas displays,
    108, *108*; establishment of, 18;
    expansion of Berkeley Pit, 63;
    Fourth of July parade floats,
    110, *110*; Franklin School,
    178–79; gardens and ethnic
    markets, 74, 76; girls on
    outing, *280*; girls softball team,
    147; Leonard Mine, *29*; 1930s
    view, *251*; St. Helena's Church,
    72, 271
Meaderville Bakery, and
    Sconfienza family, 18, 74, 76
Meaderville Mercantile, 74
"Memories of a McQueen
    Childhood": recollections
    of Steve Sherick, 249–77;
    children's work and jobs,
    268–69; cultural diversity of
    McQueen, 257–59; father's
    immigration from Croatia,
    249–54; music, 265–68;
    neighborhood boundaries
    and cultural character, 254–57;
    neighborhood camaraderie,
    264–65; opportunities beyond
    McQueen, 261–64; religious

and cultural celebrations, 271–77; restaurants, 269–70; wine making, 259–61

Mencarelli, Mary Gussino, 182

Mesopust festivities, 172, 272, *272*, 273–74, 283

Metropolitan Market, 78

Mexican cultural traditions, 181

Michaels, Sarah, 241–42

Micheletti, Connie, Constanza, and Rosella, 239

Micheletti, Lydia, 238–39

Michelotti, Mary, *280*

Mile High, Mile Deep (O'Malley), 15, 27, 70

Militia barracks, 84

Milji, Mike, 202

Miners: children's memories of, 68–69, 137; circa 1900, *229*; types of, 254

Miners' Union Day celebrations, 106–107, 294n104

Mining industry: Anaconda Company holiday celebrations, 106; care of horses, 102; children's familiarity with, 64–71; children's memories of miners, 68–69, 137; *Copper Commando* newspaper, 51, 54; decline between 1929 and 1933, 130; early development of, 15–17; gallows frames, 148, *281*, *290*; gradual reduction in, 58–63; Granite Mountain Mine fire, 34, 287, 294n72; Greater Butte Project, 58; machinery and tools of, 66; open-pit mining, 1–2, 58, 62–63, 110; Pittsmont Smelter, 67; promotions into salaried positions, 101–2; trauma of mine disasters, 287; work life in early twentieth century, 27–31

Mining landscape: children in, *65*; children's memories of, 65–68; and geography of childhood, 279–80; lack of birds, 200

Monroe school, 23

Montana Children's Home, 118

Montana Council of Defense, 36, 205, 294n80

Montana Laundry, 1

Montana School of Mines, 171, 208

Montana Sedition Act, 36

Montana Standard newspaper: among Butte dailies, 218; children's work selling, 242; East Side Neighborhood House and Junior Service League, 128; end of 1959 strike, 61; ice skating rinks, 141; Junior Service League, 129; "serenades" during labor unrest, 48, 55–56; work by Andrea McCormick, ix–x

Moore, Annie, *147*

Moore, Loretta, *147*

Morello, Julia, *147*

Moriarity, Eugene and Graten, 189

Movies, popularity of, 47–48, 167–71. *See also* names of individual theaters; Theaters

Mullen, Pat, 73

Mullen House, 230, 241

Mullins, Jerry, 167

Munroe, Jack, 24

Murphy, Mary, ix, x

Murray, Joe, Catherine, and Neamer, *184*

Mushrooms, gathering and selling, 245

Music: children in early Butte, *211*; entrepreneurial efforts of children, 265–67; at Grant School, 180–81; immigrant love of, 81, 256–57; music education, 211–15; traditional Irish songs, 243

Naranche, Eso, 180

Narodni Dom hall, 18, 273, 274

National Defense Education Act, 12

National Industrial Recovery Act of 1933, 45

National Youth Administration: creating and maintaining skating rinks, 141; introduction of, 10

Neighborhoods: camaraderie of, 282; collective identity of, 280; early history, 17–19; expansion of Berkeley Pit, 62–63, 110; as extended families, 281–82, 289. *See also* Ethnic neighborhoods

Neversweat Mine, *83*

New Age newspaper, 20, 37–38

New Deal Bar: community support, 167; Halloween celebrations, 165–66, *166*; location, 1

New Deal public policies, 10–11

New Year celebrations, 108, 277

Newsboys, 216, 219–27, *220*, 242. *See also* Butte Newsboys Club

Newspapers: Butte dailies, 218; market for, 223–24; work selling, 216, 242

Nicholls, Helen, 186–87, 278

Nicknames, tradition of, 77

Nick's Bar, 268

Nine Mile Reservoir, circa 1945, *262*

North Main Street 1939, *57*

Norton, G., 88

Novi Vinodolski, Croatia, 271

Nursery schools, 23, 41, 45, 179; and WPA work projects, 49, 130

Nursing, training for, 53

Nybell, Lynn, x

O'Connor, David J., 126–27

O'Connor, Oakie, 55

O'Connor, Patsy, 142

Odonovich, Grace Marie, *262*

O'Farrell, Babe, 142

Olsen, Arnold, 207

Olson, Robert, 152–53

O'Malley, Richard K., 15, 27, 70

O'Neil boardinghouse, 88–89

Onkalo, Ann, 152

Onkalo, John: Finntown, 84, 137; funerals in childhood, 155; Halloween celebrations, 164–65; petty thefts of wood, 151–52; winter games and sports, 139; youthful gangs, 158

Open-pit mining: beginnings of, 1–2; destruction of neighborhoods, 62–63, 110; launch of, 58. *See also* Berkeley Pit

Opera: Grand Opera House, 25; immigrant love of, 81, 256–57

Oral histories, as source material, 5, 6

Ore dumps, as playgrounds, 68, 69, *136*

Oreskovich, Millie, *262*

Orlich, Danny, *262*

Orphanages and asylums: nineteenth-century building boom, 8; reforming and improving, 111–18. *See also* Homes and orphanages

Orpheum Theater, 33, *168*

Orzo barbershop, 256

Osello, Pene, *267*

O'Sullivan, Sarsfield, 87

Overall Gang, 159–60, *162*

Ozanne, Paul, 125

Pajnich, Beans, *262*

Pajnich, Bobby and Danny, *262*, *267*

Palagi, Hazel, *267*

Palia, Mary, 189

Pappas, Irene, *184*

Park Theater, 170, 171, *225*

Parrot Flats, 80, 265

Parrot Smelter, *146*

Pascoe, T. J., 28

Passover Seder, 108

Pasties, Cornish, 74

Paul Clark Home: archival research, 4; founding and early activities, 113–16; grand opening of, 111; photos of, *112*, *113*

Pearl Harbor, 50–51

Peavy, Linda, 6–7

Pelletier, Spike, 77

Pencrazzi family, 256

Penrose, Elinore Sterrett Shields: Columbia Gardens, 174; description of Cornish pasties, 74; Holland Ice Rink, 141; mining landscape, 66–67; winter games and sports, 139–40

Pension program, for widowed mothers, 30, 44

Pentilla, Ann: English as a second language, 179; home health remedies, 94; infant mortality, 21; mining accidents, 71; secondary education; South Montana Street, 77–78

People's Theater, 218

Pet shows, 133, *134*, 142

Peters, Mike, 158

Petrin, Joey and Lavenia, *262*

Petroni, Minnie, *267*

Pfeiffer, Amanda, 123

Phillips, Mary, 131

Pierce, Dillis, Margaret, and Sally, *147*

"Pigpen" at Clark Park, 161–63

Pigs, raising and slaughter of, 78–79, 258–59

Pipestone Hot Springs, family at, 90, *91*

Pirnat, Father, 196

Pittsmont Smelter, 67

Playgrounds: copper tanks as, 144; dangers of play, 152–54; as deterrent to delinquency, 9; empty lots, 262; increase during Works Progress Administration, 50; makeshift playing fields, 148; mine yards as, 143–49, 280; ore dumps as, 68, 69, *136*; organized play for children, 126–28; "Play-go-Round" mobile playground, 133, 142; Playground Association of America, 126, 299n46; swings, circa 1950, *281*; woodyards as, 149–50

Polio epidemic of 1952, 12

Pollution, air, 73

Pomroy, Hazel, *147*

Popovich, Milt, 180

Poultices, flaxseed, 94

Poverty: and children's health, 93–94; clothing, 208; and family life, 94–98, 106; intergenerational trauma of, 286–87; language of "dependence," 298n12; letters to Santa, 202–3; petty thefts from mines and mining operations, 99–100, 151–52, 227–28, 247, 300n28; responses to malnutrition, 293n66; student writing about, 201–2; and work stoppages, 27

Pregnancy, among teenage girls, 117–18

Preschools and kindergartens, public funding for, 11

Progressive Era: aid to children, 8–9; children's progress during, 31–33; education during, 187–88; reforms on behalf of children, 112–18

Prohibition era, 160, 260–61

Public policy and child welfare: advances in, 10; Aid to Dependent Children, 49; importance of Butte to rest of Montana, 289–90; public health campaigns, 22, 42, 133; state efforts to care for neglected children, 118–21; support for playgrounds, 126–28

Public Welfare Act of 1937, 130

Punke, Michael, 34, 35

Puppet theater performances, 130, 133

Quong, Puck Huie, *19*

Race Track neighborhood, 78

Radio: children's programs, 43, 171; distraction during Great Depression, 47–48, 50

Raiha, John and Marvin, *233*

Raiha, Linda: acknowledgement, ix; Big M, 146–47; children's work and jobs, 232–33; helpful first-grade teacher, 198–99; miners' lunch-buckets, 69–70; neighborhood fights, 159; radio programs, 171

Rangatangs gang, 159

Rankin, Jeannette, 35–36

Rationing, wartime, 52–53

Receiving homes for children, 111–18, 131–33

Recreation: advances for children in 1920s, 40–42; chase and "commandoes," 138; in early twentieth century, 24–26; hiking, 137; ice hockey, 141; makeshift baseball, 147–48; neighborhood camaraderie, 135–37, 138, 163; new YMCA building in 1919, 39; Rocky Mountain Garden Club, 41–42; skating, 140–41, 141–42; skiing, *283*; swimming lessons at YMCA, 164; tobogganing, 137; winter games and sports, 135, 138–43; and WPA work projects, 49, 295n151

Religious communities: attendance at Sunday Mass, 193; Christmas celebrations among, 108, 277; Croatian Catholic and Serbian Orthodox, 80; First Communion, St. Helena's Church, 72; growth of, 17–18; Italian Catholics in Meaderville, 74–75; in McQueen Addition, 255–56, 271; parish education, 23; relief societies, 298n17; saints day celebrations, 75; youth groups, 32–33

Restaurants, children's work in, 238–42, 269–71

Resurrection of Dinny O'Dowd, 195

Rialto Theater, 169, 218, 265

Riipi boardinghouse, 86

Riley, Frank, 221

Ritchie, Willie, 153

Roaring Twenties, life in, 40–42, 203–4

Roberts, Joe: childhood in Great Depression, 47; work efforts during Great Depression, 247

Rocky Mountain Café, 239, 269

Rogers, Betty Jo, *184*

Roller-skating craze, 24

Romano, Vic, *267*

Roosevelt, Eleanor, 45

Roosevelt, Franklin D., 44–45

Roosevelt, Theodore, 32

Rose Garden Dance Hall, 272

Rosellini, Virginia, *267*

Rosenstein's Confectionery, 93, 235–36

Rowling, Marge, 208

Ruffato, Dominick, *147*

Ruffato, John, 122–23

Russell, Jack, *267*

"Rustling card" system, 34

Ruthledge, Phyllis, *184*

S & L Ice Cream Parlor, 241

Sacred Heart Parish: Sacred Heart School, 23, 63, 79, 183–84, *184*, 191, *191*; significance in East Butte, 79

Saints day celebrations, 75

Salvation Army, 27, 41

Saturday Evening Post, children's work selling, 224, 242

Saunas, 83

Savoy restaurant, 269

Sawdust from mine yards, 152

Scandinavian Fraternity and Hall, 18

Schiesser, Henry, 57–58, 213–14, 301n48

Schiesser, Jean and Karen, 213

Schmooke (miner), *255*

Schoenfeld, Otto: advocacy for children, 119–20; on child labor, 218–19; concern for girls, 124; dependent vs. delinquent children, 123

Sconfienza, John: Franklin School, 196; school and work responsibilities, 192; work in family business, 234–35, 245–46

Sconfienza family, and Meaderville Bakery, 18

Scrap metal drives, 52, *52*

Sealander, Judith, 6

Serbian immigration and community: in East Butte, 72, 80, 85; at Grant School, 179, 180; Mesopust celebrations, 172; Serbian Orthodox Christmas, 108, 277

"Serenades" during labor unrest, 48, 55–56, *56*, 103–105, *104*

Settlement house movement, 9

Sewell Hardware, 227

Sewing school: at Paul Clark Home, 114; sewing classes at Grant School, 181

Shannon, John, 161

Shannon, Kevin: acknowledgement, ix; movie matinees, 168; music and music education, 211; selling newspapers, 216, 224–25; singing in Irish bars, 243, 283

Shannon, Marion, *161*

Shea, Bridget, 242

Shea, Guinness, 155–56

Shea, John T.: Clark Park, 163; dealing with strikes and class distinctions, 100; funerals in childhood, 155–56; ice hockey games in Corktown, 141; life during Great Depression, 45–46; Miners' Union Day, 106–7; nuns as teachers, 196; youthful gangs, 158

Sheehan, Ernestine, *72*

Sheehan, Lucille Martinesso: acknowledgement, ix; circa 1925, *75*; circa 1926, *144*; Columbia Gardens, 174–75; home health remedies, 182–83; play in copper tanks, 144

Sheehy, Ed, 283

Sheehy, John "Skeff": acknowledgement, ix; benefit of intergenerational relationships, 282, 283; cinder playing fields, 147; Columbia Gardens, 176; education and career of, 208–9; high school during Great Depression, 208; importance of education, 194–95; Irish immigrant community, 88–89; mining accidents, 71; mining landscape, 65–66; mornings in childhood, 14; movie matinees, 169; music and music education, 211; Overall Gang, 160; poverty and domestic violence, 97; train tunnels, 149; woodyards, 150; work as newsboy, 222–24, 246

"Sheiks," 203–4

Sherick, Steve: at 1945 picnic, *262*; in accordion ensemble, *267*; acknowledgement, ix; Gina Zanchi as music teacher, 213; home health remedies, 183; "Memories of a McQueen Childhood," 13–14, 249–77; Mesopust celebration, 283; Miners' Union Day, 107

Sherman, Bessie Toy: Centerville and Meaderville, 72–73; Fourth of July trees in Meaderville, 109

Sherman, Bob, 230–31

Sherman School, 23

Shoeshine work, 245

Shook, Jeff, x

Shovlin, Frank, 152–53

Silva, Audrey and Bernardine, *267*

Silver Bow Café, 241–42

Silver Bow Emergency Relief Association, 44, 129

Silver Bow Homes housing development, 165

Silver Lake boardinghouse, 85
Sims, Ray and Adah, 103
Singermann (Brinig), 92–93
Sisters of Charity of
    Leavenworth, 117, 185–86
Sisters of Charity of the Blessed
    Virgin Mary, 186
Skating, 140–41, 141–42, *142. See
    also* Ice Hockey
Skiing, *283*
Slag at Pittsmont Smelter, 67
Slatt, A. and C., 88
Slavic immigration and
    community: Mesopust
    celebrations, 172, 272, *272*,
    273–74, *283*; origins of
    Bohunkus Day, 275, *276*, *277*.
    See also Croatian immigration
    and community; Serbian
    immigration and community;
    Slovenian immigration and
    community
Sledding, 139–40
Slovenian immigration and
    community: at Grant School,
    179, 180; Slovenian American
    Hall, 18
Smith, Ursula, 6–7
Smithers, C. Owen, 166
*Snow White and the Seven
    Dwarfs*, 11
Social Security Act, 10–11, 49
Society for the Prevention of
    Cruelty to Animals, 8–9
Softball, Meaderville girls team,
    147
Solat, Mike, 238
Soroptimist Home for Children,
    4, 131–33, *133*, 299n65
Spanish influenza epidemic,
    36–37, 294n87
Spencer, Ann J., *184*
Sports and games: chase and
    "commandoes," 138; duck
    pins bowling, 265; in early
    twentieth century, 24; Grant
    School Bulldogs, 180, *181*;
    high school football, 43–44,
    186, 187, 301n18; ice hockey,
    141; makeshift baseball,
    147–48; in McQueen Addition
    neighborhood, 262–63;
    Meaderville Girls Softball
    team, *147*; neighborhood

camaraderie, 135–37, 138, 163;
    organized play for children,
    126–28; ring-around-the-
    rosy 1910, *180*; Sacred Heart
    School athletes, *184*; skating,
    140–42, *142*; skiing, *283*;
    spring and summer, 142;
    swimming lessons at YMCA,
    164; tobogganing, 135; winter
    games and sports, 135, 138–43;
    youth sports leagues, 127
Sputnik space program, 11
St. Helena's Church,
    Meaderville: First Holy
    Communion, 1959, *72*; Gina
    Zanchi, 212; significance to
    Italian Catholic families,
    74–75, 271
St. James School of Nursing, 53
St. John's Day, 277
St. Joseph's Orphanage, 116–17,
    124
St. Joseph School, 211
St. Lawrence O'Toole School, 23,
    163, 185
St. Mary's Parish and School, 23,
    29, 38, 39, 192–93; class sizes
    and heating, 193; eighth-grade
    class circa 1925, *194*; first-grade
    class circa 1910, *193*; and Irish
    immigrant community, 87;
    neighborhood camaraderie,
    136; political education, 207
St. Patrick's Day at Grant
    School, 180
St. Patrick's School, *185*, 185–86,
    191
St. Philip and Jacob Society, *262*,
    270–71, 271
St. Stephen's Day, 277
Stallman, Otto, *11*
Stanaway, Marrion and B., *184*
Staples, Dr., 222
Stapleton, Guy, 22
State Board of Health, 33, 42
State Bureau of Child and
    Animal Protection: advocacy
    for girls, 124–25; on child labor,
    218–19; child welfare as public
    concern, 121; establishment of,
    119; preventing and addressing
    juvenile delinquency, 123;
    transfer to State Department
    of Public Welfare, 130

State Department of Public
    Welfare, 130
State Reform School, 123, 124;
    founding of, 118
Stefanic, Bonnie, ix, 60, 96
Stewart, Samuel V., 34
Stilts for children, 152
Stokina, Peter, 203
Stope miners, 254, 255
Stratton, Vadis: absorbing
    ethnic differences, 283;
    acknowledgement, ix;
    childhood in Great
    Depression, 46; home
    health remedies, 94; Miners'
    Union Day, 107; Race Track
    neighborhood, 78
Strikes and work stoppages: in
    1934, 100–101; in 1921–1922,
    40–41; and Aid to Dependent
    Children, 134; in April 1946,
    55–56, 100, 101, 102–105, *104*; in
    August 1959, 59–60, 278; and
    children's everyday psychology,
    285; dealing with class
    distinctions, 100–106; effect
    on families, 27, 96, 287; during
    Great Depression, 48–49
Sullivan, D., 88
Sullivan, Pat, 163
Sullivan, R., 88
Sundberg Electric, 226–27
Suominen's boardinghouse, 82
Superman comic books,
    introduction of, 11
Susak, Helen and Rosemary, *184*
Sutey, Mary, *184*
Swift, Alma, 206
Swimming: at Bell Creek, 245;
    lessons at YMCA, 164
Symon's Department Store, 169,
    223, 228

Takala, Hilea, John, and Mary,
    145
Taksa, Lucy, 7
Tarrant, Collette, 91–92
Teenage pregnancy, 117–18
Terminal Drug store, 223
Theaters: admission prices, 242–
    43; early twentieth century,
    25; films offered circa 1914,
    167; jobs for children, 218; in
    Uptown Butte, 169; weeknight

features, 171. *See also* individual theaters
Theoretical perspectives on childhood, 6–7
Tilton, Daniel W., 220
Tinsley, Maureen, 142–43
Tipperary ice cream and candy store, 256
"Tippy" baseball, 147–48
Tobogganing, 135
Tolleson-Knee, Ryan, x
Toole, Joseph K., 32
Top Hat restaurant, 269, *269*
Topography of Butte, 138–39
Tracing the Veins (Finn), ix
Track meets, 142
Trains, adventures and play, 149–51
Trapshooters, setting traps for, 267–68
Trbovich, Mary, 108
Treglown, Nicholas, 28
Treparish, Teddy, 239
Treparish, Teddy and Gino, 270
Trevena, Shirley: acknowledgement, ix; children's work and jobs, 236–37; Pearl Harbor, 50–51; wartime rationing, 52–53
Trevithick, Minnie, *145*
Triplets, first recorded birth in Butte, 21–22
Troglio, Jim, *267*
Trolley car, Columbia Gardens, *175*
Trythall, Phil, 102
Tuomala's boardinghouse, 82

Ugrin, Laurie, 95; acknowledgement, xi
Uptown Butte: character of, 167; circa 1934, *217*; landmarks of, 223; Park Theater in 1939, *225*
U.S. Children's Bureau, 10, 126, 130
U.S. Espionage Act, 205

Vaccines: polio, 12, 133; smallpox, 42
Valentino, Rudolph, 203–4

Vegetables, scavenging and selling, 245, 247
Vincent, Sister Rose, 117
Vincent, William, *145*

Waddell, Mae, 247
Wald, Lillian, 9
Walker's Café and Bar, 240
Walkerville, youthful gangs in, 158
Walsh, Jack, 208
Ward, Annie, 121
Ward, John, 185–86
Washington Junior High School, 188, *202*
Wayrenen, Ray, 82–84
Webster, Val, 241–42
Weir, L. H., 127
Wendel, Herb, 36–37
Wertham, Fredric, 210
West, Elliot, 6
White House Conference on Children 1909, 10
White House Conference on Children and Youth in a Democracy, 1940s, 11
Why Johnny Can't Read (Flesch), 11
Widows, children's memories of, 71
Wiley, Kid, 39–40
William Tell Benevolent Society, 19
Williams, Butch, *262*
Williams, George, 204
Wine making, 81–82, 259–61
Winter games and sports, 135, 138–43, *283*
Winter Garden bowling alley, 268
Women: Butte Women's Protective Union, 20, 242; Cadet Nurses Corps, 53; poverty and prostitution, 121; war production industries, 11; widowhood, 29–31, 71; WPA sewing rooms, 45, 245
Women's Christian Temperance Union, 31–32
Wood gathering, 227–28, 246

Woodville, 1930, *283*
Woodyards, 149–50
Work, Clemens, 205–6
Works Progress Administration (WPA): child care and recreational projects by, 49; employment in Butte, 45; playgrounds and sports programs, 127–28; student participation in, 207
World War I and aftermath, 33–40, 205–7
World War II: "baby boom" following, 12; coming of age during, 50–55; demand for child care, 11; end of, 55, 296n167; political education during, 209; postwar period, 55–58, 131, 209–10
Writing: home from World War II, 214–15; by students, 201–5, 206

Yankee Doodle Gulch, 263
Yegen Bank, 223
Yellowstone Park earthquake of 1959, 59
YMCA: opening new building in 1919, 39; recreation programs, 265; swimming lessons, 164; youth sports leagues, 127
Young, Robert, 188
Your Children in Wartime, 52
Youth court system, establishment of, 31

Zanchi, Gina, music and music education, 211–13, 266
Zannon, Esther, 165
Zinn, Howard, 33

About the Author

Janet L. Finn is Professor of Social Work at the University of Montana–Missoula and faculty member in the International Development Studies and Women and Gender Studies programs. She holds a bachelor's degree from the University of Montana, a Master of Social Work degree from Eastern Washington University, and a PhD in cultural anthropology and social work from the University of Michigan. She has authored and edited numerous books and articles about both Butte and childhood, including *Tracing the Veins: Of Copper, Culture, and Community from Butte to Chuquicamata* (University of California Press, 1998); *Motherlode: Legacies of Women's Lives and Labors in Butte, Montana* (Clark City Press, 2005); and *Childhood, Youth, and Social Work in Transformation* (Columbia University Press, 2009).

University of Montana–Missoula, file photo by Todd Goodrich